Buddhist Tourism in Asia

Contemporary Buddhism

MARK M. ROWE, SERIES EDITOR

Architects of Buddhist Leisure: Socially Disengaged Buddhism in Asia's Museums, Monuments, and Amusement Parks
Justin Thomas McDaniel

Educating Monks: Minority Buddhism on China's Southwest Border
Thomas A. Borchert

From the Mountains to the Cities: A History of Buddhist Propagation in Modern Korea
Mark A. Nathan

From Indra's Net to Internet: Communication, Technology, and the Evolution of Buddhist Ideas
Daniel Veidlinger

Soka Gakkai's Human Revolution: The Rise of a Mimetic Nation in Modern Japan
Levi McLaughlin

Guardians of the Buddha's Home: Domestic Religion in the Contemporary Jōdo Shinshū
Jessica Starling

Morality and Monastic Revival in Post-Mao Tibet
Jane E. Caple

Buddhist Tourism in Asia
Edited by Courtney Bruntz and Brooke Schedneck

Buddhist Tourism in Asia

Edited by

Courtney Bruntz and
Brooke Schedneck

UNIVERSITY OF HAWAI'I PRESS
HONOLULU

Publication of this book has been assisted by a grant from BDK Canada.

© 2020 University of Hawaiʻi Press
All rights reserved
Paperback edition 2021

Printed in the United States of America

26 25 24 23 22 21 6 5 4 3 2 1

Library of Congress Cataloging-in-Publication Data

Names: Bruntz, Courtney editor. | Schedneck, Brooke, editor. | Bruntz, Courtney, editor. | Schedneck, Brooke, editor.
Title: Buddhist tourism in Asia / edited by Courtney Bruntz, Brooke Schedneck.
Other titles: Contemporary Buddhism.
Description: Honolulu : University of Hawaiʻi Press, 2020. | Series: Contemporary Buddhism | Includes bibliographical references and index.
Identifiers: LCCN 2019027817| ISBN 9780824881184 (hardcover) | ISBN 9780824882846 (epub) | ISBN 9780824882822 (adobe pdf) | ISBN 9780824882839 (kindle edition)
Subjects: LCSH: Tourism—Asia—Religious aspects—Buddhism—Case studies. | Buddhist pilgrims and pilgrimages—Case studies. | LCGFT: Case studies.
Classification: LCC G155.A74 B83 2020 | DDC 338.4/7915—dc23
LC record available at https://lccn.loc.gov/2019027817

ISBN 978-0-8248-8985-2 (pbk.)

University of Hawaiʻi Press books are printed on acid-free paper and meet the guidelines for permanence and durability of the Council on Library Resources.

Cover photo: Lingyin Temple, Hangzhou, China, by Courtney Bruntz

Contents

Series Editor's Preface

AS THE FIRST BOOK-LENGTH TREATMENT OF BUDDHIST tourism in Asia, this multi-authored work breaks exciting, new ground in expanding our ever-shifting understanding of contemporary Asian Buddhism. Through themes of Buddhist imaginaries and place-making, secularizing the sacred, and commodification and its consequences, the volume's contributors explore how tourism, Buddhist communities, and religious sites constitute each other, covering everything from transnational pilgrimage to speed-dating to privatized hells. Here we encounter Buddhism as not only a "religion of peace," a spiritual pursuit, and a bastion of traditional culture, but also a state apparatus and a marketable commodity that is deeply enmeshed in the flows of globalized market capitalism. This is not a story of "traditional" versus "secularized" Buddhism, but rather one of an active and localized set of practices that engages all facets of modern life. Readers traveling the pages that follow will experience "Buddhist place-making as a dynamic mode of praxis" and "Buddhist sacred sites as constructions, reconfigurations, and reflections of multiple imaginaries." As such, this book provides detailed local studies of contemporary Buddhism that consciously engage broader theoretical conversations within the study of religion, anthropology, and modernity.

Acknowledgments

JUST AS THE DEVELOPMENT OF A BUDDHIST tourist site requires the efforts of multiple actors, so too did this volume. With the generous support from the School of History, Philosophy, and Religion (SHPR) at Oregon State University, a workshop in the spring of 2016 initiated conversations, which led to the completed work in this manuscript. We would like to extend our gratitude to SHPR for their support, and would also like to thank the China and Inner Asia Council of the Association for Asian Studies for awarding us with a grant to help fund our workshop. We would like to acknowledge all of the editors and staff who worked on this volume at the University of Hawaiʻi Press, particularly Stephanie Chun for supporting our work. Particular thanks also goes to Mark Rowe for his encouragement and insightful recommendations on the Introduction and theoretical perspectives. The University of Hawaiʻi Press' anonymous reviewers provided us with valuable insight, and their suggestions gave us guidance for editing this book and its frameworks into their final form.

Studies utilizing ethnography require time spent collecting data from interviews, participant observation, and engagement at field sites. We would like to thank members of the various Buddhist communities, tourists, and tourism operators for their willingness to participate in our studies. We are furthermore grateful to our contributors for their time and care in collecting and analyzing data for this manuscript, as well as their diligence throughout the writing and editing process. And finally, we would like to extend deep thanks to our mentors for shaping us into scholars of religious studies, as well as to our families. Courtney Bruntz is especially grateful to Richard Payne, Judith Berling, and Kristy Nabhan-Warren, and would like to thank her parents, husband Michael, and daughter Daphne for their enduring love and support. Brooke Schedneck thanks Thomas Bremer, Steven Epstein, and her Thai teacher Warisa Tananchai for conversations and feedback on issues of Buddhist tourism. William Starner and son Jet have also supported her in their own ways.

Introduction

Theoretical Landscapes of Buddhist Tourism in Asia

Courtney Bruntz and Brooke Schedneck

THE RELATIONSHIP BETWEEN BUDDHISM AND RELIGIOUS TOURISM has increasingly become an important topic, not only for academics, but for Buddhist monastics and practitioners as well. Across Asia, locations and physical sites associated with Buddhism or the historical Buddha are now part of tourism circuits, and recent tourism developments have contributed to the revitalization of Buddhist sites. With Asia becoming a top tourist destination, and recent trends such as Myanmar rapidly expanding its tourist industry and China becoming home to a highly mobile middle class, contemporary realities of tourism in this region necessarily involve sacred Buddhist sites. Buddhists, government organizations, business corporations, and individuals are taking advantage of the popularity of Buddhism by making sacred mountains, temples, relics, and Buddhist teachers "tourist-friendly" through a variety of means. In this context Buddhist sites become a cultural heritage attraction, a religious festival becomes a tourism marketing campaign, and a difficult pilgrimage route becomes a physical, spiritual, and cosmopolitan achievement.

Recent developments in South, Southeast, and East Asia have spearheaded Buddhist tourism that re-conceptualizes the meanings and values of sites associated with Buddhism, as governments are hoping to capitalize on an expansive definition of Buddhism that envelops the tradition within nation-state ideologies. In China, Mount Wutai (the mythological home of Mañjuśrī) received over one million visitors in 2001, and by 2007 that number rose to over three million.[1] Increases in traveler numbers are attributed to the efforts of local government bodies and tourism management companies that have marketed many Buddhist locations as cultural destinations. In India as well, many Buddhist locations have undergone processes of rebranding, and non-religious organizations have emphasized India as Buddhism's "homeland." As David Geary (2017) explains, a revitalization of Buddhist sites has occurred with projects directed at promoting ancient networks of Buddhist centers. UNESCO has greatly contributed to this trend by transforming sites like Bodh Gaya into World Heritage destinations. UNESCO's influence on religious tourism more broadly has been felt across Asia, including Cambodia, where the organization has worked with non-religious organizations to develop cultural tourism. Between 2007 and 2009, for example, the temple Banteay Srei—one of the most visited temples at Angkor Wat—received 1,900 persons/day during the high season and 6,500 persons/day on traditional national holidays, and visitor numbers increase each year.[2]

Efforts aimed at encouraging both domestic and international travel have led to an increase in tourist numbers across Asia. The Tourism Organization of Thailand began after World War II to develop tourism sites for international and domestic travelers, with much of their promotional activity including Buddhist-related sites and festivals.[3] As in other developing nations, tourism in Thailand offered the opportunity for foreign exchanges to boost the nation's economic sector. In many Asian nations, recent rapid economic development resulted in the creation of a middle class of travelers who had the time and financial resources to visit domestic locations. Thus in 1996, domestic trips by Thai tourists numbered 42.5 million, and projections indicated that number doubled to 97 million by 2003 (Kaosa-ard et al. 2001, 110). In addition to rising numbers of middle-class travelers, advancements in mobility and transportation have further altered the accessibility of tourist destinations. In Japan, in the late 1960s perhaps the most famous eighty-eight temple circulatory pilgrimage on the island of Shikoku received about fifteen thousand pilgrims per year. By the 1980s, this number had increased to one hundred thousand, and in the late 1990s, these numbers continued to rise (Reader 2005, 155). Such growth is linked to the development of bus tours, allowing visitors to more quickly and easily participate in the Shikoku *henro* (pilgrimage).

Through case studies of Buddhist tourist sites across Asia, this volume argues that overlapping concerns of place-making, secularization, and commodification exist in dynamic tension at Buddhist tourist sites. Through efforts of Buddhist place-making, which utilize global and domestic imaginaries of Buddhism, Buddhists creatively engage with modernity, including processes of secularization and commodification. This volume brings together Buddhist Studies scholars to generate a comparative investigation of places, identities, and practices within Buddhism's diverse tourism landscape. Our aim is to provide insight regarding how tourism works within Buddhist contexts. Our focus is not exclusively travelers and Buddhist sites, but also local people, private companies, monks, and lay officials, as well as physical and symbolic landscapes, legends, and myths. To this end, some of the overarching questions the chapters present are: How, and why, have certain routes, groups, sites, and practices associated with Buddhism been constructed and what are the effects? In what ways do travelers derive meaning from Buddhist places? How do Buddhist sites fortify national, cultural, or religious identities? In this way we give our attention to translations, innovations, and creative strategies in regard to tourism in Buddhist locations.

Although Buddhist travel has existed for centuries, much of our understanding about contemporary religious travelers and how to study them has arisen from examples within Western religious traditions. Locations of scholarship concerning religious pilgrimages have been skewed toward Christian sites in Europe such as the Camino de Santiago in Spain and the Sanctuary of our Lady Lourdes in France (Eade 1992; Eade and Sallnow 1991; Sánchez y Sánchez and Hesp 2015), as well as the Muslim pilgrimage to the Kaaba in Mecca, Saudi Arabia (Eickelman and Piscatori 1990; Tagliacozzo 2013; Tagliacozzo and Toorawa 2016). Within Asia there have been a limited number of studies concerning religious tourist sites such as Rishikesh and Bodh Gaya in India and pilgrimage sites in Japan (Geary et al. 2012; Huber 2008; Reader 2005; Rodríguez del Alisal et al. 2007; Singh 2009). Besides these few monographs on Buddhism and tourism, often Buddhism is represented by a single chapter in larger edited volumes on pilgrimage, tourism, and/or sites in Asia (Einarsen 1995; Stoddard and Morris 1997; United Nations 2003). These studies do not address the diversity of Buddhist sites and their relationships to global market forces and larger religious economies.

Despite a lack of representation in scholarship, Buddhism and Buddhist places provide an important perspective on the nature of travel to religious sites. Traditional models of tourism and pilgrimage have separated the pilgrim from the tourist, with pilgrimage referring to explicit religious activities and tourism meaning non-religious secular ones. Studies on global religious tourism showcase the divergent ways religious sites are packaged, with promotional literature marking a site for its connections to culture (to attract curious tourists) while also advertising it for spiritual cultivation (to entice religiously motivated travelers) (Olsen 2003; Shackley 2001; Shoval 2000; Timothy and Olsen 2006; Vukonić 1996). The theoretical intent of these works has been to delineate the ardent pilgrim from the interested tourist. But such an attempt is muddled by social realities, which do not neatly separate the sacred and the profane. Recent works have included a merging of the two categories. In their work on pilgrimage in China, Susan Naquin and Chün-Fang Yü (1992) suggest pilgrimage itself requires redefinition because pilgrimage has always incorporated entertainment and leisure. Tourism is not only frivolity, but as Schedneck (2015) has found, activities typically associated with serious religious pilgrimage, such as meditation, are often performed by non-Buddhists who describe themselves as tourists in Thailand. As Timothy and Olsen (2006) find, a tourist can thus simply be considered one who "travels temporarily... away from home to another region" (6). A broader understanding of tourists such as this fits our case studies. At places of Buddhist tourism, travel does not necessarily involve long distances or periods of time, and religious affiliation is not always a concern. Religious practice options are available, but it is not necessary to engage in devotion-based activities. Why is this the case? As many of our contributors demonstrate, Buddhism is a missionary religion that seeks to spread its teachings but not convert. Buddhists pride themselves on being welcoming to the international community, and the economic resources that tourism brings are an important factor. Buddhist tourism and pilgrimage cannot be neatly separated, which comes through in our investigations of Buddhist places.[4]

Additionally, the methodology of studying religious travel can also be examined through the lens of Buddhism. Methodology of religious pilgrimage falls into three approaches. The classic Turnerian approach of pilgrimage as fostering communitas and social cohesion is, of course, well known in many disciplines (Turner 1969). John Eade and Michael Sallnow (1991) draw our attention away from the Turnerian approach of communitas and instead look at pilgrimages as unique contexts and as sites of competing discourses. However, Ian Reader (2005) finds that although pilgrimage can reinforce differences and tensions between ethnic and social groups, it is often not primarily a space of competing discourses and contest, but varying understandings in dialogue and interaction with each other (29). Reader asks us to find the middle way between a group in contest and a group in total antistructural community. Buddhist places highlighted in this volume demonstrate this multivocal quality. The chapters below illustrate the concord and competition of their respective Asian locations in order to examine the ways disparate meanings operate together.

An advantage to a comparative study of Buddhist tourist locations is the ability to analyze broadly their common challenges and diverse innovations, allowing a clearer understanding of contemporary Buddhism. Although Buddhist places popular with tourists contain similar advantages and disadvantages, each site, within a particular nation-state, is diverse in the particular kinds of restraints it faces as well as the economic benefits it pursues. Contemporary Buddhist site construction is similar to language patterns. While sites, like languages, have common features and at times have symbols that replicate other locations (comparable to how languages have similar grammar constructions and cognates), they also incorporate localized forms of utilization. Languages have patterns—diverse sentence structures and phrases—molded together to create a particular meaning. Buddhist site construction is quite similar. Although a site's specific geographical features, histories, lineages, and cultures all have connections to Buddhism, they are packaged together in unique manners meant to emphasize the location's particularity. By investigating Buddhist sites of tourism, we analyze the shared struggles and varied opportunities of Buddhist sites that welcome domestic and international visitors.

In comparing this diversity of perceptions and meanings, this volume illuminates how tourism developments reflect concerns important to both Buddhists and scholarly interpretations of contemporary Buddhism. Buddhist tourism in Asia thus allows us to think about how Buddhist traditions operate in modernity. Although texts, history, and Buddhist thought inform many of the chapters, contemporary Buddhist tourism is best understood through the places where Buddhists and non-Buddhists directly encounter the religion. Buddhists are taking part in business, government, technology, and capitalism—transformations of the modern world that have especially resulted from economic transitions and international market developments. Studies have acknowledged many of the ways Buddhists have encountered modernity (Schober and Collins 2017; Heine and Prebish 2003; McMahan 2012), and few have analyzed Buddhist cultural sites entrenched in global markets (McDaniel 2017). However, none have directly addressed tourism. To analyze this, the following sections and chapters are divided into three parts: Buddhist Imaginaries and Place-Making, Secularizing the Sacred, and Commodification and Its Consequences. These are not exclusive categorizations. Authors in this volume draw on overlapping ideas from each of the three perspectives, and in many cases, chapters could fit into more than one part. However, chapters are grouped into a primary part in order to underline echoes and broader trends within the study of Buddhist tourism.

Buddhist Imaginaries and Place-Making

Because Buddhism is a global religion with multiple transnational flows enabling it to spread its varied ideas and practices, specific images regarding what Buddhism entails (i.e., robed monks, meditation, peace) have come to be associated with the religion. As discussed by Noel Salazar and Nelson Graburn (2014), imaginaries are "socially transmitted representational assemblages that interact with people's personal imaginings and that are used as meaning-making and world-shaping devices" (1). To provide a better sense, Naomi Leite (2014) defines tourist imaginaries as "those shared, composite images of a place or people, whether as general types or as particular destinations, held by tourists, would-be tourists, and not-yet tourists as a result of widely circulating imagery and ideas" (265). An imaginary of a place, other people, or a religion can be formed early in one's life, stemming from nascent experiences within one's family, elementary school textbooks, and/or media representations. In this way, as Maria Gravari-Barbas and Nelson Graburn

(2012) explain, "imaginaries can be both idiosyncratic and familial, or culturally shared. They can be instilled at such a young age that they become part of the unconscious attitudes that Bourdieu calls habitus" (1). Imaginaries, then, is an idea that connects images and texts to a site's material dimension, or an individual's thoughts to a social location. This term, for the purposes of this volume, will be used to describe the ways Buddhism is marketed and promoted to domestic and international tourists, as well as the diverse ways individual Buddhist practitioners envision their own religion.

Imaginaries, in slightly different senses, have also been referred to by Steven Collins (1998), Benedict Anderson (1983), and Arjun Appadurai (1996). Collins, in his book, *Nirvana and Other Buddhist Felicities,* uses the French term *imaginaire* to discuss a Pali *imaginaire*. He describes this *imaginaire,* using the Pali texts of the southern Buddhist tradition, as "for the most part an unchanging ideology, which was repeatedly adopted by kings in changing circumstances" (Collins 1998, 87). In his use, the Pali *imaginaire* and history do not completely coincide, but its ideas can tell us about the cultural logics of these premodern societies. In *Modernity at Large,* Appadurai (1996) uses the term imaginary as a social practice that can reveal collective representations mediated through modern media (31). Anderson (1983), in his *Imagined Communities,* analyzes nations as socially constructed, imagined into existence by members of the group using media instruments of communication (6). The imagination then is crucial for conceptualizing ideologies of the past and present that shape individuals, societies, and the representations of place.

Tourism imaginaries easily become part of collective understandings of place because of their efficacy and ability to be replicated. The imaginary of a place of Buddhist tourism is not "real" in a concrete sense, but imaginaries, much like gender as argued by Judith Butler (1990), "sediment" over time through constructed materials, tourism routes, branding, and other actions related to them. Like the concrete (physical/material) dimension of Buddhist sites, there are multiple imaginaries. At times the imaginary of Buddhism and a Buddhist place evokes images of the Buddha and Buddha statues, but at other times it conjures pictures of famous monks and worship at temples. For some people, their imaginary of Buddhism involves peace and relaxation, for others loud festivals and fun with family. Furthermore, there are both collective imaginaries for large audiences and more specific ones for local groups, and the imaginaries that tourist operators present are diverse in order to entice a wide range of visitors.

Imaginaries help to analyze the motivations of tourists and how tourist providers present Buddhism, furnishing a lens through which we can understand the diversity of contemporary understandings and representations of Buddhism. These ideas of a place, images of a site, and perceptions of culture and religion, control the travelers' choice of destination (Gravari-Barbas and

Graburn 2012, 1). John Miksic's chapter in this book, for example, examines premodern and modern garden spaces in Southeast Asia, and in particular, locations that evoke Buddhist narratives of hell. The Tiger Balm Gardens in Singapore, which have been managed by private companies and the Singapore government, exemplify the reality that imaginaries are not monolithic, but subject to individual interpretation and ascribed meanings. Private companies have disconnected Buddhist imaginaries from the site. As a result, depictions of Buddhist hell realms have been de-emphasized, while theater and rides have been added. In contrast to modern hell gardens in Thailand and Laos that have remained connected to Buddhist owners, and sites like Borobudur in Indonesia and Angkor Wat in Cambodia, which are under the protection of UNESCO as World Heritages sites, the Tiger Balm Gardens, as Miksic argues, have lost their appeal because of the missing Buddhist imaginary. This chapter demonstrates the risk of privatizing Buddhist spaces, and the importance of understanding the power of the Buddhist imaginary.

In contrast with specific imaginaries associated with the Tiger Balm Gardens analyzed in Miksic's chapter, there is a universal, collective imaginary associated with Indian Buddhist sites—an imaginary of peace. This tourist imaginary is investigated in David Geary's chapter on Bodh Gaya. In his study, this international imaginary of Buddhism as a tradition of peace is analyzed as a composite of historical, social, political, and economic developments. Such collective imaginaries have become significant in modern tourism settings, for they resonate with Buddhists and non-Buddhists alike. However, as Geary points out, an imaginary of Buddhism as "peace" has its problems. A location's imaginary dimension does not exist in isolation from its physical dimension, and the tourist gaze of Buddhism results in significant alterations to Buddhist places, commodified materials, and emblems of the tradition. Orientalist images, fantasies, and desires, as Geary discusses, are repackaged and utilized by Buddhist and Indian political leaders alike. In this way, Buddhism, not as a tradition of ritual and rules, but one of peace and non-violence, becomes an important imaginary within global tourist economies. In such economies, both specific and universal imaginaries shape physical spaces, as well as commodities and symbols associated with the tradition. A site's imaginary dimension is thus a lens through which we can understand its diverse nature.

Imaginaries also serve as a mechanism for Buddhist place-making. Drawing on Stephan Feuchtwang (2004), place-making is not the result of constructing physical structures or boundaries; instead, place-making is a process of centering. A "place" is created when there is a centering of a series of repeated actions at a particular location (Feuchtwang 2004, 4). For example, a marketplace is created from a centering of individuals focused on the buying and selling of goods. As explained by Dickhardt (2016), "building a house is not *per se* the essential element of making the house a place. Rather, it is the act of making the house a focal point of actors, their practices and their meanings which defines it as a place" (18). Building on Feuchtwang's view, Michael Dickhardt concludes that place-making is essentially a mode of praxis. Places do not create themselves but are instead created for particular purposes—to "establish sacredness... construct personal, cultural, historical, and national identities... define social spaces for religious practices... [and] incorporate groups into agendas of nation-building and of projects of civilizing and modernizing" (Dickhardt 2016, 15). Places of Buddhist tourism are therefore created from the centering of individuals and a repetition of particular practices.

What we see across our case studies is that Buddhist place-making in the midst of tourism incorporates a variety of activities, and the actions specific to a location reflect associated imaginaries. At places of Buddhist tourism imaginaries regarding Buddhist identity and practice (historically and contemporarily) are made "real." Furthermore, they are important centers for projects aimed at intentionally modernizing and globalizing the tradition, while also expressing cultural and national identities. By investigating sites of Buddhist tourism we better understand Buddhist place-making as a dynamic mode of praxis, and Buddhist sacred sites as constructions, reconfigurations, and reflections of multiple imaginaries. Furthermore, Buddhist place-making in the midst of tourism illuminates the manners in which various groups of Buddhists and non-Buddhists integrate and evoke differing imaginaries of a Buddhist site and the activities appropriate there, which at times, can result in contestations over the nature of a Buddhist place.

As will be seen in Brooke Schedneck's chapter, in northern Thailand diverse groups of tourists frequent Chiang Mai temples, which influences the manners in which Buddhism is both presented and practiced. At present, foreigners can volunteer at temples, and/or participate in temple stay and monk chat programs, in addition to simply visiting as a tourist. Chiang Mai Buddhist monks, Schedneck contends, view these encounters as opportunities to educate foreigners, and to introduce Buddhist teachings. These monks thus consider the Buddhist temple space as open and welcoming. Hence Buddhist monks have adapted temple spaces so that they are accessible places for foreign tourists to reside and visit while staying in Chiang Mai. What is clear in this work is that the way in which one imagines a religious tradition shapes how places of sacredness are configured, and in turn, configurations of place reinforce and/or challenge other imaginaries. In the case of Chiang Mai, Schedneck uncovers the divergent views held by lay Thai Buddhists and monks: the lay Buddhists regard temples as a sacred place where one displays specific values associated with being Thai, while the monks aim to project an image of openness toward all people.

Justin Ritzinger's study involves competing place-making claims regarding which mountain in China is the legitimate home of Maitreya, the future Buddha within Buddhist traditions. Buddhism's four sacred mountains are places where resident bodhisattvas are known to manifest their presence and attract visitors. However, what Ritzinger argues is that in contemporary China, while this imaginary of powerful sacred mountains remains, a site's networks, mobilities, and social and economic capital are most significant for producing authoritative claims about sacred places. This highlights the point that practices of Buddhist place-making are not abstract, but are instead intentional processes in constant motion. Ongoing place-making continuously shapes and reshapes particular sites, and they reflect broader agendas of nation-state, culture building, and globalization.

What Part I highlights is the fluidity and creativity possible within Buddhist place-making, varying interpretations over the nature and purpose of these spaces, and relationships between physical and ideological dimensions of Buddhist imaginaries. To that end, authors ask questions such as: Who has power to influence how Buddhist tourism sites are arranged and what knowledge is disseminated about the location? What representations are reinforced, what spatial practices are encouraged, repeated, and centered within Buddhist places? Which representations and practices are excluded and/or silenced, and what are the divergent viewpoints regarding a place that comes into contestation and how are these resolved? The chapters in this volume seek to untangle specifically how Buddhist imaginaries and place-making shape various locations in Asia, demonstrating how Buddhist tourist sites are entangled within particular social, political, economic, and geographic contexts.

Secularizing the Sacred

Just as place-making is a result of a mode of praxis, sacredness too is a process of sacralization. As Reader (2014) notes, rather than a definitive category in which the sacred is inherently separate from the profane, sacredness is a fluctuating classification, influenced by travelers, religious specialists, and mediators of a site. Jacob Kinnard (2014) has also drawn our attention to the multivocality and hybridity of religious spaces, which depend on the meanings and receptions constructed by diverse agents as well as the ways the sacred exists only as "products of history—specific, complex messy historical processes" (2). Thomas Tweed (2008) also encourages us to focus on the fluidity of religious spaces as well as the constant motion of religious meanings and values. Buddhist sacred places are continually being molded and altered by monastic and lay communities, managing individuals and companies, commercial operators who market symbols and meanings associated with the location, as well as domestic and international visitors.

While places of Buddhist tourism are purposefully created to establish sacredness, they are also layered with secular (i.e., non-religious) influences.[5]

We use the terms "sacred" and "secular" here not to reify a binary, but instead to point to the ways Buddhists use these categories to understand and demarcate what is internal and external to their tradition. While the terms "secular," "secularization," and "secularism," have changed meanings over the centuries, as a modern category, secular, as José Casanova (2009) contends, is used "to construct, codify, grasp, and experience a realm or reality differentiated from 'the religious'" (1049). Secularization then concerns the processes of transformation and differentiation of the institutional spheres of "the religious" from "the secular" (Casanova 2009, 1050). Finally, secularism can be a worldview, ideology, or statecraft principle. Because of this, secular, as a modern epistemic category, refers to realms of science, art, entertainment, health, the state, and/or the economy, etc., while the religious consists of ecclesiastical institutions. Within the social sciences, theories of secularization have been based on examples within Christendom; to secularize originally referred to making religious persons or things "worldly." Internal Christian secularization referred to processes seeking to spiritualize the temporal world, and externally, anticlericalism included efforts aimed at liberating secular spheres from ecclesiastical control (Casanova 2011, 56–57).

Authors within our edited volume find similar patterns at places of Buddhist tourism. Depending on the particular location and context, Buddhists might feel threatened by external secularization of religious sites, including processes in which tourism companies purposefully promote a Buddhist location for its cultural value, thus differentiating it from religion. Such efforts might seem to be an indication of decline and intrusion of the secular into sacred spaces.[6] At the same time, however, Buddhist tourism reveals that, instead of being perceived uniformly as an external threat, creating an alliance with secular forces is often a strategy Buddhists use to promote their traditions and sacred sites. Buddhists in tourist locations often find ways to compromise with secular forces. And they are doing so in order to expand networks of travelers, maintain financial viability, and educate people about Buddhist traditions. By making Buddhist sacred sites "worldly"—that is, infused with cultural ideologies, worldviews, and/or statecraft principles—Buddhists strategically aim to extend a religious site's value into secular spheres. Such efforts are not aimed at differentiating the religious from the secular, but rather entering into secular domains as opportunities to spread the religion, increase visitor numbers, and create new avenues and resources for income. As Casanova (2011) points out, historically, the secular was thought of as the residual category, or the social spheres that remained when the religious was lifted. In contrast, in modernity, the secular "appears now as reality *tout court,* while the religious is increasingly perceived not only as the residual category, the other of the secular, but also as a superstructural and superfluous additive" (55). Again, he is writing from the perspective of Western Christendom, but the encroachment of the secular on to religious sites is felt quite strongly across Asia as well. Secularization is not, however, a uniform process, and for some Buddhists, processes of secularization are not felt as encroachment but rather as opportunities for internationalization, missionization, and/or modernization. Because of their interrelatedness, the secular and the religious are thus not treated as binary categories within our case studies of Buddhist tourism. Instead, authors focus on secularization as dynamic processes that blur boundaries between religious and secular.

Many of the chapters included in Part I regarding Buddhist imaginaries and place-making uncover how secular agendas are incorporated into Buddhist site construction. Chapters in Part III, "Commodification and Its Consequences," will reveal commodification as a mode of secularization. Processes of secularization are thus embedded in all of our studies. However, chapters in Part II, focused on secularity, are grouped together to stress the challenges and opportunities tourist economies provide Buddhists.

John Marston's chapter, for example, studies Cambodian Buddhist pilgrims traveling to India and Sri Lanka, illuminating the intersections between Buddhists and secular forces—especially tour companies. In contemporary tourist economies, package tours have developed to facilitate these international trips while customizing the visit to meet the Cambodian Buddhists' expectations of a Buddhist pilgrimage. We see that the Cambodian Buddhist group Marston describes utilizes practices both from the Cambodian Buddhist repertoire of devotion, donation, merit-making, and pilgrimage, as well as adopting, perhaps temporarily, Buddhist practices that are more South Asian in their development. This chapter highlights the ways Buddhist practice can be shaped by secularization, including state agendas and economic developments. In Matthew Trew's study of the growth of tourism in Cambodia, the nation has become a place filled with imaginaries, from an ancient Buddhist past to a more recent and dark history of genocide. With surges of tourists in Asian nations, Buddhists have responded by marketing Buddhist-affiliated locations as sites tourists can add on to their travel itinerary. Cambodian Buddhists purposefully promote religious locations as tourist ones, encouraging the use of technology to feed into a symbolic economy where tourism thrives. In Trew's chapter, modern-era pagodas provide tourists with additional sites to visit following "temple fatigue" from the ancient ruins of Angkor Wat. For many Cambodian Buddhists, globalization and secularization of religious locations in the nation have created an opportunity to develop a tourist economy. With this, Cambodian Buddhist practice is changing to be more performative and accessible, and Buddhists who are secularizing sacred sites for tourism are confronted with questions of tradition, acceptable practice, and how to manage new wealth. Related to this study is Courtney Bruntz's chapter that analyzes how secular forces from the government and tourism corporations have encroached upon Buddhist spaces in China, and the ways in which monastic communities have responded. With religious tourism emerging as a means of generating income for state-owned enterprises, many Buddhist temples have been renovated or newly built for economic purposes. While an influx of tourists is financially beneficial for many temple communities, there is concern over non-religious entities commodifying Buddhism. Her study reveals ways that Buddhists are utilizing secular resources to create a variety of tourist experiences, rather than combating secular forces themselves. Notably state connections are flexed to revise policies regarding religious spaces, and technology is not only used to promote Dharma talks, temple stays, and meditation retreats, but also in some cases, to differentiate Buddhism as a modern and technologically advanced tradition.

Buddhists are thus adapting sites to accommodate an increase in tourist numbers, while also being concerned with how to survive in modern tourist economies flush with competition. This is of particular concern to Buddhists in Japan. As Ian Reader notes in his chapter, a growing pattern in Japan has included religious institutions promoting themselves as places of tourism, and doing so through commercial and governmental operators. He clarifies that premodern settings also included relationships between religious and secular institutions. However, in modern settings, tourist operations, along with accessibility to sites for recreation, have increased to the extent that Buddhist temples are confronted with issues of survival. Not only have tourist numbers declined but so too have temple memberships. A loss of income has thus resulted in temples turning to secular, commercial agencies to rebrand their relevancy. Reader traces this history, and examines the variety of reasons for which Buddhists are utilizing secular means to revitalize their sacred sites and pilgrimage routes.

Of course, it is necessary to recognize that a coupling of the religious and the secular is not particular to the contemporary. Although, within Buddhist Studies scholarship, David McMahan (2017) has analyzed the secular in the context of meditation, many of his main points can be applied to Buddhist tourism. "Classical" theories of secularization (Berger 1999) perceived secularization as a process that results in a loss of religiosity. These have been overturned in current research on religion and secularization. This shift in analysis, McMahan (2017) notes, has revealed a complex process in which both religious and secular forces work interdependently (113). Government, tourist, and cultural organizations work with Buddhists to promote sites for their cultural, historical, and religious value, while at the same time individuals and groups construct non-Buddhist places that evoke Buddhist imaginaries from texts, rituals, and practices. Buddhists, too, work with government and tourist agencies to market sacred sites to travelers, while also altering rituals, practices, and spaces to enhance contemporary relevancy. Secularity "serves as a driver of change and reconfiguration of religious belief, practice, and interpretation" (McMahan 2017, 114). Studies within this volume will indicate that the categories of secular and sacred are in flux, and their relationship is sometimes in conflict and sometimes in harmony at Buddhist sites. Chapters in Part II highlight that secularizing Buddhist sites occurs in manners specific to resources and challenges present within a nation and particular location.

This section reveals that Buddhists often view secularization as a resource for reinventing practices and spaces in order to attract diverse travelers and retain religion's relevancy. Such changes do not, of course, occur without contestation, and the development of Buddhist sites by non-Buddhist organizations has been a source of controversy.[7] Authors within this section analyze processes of secularization to ask questions such as: What are the various reasons for which Buddhists purposefully seek out associations with non-Buddhist institutions in promoting their sacred sites? How have global tourist economies altered how a site engages with secular spheres? What challenges are Buddhists addressing in this process, and how do connections with secular domains alter Buddhist practice? Chapters in Part II understand secular and religious as interrelated categories, and investigate how tourist and government agencies work in tandem with Buddhists to promote Buddhist sites as places of value for their heterogeneous religious, cultural, and historical identities. Therefore, secularization is not conceived of as a necessary part of modernity that sets Buddhism into decline. Instead Buddhism remains a part of modernity in historically and culturally specific contexts, revealing the ways that the secular and sacred can be integrated and incorporated within these case studies of Buddhist tourism.

Commodification and Its Consequences

At sites of Buddhist tourism, the secular and religious have a dynamic relationship in the activities of visitors, and this amalgamation includes consuming religious sites as commodities. Thus, not only does Buddhist place-making often include secular forces, it also involves processes of commodification. Commodification can be, of course, a manner in which Buddhist places are secularized. In religious tourism, objects and services are readily commodified (Timothy and Olsen 2006), meaning that symbols, objects, teachings, and practices connected to Buddhism are bought and sold within economic markets. This commodification is directly related to imaginaries, place-making, and processes of secularization, and given its importance, deserves its own consideration. As images associated with Buddhism shape commodities created, imaginaries are disseminated and reinforced through the practice of buying and selling Buddhist-related goods. Commodifying Buddhism is furthermore an avenue for economic profit, as commercial institutions participate in the construction of Buddhist places and Buddhist commodities. Physical objects as well as values associated with Buddhism are produced within complex historical and cultural contexts. For a pilgrim, an amulet provides confidence of protection, and a white cloth with stamps of temples visited gives hope for rebirth in the Pure Land. Commercial markets furthermore sustain Buddhist pilgrimages, as objects—talismans, particular forms of dress, prayer scrolls, Buddha statues, temple replicas, recordings of sermons, etc.—are sold as Buddhist commodities. Religious commodification is not unique to modernity, instead, in both historical and contemporary settings, tangible objects related to Buddhism coincide with religious imaginaries, sacred places, and secular (i.e., commercial) contexts.

Physical goods associated with Buddhism and its values are responsive and sensitive to changes in cultural and economic settings. Many scholars have questioned whether or not commodification results in de-sacralization, meaning that in modern settings Buddhism is exploited as a secular commodity and not a religious one (Guo 2006; Oakes 1998; Prideaux and Timothy 2008; Ryan and Gu 2009). Indeed, tourism companies and service organizations, as well as religious specialists and government actors, construct ways in which travelers consume Buddhism. To attract new visitors, tourism agencies brand Buddhist sites in a manner to make their appeal universal, and often this branding results in Buddhism becoming a commodity of culture or heritage. Examples of this include the "museumification" of Buddhist temples in China—a notion that Gareth Fisher (2011) borrows from Brian Nichols—in which temples are restored and reopened as official destinations of cultural preservation, and the rebranding of Buddhist sites as UNESCO World Heritage locales (Geary 2008). Recent government efforts to restore ancient Buddhist temples for increased tourism shape religious landscapes, and often, appropriations of Buddhism occur in conjunction with promoting national unity (Covington 2002; Philip and Mercer 1999). In tourist settings, Buddhism itself becomes a product of culture (Moran 2004), and through government commodification efforts, Buddhist sites gain cultural prestige and are recognized for their heritage value (Kaplan 2010; Kitiarsa 2008).

What we find, however, in studying commodifications of Buddhism that occur within tourism markets, is that commodifying Buddhist traditions does not inherently weaken religiosity. Brian Nichols' chapter especially interrogates this by examining Chinese Buddhist attitudes toward tourism. Specifically, he investigates whether or not tourism fits within Buddhists' own imaginaries of religiosity. Nichols places his study of contemporary debates about Buddhist tourism within Chinese Buddhist history, for relationships between Buddhists and surrounding market economies is by no means new. In modern settings, state-owned tourism corporations have commodified Buddhist sacred sites, traditions, and practices, which indeed has had significant consequences (including an increase of noise and disruption). However, such activity does not represent Buddhism and tourism in contestation but instead demonstrates negotiation and mediated cooperation.

Religions themselves can function like commercial goods, with objects, symbols, and activities bought and sold based on shifting market forces. Within Buddhist tourist destinations travelers are encouraged to consume sites associated with Buddhism in particular ways—that is, as an auspicious location, an ideal place of leisure, or both. Modernizing economies shape parameters in which religious sites are consumed, while opening locations to a diverse set of travelers. Short-term visits, for example, now often trump long-term pilgrimages. Tim Oakes and Donald Sutton (2010) point out that while improved roads have made it easier for worshipers, fewer people stay overnight at religious sites. Emerging tourist markets across Asia have further prompted religious specialists to participate in the packaging and rebranding of sacred sites so that long-term stay has more value. In the tourist economy today, visitors have access to all-inclusive packages that provide a range of options for travelers. The Temple Stay program in Korea, for example, encourages travelers to not simply visit a temple for a few hours, but instead market the experience as more worthwhile if one stays for a few nights (Jang 2009). While historically Buddhist temples and monasteries have relied on economic support from laity for survival, and Buddhist sites themselves have existed in a "gift economy" (discussed below), what separates current Buddhist tourism from the past are the market economies in which sites are entrenched. The commodification of Buddhism creates a situation in which scholars must focus on the economic contexts in which Buddhism is located, including globalized market capitalism.

Elizabeth Williams-Oerberg's chapter, for example, investigates correlations among consumerism, commodification, and the historical continuity of promoting Ladakh as an epicenter of Buddhism. Through this marketing, her research indicates an expansion of Buddhist institutions, with advertisements associating the place of Ladakh with an imaginary of peace and tranquility derived from its close connection to Buddhism. Buddhism has essentially become a unique selling point for increasing tourism, indicating that consumerism and commodification are not minimizing or diluting Buddhism's influence in Ladakh. Instead, Buddhist institutions are enhanced through government investments in tourism, while the imaginative value of Buddhism is drawn upon by numerous tourist services. This case study demonstrates that in Ladakh, tourism and Buddhism maintain a reciprocal relationship where Buddhists benefit from tourism and tourism benefits from Buddhism.

Buddhism does not just exist in the market economy, but has its own internal economy. In both Theravada and Mahayana contexts, an economy of merit refers to practices in which laity support the monastic community through giving clothing and food (*dāna*), as monks serve as a field of merit for these practitioners. It is not the monks themselves who give merit to the laity, but instead, through their ascetic lifestyle, they are a field in which the layperson's giving results in the acquisition of merit (Freiberger 2000). This is Buddhism's "gift economy." Buddhist laypersons engage in donor practices in order to gain merit that will have a positive effect on their current situation and "will negate the effects of past evil deeds and lead to beneficial future conditions, especially a good rebirth" (Adamek 2005, 135). Giving gifts to monks is a means for a layperson to earn good karma, which has historically inspired practitioners to undergo arduous journeys to faraway monasteries. When a practitioner expends much cost, time, and physical effort to traverse long distances, the benefit of such a journey is well worth the difficulty. Although the first part of Buddhism's exchange economy is based on gifts offered to monastics, the second, Buddhism's field of merit, drawing here on Bourdieu's (1971) theory of exchange, is an economy of symbolic goods in which the practitioner acquires a symbolic product.

In modern contexts, gift economies as well as an economy of symbolic goods remains, but the conditions through which merit is mediated and obtained has changed. In contemporary Japan, for example, one has the choice to physically walk the Shikoku circuit or complete the journey by bicycle, private car, public bus, or even a helicopter. One can further choose a "proxy" tour—hiring an individual to journey on one's behalf—or, if the potential pilgrim is constrained by time or money, the tour is virtually accessible through a corporate-run website. In modern settings not only do religious specialists mediate Buddhism, but so too do corporations and local members of informal sectors who sell a variety of travel offerings. For example, in Matthew Mitchell's chapter we are introduced to a model of Buddhist tourism in Japan in which Japanese travel and matchmaking companies, together with Buddhist priests, reinvent the usefulness of the temple space. Here Buddhist tourism is directed toward romance, and Buddhist rituals are marketed to young singles as efficacious for meeting one's love match. Essentially, in this process of commodification, priests and companies are connecting Buddhism to an imaginary of love, are shaping the temple space to accommodate this newly marketed image, and are marketing Buddhist temples and shrines as effective for finding love.

Buddhist sites have always been a part of surrounding market economies, with inns housing pilgrims along their journeys, teahouses providing sustenance, and shops ensuring travelers the ability to find clothing and other necessities. In this way, Buddhist sites produce a number of surrounding economies. Another distinction between current commodification and the past is the tourism market through which Buddhism is presented. New mediations of Buddhism, based on technologies and opportunities available through contemporary economic marketplaces, result in commodification particular to a site's location. Reader (2014) observes that changing political, economic, and social circumstances influence Buddhist practice, which requires Buddhists to discover new methods for economic support. In the context of this edited volume, authors investigate how shifting socioeconomic contexts influence Buddhist sites, the consequences of these alterations, and how Buddhists are responding. Such examinations encourage us to consider how visitor expectations shape Buddhist locations, and how commodification sways visitor expectations. Commodification is an avenue for us to explore Buddhist tourism as a process of interactions between Buddhist institutions and the marketplace. In this way, processes of commodification are similar to processes of secularization—they involve revitalizations of Buddhism, which authors in this volume explore. By investigating the cultural contexts in which Buddhism is sold as a physical product (statues, icons, postcards, brochures), an appealing activity (festivals, celebrations, contemplation), and a value (peace, serenity, tradition), we investigate the ways complex markets shape Buddhism and Buddhist practice and vice versa. All of the chapters within this volume address commodification in one manner or another, for through commodity construction, Buddhist sites develop along with secular influences, and imaginaries of Buddhism are made "real."

Chapter Summaries

Part I, "Buddhist Imaginaries and Place-Making," opens with David Geary's chapter, "Peace and the Buddhist Imaginary in Bodh Gaya, India," which explores the modern historical changes in the city of Bodh Gaya as it has gone from a small agricultural town to a growing international destination drawing tens of thousands of pilgrims and visitors each year. Underlying these changes to the urban and sacred landscape is the vital role of peace and its correspondence with a global Buddhist imaginary. This chapter argues that the relationship between Buddhism and peace is central to the imagination of many pilgrims, tourists, and visitors to the site and traces the multiple trajectories of this predominant discourse. In drawing attention to the work of the imagination in spaces of transnational encounter such as Bodh Gaya, this chapter critically examines the production and circulation of images and knowledge that attempt to make Bodh Gaya into a place of peace, even as Bihar, the area surrounding this sacred Buddhist location, is filled with poverty and crime.

John Miksic's study continues to discuss the imaginaries and place-making of Buddhism, but does so from the perspective of Buddhist fantasy worlds in Southeast Asia. His work focuses on the recent and fraught history of the Tiger Balm Gardens in Singapore, which has changed hands between private Buddhist owners, private companies, and the Singapore government.

He argues that these secular forces have removed part of what makes this site important, its connection to the Buddhist imaginaries of heaven and hell. Miksic locates this imaginary in large Buddhist complexes such as Borobudur in Indonesia and Angkor Wat in Cambodia. The idea of the Buddhist fantasy world has been in existence for over one thousand years, portraying the values and cosmology of Buddhism, and the more modern value of cultural heritage. Modern hell gardens in Thailand and Laos are also brought in to the comparative perspective of this chapter as an example of tourist spaces that have remained apart from the secular. In the end Miksic finds that the Tiger Balm Gardens today, even though in a new private company's hands, would do well to link the property closely to the Buddhist imaginaries of heaven and hell that have survived so well in other areas of Southeast Asia.

In "Loss and Promise: The Buddhist Temple as Tourist Space in Thailand," Brooke Schedneck discusses contrasting perceptions of foreign tourists between Buddhist laity and monks in Chiang Mai, Thailand. In this way, she highlights contestations over the nature and purpose of the Thai Buddhist temple. Case studies of inappropriate tourist behavior in temples, interviews with resident monks of temples popular with tourists, and analysis of Thai newspaper and social media, demonstrate the divergent reactions to tourists engaging in Buddhist temple space. While Thai lay Buddhists might in some cases label foreign tourists as a destructive force, Buddhist monks make use of these occasions to missionize the tradition. Considering the roles of Buddhist monastics within these temples, Schedneck analyzes the ways Chiang Mai monks portray Buddhism as a welcoming religion and display an attitude of openness. This chapter thus analyzes the contested nature of Buddhist place-making through tourism in Chiang Mai.

Finally, in "Marketing Maitreya: Two Peaks, Three Forms of Capital, and the Quest to Establish a Fifth Buddhist Mountain," Justin R. Ritzinger also explores contestation over Buddhist place-making. But instead of the nature of the Buddhist temple, this chapter investigates the competition between Mount Xuedou and Mount Fanjing to become the "true" home of Maitreya, and thus the fifth sacred mountain of China. Traditionally in China, sacred sites grew in prestige and prominence due to their perceived *ling* (spiritual power), as attested to in stories of marvelous occurrences. They grew in fame because of their ideological and physical dimensions, as sites were identified for their resident bodhisattva who would manifest their presence and work wonders. More recently, Ritzinger argues, Buddhist place-making is not simply in the court of public opinion but rests on the cultural and social capital established in each site.

Part II, "Secularizing the Sacred," begins with John Marston's "Cambodian Pilgrimage Groups in India and Sri Lanka." The phenomenon of Cambodians visiting sacred Buddhist sites in India has gained a new level of intensity since 2003 when package tours began being organized for Cambodian

Buddhists. Videos generated by the trips function as keepsakes for participants, but are also used to advertise the trips and for fundraising in support of temple building projects. This chapter analyzes a series of pilgrimage videos for the purpose of uncovering symbols and meanings generated by a Cambodian Buddhist group's trip to sites in Sri Lanka and India, and it explores the ways these Cambodian laypeople and trip leaders undertake practices as part of an imaginary of a Buddhist pilgrim. Marston examines the wider context of these pilgrimages as they are set within a package tour. This package mixes Buddhist activities with more secular ones and has been criticized by Cambodian Buddhists for the appearance of following a business model.

Next, Matthew J. Trew's "Buddhists, Bones, and Bats: Thematic Tourism and the Symbolic Economy of Phnom Sampeau, Cambodia" focuses on the increased Buddhist tourism options in Cambodia's peripheral locations. While the UNESCO World Heritage Site of Angkor Wat is the primary draw for tourists, smaller sites around the country are benefiting from this growth. A prime example is the northwestern capital of Battambang, considered to be the Buddhist heart of the country because of a unique history as a Thai tributary state. This chapter examines one of Battambang's sites—the mountain of Phnom Sampeau—for the purposes of investigating thematic tourism that is driving a growing symbolic economy. Trew argues that Buddhism's symbolic economy creates overlapping imaginaries of Buddhist place, and indicates the ways Buddhist and non-Buddhist spaces negotiate becoming part of a wider tourism network.

Courtney Bruntz's "Taking Tourism into Their Own Hands: Monastic Communities and Temple Transformations in China" focuses on how particular monasteries and monastics have made use of technology and state connections as secular resources to alter temple spaces, and to furthermore promote meditation retreats, sutra study programs, and volunteerism. With monasteries existing in consumer-driven tourism markets, many Buddhist sites have been commodified for corporate tourism purposes. Commodification on the part of commercial entities creates challenges for monks who want to ensure temples are free of cost, distinguish Buddhism as a contemplative tradition, and encourage visits not only for recreation but also devotional practice. Amidst secularization, however, avenues for making these goals a reality have arisen. Buddhists now have access to economic resources (including those from practitioners) as well as technological developments to not only transform Buddhist spaces and practices but also to transmit the tradition in efficient ways. Comparing monasteries and temples in both Beijing and Xian, this chapter contends that contemporary Chinese monastics are not opposing tourism or secular forces, but are instead taking the realities of tourism into their own hands by using secular avenues to entice visitors to temples for study, devotion, and contemplation.

Part II concludes with Ian Reader's "Turning to Tourism in a Time of Crisis? Buddhist Temples and Pilgrimage Promotion in Secular(ized) Japan," which articulates a common pattern of Japanese Buddhist temples interacting with secular and commercial concerns for economic reasons. Via case studies of the ways in which temples and pilgrimages are being promoted by Buddhist and secular state agencies, this chapter examines links between Buddhism and tourism in contemporary Japan to investigate how state participation in the promotion of temples and pilgrimages has led to an increasing emphasis on the tourist dimensions of visiting Buddhist sites. Reader emphasizes that while commercial involvements have helped revitalize local pilgrimages and Buddhist practices, there also exists a broader trend of emphasizing tourism as the main appeal of visiting or going on pilgrimage to Japanese Buddhist sites, resulting in temples losing their place in society as sacred spaces.

In Part III, "Commodification and Its Consequences," Brian Nichols' chapter "Interrogating Religious Tourism at Buddhist Monasteries in China" investigates the ways that tourism is seen as both corrosive to an environment conducive to contemplative religious practices and an economic advantage that results in temples and monasteries actively promoting themselves as tourist sites. It is tempting to read such commercially motivated behaviors as examples of commodification at the expense of religiosity, but what we now call tourism, has arguably enjoyed a long history in Buddhism. While tourism can be disruptive to religious cultivation, Nichols argues it is not necessarily at odds with Buddhism's larger goals. Nichols' study takes an emic approach and encourages scholars to consider weak and strong notions of commodification to better understand complicated relationships between Buddhism and tourism.

Matthew Mitchell's "How I Meditated with Your Mother: Speed Dating at Temples and Shrines in Contemporary Japan," explores the romantic world of Japanese temples. Recently a number of groups have formed that cater to young, unmarried women and men looking to connect over the meditation cushion. Mitchell discusses the goals and activities of these groups of young Japanese tourists, which not only includes staying at temples, doing Zen meditation (*zazen*), copying sutras, and enjoying vegetarian temple food, but also connecting with other participants. This intentional commodification of Buddhist sites, Mitchell contends, is in order to mobilize young Japanese into visiting forgotten temples and shrines. Hence tourist organizations and priests work together to market sacred sites as locales of Buddhism's "traditional roots" while also rebranding them as romantic locales, perfect for finding love.

Part III concludes with Elizabeth Williams-Oerberg's "Buddhism: A Unique Selling Proposition (USP) in Ladakh," which investigates the ways Buddhism has been promoted as a USP by Ladakhi government officials in order to stimulate increased spiritual tourism to the region. Significant amounts of money and materials have been invested in renovating Buddhist temples with the aim of attracting foreign and domestic tourists to the region and thereby stimulating economic activity. This chapter highlights the ways that the imaginary of Buddhism as a peaceful and serene religion is clearly connected to tourism business discourses. As Ladakh's USP, Buddhism becomes the background to which all other aspects of Ladakhi culture are connected.

Buddhist landscapes in Asia have been shaped by wider trends in the region. Demands for tangible Buddhist items and intangible Buddhist services are a necessity, in some cases, of receiving support from secular institutions, including private businesses and governments, along with shifting global and local imaginaries of Buddhism. Commodifications of Buddhism can contribute to debates about secularizing the tradition while reinforcing a variety of Buddhist imaginaries. By studying Buddhist sites of tourism, we can understand common struggles and opportunities that contemporary Buddhists face. Further, we can analyze Buddhism as a dynamic tradition that includes patterns across geographical spaces as well as particularities of diverse local traditions. The following chapters investigate contemporary ways aspects of this tradition have become entrenched in tourist markets to emphasize how Buddhist places are imagined, secularized, and commodified.

The chapters in this book represent current studies being done on Buddhist tourism in Asia, the first of its kind. Our goal is to set some of the terms of this emerging conversation and lay out some of the theoretical landscapes of the relationship between Buddhism and tourism. Because of this, this volume is not an overview of case studies from all areas of Asia, as we are unfortunately missing chapters on parts of Southeast, Inner, and East Asia. It is our hope that future scholarship from these absent parts of Asia will build on the ideas set forth here.

Notes

1 For more on visitor numbers, see: UNESCO, 2009, *Nomination File,* http://whc.unesco.org/uploads/nominations/1279.pdf.

2 For more on the management plan of Angkor Wat see: United Nations Educational, Scientific, and Culture Organization, APSARA, and Godden Mackay Logan Heritage Consultants, 2012, *Angkor World Heritage Area Tourism Management Plan,* whc.unesco.org/document/134601.

3 In a search for "Buddhism" under Attractions on the Tourism Authority of Thailand website, the list totals just under 100. See: Tourism Authority of Thailand, accessed August 24, 2018, https://na.tourismthailand.org/Attraction/Search?lifestyle_id=3&cat_id=&subcat_id=&view=&keyword=Buddhism&sort=0&page=10.

4 In this volume, at times authors refer specifically to a pilgrimage, doing so because their interlocutors use this term. In such cases, pilgrimage refers to any journey to a sacred place in order to primarily perform a religious act. Religious tourism is often viewed by our interlocutors more broadly—as an activity that can include pilgrimage as well as a diverse range of activities connected with visits to a sacred site, including devotion, sightseeing, cultivation, and leisure. When

referring to sacred sites, we specifically mean spaces that are labeled as such by Buddhist themselves. Contributors to this volume do not impose an identification of "sacred" on to studied sites, but instead use the markers of their Buddhist interlocutors to understand the sacred in each Buddhist context.

5 Our use of the terms "secular," "secularizing," and "secularization" here refer to the ways that Buddhists engage with non-Buddhist, non-religious groups, in order to create and promote tourism. In our chapters, contributors discuss the ways Buddhists enter into partnerships with both governments and private companies in order to increase tourism possibilities.

6 Schober and Collins (2017) discuss the ways Buddhists view the term secular as mostly consisting of the government and its relationship to multiple religions within the same nation-state. Most recently, this secularism has produced anxiety that Buddhism is in decline and under threat within Buddhist nationalist flash points of Myanmar, Sri Lanka, and southern Thailand (10).

7 For the case of Tibet, for example, see Makley (2018).

References

Adamek, Wendi. 2005. "The Impossibility of the Given: Representations of Merit and Emptiness in Medieval Chinese Buddhism." *History of Religions* 45 (2): 135–180.

Anderson, Benedict. 1983. *Imagined Communities: Reflections on the Origin and Spread of Nationalism.* London: Verso.

Appadurai, Arjun. 1996. *Modernity at Large: Cultural Dimensions of Globalization.* Minneapolis: University of Minnesota Press.

Berger, Peter L., ed. 1999. *The Desecularization of the World: Resurgent Religion and World Politics.* Grand Rapids, MI: Wm. B. Eerdmans Publishing Company.

Bourdieu, Pierre. 1971. "Le marché des biens symboliques" (The market of symbolic goods). *L'année sociologique* 22: 49–126.

Butler, Judith. 1990. *Gender Trouble: Feminism and the Subversion of Identity.* New York: Routledge.

Casanova, José. 2009. "The Secular and Secularisms." *Social Research* 76 (4): 1049–1066.

——. 2011. "The Secular, Secularization, Secularisms." In *Rethinking Secularism,* edited by Craig Calhoun, Mark Juergensmeyer, and Jonathan Vanantwerpen, 54–74. Oxford: Oxford University Press.

Collins, Steven. 1998. *Nirvana and Other Buddhist Felicities: Utopias of the Pali Imaginaire.* Cambridge and New York: Cambridge University Press.

Covington, Richard. 2002. "Sacred and Profane." *Smithsonian* 33 (9): 80–89.

Dickhardt, Michael. 2016. "Religion, Place and Modernity in Southeast and East Asia: Reflections on the Spatial Articulation of Religion with Modernity." In *Religion, Place and Modernity: Spatial Articulations in Southeast Asia and East Asia,* edited by Michael Dickhardt and Andrea Lauser, 1–36. Boston: Brill.

Eade, John. 1992. "Pilgrimage and Tourism at Lourdes, France." *Annals of Tourism Research* 19: 18–3.

Eade, John, and Michael Sallnow, eds. 1991. *Contesting the Sacred: The Anthropology of Christian Pilgrimage.* New York: Routledge.

Eickelman, Dale F., and James Piscatori, eds. 1990. *Muslim Travellers: Pilgrimage, Migration, and the Religious Imagination.* Berkeley: University of California Press.

Einarsen, John, ed. 1995. *The Sacred Mountains of Asia.* Boston: Shambhala.

Feuchtwang, Stephan. 2004. "Theorising Place." In *Making Place: State Projects, Globalisation and Local Responses in China,* edited by Stephan Feuchtwang, 3–32. London: UCL Press.

Fisher, Gareth. 2011. "Morality Books and the Regrowth of Lay Buddhism in China." In *Religion in Contemporary China: Revitalization and Innovation,* edited by Adam Yuet Chau, 53–80. New York: Routledge.

Freiberger, Oliver. 2000. "Profiling the Saṅgha: Institutional and Non-institutional Tendencies in Early Buddhist Teachings." *Marburg Journal of Religion* 5 (1): 1–6.

Geary, David. 2008. "Destination Enlightenment: Branding Buddhism and Spiritual Tourism in Bodhgaya, Bihar." *Anthropology Today* 24 (3): 11–14.

——. 2017. *The Rebirth of Bodh Gaya: Buddhism and the Making of a World Heritage Site.* Seattle: University of Washington Press.

Geary, David, Matthew R. Sayers, and Abhisek Sing Amar, eds. 2012. *Cross-disciplinary Perspectives on a Contested Site: Bodh Gaya Jataka.* London: Routledge.

Gravari-Barbas, Maria, and Nelson H. H. Graburn. 2012. "Tourist Imaginaries." *Via@: International Interdisciplinary Review of Tourism* 1:1–5.

Guo, Chao. 2006. "Tourism and the Spiritual Philosophies of the 'Orient.'" In *Tourism, Religion and Spiritual Journeys,* edited by Dallen J. Timothy and Daniel H. Olsen, 121–138. NewYork: Routledge.

Heine, Steven, and Charles S. Prebish, eds. 2003. *Buddhism in the Modern World: Adaptations of an Ancient Tradition.* New York: Oxford University Press.

Huber, Toni. 2008. *The Holy Land Reborn: Pilgrimage and the Tibetan Reinvention of Buddhist India.* Chicago: University of Chicago Press.

Jang, Eunhwa. 2009. *Journey to Korean Temples and Temple Stay.* Seoul: Her One Media.

Kaosa-ard, Mingsarn, David Bezic, and Suzanne White. 2001. "Domestic Tourism in Thailand: Supply and Demand." In *The Native Tourist: Mass Tourism Within Developing Countries,* edited by Krishna B. Ghimire, 109–141. New York: Earthscan Publications Ltd.

Kaplan, Uri. 2010. "Images of Monasticism: The Temple Stay Program and the Rebranding of Korean Buddhist Temples." *Korean Studies* 34:127–146.

Kinnard, Jacob, N. 2014. *Places in Motion: The Fluid Identities of Temples, Images, and Pilgrims.* New York: Oxford University Press.

Kitiarsa, Pattana, ed. 2008. *Religious Commodifications in Asia: Marketing Gods.* New York: Routledge.

Leite, Naomi. 2014. "Afterword: Locating Imaginaries in the Anthropology of Tourism." In *Tourism Imaginaries: Anthropological Approaches,* edited by Nelson Graburn and Noel Salazar, 260–278. New York: Berghahn.

Makley, Charlene. 2018. *The Battle for Fortune: State-Led Development, Personhood, and Power among Tibetans in China.* Ithaca, NY: Cornell University Press.

McDaniel, Justin. 2017. *Architects of Buddhist Leisure.* Honolulu: University of Hawaiʻi Press.

McMahan, David. 2017. "Buddhism and Global Secularisms." *Journal of Global Buddhism* 18:112–128.

——, ed. 2012. *Buddhism in the Modern World.* New York and Abingdon, Oxon: Routledge.

Moran, Peter, ed. 2004. *Buddhism Observed: Travelers, Exiles and Tibetan Dharma in Kathmandu.* New York: RoutledgeCurzon.

Naquin, Susan, and Chün-fang Yü, eds. 1992. *Pilgrims and Sacred Sites in China.* Berkeley: University of California Press.

Oakes, Tim. 1998. *Tourism and Modernity in China.* New York: Routledge.

Oakes, Tim, and Donald S. Sutton, eds. 2010. *Faiths on Display: Religion Tourism, and the Chinese State.* Lanham, MD: Rowman and Littlefield.

Olsen, Daniel H. 2003. "Heritage, Tourism, and the Commodification of Religion." *Tourism Recreation Research* 28 (3): 99–104.

Philip, Janette, and David Mercer. 1999. "Commodification of Buddhism in Contemporary Burma." *Annals of Tourism Research* 26 (1): 21–54.

Prideaux, Bruce, and Dallen J. Timothy. 2008. "Themes in Cultural and Heritage Tourism in Asia and the Pacific." In *Cultural and Heritage Tourism in Asia and the Pacific,* edited by Bruce Prideaux, Dallen J. Timothy, and Kaye Chon, 1–16. New York: Routledge.

Reader, Ian. 2005. *Making Pilgrimages: Meaning and Practice in Shikoku.* Honolulu: University of Hawai'i Press.

———. 2014. *Pilgrimage in the Marketplace.* New York: Routledge.

Rodríguez del Alisal, Maria, Peter Ackermann, and Dolores P. Martinez, eds. 2007. *Pilgrimages and Spiritual Quests in Japan.* New York: Routledge.

Ryan, Chris, and Gu Huimin, eds. 2009. *Tourism in China: Destination, Cultures and Communities.* New York: Routledge.

Salazar, Noel B., and Nelson Graburn, eds. 2014. *Tourism Imaginaries: Anthropological Approaches.* New York: Berghahn.

Sánchez y Sánchez, Samuel, and Annie Hesp, eds. 2015. *The Camino de Santiago in the 21st Century: Interdisipinary Perspectives and Global Views.* New York: Routledge.

Schedneck, Brooke. 2015. *Thailand's International Meditation Centers: Tourism and the Global Commodification of Religious Practices.* New York: Routledge.

Schober, Juliane, and Steven Collins, eds. 2017. *Theravāda Buddhist Encounters with Modernity.* New York: Routledge.

Shackley, Myra. 2001. *Managing Sacred Sites: Service Provision and Visitor Experience.* London: Thomson.

Shoval, Noam. 2000. "Commodification and Theming of the Sacred: Changing Patterns of Tourism Consumption in the 'Holy Land.'" In *New Forms of Consumption: Consumers, Culture, and Commodification,* edited by Mark Gottdiener, 251–262. Lanham, MD: Rowman and Littlefield.

Singh, Shalini, ed. 2009. *Domestic Tourism in Asia: Diversity and Divergence.* London: Earthscan.

Stoddard, Robert H., and E. Alan Morris, eds. 1997. *Sacred Places, Sacred Spaces: The Geography of Pilgrimages.* Baton Rouge: Louisiana State University.

Tagliacozzo, Eric. 2013. *The Longest Journey: Southeast Asians and the Pilgrimage to Mecca.* New York: Oxford University Press.

Tagliacozzo, Eric, and Shawkat Toorawa. 2016. *The Hajj: Pilgrimage in Islam.* New York: Cambridge University Press.

Timothy, Dallen, J., and Daniel H. Olsen, eds. 2006. *Tourism, Religion and Spiritual Journeys.* New York: Routledge.

Tuan, Yi Fu. 1977. *Space and Place: The Perspective of Experience.* Minneapolis: University of Minnesota Press.

Turner, Victor, W. 1969. *The Ritual Process: Structure and Anti-Structure.* Chicago: Aldine Publishing Company.

Tweed, Thomas. 2008. *Crossing and Dwelling: A Theory of Religion.* Cambridge: Harvard University Press.

UNESCO. 2009. *Nomination File.* http://whc.unesco.org/uploads/nominations/1279.pdf.

United Nations. 2003. *Promotion of Buddhist Tourism Circuits in Selected Asian Countries.* New York: United Nations Publications.

Vukonić, Boris. 1996. *Tourism and Religion.* Oxford: Pergamon Press.

PART I

Buddhist Imaginaries and Place-Making

1

Peace and the Buddhist Imaginary in Bodh Gaya, India

DAVID GEARY

Barefoot in the gardens of Buddha. Visit to a holy place where peace is pervasive.

The Province, *Vancouver, April 20, 2008*

A range of low forested hills silhouette the small hamlets flanking the glistening, sandy banks of the river. Monks and nuns rub shoulders with tourists and believers from all over the world. An all-pervading calm envelops the town, giving visitors a sense of peace.

Bihar State Tourism Pamphlet, 2006

"Absolute peace and calmness"

What a wonderful place. Once we had walked into the heart of this site we looked at each and agreed that a calmness had overcome us. I am so glad to have shared my day at this beautiful place with the many Buddhist pilgrims.

Tripadvisor, reviewed April 25, 2016

IT IS WELL KNOWN THAT THE IMAGINATION plays an essential role in tourism. As Salazar and Graburn (2014) write, "tourism involves the human capacity to imagine or to enter into the imaginings of others. . . . Seductive images and discourses about peoples and places are so predominant that without them there probably would be little tourism, if any at all" (1). For diverse Buddhist and non-Buddhist visitors to Bodh Gaya, there are certain ideas and images in circulation that enframe the place of the Buddha's enlightenment prior to physically visiting the site. In this chapter I will argue that peace is a central motivation for many Buddhist pilgrims and tourists to Bodh Gaya, which adheres to an expansive and globally circulating image of Buddhism. But why peace? And why travel so far to experience it?

As several scholars have noted (Appadurai 1996; Brennan 2004; Salazar and Graburn 2012), the role of the imagination from a distance is key to understanding the allure of these new global tourist landscapes, the various meanings associated with place, as well as the socioeconomic interactions that arise from that signification. Unlike sex tourist destinations, for example, where foreigners can pay to fulfill their sexual fantasies (Brennan 2004), the commodification of peace is somewhat of a red herring. The concept of peace conjures a complex range of meanings that is often used as a point of reference, an empty "other" defined by an absence or cessation of war and violence (Williams and McConnell 2011, 928). Peace can also operate at various scales that include "inner" subjective domains of experience, such as meditation and quietude, and "outer" expressions of peace and peace-building campaigns related to social justice, geopolitical diplomacy, and post-conflict resolution. Thus, the desire for peace is not simply an internalized wish and form of embodied self-cultivation that mirrors the calm and serene image of the Buddha's comportment. It is also an idealistic construct that denotes something universal and is mobilized like a "charismatic package" (Tsing 2004, 227) across localities and cultures through tourism marketing, media, and social practices by Buddhist groups themselves.[1]

If peace is central to Buddhism and the tourism imaginary in Bodh Gaya, it is not without its analytical challenges. Where does this image of peace come from, and how does it motivate individual and collective desires toward the sacred? How do certain images and representations of Buddhism circulate around the globe and what material impact do they have on particular places and local lives? The origins of tourism imaginaries are complex and difficult to identify, as Salazar and Graburn (2012) point out, especially if they have been in circulation for a long time. Situated within wider sociocultural frameworks (Hutnyk 1996), tourism imaginaries bring together the "ideational and material" realms in mutually constitutive ways that are often projected on to a destination (Leite 2014, 269). Thus, following Salazar and Graburn (2012), it is important to bring historical and ethnographic methods to bear on the "multiple conduits through which they [tourism imaginaries] pass and become visible in the form of images and discourses," as well as how they are embedded in distinctive social and political relationships at the local level (2).

Bringing the material and ideational realms together, in this chapter I show how a Buddhist imaginary of peace in Bodh Gaya emerges from nineteenth- and twentieth-century discourses. These new articulations have led to a modern reformulation and decontextualized view of Buddhism as a rational and enlightened religion of universal appeal due to its emphasis on compassion, self-discipline, and peace. This image of Buddhism has become particularly pronounced in the West alongside the emergence of prominent "engaged" Buddhist leaders such as Nobel Peace Prize winner, the Fourteenth Dalai Lama Tenzin Gyatso, and Vietnamese Zen monk Thich Nhat Hanh. Not only have various Buddhist leaders and communities utilized Bodh Gaya's sacred ground for the projection of an apolitical and non-violent image in line with these earlier Orientalist discourses, the emphasis on peace is also central to the Indian government. The government's efforts to capitalize on the development prospects of Buddhist pilgrimage and spiritual tourism serves to enhance India's broader vision of "soft power" (Nye 2003, 2013).[2]

What I want to emphasize is that Bodh Gaya is a global pilgrimage and tourist destination that relies on a particular place-making myth and image of Buddhism as a religion of peace. Given the rapid development and social change that is taking place in Bodh Gaya this also has consequences for everyday socio-spatial relations in the surrounding area. While much has been written about the idealized relationship between Buddhism and peace, less research has explicitly addressed how peace as an assemblage of disparate elements becomes grounded and reproduced in places, bodies, and the micropolitics of everyday life (Williams 2013, 232).

Is Buddhism a Religion of Peace?

> All beings fear death and they all fear the pain of a club. Think: how do they make you feel? Then do not kill and do not club; live peacefully with all beings and do not add to the violence of this world. Harm no one here and you will pass your next life in peace.
>
> *Buddha, Dhammapada*

In this modern era, Buddhism is frequently described as a religion of peace and non-violence. In the global circulation of Buddhist images and iconography there is perhaps no greater signifier of the religion than Siddhartha Gautama sitting in sublime contemplation beneath the Bodhi tree in what is known as Bodh Gaya today. For forty days, it is believed, the future Buddha sat pondering the nature of suffering and the root of its causes among all sentient beings. Through his stillness and meditative awareness, he conquered all distractions and removed all traces of ignorance before bathing in the sublime experience of enlightenment (or *bodhi*, "awakening"). Thus, as the navel of the earth and victory throne of all buddhas (*vajrasana*), Bodh Gaya has become, arguably, the most important Buddhist pilgrimage site in the modern era and the center of an emerging world Buddhism (Geary 2014). And, in the imagination of many Buddhist pilgrims and global travelers to the place of the Buddha's epiphany, the ineffable experience of enlightenment is reified as a transcendent ideal and metaphorically described as a direct experience of peace.

Although it is not the goal of this chapter to disentangle the complex translations, connotations, and meanings surrounding the Buddha's awakening or to verify its authenticity in relation to Bodh Gaya's sacred space, what interests me is a historical and religious contextualization of peace and how this has become conflated with the place of the Buddha's enlightenment in the modern era. According to Selwyn (1996), all places and people that are the objects of the tourist gaze (Urry 1990) reflect certain idealized images or mythic "stories" that are drawn from a variety of sources and "serve to connect specific destinations with more general preoccupations and desires in the tourist's own society" (cited in Leite 2012, 265). This view is in line with place-making as discussed in the Introduction. Places are the centering of repeated actions, which are inevitably shaped by idealized images and stories. In the context of Bodh Gaya's rediscovery and global reimagining as the place of the Buddha's enlightenment, it is important to situate this genealogy within the broader discourse of the Orient that derives from nineteenth-century interpretations of non-Christian religions.

It is well known that tourism marketing in Asia relies on the repackaging and circulation of Orientalist images, fantasies, and desires (both locally and globally inspired). In the context of these traveling images, India has long been romanticized as a spiritual utopia, a place of self-discovery and ancient wisdom, which has led to the familiar binary of the "spiritual East" and "rational West" (Geary 2013; Schedneck 2013; Singer 1972). It is for these reasons that Bodh Gaya as the central place of Buddhism is uniquely situated in terms of the "cultural symbolic of the mystical east" (King 1999,1). The metanarrative of peace can be read as one constituent element of a larger imagined geography of spiritual tourism that accompanies Occidental fantasies of the East, and India in particular. Although the search for peace is by no means a Western phenomenon, as I will demonstrate shortly, the desire for spiritual enrichment through an Eastern "Other" has long resonated among Western travelers.

Among early Western scholars and Orientalists, there was a strong Victorian fascination with Gautama Buddha's humanizing character and heroic qualities that came to resemble an ideal Victorian gentleman. Through a process of textualization, as Almond (1988,132) writes, the Victorian interpretation involved assimilating Buddhism insofar as it correlated with normative Victorian ideas and values, and rejecting Buddhism so far as it was incommensurable with these values, such as the theme of suffering and pessimism around the annihilation of the individual. This latent image of an ideal Buddhism assembled from ancient texts and scriptures was also enhanced and exaggerated in opposition to the ritualistic and hierarchical orthopraxy of Hinduism in the Indian subcontinent, as well as the presumed moral degradation of Buddhism outside India over time. Thus, comparable to Martin Luther, the Buddha was seen as a great social reformer who proclaimed the equality of all men, and had a significant "humanizing and civilizing influence throughout Asia" (Almond 1988, 130), "one of calm and sweet majesty, of infinite tenderness and compassion, and of perfect moral freedom" (70).

These imaginative reconstructions based on Occidental fantasies and myths have provided fertile ground for the making of Buddhist modernism as it's received in the West. As discussed by David McMahan (2008), from the nineteenth century onward, a Westernized view of Buddhism appears as a religion "in which you don't have to believe anything in particular or follow any strict rules, you simply exercise compassion and maintain a peaceful state of mind through meditation" (4). Thus, for many North Americans and Europeans what they understand as "Buddhism" according to McMahan (2008), is actually a "modern hybrid tradition with roots in the European Enlightenment no less than the Buddha's enlightenment, in Romanticism and transcendentalism as much as the Pali canon, and in the clash of Asian culture and colonial powers as much as in mindfulness and meditation" (5). Although it is tempting to see these modernizing forms of Buddhism as an "exclusively western project or simply a representation of the eastern Other" (McMahan 2008, 6), there were also a number of important Asian Buddhist reformers who have helped bring this complex mixture of different cultural and intellectual currents to the foreground, including the emphasis on peace. A few examples will help to illustrate the point.

Under the influence of colonialism and an emerging nationalist movement throughout various parts of Asia, several Asian elites and Buddhist reformers actively sought to align their religious traditions with certain discourses of modernity, hoping to build their own authority and legitimacy on the international stage (Schedneck 2013, 41). In the postcolonial Indian context, for example, this image and idealization of Buddhism as an ancient faith marked by rationality, non-violence, and an egalitarian message was one that resonated with the first prime minister of India, Jawaharlal Nehru, who looked to the "historical Buddha" and Emperor Asóka as embodiments of moral virtue for India's newfound secular state. The strategic use of Buddhist heritage and Gautama Buddha's pacifying qualities helped to project India as a moral authority as well as strengthen economic links and diplomacy within the region. There were also a number of more specific events in this history of postcolonial India that has contributed to this moral and inclusive discourse. This includes Nehru's leading role in the Non-Aligned Movement following the Bandung Conference of April 1955 (often described as the "Third Way") that provided an alternative to the Cold War division, as well as the Indian government's active role in the yearlong International Buddha Jayanti celebrations in 1956–1957 where several major events were dedicated to world peace (Geary

2014). What is also significant about this modern interpretation of Buddhism alongside India's constitutional commitment to secularism, is that it does not present Buddhism or Buddhists, "as particularly threatening or problematic by adherents of India's other religious communities and their leaders" (Singh 2010, 194), namely Hinduism and Islam.

Evident in any library catalogue search, the relationship between Buddhism and peace became more pronounced throughout the twentieth century, especially in the post–World War II period. As Ian Harris writes, within this burgeoning writing genre among Buddhist scholars and practitioners, there is a strong tendency to "transpose an individualist and subjective understanding of peace into the socio-political domain that is consistent with the tenets of 'protestant Buddhism'" (2009, 22). Although this discourse can be traced back to modern Buddhist reformers like Anagarika Dharmapala and others, it is also consistent with the growth of a "global liberal religiosity" that has created new ground for Buddhist leaders to reformulate and reconceive their traditions in universal and humanistic terms (Harris 2009, 23). Like the influence of "spirituality" as discussed by David McMahan (2012), the supposed universality of peace that lies at the moral core of *all* religions was quickly adopted by many cosmopolitan representatives of Asian traditions who utilized the terminology as "an important vehicle by which non-Western traditions presented themselves to the broader world, constituting themselves as 'world religions'" (3). It was also central to the founding of several transnational Buddhist organizations that emerged in the aftermath of World War II such as the World Fellowship of Buddhists (founded in 1950), the World Buddhist Sangha Council (founded in 1966), and most importantly, the Asian Buddhist Conference for Peace in the 1970s (Harris 2009, 23–24). In all of these cases, international forums and meetings among Buddhists were dedicated to world peace.

Although various scholars (Arisaka 1996; Victoria 2006) have pointed to a high level of collusion between some prominent Japanese Buddhists and the general war effort, this was followed by a radical shift toward peace activism after 1945 (Harris 2009; Stone 2000). One significant Japanese Buddhist traveler-monk who played a leading role in the propagation of world peace following World War II was Nichidatsu Fujii, known popularly as Fujii Guruji (1885–1985), founder of the Nipponzan-Myohoji order. Born on the island of Kyushu, Fujii was attracted to the Lotus Sutra and teachings of Nichiren, who had predicted that the Buddha Dharma would return to India. Inspired by this prediction he set out on his mission to India in the early 1930s, and later spearheaded a movement to build Peace Pagodas (*Shanti Stupa*) in Japan, India, and throughout the world—all dedicated to world peace. The first Peace Pagodas were built in the Japanese cities of Hiroshima and Nagasaki following the devastation of the atomic bombs. This was followed by the 1965 construction of the World Peace Pagoda on the top of Ratnagiri Hill in Rajgir in the North

Indian state of Bihar. Throughout his life, and continuing after his death in 1985, Fujii Gurujii and those connected to his movement have erected at least eighty stupas or Peace Pagodas around the world.

Over the last thirty years, the discourse of world peace (Tib. *dzamling zhi-de*) has also been adopted on the modern international stage by various proponents of the Tibetan cause, most notably His Holiness the Fourteenth Dalai Lama (Mills 2009).[3] Following the Chinese invasion of Tibet in 1959 and its resulting diaspora of Buddhist monks, many of whom reside in India and undertake pilgrimage to Bodh Gaya every winter season, the Mahabodhi Temple and its surroundings have become important ceremonial staging grounds for large ritual gatherings such as the Kalachakra (Dukhor Wangchen) Initiation and the Monlam or Great Prayer for World Peace. Because one's ritual actions are believed to multiply in a sacred place like Bodh Gaya, these ritual events are believed to generate vast amounts of religious merit among participants. Although both the Kalachakra and Monlam have a long history in the Tibetan plateau as key rituals of the Gelukpa monastic tradition, Toni Huber (2008) suggests that since the 1980s there has been considerable innovations in the ritual activities staged in Bodh Gaya, especially with respect to the Monlam or the Great Prayer Festival for World Peace that has now been adopted by the other three main schools of Tibetan Buddhism in Indian exile.

The strategic staging of these ritual gatherings at the symbolic center of the Buddhist universe (as well as other major Buddhist holy sites), including the rhetorical emphasis on "World Peace" by the Tibetan exile organizers, is significant, according to Huber, because it coincides with a major shift in Tibetan exile self-representations (2008, 363). In Huber's words, "Throughout the 1980s and 1990s, an increasingly sophisticated Tibetan exile discourse on world peace and the projection of an essentially non-violent Tibetan national identity and history were deliberately cultivated by the Tibetan government-in-exile and its supporters and publicly represented in various ways" (363). The Tibetan identification of these rituals for world peace on the global stage, not only builds on an early precedent set by Buddhist modernists and international Buddhist movements, but they also serve "to reinforce the perception of Tibetan religion as a unique and significant resource which may serve a universal purpose" (Huber 2008, 363).

By way of contrast to Huber, Martin Mills (2009) argues that the proliferation of Tibetan World Peace discourse by the Tibetan government-in-exile and Western followers, is not just a rhetorical strategy, but in fact a continuation of established facets of Buddhist ritual practice that are organized around traditional Tibetan understandings of righteous kingly sovereignty. Rather than innovations built on Western, secular interpretations of peace or borrowed elements of a New Age discourse, there are clear continuities with traditional Tibetan interpretations of ritual practice that hark back to the early imperial period of Tibetan history. Of central importance for the Dalai Lama and other high-ranking lamas, is the idea that specific rituals, including the consecration of stupas, inscribe the landscape with the presence of particular buddhas that "positively influence the moral and geomantic environment in which they are performed" (Mills 2009, 23). Regardless of whether these ritual actions are a reflection of traditional Tibetan modes of ritual statecraft or new creative self-representations among a diaspora hungry for international recognition and support, they have strengthened the image of Buddhism as a religion of peace that has consequences for how Bodh Gaya is shaped as a place of global pilgrimage and tourism.

Although these Tibetan renditions of religiosity have been particularly significant since the 1980s, they are not the only Buddhist community or Buddhist leaders to assert or utilize world peace as a vehicle for social reform and the projection of a universal morality based on Buddhist teachings and/or perspectives. Like the Fourteenth Dalai Lama, other living global saints, peace activists, and socially "engaged" Buddhist leaders—such as Vietnamese Zen monk Thich Nhat Hanh, Thai Sulak Sivaraksa, and Cambodian monk Maha Ghosananda—have also played a key role in asserting the importance of cultivating inner peace as a precondition for bringing about lasting world peace. As a result of the unique circumstances in Burma/Myanmar, Nobel Peace Prize winner and politician Aung San Suu Kyi has also been a major voice in this milieu advocating for non-violence in the struggle for democracy.

Let us return to the main question of this section: is Buddhism a religion of peace? Like other major world religions, Buddhism has a set of guiding moral precepts such as the concept of *ahimsa*—abstaining from killing living creatures—that is believed to be intrinsic to the teachings of the Buddha. Buddhists believe that peace can be attained once all suffering (*dukkha*) ends. These moral precepts that adhere to a set of teachings called the Four Noble Truths are also strengthened by a tool kit of meditation practices and techniques designed to transform and eliminate unwholesome thoughts such as hatred, anger, and rage that may contribute to violence. While most Buddhists practice non-violence and do not support war efforts, the Buddha's teachings and moral guidelines are not separate from the broader social and political conditions in which Buddhists live. Due to the historical connections between state power and religious patronage this has led to bloodshed and the moral justification of violence in several parts of the Buddhist world. Part of the reason why this is the case, according to Charles Keyes (2007) is that members of the Buddhist sangha who exemplify and teach the Dharma to others, have always relied on the economic support of the laity and the protection of state rulers and kings (147).

Although Buddhism is often imagined, especially by Westerners, as a religion of radical world-rejection centered on meditation and achieving detachment from the world, Buddhism has always been, and continues to be, embroiled in sociopolitical conflicts of the countries where Buddhists reside (Jerryson 2011; Keyes 2007). This has become even more apparent in recent decades, especially in Thailand, Burma, and Sri Lanka, where social and economic grievances have enflamed communal tensions, with lay Buddhist followers and radicalized monks denouncing and targeting Muslim minorities and destroying mosques. In short, Buddhism is not, as is often assumed, solely based on the doctrines and platitudes of its popular leaders, a religion of peace. Buddhists are not immune from "the same human spectrum of emotions, which includes the penchant for violence" (Jerryson 2010). So, in the context of Bodh Gaya, perhaps we have to look elsewhere for contributing factors that go beyond this one-sided image of Buddhism and analyze the ways peace is expressed within broader socioeconomic forces at the local and global level.

Spiritual Tourism and Everyday Peace in Bihar

How is the aspiration for peace articulated within tourism development and increased commodification in Bodh Gaya? Due to the reification of the sacred and profane as separate ontological categories in the social sciences, the economic aspects of religious travel have been one of the least studied topics in relation to the field of pilgrimage (Timothy and Olsen 2006; Vukonic 2002). This is particularly pertinent in the South Asian context where there has long been a blurring of the sacred and commercial realms. Although pilgrimage has been for a long time an economic driver and remains so today, increasingly we are seeing new pressures related to the global economy that are leading to the commodification of space, including sacred space, to meet the desires of the tourist gaze.

When sacred places and the consumption of certain religious practices become a marketable commodity, it creates spiritual tourism: a much larger field of (re)creation and tourism that includes the popular expansion of meditation retreats, yoga centers, ashrams for the guru-seeking, alternative medicine destinations, spa treatments, and other transnational spaces geared toward practices of well-being, relaxation, and spiritual enrichment. Although religious travel, such as pilgrimage, has a long history in many parts of the world, the commodification of sacred places and the lure of the spiritual tourist has also become a key strategy deployed by various state governments due to its economic potential. Like the subsequent rise in dark tourism directed to places identified with death and suffering in the modern era, such as Auschwitz, Ground Zero in New York, and the Killing Fields in Cambodia (see Matthew Trew, this volume), spiritual tourism directed toward practices of well-being and psychosocial nourishment represents the other spectrum of the tourist gaze. The emphasis on spirituality is also important in the context of tourism, according to Timothy and Olsen (2006), because it can be interpreted as a dis-embedding of religious tradition and a "secularizing trend towards more privatized and pluralized experience" where people are no longer constrained by religious dogma, hierarchy, and authority (4–5). Whereas religion has institutional connotations, prescribed rituals or worship, and established ways of believing, spirituality suggests a more experiential and intangible dimension that has to do with deep motivations for life meaning, change, and wholeness that functions well in secular markets (Carrette and King 2005; McMahan 2012; Schedneck 2013).

Thus, as an important and growing segment of international tourism, some of the factors contributing to religious and spiritually motivated travel, according to Timothy and Olsen (2006), include investments in mass transportation, such as new railways and airports; the restoration of ancient sites; a sense of dislocation as a result of rapid global and social change; and an increasing number of people who are in search of meaning and answers to fundamental questions about the human experience, such as emancipation from suffering, a desire for peace, and the transformation of consciousness (3–6). Reasons why people are drawn to Buddhism in particular is its association with meditation and other interior states of psychological contentment that provide relief and guidance in the face of growing violence in the media, as well as the threat of ISIS and terrorist activities in many parts of the world. The emancipatory potential of Buddhism appears to resonate with these broader developments because pilgrims and non-Buddhist travelers not only seek an emotional and temporary release from the mundane world of everyday social structure and disenchantment (Turner 1973), but Buddhism can also provide a radical critique of capitalism due to its underlying ethos of renunciation, including the soteriological goal of nirvana that involves the extinguishing of all attachments, cravings, and desires. It is not surprising that among many Western Buddhist pilgrims and practitioners that I spoke with in Bodh Gaya, when the search for peace and personal transformation is most desired, the commercial excess and consumerism is bemoaned the greatest. The irony of course is that a strong market presence has emerged in Bodh Gaya (and elsewhere) around Buddhist aspirations for non-desire and liberation from consumerism. If non-desire is the base, the drive to conquer desire creates more surplus value.

Given that spiritual tourism is an emerging phenomenon that contributes to the Buddhist imaginary of peace in Bodh Gaya, another important factor is the town's location in the North Indian state of Bihar. Tourism imaginaries, as Salazar and Graburn (2012) suggest, are often structured by dichotomies. Because tourism imaginaries do not exist in a vacuum, they have to contend with other circulating images and ideas that may help to reaffirm or reinforce particular views of a place or peoples. Among the various guidebooks, travel narratives, newsprint media, and interlocutors I spoke with in Bodh Gaya, there is an important juxtaposition between the various representational practices that enframe the place of the Buddha's enlightenment, and the broader subcontinental image of Bihar that evokes revulsion and disdain—a place that is feared, despised, and morally bereft. Despite Bihar's remarkable cultural legacy as the "land of *viharas*," as well as more recent efforts to rebrand its image as "Blissful Bihar" in tourism promotional materials, it remains a densely populated and impoverished rural state with a large out-migration of workers that has contributed to discrimination and marginalization of Biharis throughout India.

Drawing a parallel with earlier images of Sicily among the Indian states, Arun Sinha goes as far as to describe Bihar as "extremely violent, subversive, perilous, ungovernable; a place where human life was as cheap as in a spaghetti Western" (1991, 10). Not only is Bihar's countryside associated with caste violence and lawlessness but the swelling cities of Patna and Gaya have also gained popular notoriety for their political/criminal nexus and kidnapping economy, as evident in weekly print-media and recent Bollywood films such as *Apaharan* (2005) and *Gangajal* (2003). A paradigmatic political figure who encapsulates this image of Bihar is none other than Lalu Prasad Yadav—a crass and uncouth low-caste politician who ruled the state as chief minister for fifteen years. As an object of ridicule and a popular national icon, Bihar and Lalu's rise to fame are important because they provide a marked juxtaposition to the moral superiority of the Buddha and the desire for peace that many seek in their journey to Bodh Gaya.

Although it is not the aim of this chapter to separate "myth" from "reality" in the popular rhetoric surrounding Bihar, what is evident in these representations of Bihar is that it has long been regarded as difficult terrain for the forces of capitalism and economic development. Unlike the shining model and success of Kerala as a tourist destination to the south, Bihar's position of alterity and marginality finds a unique consort with the transnational desires and opportunities presented by Buddhism and spiritual tourism in the late twentieth and early twenty-first century. Up until recently Bihar's unfavorable image and reputation had in many ways served as a deterrent for visitors to Bodh Gaya. Fear of bandits, *Naxalites* (Maoist insurgents), and poor infrastructure have arguably helped to insulate this small rural town with a spiritual aroma of peace without mass tourism and commercialism. However, the surging forces of transnational capital as a result of increased transportation (including a new international airport) and a new chief minister elected on a platform of anti-corruption and robust development, has brought greater attention to Bodh Gaya's globalizing prospects as a pilgrim and tourist destination.

In line with this structuring dichotomy are two important developments that have helped to strengthen and reinforce the Buddhist imaginary of peace at the local level in recent years. Of primary importance is the everyday host-guest relations in the marketplace that plays a critical role in shaping the experience of Bodh Gaya. In the Bodh Gaya Block (surrounding villages) nearly 80 percent of the social demographic is comprised of scheduled caste/tribes and "other backwards castes" from both Hindu and Muslim religious backgrounds. As one of the poorest districts in the country, outside of the agricultural sector a significant section of this population relies on the formal and informal tourism market for their livelihood. Thus, in order to distance themselves from the negative image of Bihar, many of the employers in the bazaar have an acute sensitivity and awareness about upholding an ethic of hospitality that speaks in subtle ways to the rhetoric of peace. This ethic is best encapsulated in the vernacular phrase *atthiti bhagwan hai,* "guest is god," that helps to ensure continuing economic prosperity and opportunities through pilgrimage-based tourism. As one local shopkeeper explained to me: "If the system is disturbed the money will go. Hindus, Muslims, Buddhists—if they fight the business will die out. In Bodh Gaya you will not find as many people cheat you or try and steal. Everyone is cautious that this business environment should not be disturbed."

While much has been written about contestation in Bodh Gaya, especially with respect to management of the Mahabodhi Temple (Geary, Sayers, and Amar 2012), it is important to emphasize that everyday inter-community life in Bodh Gaya is more often characterized by cooperation, exchange, and amity, than conflict. Similar to the work of Philipa Williams and her study of the silk industry in nearby Varanasi, the circulation of economic capital at the local level is therefore "integral to the possibility as well as the necessity of everyday peace being sustained" in Bodh Gaya (2013, 235). While this is a different motivation for peace than the goal of many Buddhist pilgrims and spiritual tourists to Bodh Gaya, it demonstrates how the economic and religious aspects of place are mutually reinforcing.

Not only do tourism imaginaries rely on hospitality at the local level to reaffirm particular desires and/or images of place, they are also hinged on more official representations such as the 2002 designation of the Mahabodhi Temple complex as a UNESCO World Heritage site. The strengthening of international diplomacy and the importance of promoting world peace has long underlined the vision of the United Nations with its foundational goal of establishing a culture of "peace in the minds of men." As defined by the United Nations, a "culture of peace is a set of values, attitudes, modes of behavior and ways of life that reject violence and prevent conflicts by tackling their root causes to solve problems through dialogue and negotiation among individuals, groups and nations."[4] Paired with tourism development, the United Nations, the World Bank, and the World Tourism Organization have all lauded the benefits of UNESCO World Heritage as a "mechanism for world peace" that promotes understanding among peoples, helps to conserve places of outstanding universal value, and contributes to the exchange of visitors (Chambers 2009). Through the protection of natural and cultural heritage around the globe UNESCO rhetorically positions all of humanity as a global family and community of heirs with peace and peace building at the center of its mission.

As part of my ongoing research in Bodh Gaya over the last twelve years, I have been looking at the spatial politics generated by both the rapid economic development under globalization and the linked conservation demands placed upon the built environment to safeguard Bodh Gaya's material past. As part of the stipulation for the site's admission on the World Heritage list in 2002, this international designation also set in motion a number of contingent development plans and conservation initiatives that seek to rehabilitate and beautify the urban center through the implementation of a two-kilometer buffer zone that is also referred to as a "zone of peace" around the Mahabodhi Temple. What seems at the surface antithetical to the goals of UNESCO, in 2007 and 2013, the state-municipal and regional authorities in Bodh Gaya proceeded to demolish a number of buildings, street-side stalls, and commercial shops along the footpath and have proposed relocating a large segment of residential dwellings. These recent actions by the state administration to remove "encroachments" has brought growing strife and resistance among local groups in connection with the recent international conservation demands that have the capacity to undermine the ethics of hospitality and inter-community amity described above.

In many ways, these changes to Bodh Gaya's landscape reflect similar processes in other Indian cities (and around the world), which have also witnessed a rapid integration of global consumer markets and commodity networks that have fostered more competitive interactions over public space. The pressures of market liberalization coupled with the efforts to ensure a city's position in the new global economy of tourism have led to the creation of extra-governmental spaces of production, such as "Special Economic Zones," and protected spaces whereby neo-liberal reforms merge and intersect with global conventions and transnational conservation agendas as posed by UNESCO. Thus, in seeking to uphold universal ideas and values associated with World Heritage, places like Bodh Gaya have also become significant registers to rid streets and public lands of squatters and encroachers, and to reclaim public space for the use of "proper citizens" (Chatterjee 2004). The irony is that on the one hand UNESCO seeks to establish a culture of peace through World Heritage and its model of global citizenship, while at the same time World Heritage provides an alibi for rehabilitating urban spaces that is often in direct conflict with the demands of local people who compete for capital, jobs, and access to livelihood. In other words, although tourism imaginaries have a "capacity to become natural or to naturalize what they represent" (Salazar 2010, 142), they are not detached from social realities of place and are often contingent on the local context and the broader moral-commercial ethos that sustains the environment for pilgrims and tourists.

Peace is central to the Buddhist imaginary in Bodh Gaya and correlates with its rise as a place of global tourism and pilgrimage. Not only is peace a central aspiration for pilgrims and visitors to the place of enlightenment, but it also forms an important backdrop for certain encounters, transactions, and negotiations in and around Bodh Gaya. There are many visitors and residents of Bodh Gaya who would argue that the site is inherently peaceful due to the grace of Lord Buddha and his auspicious awakening *at this spot* over twenty-five hundred years ago. When I asked a local caretaker of the Mahabodhi Temple grounds, why the place remains peaceful he said: "It is the Buddha. Even his name is enough to calm people. They say he is still a living force." This may very well be the case, but as I have suggested here, the Buddhist imaginary of peace in Bodh Gaya rests on a complex web of social, economic, and geographic causes and conditions.

Buddhism has been constructed as a religion of peace in a number of different ways, which owes a great deal to the conditions of modernity, especially after World War II and more recently, international media, and the heightened awareness of violence and terror in various parts of the world. Despite the reality of radicalized monks and state violence in several Buddhist countries, this one-sided image continues to be sustained, especially in the West, but also by various prominent Asian Buddhist leaders and ritual communities of practice such as the Tibetans who utilize Bodh Gaya's sacred space for their ritual events in the name of world peace. The role of peace, as I have discussed, is also central to World Heritage, tourism promotion, and the spatial integration of the temple town that involves various social relationships and interlocking webs of meaning that contribute to this image of place.

Most importantly, the shadow of poverty and the local demands for livelihood are decisive factors in stabilizing Bodh Gaya as an alleged "zone of peace" in the first place. If an ideal Buddhist state of existence comes through living in harmony with everything (sentient or non-sentient) in the universe, this involves a better appreciation of the multiple influences and interconnections that compel peace as a collective product. Although there can be no question, as Ian Harris (2009) writes, "that the proper practice of Buddhism fosters a personal, subjective or inner feeling of peace in the individual practitioner it is a little more difficult to determine whether Buddhist practice actually creates peace in the social or political domain" (22). As a transnational place undergoing rapid change, a better appreciation and understanding of the sacral-commercial ties and conditions that inform Buddhist tourism in Bodh Gaya may be a step toward the realization of peace.

Notes

1 Following the work of anthropologist Anna Tsing (2004), she shows how environmental activism "moves in 'charismatic packages,' allegorical modules that speak to the possibilities of making a cause heard… formed in a political and cultural location that gives their stories meaning" (227). Peace building, like environmental activism, in other words, can be seen as a model of solidarity that travels unmoored from their place of emergence and becomes reattached as allegories within "new fields of meaning and of social action to make a difference in its new home" (228).

2 Soft power is a concept developed by Joseph Nye that suggests the ability to attract and co-opt through the appeal of culture, political values, and foreign policies, rather than through coercion (hard power), using force, or giving money as a means of persuasion. Throughout the twentieth century, but especially following India's independence in 1947, the civilizational legacy of Buddhism and the Asoka-Maurya past has been adopted as a key cultural resource for diplomacy in the region, especially following India's Look East Policy that was initiated in 1991.

3 As a central plank of His Holiness' international political profile, as well as for senior Tibetan lamas, there is no denying the influence of this world peace rubric within Tibetan affairs, which extends well beyond Bodh Gaya. Other examples include the Fourteenth Dalai Lama's Five Point Peace Plan for the future of the Tibetan state as a neutral demilitarized Zone of Peace, the World Peace Vase Project carried out by Dilgo Khyentse Rinpoche and Dzongsar Khyentse Rinpoche since 1987, and the Stupas for World Peace initiative, constructed under the auspices of Akong Tulku Rinpoche and Penor Rinpoche since 1990, among others (Mills 2009).

4 UN Resolutions A/RES/52/13: Culture of Peace; and A/RES/53/243, Declaration and Programme of Action on a Culture of Peace.

References

Almond, Philip C. 1988. *The British Discovery of Buddhism.* Cambridge: Cambridge University Press.

Appadurai, Arjun. 1996. *Modernity at Large: Cultural Dimensions of Globalization.* Minneapolis: University of Minnesota Press.

Arisaka, Yoko. 1996. "The Nishida Enigma: 'The Principle of the New World Order.'" *Monumenta Nipponica* 51 (1): 81–105.

Brennan, Denise. 2004. *What's Love Got To Do With It: Transnational Desires and Sex Tourism in the Dominican Republic.* Durham, NC: Duke University Press.

Carrette, Jeremy R., and Richard King. 2005. *Selling Spirituality: The Silent Takeover of Religion.* New York: Routledge.

Chambers, Erve. 2009. *Native Tours: The Anthropology of Travel and Tourism.* Long Grove, IL: Waveland Press.

Chatterjee, Partha. 2004. *The Politics of the Governed: Reflections on Popular Politics in Most of the World.* New York: Columbia University Press.

Geary, David. 2013. "Incredible India in a Global Age: The Cultural Politics of Image Branding in Tourism." *Tourist Studies* 13 (1): 36–61.

——. 2014. "Rebuilding the Navel of the Earth: Buddhist Pilgrimage and Transnational Religious Networks." *Modern Asian Studies* 48 (3): 645–692.

Geary, David, Matthew R. Sayers, and Abhishek Singh Amar, eds. 2012. *Cross-disciplinary Perspectives on a Contested Buddhist Site: Bodh Gaya Jataka.* London: Routledge.

Harris, Ian. 2009. "Is Buddhism a Religion of Peace? Reflections on Conflict and the Buddhist Political Imagination." *Buddhist Approach to Political Conflict and Peace Development,* UNDV Conference, volumes 4–6, May 2552/2009, Thailand, 12–26.

Huber, Toni. 2008. *The Holy Land Reborn: Pilgrimage and the Tibetan Reinvention of Buddhist India.* Chicago: University of Chicago Press.

Hutnyk, John. 1996. *The Rumour of Calcutta: Tourism, Charity and the Poverty of Representation.* London: Zed Books.

Jerryson, Michael. 2011. *Buddhist Fury: Religion and Violence in Southern Thailand.* New York: Oxford University Press.

——. 2010. "Monks with Guns: Discovering Buddhist Violence." *Religion Dispatches.* Last modified January 12, 2010. http://religiondispatches.org/monks-with-guns-discovering-buddhist-violence/

Keyes, Charles F. 2007. "Monks, Guns, and Peace: Theravada Buddhism and Political Violence." In *Belief and Bloodshed: Religion and Violence across Time and Tradition,* edited by James K. Wellman Jr., 145–163. Lanham, MD: Rowman & Littlefield Publishers.

King, Richard. 1999. *Orientalism and Religion: Post-Colonial Theory, India and "The Mystic East."* New York: Routledge.

Leite, Naomi. 2014. "Locating Imaginaries in the Anthropology of Tourism." In *Tourism Imaginaries: Anthropological Approaches,* edited by Noel B. Salazar and Nelson H. H. Graburn, 260–278. New York: Berghahn Books.

McMahan, David L. 2012 "The Enchanted Secular: Buddhism and the Emergence of Transtraditional 'Spirituality.'" *The Eastern Buddhist* 43 (1): 205–223.

——. 2008. *The Making of Buddhist Modernism.* New York: Oxford University Press.

Mills, Martin. 2009. "This Circle of Kings: Modern Tibetan Visions of World Peace." In *Boundless Worlds: An Anthropological Approach to Movement,* edited by Peter Wynn Kirby, 95–114. New York: Berghahn Books.

Nye, Joseph. S. 2013. "Hard, Soft, and Smart Power." In *The Oxford Handbook of Modern Diplomacy,* edited by A. F. Cooper, J. Heine, and R. C. Thakur, 559–574. New York: Oxford University Press.

——. 2004. *Soft Power: The Means to Success in World Politics.* New York: Public Affairs.

Salazar, Noel B. 2010. *Envisioning Eden: Mobilizing Imaginaries in Tourism and Beyond.* New York: Berghahn Books.

——. 2012. "Tourism Imaginaries: A Conceptual Approach." *Annals of Tourism Research* 39 (2): 863–882.

Salazar, Noel B., and Nelson H. H. Graburn, eds. 2014. *Tourism Imaginaries: Anthropological Approaches.* New York: Berghahn Books.

Schedneck, Brooke. 2013, "The Decontexualization of Asian Religious Practices in the Context of Globalization." *Journal for Cultural and Religious Theory* 12 (3): 36–54.

Selwyn, Tom. 1996. *The Tourist Image: Myths and Myth Making in Tourism.* Chichester: Wiley.

Singer, Milton. 1972. *When a Great Tradition Modernizes: An Anthropological Approach to Indian Civilization.* New York: Praeger Publishers.

Singh, U. 2010. "Exile and Return: The Reinvention of Buddhism and Buddhist Sites in Modern India." *South Asia Studies* 26 (2): 193–217.

Sinha, Arun. 1991. *Against the Few: Struggles of India's Rural Poor.* London: Zed Books.

Stone, Jacqueline. 2000. "Japanese Lotus Millenarianism: From Militant Nationalism to Contemporary Peace Movements." In *Millenialism, Persecution and Violence: Historical Cases,* edited by Catherine Wessinger, 261–280. Syracuse: Syracuse University Press.

Timothy, Dallen, and Daniel Olsen, eds. 2006. *Tourism, Religion and Spiritual Journeys.* New York: Routledge.

Tsing, Anna Lowenhaupt. 2004. *Friction: An Ethnography of Global Connection.* Princeton: Princeton University Press.

Turner, Victor. 1973. "The Center Out There: Pilgrim's Goal." *History of Religions*, 191–230.

Urry, John. 1990. *The Tourist Gaze: Leisure and Travel in Contemporary Societies.* London: Sage.

Victoria, Brian. 2006. "D.T. Suzuki and Japanese Militarism: Supporter or Opponent?" In *Buddhism and Violence,* edited by Michael Zimmermann, 159–194. Lumbini: Lumbini International Research Centre.

Vukonic, Boris. 2002. "Religion, Tourism and Economics: A Convenient Symbiosis." *Tourism Recreation Research* 27 (2): 59–64.

Williams, Philippa. 2013. "Reproducing Everyday Peace in North India: Process, Politics, and Power." *Annals of the Association of American Geographers* 103 (1): 230–250.

Williams, Philippa, and Fiona McConnell. 2011. "Critical Geographies of Peace." *Antipode* 43 (4): 927–931.

2

Imaginaries of Buddhist Fantasy Worlds in Southeast Asia

The Decline of Tiger Balm Gardens of Singapore in Comparative Perspective

JOHN N. MIKSIC

IN THE SECOND HALF OF THE FIRST millennium CE, depictions of Buddhist fantasy worlds, which one might classify as physical manifestations of a Buddhist imaginary[1] (Salazar and Graburn 2014), began to appear in China and Southeast Asia. In the twentieth century such sites have also become common in many parts of Asia (McDaniel 2016). These "fantasy worlds" are populated by fanciful beings and artistic motifs based on a number of Buddhist texts. Fantasy worlds in early Southeast Asia drew on several themes, but by the twentieth century one theme came to dominate: that of heaven and hell. One of the most elaborate of these is Singapore's Tiger Balm Gardens, also known as Haw Par Villa, originally constructed in 1937. For much of its history, Tiger Balm Gardens was a privately owned site open to the public as an act of charity and Buddhist merit-making. In the 1980s it was commercialized, but this experiment resulted in the loss of over 100 million USD. The Gardens then reverted to its former status as a public garden, with minimal maintenance. In 2015 the Gardens were put under the management of a private company, with the intent of retaining as much of the site's heritage value as possible.

I will trace the waxing and waning popularity of the Tiger Balm Gardens and argue that because the secular aspects of the site are highlighted for visitors, these Gardens are not as popular as other Asian fantasy worlds that do heighten specific Buddhist imaginaries in Southeast Asia during the past twelve hundred years.[2] In this volume's Introduction the fluidity of religious places is emphasized, Bruntz and Schedneck making note of the ways in which secular forces shape meanings and values associated to and with religious sites. In the case of fantasy worlds, these destinations are among the most popular sites of visitorship by Buddhists and non-Buddhists alike, both as places of pilgrimage, and as sites of tourism. The major sites to be discussed in this chapter, in addition to the Tiger Balm Gardens are Borobudur (Java, built ca. 780–850); Angkor Wat (Cambodia, ca. 1110–1150), and modern hell gardens within Thailand and Laos. Through a comparative overview of ancient and contemporary depictions of heavens and hells, this chapter investigates intersections between Buddhist narratives and secular influences, in order to uncover what is lost when the power of the Buddhist imaginary, in secular and sacred contexts, is minimized.

Tiger Balm Gardens: A Brief Overview

In 1983 Singapore's Chinatown was the most popular tourist attraction in the country. The resort island of Sentosa was the second-highest ranked destination. The third was a garden, but not the Botanical Garden, which has since become Singapore's first property to be inscribed on UNESCO's World Heritage list, nor was it Gardens by the Bay, which in 2018 is Singapore's most iconic attraction; that garden had not even been planned yet. Singapore's most popular garden thirty-five years ago was the Tiger Balm Gardens. It is named after a patent medicine still widely used for minor ailments.

The Tiger Balm Gardens are one of the most incredible conflations of religion, moral philosophy, and commodification ever built. When they were created, overseas Chinese were becoming as wealthy as their European overlords. They built huge mansions in the major cities of Southeast Asia, combining elements of European and Chinese styles. Two brothers also built Gardens that they opened to the public. These Gardens combined elements of Chinese garden art such as rockwork, islands, grottoes, and vegetation, with a conglomeration of Chinese and Buddhist mythology, including such Buddhist themes as the Journey to the West undertaken by Xuanzang to obtain sutras, the Western Paradise of Amitabha, and the story of Guanyin, a Chinese adaptation of Avalokiteśvara.

The builders of the Tiger Balm Gardens, Aw Boon Haw and Aw Boon Par, were born in Rangoon (now Yangon), in British-ruled Burma (now Myanmar). The Aw family's wealth sprang from a business venture in Burma focused on a medicinal salve that they marketed under the brand name Tiger Balm. This symbol adorned many objects, from bottles and packages to the automobiles they drove. The brothers moved their company's head office to Singapore in 1926, and in 1932 to Hong Kong. Aw Boon Par died in 1944; Aw Boon Haw died in 1954. In 1971 the family sold the company to Slater Walker Securities of London.[3]

The brothers fashioned themed gardens in both Hong Kong and Singapore. The Hong Kong Garden was built in the urban area of that colony in 1932. In 1937 another garden was constructed in Singapore, which was Aw Boon Par's place of residence. The family had a large mansion near Orchard Road, but the Singapore garden was located several kilometers out of town, in a hill overlooking what was then a small fishing village on a sandy beach. In the 1930s this garden was a place to escape the city and enjoy the sea breeze. Now it is out of sight of the ocean; a container port has been built on reclaimed land between the hill and the sea. Poetry in Chinese characters displayed on the traditional Chinese gateway to the park praising the sea now seems incongruous.

A house in Art Deco style was built on top of the hill. A garden on three terraces below the summit was open to the public. The site's name, Tiger Balm Gardens, was partly adopted in order to market the company's products; statues of a boy and girl tiger dressed in human clothes still proffer jars of Tiger Balm ointment. Tiger imagery occurs in several parts of the Gardens, but in the context of mythological tableaus. The tiger is a popular symbol in Singapore; the country's most popular beer is called Tiger, as is the country's national soccer team. Wild tigers were still found in Singapore in the nineteenth century. The Art Deco house has long vanished. What remains is a fantasy world composed of statues of deities, humans, and animals, many of which are acting out fables relative to human morality. The sources of inspiration for the sculptures and landscapes include Buddhism, Daoism, Chinese folklore, and such icons as Japanese sumo wrestlers, Thai classical dancers, and the Statue of Liberty. There is no clear pattern in the distribution of tableaus. The family added new exhibits as the spirit moved them over the years, and more were added after the site was acquired by the Singapore government in 1985. There are few signs to explain to the visitors what the tableaus signify. It seems that the Aw family assumed that the main visitorship would come from the segment of the local population familiar with these themes, and the subsequent developers of the site did not rectify the situation.

In 1983, when the Gardens were still a very popular destination, most visitors were local, but many were not Chinese. Photographs and conversations with Singaporeans who visited the Gardens during that period indicate that the Gardens were popular with people from many different cultural backgrounds. Malays, Indians, Europeans, and others were equally likely to be found in large family groups enjoying the country air on weekends. Natural features were certainly part of the site's attraction, as was the sheer novelty of the tableaus; other media such as television or computers had yet to usurp the role of the outdoors as a source of diversion and pleasure. However, one common thread unites all Singaporeans when they recount their memories of visiting the Tiger Balm Gardens: the Ten Courts of Hell. Generations of Singaporeans of all religions brought their children to visit the Gardens in order to scare them into obedience by showing them depictions of damned souls in torment. Almost all Singaporeans born before the year 2000 were taken on this rite of passage, facilitated by the fact that it was a free source of entertainment in a parklike setting outside the urban area.[4]

The vast majority of visitors are unaware of the strength of the link between the Ten Courts of Hell, the Gardens as a whole, and Buddhism. Most people view the Gardens as a remnant of a fantasy world created by a rich Chinese family to indulge their idiosyncratic whims. As the distance between the impressions of the 1930s and the present widens, people find it increasingly difficult to understand the motivations of the builders of the Gardens. The majority may assume that the Gardens were nothing but a means of selling patent medicine. If one visits Myanmar today, however, one may begin to suspect that the Tiger Balm Gardens was constructed with a very different purpose in mind: the acquisition of merit by honoring the Buddha, by giving pleasure to other beings, and by instilling moral virtues. A large proportion of the activities of the population in Myanmar is still driven by the quest for merit. One major motive for the construction of the Tiger Balm Gardens was probably to ensure good rebirths for the Aw family. This is an example of what a newly wealthy Southeast Asian Chinese family chose to do with their fortune in the 1930s. Others built schools or hospitals; the construction of a public park was seen as no less meritorious.

It is also significant to note what the Gardens do *not* contain. The iconography omits two folk deities who are among the most popular among the overseas Chinese community: Mazu and Toh Peh Kong. Mazu is a female deity who has been popular among emigrants from South China for centuries. A large statue of her stands in the Guangzhou Provincial Museum as well as in old Singapore temples. She is particularly associated with the sea, ships, and sailors. Toh Peh Kong shrines are found in most Chinese communities in Southeast Asia. One of the most important sites of folk religion in Singapore today is a shrine to Toh Peh Kong on Kusu Island built sometime in the early nineteenth century (Comber 1958, 33; Choo 2016). These deities are regarded as protectors, but they do not lend themselves to any program of moral instruction and are not found in Buddhism, which may explain why they were not incorporated into the Tiger Balm Gardens.

I do not make this argument purely for the sake of reconstructing history, even though it is important to arrive at correct interpretations of people's past actions in order to understand human behavior today. At least as important are the questions of whether the Tiger Balm Gardens should be preserved, and if so, why and how? What are the values of the Gardens that can and should be preserved? How much of the significance of the Gardens is visible to someone who visits to view the tableaus, and how much of the Gardens' meaning is hidden? What kind of awareness on the part of the visitors is necessary in order to derive full benefit from the visit? In order to survive, it seems likely that the Gardens will have to generate revenue. Perhaps with the development of a wider perspective as time passes, the public will arrive at a greater appreciation of the value of the Gardens as a site depicting Buddhist narratives, and political support for the preservation of the site by the government will rise. In the near term, however, there is a danger that unless more secular elements can be grafted on to the Gardens, the heritage attributes of the site may be lost due to redevelopment. By calling attention to the Buddhist attributes of the Tiger Balm Gardens and the link between this Garden and other famous Buddhist fantasy worlds, it may be possible to develop a greater sense of awareness and appreciation for the Gardens as part of a much larger Buddhist imaginary.

An Unsuccessful Attempt at Commercialization, a Period of Hibernation, and a New Beginning

A few months before he died in 1954, Aw Boon Haw decreed that the Tiger Balm Gardens should continue to be open to the public free of charge and not be sold or privatized for twenty years. In 1986 the Aw family donated it to the nation, on condition that the name should not be changed and the memorials to family members should remain intact.[5] After the government acquired title to the Gardens, the Singapore Tourism Board (STB) was given the task of commercializing them. They hired a company that had conducted feasibility studies for Disneyland in the United States, whose plan called for converting Tiger Balm Gardens into a theme park of Chinese mythology. Another company with connections to Walt Disney Productions proposed an "Imperial Path," which would use the "dark ride" technology common at Disneyland to tell the story of China from the Shang to the Qing Dynasties. This was not built, but major additions to the Gardens were approved, including theaters that used animatronics to tell stories of Chinese mythology, bearing no relationship to Buddhism or Singapore, as was a waterslide in the shape of a dragon, which became the new emblem of the park (Yeoh and Teo 1996).

The contract to build and operate the park was given to a local consortium called International Theme Parks (Ltd.) in 1988. A sum of eighty million Singaporean dollars was spent on redeveloping the site. Many of the old sculptures, including the Ten Courts of Hell, were demolished. According to a *Straits Times* 1986 article two consultants from China considered the "scenes of sex and gore" too violent for children (as cited in Huang and Hong 2007, 56). The displays were dense in their depictions of blood, dismembered bodies, and people engaged in illicit sexual activity. They were eventually recreated, in less graphic form, in an area of the Gardens that had originally formed a swimming pool. Later more dioramas depicting moral lessons were recreated on the walls of what was formerly the changing room for the swimmers and along the path leading to it from the new Courts of Hell. Re-enactors were hired to stroll the grounds, and restaurants were opened. Admission charges of eighteen Singaporean dollars were levied, a significant amount in 1990. The site was no longer a garden; it was Haw Par Villa Dragon World.

The theme park approach based on a simplified presentation of Chinese culture was not a commercial success. The company lost millions of dollars, and eventually returned the site to the government in 2001. The dragon ride was demolished, but a large amphitheater, unused since then, still stands. The park returned to its role as a public garden. A company called Orient Management maintained the sculptures and tableaus under license from the Singapore Tourism Board. The company was staffed by Singaporeans who performed their duties largely as a labor of love. In 2005 a museum called Hua Song was added to the park, along with a high-end Chinese restaurant. The museum, which featured excellent exhibits telling the story of the overseas Chinese diaspora, was launched together with a massive reference book, *The Encyclopedia of the Chinese Overseas*.[6] Unfortunately ticket receipts from the museum could not cover the cost of its maintenance, and it was closed in 2012.[7] The restaurant had already failed.

What went wrong? Was the attempt to convert the Gardens into a secularized and commercially viable venture doomed from the start? The Gardens' privatization, denatured of its important Buddhist components, and subsequent demise coincided with the birth of Internet culture. Was its failure the result of changing tastes, or was it due to faulty planning? In the 1980s, China was still a daunting place for foreigners to visit. The Singapore Tourism Board thought it would be possible to position Singapore as a condensed version of mainland Chinese culture. Other projects implemented in Singapore at this time included Tang Dynasty and Ming Dynasty "villages," which also proved to be commercial failures. In actuality, China opened up rapidly in the late 1980s, and tourists rapidly began to visit the actual sites rather than replicas of them in equatorial Southeast Asia.

Huang and Hong (2007) argue that one of the main reasons for the failure of the venture was that it focused on an ersatz version of mainland Chinese culture, rather than an authentic story such as the underappreciated ascent of the overseas Chinese, who have created their own unique society over the past seven hundred years. A 1979 editorial in *The Straits Times* newspaper expressed a somewhat condescending view that was common in certain quarters:

> It [The Villa] may not be an image about what we are particularly proud . . . it has no distinct historical value, but it certainly has a remarkably distinctive style. Not everyone may care for the colour scheme or the themes of the tableaux, or the quality of the figure

> work. But where else can the Singaporean and the foreigner find such a rich and sometimes vulgar representation of man's imagination, dreams and fears? (as cited in Huang and Hong 2007, 56)

The view espoused by this *Straits Times* editorial reflects one point of view, but it may not be representative of the majority of Singaporeans, then or now. According to a survey in 2000, published in *The Straits Times,* 85 percent of respondents felt that the Gardens were "part of Singapore's heritage" (as cited in Huang and Hong 2007, 72). In 2001 the well-known Singaporean author Catherine Lim wrote a novel, *Following the Wrong God Home,* in which Haw Par Villa was both a "repository of tradition and a refuge from conventions" (Huang and Hong 2007, 68). The history of Tiger Balm Gardens is interesting for several reasons. One of these is the differing reactions it arouses within Singapore society. The disparaging attitude toward the Gardens is less and less frequently expressed. On the contrary, the endeavor to preserve the Gardens is increasingly supported by members of the Singapore public who believe that it does represent a period in the formation of a Singapore identity that is relevant to the present.

In August 2015 the government tendered the Gardens to a local company called Journeys. This is one of several companies under unified management that have conducted historical tours of Singapore sites for twenty years. They have been successful in generating enough income from educational tourism to maintain other heritage sites in Singapore. Sites under their purview include the Battlebox, a British World War II command center on Fort Canning, Singapore,[8] and the Chinatown Heritage Centre.[9] One of the company's new ideas for the Gardens is advertised as "Hell's Museum," which is scheduled to open officially in June 2018. This attraction is described as a place where visitors will learn about "Asia's death rituals, funerary practices and various religious beliefs on the afterlife" (Zaccheus 2017).

Many Singaporeans feel that the Tiger Balm Gardens is an important site of their heritage, one that transcends religious and ethnic boundaries. The Singapore government, however, has not shown a willingness to subsidize the Gardens in the long term. The Journeys company has shown an unusual aptitude in managing similar properties in Singapore; one hopes that they will be successful in this instance too. One of the most promising approaches to reviving the fortunes of the Gardens would seem to lie in exploiting the link between this particular garden, the historical role of the Southeast Asian garden in general, Buddhist gardens in particular, and the ironic symbolism of hell in a garden, a juxtaposition that has been replicated numerous times in Southeast Asian history. The potential of this approach does not yet seem to have been appreciated by the interested parties.

It can be argued that the ultimate resolution of the attempt to generate financial as well as social support for the preservation of this Buddhist fantasy world probably lies in a return to the original Buddhist focus of the Gardens, in which Buddhism and the Ten Courts played a major role. Letters to the forum page of *The Straits Times* regarding Singapore tourism policy imply that the elements of the Gardens that are intrinsic to authenticity, including as many original artifacts as possible, will be instrumental in drawing upon the wider Singapore society for support.[10] It is undeniable that mistakes were made in the past. It is not surprising that reliance on foreign consultants who had little or no knowledge of Singaporean or Southeast Asian heritage led to a failure of that particular form of commodification. The original plan was flawed in its marketing and its attitude toward authenticity. A new plan that incorporates mythology and Buddhism in a coherent and accurate manner may succeed. One problem is that the original concept of the 1930s relied heavily on the assumption that visitors would be able to identify iconic figures in the stories narrated by the tableaus and sculptures. The development of a visitor center, similar to a museum, and the incorporation of new technology including smartphones and other portable devices, should make it possible to compensate for the current lack of ability to decipher the manifestations of the old significances and even enhance them.

The Tiger Balm Gardens as Buddhism and Folk Religion

In an ironic but significant note, a small nook at the edge of a small forest near the old swimming pool has a new addition, provided by an anonymous person or group: a shrine with idols and incense burners. This is a frequent phenomenon even in hypermodern Singapore: folk religions with Chinese, Daoist, and Buddhist characteristics (such as Guanyin statues) continue to appear mysteriously in the interstices of modern urban life. One of the main unspoken assumptions of the Singapore government, as is apparent from the strategy pursued by its agency, the Singapore Tourism Board, is that folk religion is unacceptable, perhaps because it seems unsophisticated. In the nineteenth century, over one hundred Muslim shrines to devout Muslims with supposed powers to help the living (*keramats*) were constructed in Singapore (Muhammad Zain bin Mahmood 1959). All but four of these (Keramat Iskandar Shah, Keramat Habib Noh, Bukit Purmei, and Kusu Island) have been demolished. Other small spirit shrines appear from time to time, but sooner or later are "cleared away" by officials. It seems difficult for government decision makers to accept unorganized religious expressions as legitimate. It is likely that many Singaporeans would classify the Ten Courts of Hell as an extreme example of such informal religious expression, differing from the smaller shrines mainly in the scale of its construction and its association with a well-known family that embodies entrepreneurial virtues espoused by the government.

The Tiger Balm Gardens contain no Buddhist prayer hall and has never had any resident monks. According to Justin McDaniel (2016), the lack of any overt Buddhist place of worship has caused the Gardens to be neglected by students of religion, art, and architecture (84). Aw Boon Haw was not interested in establishing a temple; this would have conflicted with what I think was his broader aim, which was to earn merit by teaching. The Ten Courts of Hell site has succeeded in attracting visitors of a wide range of non-Buddhist backgrounds for precisely this reason. This does not however make the Courts Chinese rather than Buddhist. As the next section will show, depictions of the Courts of Hell have a long history in the Buddhist world of Southeast Asia, a history in which gardens are heavily implicated as well.

Tiger Balm Gardens now contain about fifteen major tableaus, plus numerous individual sculptures. Some of the most elaborate tableaus, aside from the Ten Courts, depict Chinese versions of Buddhist-related texts such as *Journey to the West,* the famous story of the Tang Dynasty monk Xuanzang, who goes to India to acquire Buddhist scriptures. Others are completely unrelated to Buddhism, such as the story of *Lady White Snake* and the *Battle of the Eight Immortals beneath the Sea*. The choice of this story may have been related to the theme of the sea, which permeates much of the Gardens and would have made much more sense when one could see, hear, and smell the ocean while viewing the tableau. The Gardens depict these narratives as seamlessly integrated into a worldview in which Buddhism plays a major role.

The current Ten Courts of Hell is relegated to the southeastern corner of the site. Originally it was near the center of the Gardens, in an underground grotto that added to the impact of the display. Despite its marginalization in Dragonworld in 1988, the Courts remain one of the most popular sites in the Gardens. The Ten Courts of Hell are no longer in an artificial underground grotto. The visitor now enters a less dramatic cave-like structure above the ground made of cement, reached via a pathway between two artificial mountains. Miniature severed heads on pikes set the stage for what is to follow. A tiger peers out of a cave. This is both a reference to Tiger Balm, and to the folk belief that tiger spirits still guard certain locations in Singapore.

The story of the Ten Courts then unfolds as the visitor follows a pathway through the cave. Signs in English and Chinese describe the Three Worlds (an important Buddhist theme, to be described further below), depicted in the form of three bridges; the judgment by Yama, god of the underworld; the various courts, the crimes that they judge, and the punishments, accompanied by plaster dioramas depicting the tortures appropriate for each crime. At the end of a passageway, one reaches a depiction of the end of the tortures, the drinking of the tea of forgetfulness, and the rebirth of the soul. Upon leaving the Courts of Hell, one comes to a round structure with more recreated dioramas depicting various virtues and vices, set in a cityscape vaguely resembling Singapore in the 1930s, inhabited by people wearing costumes of that period. There is no sign indicating the fact that this was once the site of the family swimming pool.

The decision of commercial developers to de-emphasize the Ten Courts of Hell as a religious element and increase secular attractions such as a theater, seems in retrospect to have been a serious mistake. This was the main site of memory formation for people from the generations who visited the park. The decision by the company Journeys to return to the theme of death has raised concerns for some observers, such as Paulin Straughan (Zaccheus 2017), but it is undeniable that this topic is one of intense fascination for the general public. Museum displays involving mummies from Egypt have been some of the most visited in Singapore; an exhibition entitled Khazanah Kubur (Treasures from the Grave) was similarly popular in the Muzium Negara in Malaysia. It may be argued that a focus on death and funerary rituals misses much of the point of the Ten Courts of Hell. Although exhibitions on cultural attitudes toward death in Asia may hold some appeal, the experience of the last fifteen hundred years suggests that it would be advisable to focus on the theme of rebirth, rather than death as a permanent end to life. This is the intent of the Ten Courts of Hell: to emphasize the Buddhist message of death as a stage in a series of rebirths leading to ultimate enlightenment.

Heavens and Hells in the Buddhist Imaginary

The depiction of scenes from hell has existed in Buddhism for over one thousand years. These graphic illustrations of judgment and punishment attract millions of visitors per year to ancient and modern sites, mainly in Southeast Asia. The evolution of the depictions of hell over this millennium provides an interesting alternative view of the Buddhist imaginary, which normally focuses on the positive, serene aspects of Buddhism. These depictions were often if not always set in gardens or parks, thus creating a striking juxtaposition of hell as part of heaven rather than separate from it. The commodification of these tangible manifestations of Buddhist narratives has evolved in ways that exhibit some unusual twists and turns. It seems that the threat of gruesome punishment for misdeeds exerts the most powerful attraction on modern visitors to these sites, rather than the promise of an almost eternal period of blissful existence before the final entry into nirvana. Depictions of heaven are certainly present, but they tend to be static and iconographically limited to a few standard images such as the residence of the Buddha, and paradisiacal gardens with flowers, trees, birds, deer, and heavenly musicians, and people with dreamy expressions. Depictions of hell in contrast are dynamic, with many scenes depicting violent actions and a range of vivid emotions, mainly fear and agony.

Southeast Asia can make a convincing claim to have developed the oldest, most numerous, and most elaborate fantasy worlds devoted to illustrating Buddhist precepts set in the context of everyday life. One problem that the modern scholar who attempts to interpret these visual narratives has to surmount is the need to reconstruct the mentalité of the visitors to the site for whom these projects were originally designed. How were these imaginaries meant to be used, and by whom? We have no records to help us in this endeavor, so we can only theorize on the basis of inferences from contemporary scholarly models. One of the foremost practitioners of this mode of inquiry, Salazar (2012), points out that imaginaries can only be studied through the media in which they are externalized and portrayed. These textual and visual media can be items of merchandising such as icons, newspapers and magazines, exhibitions in museums, websites, and films, among many others. Unfortunately for our study, Salazar does not mention the most important medium of all for disseminating detailed concepts of religious imaginaries: religious structures, or in the case of Buddhism, temples. He does, however, provide some guidance for those of us who are engaged in this pursuit by calling attention to the need for "theoretical frameworks that allow a comprehensive study of inner dynamics that transcend the unproductive binary opposition between the economic global and the cultural local" (Salazar 2012, 866). Within the general framework of Buddhism as an organizing principle, one can go further to identify certain tropes or themes that appear frequently in centers of Buddhist visitation and pilgrimage in different parts of the world. These punishments take place in a kind of purgatory often portrayed in extremely graphic form.

Early Buddhist practitioners apparently felt a need for images of hell as part of depicting Buddhist teachings. The original iconography of Buddhism did not supply this. Images of hell eventually appeared in Buddhist art in several areas, but in Southeast Asia, attempts to create fantasy worlds incorporating hell were particularly energetic and successful. Buddhist temples are usually signposted with many emblems meant to identify them as microcosmic representations of heaven. Compared to heaven, hell was rarely depicted in early Asian art. The term *naraka,* "hell," appears in the *Mahābhārata* (Doniger 2009, 280). The text suggests that a visit to hell was a rite of passage for kingship. The same appears to have applied to early Buddhism (Goh 2015, 98). More elaborate versions of hell appear in later texts such as the *Manusmrti* and the *Bhāgavata Purāṅa* (Jacobsen 2009, 390–391), but hell did not play an important role in early Indian art. Hindu and Buddhist concepts of hell seem more akin to purgatory in Catholic traditions, with the added complication that a Buddhist could envision endless cycles of torment in hell before achieving enlightenment. Buddhist hell is not the domain of a rebel angel; it is part and parcel of the path to heaven.

The first images of hell in Asian art may have appeared in China during the Han Dynasty (206 BCE–CE 220) (Goh 2015, 92), but none survive. No evidence of Chinese influence on Southeast Asian depictions of hell is discernible.

It is true that overseas Chinese were some of the greatest sponsors of imaginaries that depict the courts of hell, but this may be due to a fortuitous combination of a general Chinese concern with morality (also found in Confucianism) and the strongly Buddhist social milieu in which the overseas Chinese found themselves. Examples from Indonesia, Cambodia, and Thailand help to illustrate the context in which the modern fantasy world of Tiger Balm Gardens fits.

Borobudur

The oldest and largest surviving example of a fantasy world focused on a connected narrative rather than a single scene or situation, Borobudur, is one of the most elaborate Buddhist monuments in the world. The monument bears 1,350 reliefs depicting *Jatakas, Avadanas,* the *Lalitavistara,* the *Gandavyuha,* and the *Bhadracari.* A series of 160 bas-reliefs carved on the base of the structure illustrates the *Mahakarmavibhangga* "The Great Classification of Actions," with scenes of bliss contrasting with fearsome torture in hell depending on one's acts in previous existences.

Ancient Javanese temples such as Borobudur were associated with gardens (Sri Soejatmi Satari 2008). Salazar (2012) refers to the importance of paradisiacal environments and vanished Edens as one of the most common elements of imaginaries of tourism (866). As examples, he cites Borobudur and the Taman Sari, both in central Java.[11] This connection between heaven and hell as two parts of the same reality rather than opposing kingdoms is a particular characteristic of Asian Buddhist imaginaries. This nuanced appeal to humans to accept one's lot in this existence in hope of attaining a better incarnation may have been acceptable to past Asian societies, but it may be losing its attraction in the modern world, in which upward mobility in this life is increasingly possible. This may partly account for the loss in popularity of the Tiger Balm Gardens, but it is also possible that this decline in popularity is due to improper commodification by the Singapore government which severed the link between the site and Buddhism. Borobudur is now probably more popular than it has ever been in the past.

Borobudur is a contender for the title of largest Buddhist monument in the world. It was built over a period of about seventy years between 780 and 850 CE. The oldest Indonesian text on Buddhism, the *Sang Hyang Kamahāyānan Mantranaya,* dates from around 1000 CE (De Jong 1974). Javanese Buddhism seems to have been undergoing rapid evolution during this period, when a Buddhist queen married a Hindu king. The monument's complex design incorporates various references to mountains, stupas, and mandalas (Miksic 1990). The Buddha gave sermons on mountains, perhaps the best known of which is the *Saddharmmapundarika* (Lotus Sutra). The stupas represent the Buddha's passing from existence to nirvana. The mandala as an aid to meditation has long been popular in northern Buddhism (China, Japan, Nepal, and Tibet), and Javanese architects integrated it into the design of Borobudur.

The site is now a UNESCO World Heritage listed property that attracts over one million visitors each year, the majority of whom are Javanese Muslims who consider Borobudur an important source of cultural pride and a place of recreation. The main appeal of Borobudur for them lies in their own imaginaries of Javanese heritage rather than those the ancient designers had in mind. Unfortunately no Indonesian-language guidebook to the monument is available. Some Indonesian visitors hire local guides who explain the meaning of the reliefs to their clients, but most Indonesians come to Borobudur to marvel at the beauty of the carvings and to enjoy the view of the countryside from the top of the monument.

Borobudur no doubt was meant to evoke various imaginaries. One of them would have been a mountain such as the Mount of Eagles (*Grdrarashtra-kuta*) where the Buddha was said to have recited the Lotus Sutra. The structure resembles a terraced mountain with staircases leading to the summit from all four cardinal directions.[12] The upper section consisting of three round terraces with 108 hollow perforated stupas and a large central stupa may be meant to evoke the Lotus Sutra. One source of the lasting appeal of the *Saddharmma-pundarika* is the fantastic imagery contained in its language. This sutra has inspired many visual depictions, though not connected pictorial narratives.[13] Favorite themes in Asian depictions of the sutra include the ray of light that shoots from Shakyamuni's forehead, which lights up all the realms from Avici Hell to Akanistha Heaven and all the beings who live in them, engaged in all kinds of actions (Tanabe 1988).

No inscriptions survive to tell us how Borobudur was planned or used. Some believe that the monument was built as an educational device for devotees on religious pilgrimages. This would explain the 1,350 large bas-relief carvings illustrating various texts on the terrace walls and balustrades. The most significant text for our purpose is the *Mahakarmavibhaṇga,* which is narrated in 160 panels on the exterior base of the monument.[14] When the first stage of the monument was finished around 820 CE, this was the only relief series visible to people outside the monument. All the relief series on the terrace walls are hidden behind balustrades; they require knowledge of esoteric Buddhist literature to decipher, which increases as one ascends to higher levels of the monument. It is possible that only certain people were allowed to climb the staircases and view the reliefs on the terraces, and that access to each level was increasingly restricted as one climbed higher.

It has also been proposed that Borobudur was designed to represent Buddhist cosmology as portrayed in the Three Worlds (Tri Buana or Tri Bhumi)—the underworld of ghosts, the middle world of humans, and the upper world of the gods.[15] Other theories provide different explanations for the choice of the *Mahakarmavibhaṇga* as a text to depict, and its location on the monument's base. The *Mahakarmavibhaṇga* reliefs on Borobudur depict good deeds and the resulting rewards. Carvings of heaven are standardized and repetitive, whereas the hells are highly varied. The version of the text depicted at Borobudur probably incorporated various levels of hell, but this is not clear from the reliefs. In Sanjiva Hell, for instance, those who fought with others during their lives are condemned to fight each other with hands that have grown iron nails, while both are attacked by a bird with a metal beak. In Raurava Hell, killers of innocent people are impaled on thorns of huge trees. Those who hunted birds are made to walk through a Sword Tree Forest in which the leaves are daggers that fall on the hunters. Tormented souls walk on spears, through burning water, or are reborn as ghouls.

Angkor Wat

After the construction of Borobudur, three hundred years passed before another Southeast Asian kingdom used massive relief carvings to depict a fantasy world. This took place at the World Heritage Site of Angkor Wat. The relief carvings and literary subjects of the Angkorian reliefs differ from those of central Java in important respects. Rather than dividing narrative depictions into sections like a cartoon or film strip, the Khmers designed synoptic scenes in which action takes place simultaneously over a distance of sixty meters. On the west side of Angkor Wat, two sixty-meter-long panels depict tumultuous battle scenes from the *Mahabharata* and *Ramayana,* Hinduism's two great epic poems. On the south side, two more sixty-meter-long panels depict processions. The western panel depicts the king leading his army in a procession. The eastern panel is devoted to the Three Worlds of Buddhist cosmology. The action begins at the western end of the wall with a procession of the souls of the dead who are marching toward a point where the level road diverges into three levels.[16] A staircase leads up to a place labeled by an inscription on the relief as *svargga,* "heaven." In the middle is a level path for those who are to be reborn in this world. At the bottom level is a hole into which evil-doers are thrown headfirst by horrifying demons into what is conveniently labeled *naraka.* In the midst of these three levels is Yama, god of the underworld and judge of the dead, assisted by two officials, labeled with the inscriptions *vrah* Dharmma and *vrah* Citragupta. *Vrah* is a Khmer title; these may represent actual officials of Angkor who were singled out for special notice by the designer of the reliefs. Unfortunately, this conjecture cannot be proven.

The Angkor Wat relief is the oldest known visual depiction of the Buddhist idea of the Three Worlds. References to the Three Worlds are found on twelfth-century clay votive tablets from Bagan and Dawei, Myanmar, but no depictions of the concept in graphic form are known from Myanmar until the sixteenth to eighteenth centuries (Goh 2015, 105). In the fourteenth century a Thai text was devoted specifically to explicating this doctrine (Phraya Lithai 1982). The heavens of Angkor Wat are divided into thirty-seven types represented by thirty-seven palaces with three rooms in each (le Bonheur 1995).[17] The thirty-two hells, with categories of crimes and punishments spelled out in detail by inscriptions, provide an interesting insight into the types of crimes of which twelfth-century Khmers could conceive. The number thirty-two is more congruent with Buddhist numerology than Hinduism, which designate hells in multiples of seven (Roveda n.d., 46). The punishments indicate a particular concern for the preservation of gardens: one hell is reserved for those who steal flowers from Siva's garden. Another is dedicated to punishing those who illegally cut down trees. Those who vandalize wells and gardens constitute another category deserving special punishment.

Given the differences in the religious contexts in which the hell reliefs appear at Angkor Wat and Borobudur, it is interesting that the sculptors employed very similar imagery to depict some punishments such as the leaves and grass in the form of knives. As at Borobudur, the punishments at Angkor Wat are graphically depicted, with the suffering of the souls vividly portrayed. As at Borobudur, it is not clear who would have comprised the audience for these reliefs. We might suspect that such massive expenditures would have been aimed at the masses, but no written descriptions survive to enable us to solve this riddle. Also like Borobudur, Angkor Wat has been listed as a UNESCO World Heritage Site. Along with being safeguarded and supported by UNESCO since 1992, the site receives over a million visitors each year. Borobudur and Angkor Wat demonstrate the ways that ancient structures have a place in modern society as cultural heritage. However, the Tiger Balm Gardens, not being as ancient, and losing some of its authenticity and Buddhist connections through privatization and government involvement, cannot be placed into the category of cultural heritage.

Gardens in the Buddhist Imaginary

These examples demonstrate the immense imaginaries that Buddhists in Southeast Asia have been able to draw upon. These fantasy worlds are inspired by particular texts and generate further imaginaries through their visual depictions in leisure gardens. Both heavens and hells exist in these Buddhist gardens in order to portray the results of good actions and bad. Gardens played an important and widespread role in Buddhism and early Southeast Asian society. It is not unusual to find depictions of hell set in Southeast Asian contexts (Schopen 2014). Gardens played important roles in the story of the historical Buddha: he was born in one at Lumbini, and gave his first sermon in one at Benares. In

Indonesia, with its equatorial climate and luxuriant vegetation, the trope of the garden as a place where certain types of special events take place was even more pronounced during the period of classical (pre-Islamic) culture than in India.

Buddhist rulers in early Southeast Asia built gardens as a means of making merit. In the seventh century a Buddhist Sumatran ruler inscribed a rock edict praising a garden that he had caused to be created and piously expressed the Buddhist wish that the merit thus obtained would be shared among all living beings (Coedès 1992). A fourteenth-century inscription from West Sumatra describes the king's palace as being in Nandanawana, named after the main park in Tawatimsa heaven, where the gods went for amusement, the last heaven before nirvana. *Cakravartin* (world conqueror) kings are supposedly reborn there after death. This garden is also described at length in the Sri Lankan *Culawangśa,* set in a Buddhist society (De Casparis 1990).

Garden imagery was pervasive in early Southeast Asian imaginaries. It is likely that Southeast Asian temples were surrounded by well-tended grounds including planned planting schemes, just as they are today. Hells were not depicted in separate places but usually inserted into the garden environment. Hells and gardens is a strange juxtaposition, but one that recurs frequently in Southeast Asia. Ancient Southeast Asian gardens were designed as places for recreation, as places for contemplation and meditation, and as symbols of the universe. In physical form, Southeast Asian gardens do not reflect Chinese or Indian garden designs. Chinese gardens are influenced by Daoism; elements such as pavilions and bridges, grotesque objects such as dwarf trees and strangely shaped rocks, are placed seemingly at random. Surviving Indian garden designs fall at the opposite end of the spectrum; they were influenced by the Persian Chahar Bagh, which reproduces in miniature the division of the world into four symmetrical quarters. Southeast Asian gardens lie between these two poles. In Indonesian garden philosophy and symbolism, nature shaped by humans served to produce a more perfect environment for people to enjoy and meditate on the meaning of life, and the relationship between the seen and unseen aspects of existence (Lombard 1967, 1969). Rather than bridges over streams, which were popular in China, garden designers in early Southeast Asia built pavilions on islands in the middle of man-made pools. Large flat stones representing the seats of ascetics were placed on top of artificial hills, the interiors of which were laced with caves. The role of the garden in the Buddhist imaginary of Southeast Asia as a setting for images of hell is thus part of its cosmological significance.

Modern Hell Gardens in Thailand and Laos

The practice of constructing Buddhist imaginaries in gardens continued to flourish in Southeast Asia in the twentieth century. The new imaginaries reflect the concerns of the growing Southeast Asian middle and upper classes. Many members of these classes were of Chinese ancestry. Modern hell gardens are not only found in Singapore, but also in Laos and Thailand. In Thailand, websites list more than twenty "Buddhist Hell Gardens."[18] Several have been built by rich laypeople in order to gain merit. Their design includes numerous features obviously intended to attract local tourists. They tend to be in areas far from Bangkok. Most of them make more or less direct references to the law of karma. One of the earliest fantasy worlds associated with Southeast Asian monasteries was the Buddha Park Garden in Vientiane, Laos (Maizels 2007, 218–219). This garden depicts Buddhist and Hindu deities, Chinese and Thai mythological beings, and a globe representing the Three Worlds. It was built by a charismatic Buddhist leader, Luangpu Boonlour Sureerat, in 1958.

Wat Khaek Buddha Park located in Nong Khai, Thailand, was established by the same man after Laos was taken over by a Communist government in 1977 (Maizels 2007, 220–221). Its depictions include dogs in human garb, illustrating the evils of vices such as drinking and gambling. Most of the displays in this garden consist of unpainted concrete sculptures of enormous size. Many of them have long incised inscriptions in Thai on their bases. The attack of Mara's army and the attempted seduction of Sakyamuni by Mara's daughters are major exhibits. One of the more interesting sculptures is a *dharmacakra* (wheel of the law).[19] In a concession to Thai popular culture, the statues that correspond to the various guardians of birth dates are displayed along with places where one can burn incense to them for good luck.[20] One of the more graphic reminders of the Buddhist admonition that all appearance is illusory consists of two statues. One depicts two amorous young people on a bench; the next depicts two skeletons in the same pose.

The Thai and Laotian hell gardens resemble Tiger Balm Gardens in that they depict a range of imaginaries, not just Buddhist ones. Even in Buddhist monasteries such as Wat Rong Khun, murals depict hell, Brahmanic deities, and figures from popular culture such as cartoon figures (McDaniel 2016, 119). The number of modern hell gardens in Thailand indicates there is an audience among domestic and international tourists for these seemingly strange mixes of three-dimensional morality narratives. None of these gardens mentioned above have been part of any kind of privatization. Unlike the Tiger Balm Gardens, they remain connected to the lay Buddhists and Buddhist monks who had the vision to create these hell gardens.

The idea of hell and damnation as attractive subjects for tourism seems at first glance to fly in the face of logic. It is, however, possible to demonstrate that rather than repelling tourists, such depictions are not only popular in modern Southeast Asia, they have been popular for over one thousand years. It is impossible to rediscover how people in ancient times experienced these installations, but their frequency and the amount of resources and expertise lavished on them indicate that for the rulers of the past, these graphic horror shows were considered to be both necessary and beneficial in attracting people to visit them and absorb the lessons behind them. It is possible to see who visits these displays today and to ask them why they do so; it is not possible to assume that the same motives that prompt people to visit these sites are exactly the same as those that operated in the ninth century in Java, or the twelfth century in Angkor, Cambodia. We can speculate on the degree of similarity and difference between the past and the present, but it is difficult to calculate the degree of confidence we can have that our conclusions are correct. What is highly probable is that at least some factors in the development of these imaginaries of pain and suffering are common to both past and present ideas about how such depictions should be designed.

The possibility of making at least some analogies between past and present is heightened by the fact that the majority of people who visit Borobudur, Angkor Wat, Wat Khaek, and Tiger Balm Gardens are local tourists or tourists from Asia, rather than people from other cultural groups. Whether this generalization betokens a fundamental difference in the attitudes toward these sites between Asians and others, is difficult to determine. What is interesting is that the strong link between these sites and Buddhism is *not* depicted, nor emphasized in tourist literature. Each site seems to be assumed to be a purely local expression of traditional origin rather than an expression of a universal set of teachings shared among Javanese, Khmer, Thais, and overseas Chinese. Thus there is a process of secularization occurring at these sites, in which Buddhist narratives of hell are installed and displayed, but the link between the sites and Buddhism is lost.

A factor that may help to explain the very long shelf life of imaginaries of Buddhist purgatory is that the sites do not move. Tourists often like to assume that the sites they visit were built and patronized by people who were pure examples of a local culture, into which modern visitors can insert themselves in order to experience authenticity lacking in their everyday lives. It is quite probable that mobility of people in the past was much lower than today, but the widespread nature of the doctrines behind the hell scenes and even some of the modes of depiction of some of the tortures suggest that they were created by people who themselves may have traveled, or come into contact with moveable objects—paintings on perishable materials such as palm leaves, which would have provided a kind of cosmopolitan experience for the designers and craftsmen in Java or Cambodia. The people in the reliefs of Borobudur and Angkor Wat in particular are sufficiently lifelike and naturalistic that they may be close to photographs of actual people, thus presenting frozen moments in time and creating a kind of temporal ambiguity (Barthes 1972; Lowenthal 1985).

The long life of Buddhist views of hell provides an unusual opportunity to trace the longevity of particular attitudes toward society and religion. It is interesting to ponder the question of whether visitors to these sites in Southeast Asia would be positively or negatively influenced by the knowledge that what they see at a particular site is not purely a local expression; all these sites form part of a network of symbolism and a common attitude toward the necessity of making people behave properly by threatening them with dire supernatural punishment in the afterlife, rather than through an appeal to reason. They were inspired by Buddhist texts and stories, but their execution is based on individual and communal interpretations. In modern settings, Borobudur and Angkor Wat will continue to be popular due to their stamps of approval from the secular institution UNESCO, along with the wide variety of imaginaries depicted, including morality tales from Buddhism, Hinduism, and explications of Buddhist cosmology. Human beings seem to prefer imaginaries composed of an unpredictable mix of ingredients, like a county fair, rather than a rigidly structured collection of nearly identical elements. Museum designers have begun to understand this, and to incorporate this mentality into their exhibition designs. This attribute, if properly maintained, should enable the Tiger Balm Gardens to survive and revive its former popularity.

Would the Tiger Balm Gardens become more or less popular if the Ten Courts of Hell were linked to a general school of Buddhist thought, rather than the idiosyncratic vision of an overseas Chinese businessman in the 1930s? Put another way, would it become more or less popular if its connections to Buddhism were emphasized? This is a question that the company Journeys, which now operates the Gardens, would do well to ponder. The fact that the display of hell continues to draw visitors, and to inspire new construction in Thailand, suggests that this experience may be much more influential than theme parks based on movie franchises, which are constantly being created, flourishing for a while, then disappearing or giving way to yet newer exhibits. Although fewer people may believe in the reality of an underworld where souls are tormented by demons, the theoretical reasons for encouraging moral behavior symbolized by these hell depictions may still be sufficiently valid that this form of Buddhist tourism will continue to develop in the future.

Notes

1 In this chapter, the term "imaginary" will be used rather than "imaginaire" to distinguish its connotation from that associated with Pali literature.

2 The Haw Par Villa combined the names of the two brothers, Aw Boon Haw and Aw Boon Par. Originally the Villa was composed of two sections: the family's private dwelling, or villa, and the public Tiger Balm Gardens. After the family gave the property to the Singapore government, the Gardens expanded to comprise the entire property. Thus, the two names historically denoted two parts of the site, but now they are synonymous.

3 See: Aw Boon Haw, accessed February 13, 2018, http://eresources.nlb.gov.sg/infopedia/articles/SIP_789_2004-12-23.html; Brandel and Turbeville 1998.

4 The information about the typical visitor experiences over time is based on my decades of living, teaching, and researching in Singapore. I visited Tiger Balm Gardens for the first time in 1976. Since I moved to Singapore in 1987, I have taken hundreds of students on field trips to the Gardens. Among Singapore students at the National University of Singapore, 95 percent of those whom I have queried said that they had been brought to the Ten Courts of Hell as young children, and that their parents had pointed out the tableaus about specific punishments connected with relations between children, parents, and teachers. This is true regardless of ethnicity.

5 The Gardens includes four stupa-shaped structures. The largest, placed on top of the hill on which the Gardens is built, honors Aw Boon Haw's parents. The next two commemorate Aw Boon Haw and Boon Par; a small one is dedicated to Aw How, Boon Haw's son, who died in 1951 (Yeoh and Teo 1996).

6 General Editor: Lynn Pan; published by Archipelago Press/Landmark Books for the Chinese Heritage Centre, Singapore, 1998.

7 Some of the exhibits were moved to the Chinese Heritage Centre, which is attached to Nanyang Technological University, Singapore. It is possible that the Hua Song Museum may be revived (Channel News Asia 2015; Lim 2017).

8 See: The Battlebox, accessed November 12, 2018, www.battlebox.com.sg.

9 See: Chinatown Heritage Centre, accessed November 12, 2018, www.chinatownheritagecentre.com.sg.

10 See: "Chinatown 'won't become a theme park,'" *The Straits Times,* December 12, 1998.

11 On Taman Sari and the significance of gardens in premodern Indonesian culture, see Miksic 2008. For an example of a royal garden from seventeenth-century Sumatra, see Shiraishi 1990.

12 The custom of building sanctuaries on terraced mountain slopes predates the introduction of South Asian cultural elements to Java in the early centuries CE.

13 The *Gandavyuha* has inspired numerous pictorial representations. See Fontein 1967.

14 The oldest texts on *Karmavibhaṅga* are found in Chinese translations of the *Śuka-sūtra;* these translations were made in the third, fifth, sixth, and tenth centuries (Chandra 2009, 143).

15 Within Buddhist cosmology there are thirty-one realms of existence wherein beings can be reborn. These include realms of hell, ghosts, animals, humans, and gods.

16 Would the term "spirits" be more appropriate than "souls" in a Buddhist context? The terms *jiva* and *atman* are used to refer to that which is transferred from one body to another at the time of transmigration; what is extinguished upon entry to nirvana is normally translated "soul" in English. For Buddhist theories of the soul, see Warder 1980, 119–126.

17 The idea of hell as comprising a court like those of mankind seems to have begun in second-century China (Goh 2015). By the early tenth century, the specific concept of ten courts with ten kings existed there (Teiser 1988, 1993). The Sutra of the Ten Kings (*Shiwangshengqi jing*) was composed in the early tenth century, possibly in 926, but the contents may be much older (Teiser 1993, 121; Goh 2015, 99). The concept of the three worlds was not important in China, unlike Southeast Asia (Miksic 2013, 148–151).

18 A search under Hell Garden Thailand on February 12, 2018, turned up numerous websites. For example, see: Trip to the Buddhist Hell Gardens of Thailand, horrorfanzine.com/trip-to-the-buddhist-hell-gardens-of-thailand.

19 Such sculptures were popular in the ancient kingdom of Dvaravati, which ruled central Thailand in the first millennium CE.

20 This is connected to the much more important shrines at stupas in Myanmar.

References

Anon. 1998. "Chinatown 'won't become a theme park.'" *The Straits Times*. December 12.
Barthes, R. 1972. *Mythologies*. Translated by A. Lavers. New York: Hill and Wang.
Brandel, Judith, and Tina Turbeville. 1998. *Tiger Balm Gardens: A Chinese Billionaire's Fantasy Environments*. Hong Kong: Aw Boon Haw Foundation.
Chandra, Lokesh. 2009. "The Hidden Base in the Cosmography of the Borobudur." In *Uncovering the Meaning of the Hidden Base of Candi Borobudur*, 137–161. Jakarta: Pusat Penelitian dan Pengembangan Arkeologi Nasional.
Channel News Asia. 2015. "STB appoints Journeys to run Haw Par Villa." https://www.channelnewsasia.com/news/singapore/stb-appoints-journeys-to/2065580.html.
Choo Ruizhi. 2016. *The Dioramas of Haw Par Villa*. Singapore: National University of Singapore Press.
Coedès, G. 1992. "Malay Inscriptions of Sriwijaya." In *Sriwijaya: History, Religion, and Language of an Early Malay Polit*, edited by George Coedès and Louis-Charles Damais, 41–92. Kuala Lumpur: Malaysian Branch of the Royal Asiatic Society, Monograph No. 20.
Comber, Leon. 1958. *Chinese Temples in Singapore*. Singapore: Eastern Universities Press.
De Casparis, J. G. 1990. "An Ancient Garden in West Sumatra." *Saraswati Esai-Esai Arkeologi. Kalpataru* 9: 40–49.
De Jong, J. W. 1974. "Notes on the Sources and the Text of the *Sang Hyang Kamahāyānan*." *Bijdragen tot de Taal-, Land- en Volkenkunde* 130 (4): 465–482.
Doniger, Wendy. 2009. *The Hindus: An Alternative History*. New York: Penguin.
Fontein, Jan. 1967. *The Pilgrimage of Sudhana: A Study of* Gaṇḍavyūha *Illustrations in China, Japan and Java*. The Hague: Mouton.
Goh Geok Yian. 2015. "Southeast Asian Images of Hell: Transmission and Adaptation." *Bulletin de l'École française d'Extrême-Orient* 101:91–116.
Huang Jianli and Hong Lysa. 2007. "Chinese Diasporic Culture and National Identity: The Taming of the Tiger Balm Gardens in Singapore." *Modern Asian Studies* 41 (1): 41–76.
Jacobsen, Knut A. 2009. "Three Functions of Hell in the Hindu Traditions." *Numen* 56:385–400.
le Bonheur, Albert. 1995. *Of Gods, Kings, and Men: Bas-Reliefs of Angkor Wat and Bayon*. London: Serindia Publications.
Lim, Irene. 2017. "Har Par Villa (Tiger Balm Gardens)." Accessed February 22, 2017. http://eresources.nlb.gov.sg/infopedia/articles/SIP_560_2004-12-14.html.
Lombard, Denys. 1969. "Jardins à Java." *Arts asiatiques* 9:135–184.
——. 1967. *Le Sultanat d'Atjéh au temps d'Iskandar Muda 1607–1636*. Paris: École Française d'Extrême-Orient.
Lowenthal, D. 1985. *The Past Is a Foreign Country*. Cambridge: Cambridge University Press.
Maizels, John. 2007. *Fantasy Worlds*. Bonn: Taschen.
McDaniel, Justin. 2016. *Architects of Buddhist Leisure: Socially Disengaged Buddhism in Asia's Museums, Monuments, and Amusement Parks*. Honolulu: University of Hawai'i Press.
Miksic, John N. 1990. *Borobudur: Golden Tales of the Buddhas*. Singapore: Periplus.
——. 2008. *Gardens in Java*. Translation of Lombard, "Jardins à Java." Jakarta: Pusat Penelitian dan Pengembangan Arkeologi Nasional.
——. 2013. *Singapore and the Silk Road of the Sea*. Singapore: National University of Singapore Press.
Mohammad Zain bin Mahmood. 1959. *A Study of Keramat Worship*. Honours thesis, University of Malaya, Singapore.

Phraya Lithai. 1982. *The Three Worlds According to King Ruang: A Thai Buddhist Cosmology*. Translated by F. E. Reynolds and M. Reynolds. Berkeley, CA: Center for South and Southeast Asian Studies, Berkeley Buddhist Studies Series No. 4.

Roveda, Vittorio. n.d. *Sacred Angkor: The Carved Reliefs of Angkor Wat*. Bangkok: River Books.

Salazar, Noel. 2012. "Tourism Imaginaries: A Conceptual Approach." *Annals of Tourism Research* 39 (2): 863–882.

Salazar, Noel B., and Nelson Graburn, eds. 2014. *Tourism Imaginaries: Anthropological Approaches*. New York: Berghahn.

Schopen, Gregory. 2014. "The Buddhist 'Monastery' and the Indian Garden. Aesthetics, Assimilations, and the Siting of Monastic Establishments." In *Buddhist Nuns, Monks, and Other Worldly Matters,* edited by Gregory Schopen, 224–250. Honolulu: University of Hawai'i Press.

Shiraishi, Saya. 1990. "A Study of Bustanu's-Salatin (the Garden of the Kings)." In *Reading Southeast Asia,* edited by Takashi Shiraishi, 41–55. Ithaca, NY: Cornell University Press.

Sri Soejatmi Satari. 2008. "Ancient Gardens and Hindu-Buddhist Architecture in Java." In *Interpreting Southeast Asia's Past: Monument, Image and Text,* edited by Elisabeth A. Bacus, Ian Glover, and Peter D. Sharrock, 122–132. Singapore: National University of Singapore Press.

Tanabe, Willa J. 1988. *Paintings of the Lotus Sutra*. New York: Weatherhill.

Teiser, Stephen. 1993. "The Growth of Purgatory." In *Religion and Society in T'ang and Sung China*, edited by Patricia Buckley Ebrey and Peter N. Gregory, 115–145. Honolulu, University of Hawai'i Press.

——. 1988. "'Having Once Died and Returned to Life': Representations of Hell in Medieval China." *Harvard Journal of Asiatic Studies* 48 (2): 433–464.

——. 2006. *Reinventing the Wheel. Paintings of Rebirth in Medieval Buddhist Temples*. Seattle: University of Washington Press.

Warder, A. K. 1980. *Indian Buddhism*. New Delhi: Motilal Banarsidass.

Yeoh, B., and J. Teo. 1996. "From Tiger Balm Gardens to Dragon World: Philanthropy and Profit in the Making of Singapore's First Cultural Theme Park." *Geografiska Annaler* Series B Human Geography 78 (1): 27–42.

Zaccheus, Melody. 2017. "Peep into Har Par Villa's Death Museum." *The Straits Times,* October 28.

3

Loss and Promise

The Buddhist Temple as Tourist Space in Thailand

BROOKE SCHEDNECK

ACCORDING TO RECENT MEDIA REPORTS, TOURISTS ARE disrespecting Buddhist sites in Thailand through inappropriate behaviors, causing negative impressions of tourists among the regional lay Buddhist population. When captured on social media, these instances are often followed by shock and outrage throughout the Thai Buddhist public sphere. In this chapter, I first focus on two case studies. The first is an incident that occurred in December 2014 when a young foreign couple conducted a yoga practice session in the space of a famous Chiang Mai city temple, Wat Suan Dok. The second occurred in August 2016, at a famous temple in Phukhet, Wat Chalong, when a Russian woman was videotaped and photographed wearing a see-through beach cover-up revealing her bikini underneath. But while these kinds of tourist behavior garner media attention, cultural misunderstanding is far from the only result of such encounters. In many temples popular with tourists, Buddhist monks contend that the presence of tourists can be both positive for the religion and beneficial for the tourists.

Religion and tourism have a contested relationship but also a mutually beneficial and entangled one. At Buddhist temples that often host tourists and practitioners, leaders must contend with overlapping ideas of the purpose of a space that can be used for devotion and recreation, ritual and leisure, education and relaxation. To demonstrate this, I will focus on two different voices in reaction to foreign tourists—the Thai lay Buddhist public as demonstrated by viral media stories, and Buddhist monks. The Thai lay Buddhist public view, broadly conceived, as we will see, often portrays a more negative view of tourists, while Buddhist monks demonstrate understanding of tourist behavior. Because of these differing perceptions, below I note both some contestations toward tourists, which have been popular in Thai Buddhist social media, and the attitude of openness toward tourists by northern Thailand's Buddhist monks. Because these monks interact with tourists on a regular basis, they have a different reaction to tourist behavior than the wider Thai Buddhist society. In creating this contrast, I do not mean to set up a stark binary between Thai lay Buddhists and monks. Of course it is difficult to represent *the* lay perspective and *the* monastic one about tourists. Instead I am comparing particular responses to tourism in temples as seen in media, shared and commented upon by Thai lay Buddhists, and the particular population of monks in northern Thailand who are located in city temples popular with tourists.

These interactions between monks and tourists are facilitated by what I term "Buddhist exchange" programs. Since the early 2000s these programs have formed in Buddhist monastic educational settings, offered by both international tourism companies affiliated with Buddhist monastic community leaders and directly through local temples. During these exchanges, international tourists and Buddhist monks interact within the contexts of volunteering in a temple, English conversation practice, joining a Buddhist community, and temporary ordination. Within these interactions, there is a conscious effort by Buddhist monks to promote Buddhism as a welcoming religion. For example, while I was complaining to a Thai monk in Wat Chedi Luang Worawihan, Chiang Mai, about the inappropriate clothing of the tourists walking by, the monk responded, "They don't know how to act in the temple. We have to teach them. If I go to Europe, it's a different culture for me. I don't know all the rules there." With much more compassion than I had displayed, this monk demonstrated openness to tourist behavior of non-Buddhists who had not yet learned how to act respectfully in the temple environment.

But it is not just their familiarity with tourists that allows monks who participate in Buddhist cultural exchange programs to have such a different reaction to them. These city monks in Chiang Mai also have a different imaginary of the purpose of the temple than the broader Thai public demonstrates on social media because, for them, the temple is a space to welcome non-Buddhists, a place to demonstrate the values of Buddhism and to spread the religion. For many Thai lay Buddhists who discuss these issues on discussion boards, news outlets, and blogs, however, the temple is a sacred place where one can engage in many kinds of merit-making activities.[1] This view of the temple is less encompassing of tourists, who represent the perceived secularity of sacred sites. In this way Thai Buddhist media introduces contestation over the proper decorum at sacred sites and the appropriate ways to respond to the sacred. While the monks I have talked to are not as concerned with the secular entering into temples through tourists, they believe that once a non-Buddhist begins to understand Buddhism and Buddhist teachings, an understanding of how to dress and present oneself in sacred spaces will naturally follow. By situating these two perspectives in conversation, this chapter argues that the main factor to consider with regard to Buddhist place-making is the ambivalence of tourism, the loss and promise tourism represents for Buddhist temples. Before examining the promise of tourism as seen by some Buddhist monks, I first discuss its loss characterized by inappropriate tourist behavior as debated by members of the Thai lay Buddhist public in social media.

Contestations of Tourist Behavior

Recent anthropological work and global Buddhist media have also found tourism to be a double-edged sword. In his study of the Temple Stay program in Korea, Uri Kaplan has recorded both positive and negative reactions to tourism. Korean monks complain about the temple environment disrupted, Buddhist activities diminished, and solitude ruined, because of noisy tourists (Kaplan 2010, 131). However, on the other hand "temples have realized the economic possibilities of joining the tourism trade, and temples today are not only charging entrance fees, but also managing hotels and restaurants in the tourist villages outside the temples' gates" (Kaplan 2010, 131). Tourism can be disruptive but it can also be lucrative. Reports from recent global Buddhist media capture this complexity. We find tourism threatening the stability of McLeod Ganj, the Tibetan diaspora in India, through stimulating the construction of low-quality buildings to accommodate those wishing to take part in teachings by the Dalai Lama and other high-ranking Tibetan Buddhist leaders (Lewis 2017). But in Japan, tourism is used as a source of hope for the future viability of rural Japanese Buddhist temples that are becoming less important to communities at the local level (Lewis 2016). Although much research on religion and tourism has focused on the negative sides of religious tourism as a damaging influence, tourism represents two poles within religious spaces—destruction and hope, loss and promise, and, as I show here, contestation and openness.[2]

The Thai lay Buddhist reaction to foreign tourists, represented in various media outlets, can be analyzed from theories of contestation about religious and sacred space. Following David Chidester and Edward Linenthal (1995) in their analysis of American sacred space, John Eade and Michael Sallnow (1991) in their discussion of Christian pilgrimage, and Jacob Kinnard's (2014) multisite study of sacred places, I discuss the ways the Buddhist temple as a tourist location becomes a space of contest over the legitimate ownership of the sacred. Some Thai Buddhists assert, through blogs and comments, their articulations of power and authority over the temple space. Images and videos of foreign tourists using the space of the temple in ways that are considered disrespectful by some Thai lay Buddhists are often shared on social media.

When tourists act inappropriately in Thai Buddhist temples, this is often captured on social media and followed by shock and outrage. In December 2014, a group of tourists engaged in a yoga practice session in the space of the famous Chiang Mai city temple, Wat Suan Dok, was widely discussed. A Thai forum called CM108 showed multiple pictures of these tourists stating, "These pictures are inappropriate (*phāp mai mǫsom*) due to monks and novices and Buddhists who, when entering the temple, must focus (*tǫng samrūam*) on their speech and hearts" (CM108 2014).[3] One commenter on this forum wrote, "Thai people know what is appropriate [in the temple space]. We need to be brave to admonish (*taktūan*) them [tourists]. If you can or cannot speak English, it doesn't matter. Just to say 'No, no, no good,' is enough. I believe every person can say these basic words in English" (CM108 2014). These images continued to be reproduced on social media and Thai news outlets. One called Kapook! Hilight News titled their article: "Foreigners practice yoga poses in Chiang Mai temple—is it appropriate?" The article goes on to explain the shock of Thai Buddhists at foreigners conducting such activities in a place Thai Buddhists consider sacred. It states that when the foreigners were having a fun time (*yāng sanuk sanān*) doing their yoga poses this caused "the people passing to question and wonder are the actions of these two foreigners appropriate? And why is no one brave to go and admonish them?" (Kapook! Hilight News 2015). To the Thai Buddhist public, as seen from these comments, yoga is viewed as a secular activity done for fun and entertainment. The amusement these tourists are having is in turn distracting, they believe, to both monks and Thai Buddhist laypeople, who act as if the temple is a sacred, religious space. To the foreign tourists, perhaps yoga and a Buddhist temple are seen as an appropriate pairing, but for Thai Buddhists this is an affront to the sacred through the encroachment of the secular.

In August 2016, at a famous temple in Phukhet, Wat Chalong, a Russian woman was videotaped and photographed wearing a see-through beach cover-up revealing her bikini underneath. The image went viral and resulted in a cultural education seminar by Thai police and an apologetic *wai* (gesture of respect and greeting in Thailand) from the Russian woman to the Thai public (Coconuts Bangkok 2016). In Thai media coverage, the description of the dress details its characteristics as sexy, see-through, and so thin that you are able to see her undergarments clearly (*yāng chat čhēn*) (Sanook.com 2016). In an article titled "Big Drama: Foreign Woman Wears Very Thin See-through Outfit in a Famous Phukhet Temple," the media outlet states that the problem is there is "no official (*čhaonātī*) to take care of this temple, check, and recommend (*næ kǣ*) to foreigners how they should behave in the temple. And this has caused the Buddhist people to see how this foreign lady acted inappropriately"

(Sanook.com 2016). This article empathizes with the tourists and local Thai people who enter the temple in order to worship and ask for blessings from the important statues of Luangpau Chaem and Luangpor Chuang located there, but instead are distracted by a foreign woman dressed sexily (*tǣng kāy wāp wiu*) and who is not concerned (*yæ̂ sæ̂*) about who could see her (Sanook.com 2016). Instead of witnessing this disrespect, this media outlet states that everyone should look appropriate in a temple because this is a sacred (*saksit*) place. Again, the tourist represents the secular in the form of beachwear, entering the temple. To think that one can go from the beach directly to the temple, as this Russian tourist did, is to equate the secular and the sacred. For Thai Buddhists, the temple and beach are compartmentalized into two very different spheres.

In the end of this piece, Sanook.com (2016) lists another problem with Chinese tourists, who regularly come to take pre-wedding photos at this temple, kissing, hugging, and wearing inappropriate outfits. Using the temple for a wedding photo shoot has become a problem in Chiang Mai as well with signs posted in the picturesque historic stupa of Wat Chedi Luang stating "No Wedding Photo." Marriage and romance, again representative of the secular, are perceived as antithetical to the temple space. These issues of inappropriate behavior and clothing are problematic in Thailand because of a highly held value called *kalatesa,* which loosely translated means, "time and place." Penny Van Esterik (2000) explains this important aspect of Thai etiquette as a "noun that means proper, suitable or balanced according to dictionary definitions, and politeness, appropriateness, or context according to Thai informants" (36). Having *kalatesa* is a good quality that indicates an individual values orderliness in social relations, understands the context of their space and time, and matches their behavior and appearance to this context. Tourists behaving in ways that display a lack of *kalatesa* are offensive to Thai Buddhists who see the temple as a space that requires one to dress modestly and act in a quiet, reserved manner. Because of this, their actions demonstrate that they do not understand the importance of their outward appearance, recognize the temple's proper context, nor can they match their behavior and dress to this space. From the perspective of *kalatesa,* tourists do not understand the sacred nature of the temple and treat it as any other secular space. Conversely, having *kalatesa* allows Thai Buddhists to assert their authority on Thai Buddhist sacred space. They treat the temple as separate from secular spaces and recognize the ways they should act and behave in order to complement this sacredness.

It is for this reason that many temples popular with tourists facilitate an understanding of *kalatesa* by employing staff to check the dress of tourists and place signs at the entrance displaying pictures of proper dress, and charge a fee to enter, such as Wat Phra Si Rattana Satsadaram (Wat Phra Kaew) and Wat Phra Chetuphon (Wat Pho) in Bangkok and Wat Prathat Doi Suthep and Wat Chedi Luang in Chiang Mai. Another temple that utilizes signs is Wat Palad, a popular hiking destination and temple with scenic views. While Thai Buddhists usually arrive at the temple in proper dress and with offerings for the monks, tourists, especially in the early morning, reach Wat Palad as groups of hikers, having finished their exercise. There are many signs indicating to the hikers to keep quiet and behave appropriately in this space. Occasionally a monk will be assigned to tell the hikers to wrap a sarong around their shorts but for the most part the temple has adapted to its diverse population of foreign hikers along with Thai Buddhist benefactors and meditators. With a coffee shop installed in 2016 and nine baht (.25 USD) going to the temple out of every purchase, this temple has found a way to be open to tourists. As tourist service providers make it easy to visit Buddhist temples as part of any tourist experience, temples institute strategies to utilize the resources tourism brings. If the destructive forces of tourism can be managed and the lucrative aspect enhanced, tourism does not pose a problem. The challenge, then, for Buddhist temples that are popular with tourists, is to create ways to make the space open to tourists while also maintaining the sacredness and familiarity of the place for Buddhists.

Comparing Buddhist tourism management strategies of temples in Chiang Mai, Thailand, with Luang Prabang, Laos, is instructive. Through detailed interviews with tourists, Lenaerts (2015) has found that in Luang Prabang's temples, visitors felt like they were in a zoo watching the monks and interfering with their lives (65). Tourists in Luang Prabang also complained that the signage in temples was not adequate so that they did not know where was restricted and where they were welcome (Lenaerts 2015, 73). Additionally, despite past information campaigns about the famous almsround in Luang Prabang, it remains a problematic event with visitors not respecting the rules and locals selling low-quality food for the tourists to give to the monks (Lenaerts 2015, 72). In contrast, visits to many of Chiang Mai's temples are designed so that the visitor knows which spaces are for the public. With signage and staff at many temples on the tourist map, managing and directing the behavior of tourists, it is not difficult to interpret the basic level of respectful behavior expected. Aside from rare instances of yoga practice sessions and beachwear in temples, Thai temples' attempts to control tourist behavior have been mostly successful.

Temple signs indicating appropriate bodily comportment are aimed at conduct and dress, but do not help to explain the symbols of Buddhist art and architecture, the purpose of the monastic life, or the meaning of lay Buddhist practice. If tourists are interested in these aspects, further encounters with Buddhism are needed. Short visits to temples can indicate possibilities of tension between tourists and Thai Buddhists; however, with more close interactions and encounters between monks and tourists, instead of conflict or even ambivalence, we see an intentional welcoming and open approach to tourists. More than just not posing a problem and becoming a source of income,

Buddhist monks in some Thai temples see other important benefits to tourism that the rest of the chapter explicates.

Buddhist Encounters in Northern Thailand

Chiang Mai is Thailand's northern capital and is known as "the city of a hundred temples." Chiang Mai is a Buddhist tourism destination because of the density of temples and the accessibility of its monks (Choe and O'Regan 2015, 199). Because the tourist industry is an important part of the economy in Thailand's largest northern city, it is an ideal location to study tourist encounters with Buddhism.[4] Most tourists arrive in Chiang Mai city by plane, bus, or train from Bangkok, but this medium-sized city, with a population of nearly two hundred thousand, is becoming increasingly accessible with direct flights from many locations in Asia.[5] Much of the imaginaries of the city itself are also linked with Buddhism. Travel magazines, such as *Travel + Leisure,* that list Chiang Mai as a top destination, do so with photos of solitary monks walking in a lush temple space.[6] *Condé Nast's Traveller* also opens its guide to Chiang Mai with a similar photo of a lone monk, dog, and bird walking between temple buildings. Chiang Mai natives themselves also seek to promote these ideas of their city through its application to become a UNESCO World Heritage Centre. In 2015 Chiang Mai was added to the list of Tentative UNESCO World Heritage Sites. In the list of nominated properties in the city's submission to officially receive this distinction, over seventy sites are Buddhist temples (UNESCO 2015). Because Chiang Mai is touted as a top tourist destination and cultural heritage center, with visiting Buddhist temples as one of the principal activities, tourist encounters are frequent for the city's monks.

Within Chiang Mai city are two Buddhist universities representing the two sects of Thai Buddhism.[7] The monks who attend these universities are from various provinces in northern Thailand, and move to Chiang Mai city for their education. Young men from similar populations also enter the middle and high schools for novice monks, which are located both inside and outside the city. Farther north on the border between Thailand and Myanmar we find members of ethnic minority groups in Thailand such as the Shan, Karen, Palaung, and others also moving to Chiang Mai city in order to take advantage of the education ordaining as a novice monk affords. Besides the Thai population, international monk students take part in the English programs offered at these universities. Young monks from many Asian countries including Bangladesh, Cambodia, Laos, Myanmar, Nepal, Vietnam, choose to attend university in Thailand in order to learn about Buddhism and secular subjects in English, something not as accessible in their countries. Because of all of these educational opportunities, there are many Thai, ethnic minority, and international monks who are eager to converse with international visitors.

Besides visiting temples, there are numerous opportunities to engage further with Buddhism and its representatives through Buddhist cultural exchange programs, with opportunities to experience life in a Buddhist temple. The size and scope of Buddhist exchange programs vary depending on the nature of the exchange. These programs are all locally produced and do not emerge out of formal sangha structures. I have identified four kinds of programs, which have different focuses and levels of engagement. First, the Monk Chat program allows tourists to learn about the monastic life and Buddhism through providing informal conversations with monks. Second, English teaching opportunities in temple schools accept foreign volunteers to enter into monastic classrooms. Third, gap year and study abroad experiential learning opportunities for educational groups stay for several days in a temple setting to learn a Buddhist way of life. Fourth, any individual can join a Temple Stay and Retreat program that allows those interested to become part of a Buddhist community by living in a Buddhist temple with the possibility of ordaining for male participants. These programs all facilitate encounters between international visitors and monks within immersive experiences ranging from an hour to several months. The majority of the international visitors to these programs are English-speakers from the United States, Europe, Australia, and New Zealand with a minority from East Asia. During periods of fieldwork from June to September 2010 and ongoing fieldwork since May 2013,[8] I investigated these programs that facilitate religious encounters between international travelers and Buddhist novices and monks. My data draws from interviews of facilitators and participants in the programs and participant-observation.

The Monk Chat program is available in three temples in Chiang Mai (Wat Suan Dok, Wat Srisuphan, and Wat Chedi Luang) for tourists interested in learning about Buddhism from monks who are college students. This program began in 2000 for the purpose of giving monks a chance to practice their English and teach about Buddhism.[9] During Monk Chat sessions there are usually between five and ten monks having small group conversations with ten to thirty tourists seated at rectangular tables.[10] Tourists learn about this program through guidebooks, online recommendations, or the Monk Chat websites.[11]

There are numerous opportunities to teach novice monks in temple schools in northern Thailand. My research focuses on the Future Sense Foundation's "Teaching English to Buddhist Monks Program."[12] In this program, participants have the opportunity to live with and teach English to Buddhist novices and monks in the Doi Saket district, forty minutes outside of Chiang Mai. Since its inception in 2014 the program has placed over one hundred volunteers in Buddhist temples each year for varying lengths of time, arriving in groups or individually.[13] From interviews with program coordinators and volunteers, their motivations for participating in the "Teaching English to Buddhist Monks Program" normally include gaining teaching experience, making a contribution, and pursuing an interest in Buddhism.[14]

Another exchange program that allows foreign guests to live on-site is located in a Dhamma center located three and a half hours outside of Chiang Mai city, in the town of Wieng Haeng, called Plik Wiwek. Founder and head monk of Plik Wiwek is Phra Ajahn Dr. Thani Jitawiriyo. Situated near the border of Thailand with the Shan State in Myanmar, Ajahn Thani established this center in order to give a home to the many orphan and poor boys in the community. Because of this situation, Plik Wiwek has a number of international networks that allow for foreign volunteers and students to learn from and contribute to the space, including gap year programs and college study abroad trips.[15]

The most immersive program, the Temple Stay and Retreat Program, is located within Wat Sri Boen Ruang in the town of Fang. This temple is also not located near a tourist area, so the program brings interested individual travelers to Fang, three hours outside of Chiang Mai city. The participants, for the most part, find out about this opportunity through the program's website.[16] Wat Sri Boen Ruang has about fifty novices in residence and about one hundred novices that attend the school on the monastery grounds. Abbot of this temple, Phra Ajahn Dr. Abhisit Pingchaiyawat estimates that 70 percent of novices at Wat Sri Boen Ruang are poor or have family problems.[17] Because of the nature of this monastic community who would benefit from exposure to international visitors, Phra Ajahn Dr. Abhisit created this program where foreign guests come to live at his temple.[18] This program is offered by donation that helps the maintenance of the facilities as well as Phra Ajahn Dr. Abhisit's development projects for Fang.[19] Instead of managing the program himself, Phra Ajahn Dr. Abhisit has program coordinators and other local volunteers to promote and orient the guests.

The main appeal of all of these programs derives from the religious and cultural exchange, and the perceived difference of both groups of participants, monastics and foreign travelers. All of these programs allow for sustained engagement with the other. Instead of a short visit where proper dress and behavior might not be understood, tourists in these programs interact with the temple space and Buddhist monks in a much more intimate way. When we look at this level of engagement, instead of the possibility of contestation, openness to the other is the dominant sensibility.

Openness to Tourist Encounters

Some tourists are not satisfied with a short visit to a single temple but want to understand more about this complex religion—what its symbols mean and what the monastic life is like. Because of this, exchange programs convey a sense of openness during the encounter through an emphasis on sampling and experimentation. Buddhist exchange programs give tourists options to engage with the religion at a variety of levels. This serves to portray Buddhism as welcoming and makes Buddhist temples attractive places for exchange. The coordinators of the Future Sense Foundation volunteer teaching program have used this kind of language in their promotion, emphasizing that their volunteers have limitless opportunities to learn about Buddhism and meditation, if one chooses. The webpage for the Teaching English to Monks program states:

> As a volunteer living in a Wat you have several unique opportunities. You can observe the daily life of the monks and experience how they live, what they think and what they feel. Although there are no scheduled classes or seminars, the monks are eager to teach about Buddhism so the potential to gain knowledge and insight is endless! . . . Outside of the classroom we encourage all volunteers to take advantage of living and being at a Buddhist temple by exploring the grounds, meeting and speaking with the monks, and taking part in all of the school/temple activities. The monks are eager to share their knowledge about Buddhism, but it is up to you to engage and talk with them.[20]

In this way, religious learning and practice is constructed not as a formal part of the program, but an added benefit. As we will see all of the Buddhist exchange programs emphasize that the choice and interest to learn has to come from the tourist.

Phra Maha Insorn, principal of Wat Nong Bua's monastic school, echoed the sentiments of this advertisement in an interview stating that the first objective in receiving volunteers at the temple is teaching English. He reminded me that the temple does not compel volunteer teachers to learn anything about Buddhism. But at the same time he also was clearly excited to talk about the possibilities that the volunteer teachers have to practice Buddhism. Phra Maha Insorn stated that there are not many opportunities if the group comes for a short time but if they stay for a couple of months, they can get a sense of what it's like to be a Buddhist.

In response to these possibilities of sampling and experimentation, the volunteers are often impressed with Buddhism. In my participant-observation and interviews with the Future Sense Foundation volunteers in summer 2016, they commented that they enjoyed being able to access aspects of Thai culture they would never be able to see on a regular visit to Thailand. Volunteers enjoyed observing the beginning of the rains retreat (*khao phansā*) and seeing their students as religious figures. They feel like they are a part of the community and even noted that it was strange to see their novice students chanting and receiving offerings while remembering them misbehaving in class. In response to my question about what he has learned about Buddhism, Tom, a twenty-two-year-old college student and volunteer for two weeks as part of an internship with Australian Catholic University, said: "I learned how welcoming Buddhists are. They not only welcome us to come into their classrooms and attend any ceremony at the temple, they are also open to our non-traditional methods of teaching where we get the novices running around and yelling. They accept it all because they think it's good for the kids." Kim, a twenty-four-year-old recent college graduate from America, who had volunteered individually for two weeks in 2015, had a similar opinion, stating:

> I have always found Buddhism interesting and love how accepting and peaceful they are. I have experienced many different forms of religion where the believers shove their ideas down others' throats, but I never experienced this with Buddhism. The monks were very happy to explain their beliefs and way of life, but never tried or expected me to change mine.

The reception from volunteers also identifies Buddhism as a welcoming religion. The monks who take part in these exchange programs want non-Buddhists to see what it's like to be a Buddhist, while the foreign participants are impressed by the ability to experiment with the religion.

At each of these programs aspects of Buddhism are taught through various means as a way for foreign tourists to sample taking on the worldview of a Buddhist. This commitment to teaching tourists about Buddhism is evident in the effort of Monk Chat monks and their university teachers. In August 2016, a symposium for Monk Chat monks titled "How to Teach Buddhism to Non-Buddhists" was held at Wat Suan Dok. During these two days, experienced teachers of Buddhism, lay and ordained, Western and Asian, were asked to summarize their strategies for teaching Buddhism.

In talking to the students at this symposium about their goals for their Monk Chat conversations they emphasized these same ideals of presenting Buddhism as open and welcoming. Novice monk Pon from Laos said his goal is to "show the Buddhist way of life and teachings of Buddhism." Phra Som from Thailand stated that "if they don't want to be Buddhist that is fine but I want to show them who I am and what is Buddhism. If they already know about Buddhism, then I want to help them understand more." Phra An from Vietnam stated that his goal is "to teach the Four Noble Truths and help them be happy." Through programs like this, Buddhists seek to present Buddhism as a welcoming religion. They display this openness to tourists by making the place of the Buddhist temple accessible to non-Buddhists to learn and experiment with Buddhist practices and lifestyles. While the Thai Buddhist public focuses on the value of proper behavior (*kalatesa*) in a sacred space, the Buddhist monks I have spoken to in northern Thailand are more interested in creating encounters that demonstrate the temple is a welcoming place.

Factors Contributing to Openness

Because most of these international visitors are English-speaking Westerners, they are part of "the allure of the West as a charismatic and appealing cultural site" (Harrison 2010, 3).[21] Their presence not only brings possibilities of English conversational practice but also prestige to a temple community to which foreigners would travel and stay for extended periods. As well whiteness is preferred in Thailand as a consequence of imperialism and complex racial ideologies that originate from both national and international sources. This explicit connection between the Westerner and the modern must, of course, have a significant impact on how we conceptualize intercultural exchanges in the postcolonial period. In this section I will investigate two characteristics that I argue are most important for the welcoming reception of particular foreigners who have demonstrated interest in Buddhism: the fact that most of the foreigners are perceived to be Christian, and the Buddhist value of spreading the teachings.

An important part of the openness displayed to Western groups of foreigners is that they are assumed to be Christian. Among Buddhist monks participating in these programs there is a general sense that Christianity is the dominant religion of the foreign participants. From my dozens of interviews and conversations with novices and monks who encounter foreigners through these programs, to them, typically, a white European or North American is Christian. Besides equating whiteness with Christianity, a second typical assumption is that Christians are not totally committed to their faith. Because of these two assumptions, Buddhist monks sense that the Buddhist religion is different and interesting to tourists. In this way Christians are seen as part of a group that could come to know and practice Buddhism, even if they do not convert to the religion. When asked why they think Christians are interested in Buddhism, one novice in the Temple Stay and Retreat Program at Wat Sri Boen Ruang responded, "I read on the internet that Christians are interested in Buddhism because it helps them know how to reach happiness. They want to see the difference between Buddhism and Christianity." This population is seen as modern and curious, but most of all, interested in learning about Buddhism.

The novice monks who live in the Dhamma center in Wieng Haeng called Plik Wiwek discussed the differences between the foreigners that come to stay with them and Thai Buddhist groups that also are hosted here.[22] In their descriptions they praise the foreigners, explicating the attributes they valued. Novice Jaem characterized the foreigners who come to Plik Wiwek as

> wanting to practice more than Thais. Thais don't want to [practice] and are not interested in Buddhism.... The foreigners are mostly Christian but interested in Buddhism much more than Thais. If they lived in Thailand they would like to be Buddhist because they can understand more about themselves (*rūčhak tūa ēng*) in the temple environment (*singwǣtlǭm khǭng wat*) and can practice (*patibhattham*). There are no opportunities in Christianity for this practice. But they have Christian families so they are Christian.

Novice monk Arm generalized that all foreigners who visit Plik Wiwek "are Christian because that is what European and American people usually are. But there are some who want to be Buddhist because Christians can change to be Buddhist (*plīan pen chāw phut dai*)." They characterize the foreigners they encounter as essentially Buddhists who happened to grow up in Christian areas.

At Plik Wiwek, the novices and monks have many opportunities to interact with and observe the foreigners who come to stay. They admire their efforts in learning about Buddhism and noted that, as they stay longer, as Phra Borowet put it, "they can get peacefulness (*khwām sangob suk*)." He continued that

> the foreigners want to know about their [own] life (*rū chīwit khǭng tūa ēng*) and who they are... that is why they come [to stay at Plik Wiwek] but Thai people just want to play games... the foreigners want to know everything (*yāk rū tukyāng*), they want to know about the center, they want to know what it's like to be ordained because they don't have opportunities at home.

The monks at Plik Wiwek infer that the foreigners are more interested than the Thai people because they never saw Buddhism or Buddhist people before and this makes them curious about the religion, its practice, and monastic life. All of the novices and monks I interviewed here had these kinds of positive views about foreigners and the Christian religion.

The novice monks at Wat Nong Bua who have experience with the volunteer teachers from Future Sense Foundation, also characterized the volunteers as mostly Christians. Novice Sen stated that "when staying here the volunteers can become calmer, more relaxed (*sangob khưn sabāy khưn*). They did not know how to do these things at first but now they do." These Buddhist exchange programs then, from the monks' and novices' points of view, improve the foreign participants' lives, aiding them to become better people. Because of the perception that these foreign participants are open to Buddhism, these same Buddhist monks feel it is their responsibility to meet this demand with explanations and teaching in order to spread Buddhism. The fact that most of the participants in these Buddhist exchange programs are Westerners, perceived to be Christian, and thus open to adding elements of Buddhism to their lives, are the most significant reasons for Buddhists' openness to tourists in these spaces. In comparison with the contestation seen within Thai social media, openness within northern Thai Buddhist temples to tourist engagement with Buddhism demonstrates the opposite end of Buddhism's relationship with tourism. Monks seek to teach the foreigners proper behavior and the appropriate response to the nature of sacred space. For these monks, tourists are not threatening Buddhist sacredness by bringing the secular into temple, but simply not yet adopting a Buddhist way of life.

Through this variety of responses, we can see that reactions to tourists in Thai Buddhist temples fluctuate from contestation to openness, demonstrating the loss and promise of Buddhist tourism. The Thai Buddhist public asserts authority over *kalatesa* in their media discussions, and encourages regulation of foreign tourists' appearance in temple spaces. Buddhist monks are interested in engaging with the tourists' curiosity about the religion. These differing views generate questions about the nature of sacred space and Buddhist place-making. What sort of place is the temple? Is it a sacred place for Buddhists that must be protected from disrespectful actions or is it a tourist space where leisure can be accommodated? As Jacob Kinnard (2014) has argued, spaces are in motion; their nature is messy and hybrid. Temples are eclectic places that can function in a variety of acceptable ways. Although I have highlighted two dominant perspectives here, the Buddhist temple in Thailand can be many things to the Buddhist practitioner and the non-Buddhist tourist alike. It can be a place to understand Buddhist teachings, make merit through donations, be in close proximity to a sacred object such as a relic of the Buddha, take pictures of mural paintings and ornate temple buildings, or to enter into a peaceful setting within nature.

Speaking of religious sites in general, Daniel Olsen asserts that "Many managers [of religious sites] would prefer to give access only to a small number of believers because of the physical impacts tourism causes" (2006, 108), and that "the main focus of religious site custodians is to preserve the emotive qualities of the place as a way of creating and maintaining an atmosphere conducive to worship and contemplation" (106), in order to meet the expectations of those religiously motivated. Thai temples, in contrast, instead of closing off the space to visitors, feature lots of activity, which makes them important sites of encounter between cultures. As Justin McDaniel observes, temples in Thailand are not all sanctimonious and solemn. He writes the following description not about tourists but about Thai Buddhists:

> Most monasteries and monastery museums are not somber places where monks strictly enforce particular ways of performing rituals.

> Even during sermons and liturgical chanting, people can be seen chatting in the corner, wandering around the grounds, talking on cell phones, eating, and flirting.... These are not places of forced spirituality, ethical directives, or detached repose. (2011, 167)

When studying religion and tourism, we cannot let Western religious attitudes toward the sacred dominate our categories, assumptions, and analysis. It might be assumed that, for all religious spaces, the most significance would be placed on quietude and careful listening. However, very few Buddhist temples are meditation centers where this would be necessary. It seems what is primarily important to the Thai lay Buddhist public is modesty of dress and appropriate behavior following *kalatesa*. Thai Buddhists who don't display this proper decorum would also be looked down upon. They would be perceived to be not demonstrating their Thainess (*khwaam ben Thai*). On the other end of the spectrum, in my conversations with Buddhist monks who participate in exchange programs, they are very proud and defensive of the perception that Buddhism is a welcoming and open religion. They understand the temple as a space where all people can learn how to calm their minds and how Buddhist teachings and practice can improve their lives. For Thai Buddhists the temple is a space of ritual and merit-making, and for monks it's also a place to missionize and show the values of the religion.

In Buddhism there is no formal publication or statement about how the religion views tourism; however, attitudes toward tourism can be seen implicitly as an expression of economic realities and an extension of Buddhist beliefs and practices. Because tourism is not restricted in Buddhist temples in Thailand we can conclude that Buddhists, for the most part, view tourism in a positive way, as demonstrated by the opportunities not only to enter a Buddhist temple space but also to encounter representatives of the religion. While instances of inappropriate behavior in temples have caused Thai Buddhists to think critically about tourism, Buddhist exchange programs demonstrate openness through offering a variety of opportunities for international visitors to sample and experiment with Buddhist ideas and worldview. In this way, interactions between tourism and Buddhism represent both loss and promise as temple spaces are contested but also reinvented in creative and interesting ways.

Notes

1. In most Thai temples there is an abundance of ways to make merit, from making offerings to monks to chanting before a Buddha statue. For an overview of ways to make merit see Schedneck (2015, 66–67).
2. See Timothy and Olsen (2006, 12) for a summary of scholarship highlighting the negative aspects of religious tourism.
3. The Romanization system I use for quotes from interviews and Thai sources follows a simplified version of that used by the Library of Congress.

4 According to the Thailand Authority of Tourism (TAT), in 2015, Chiang Mai received 2.8 million international visitors and its hotels have more than 40,000 rooms. (http://www.tatnews.org/chiang-mai-tourism-stakeholders-reiterate-readiness-in-welcoming-chinese-tourists-and-all/). Chiang Mai has become attractive recently as it has won a number of awards from Travel magazines including *Travel + Leisure* and *Condé Nast*. In *Travel + Leisure's* 2016 list of top cities Chiang Mai came in number two out of fifteen (http://www.travelandleisure.com/worlds-best/cities#charleston). And in 2014, the city was voted among the Top 25 Cities in the World by *Condé Nast Traveller*'s Readers' Choice Awards (http://www.tatnews.org/bangkok-and-chiang-mai-named-worlds-top-25-cities/).

5 Chiang Mai International Airport is expected to service about 12 million passengers by 2020 (UNESCO Bangkok 2011).

6 *Travel + Leisure* named Chiang Mai second best city in the world in 2010 and 2016.

7 The two sects in Thai Buddhism are *mahanikai* and *thammayutnikai*. Mahamakut Buddhist University located at Wat Chedi Luang, is part of the *thammayutnikai*. Mahachulalongkorn Rajavidyalaya Buddhist University, located at Wat Suan Dok, is part of the *mahanikai*.

8 I have lived, conducted research, and worked in Chiang Mai, Thailand, since 2009 and have had ongoing opportunities to participate and observe these programs. Instead of intense periods of fieldwork, I interviewed participants, monks, and mediators of these programs on an ongoing basis.

9 The Monk Chat program began in Wat Suan Dok in 2000. Wat Chedi Luang followed this trend next with their Monk Chat program beginning in 2005. Wat Srisuphan started their program in 2008. I conducted interviews at Monk Chat from January to May 2016.

10 Phra Saneh Dhammavaro, one of the founders of Monk Chat, relates its purpose in a small book. He writes that its aim is to

> fulfill the aspiration of the foreigners whom approached [*sic*] monk at Wat Suandok with a lot of doubts and questions regarding Buddhism, Buddhist way of life, life of monk and meditation etc. So the main purpose of the Monk Chat Programe [*sic*] are 1) to provide and [*sic*] opportunity for the foreigners to chat with monks informally on general topics, 2) to provide and [*sic*] opportunity for the foreigners, monks and novices to learn, exchange and discuss the general ideas on Buddhism, Buddhist way of life and Thai culture, 3) to provide and [*sic*] forum for monks and novices to exchange ideas with people from different cultures, faiths and ways of life.

11 Wat Suan Dok's Monk Chat program has a website: http://www.monkchat.net. The other two programs rely on Facebook groups that the leaders continually update with photos and videos.

12 During the beginning of my research this program was called the Wat Doi Saket Project. This project was founded in 2009 when the abbot asked ATMA SEVA, the NGO Wat Doi Saket has worked with since 1990, for increased English learning opportunities for the resident monks. However, starting in January 2014, the staff has affiliated with Future Sense Foundation and changed names.

13 The program maintains an affiliation with Phra Maha Insorn Khunawuttho, principal of the school at Wat Nong Bua, Doi Saket, Chiang Mai. I conducted interviews with staff and volunteers there between June 2016 and August 2016.

14 The costs for this program vary depending on how long one stays. If one stays for two weeks the cost is around 1,500 USD and each additional week costs $350. The Future Sense Foundation offers an English-teaching curriculum as well as airport transfer, accommodation, some food costs, trips, and support for any emergencies or concerns. This volunteer fee covers a donation to the temple and supports a

scholarship fund. Some volunteers also bring souvenirs from their home country or notebooks, books, and pencils to donate to monks or the school library.

15 These groups stay for varying lengths of time, from a few days to two weeks. They participate in activities such as teaching English to novice monks, learning meditation, chanting with the monks, visiting temples close to the Thai border with Shan State, Myanmar, and farming with the novice monks. I interviewed novice monks, monks, and Ajahn Thani there from July 14 to July 17, 2016.

16 See: Temple Stay and Retreat website, http://www.templeretreatthailand.com, accessed August 26, 2014. I conducted interviews at Wat Sri Boen Ruang on November 10, 2009, March 2, 2010, October 10, 2013, and conducted participant-observation of the program and further interviews during an extended stay from August 24 to September 28, 2014.

17 Phra Ajahn Dr. Abhisit grew up in this community of downtown Fang and returned to take the position of abbot upon the death of his teacher, the former abbot. I interviewed him at Wat Sri Boen Ruang on October 17, 2013.

18 There are five main objectives the program hopes to offer to its participants: 1) the opportunity to live in a temple, 2) learn the basics of Buddhist beliefs and practices, 3) participate in a meditation retreat nearby the temple, 4) interact with the novice monks and help them become comfortable with the basics of English, and 5) ordain as a novice monk.

19 Phra Ajahn Dr. Abhisit's Best Together Foundation (http://www.bcdcfang.org) has a number of projects to aid the people of Fang including a health center, park, and scholarships for local children.

20 See: GapGuru, Future Sense website: http://www.gapguru.com/GapYearProjects/Teach-Buddhist-Monks-Thailand.

21 Although there has been a recent influx of Chinese tourists to Chiang Mai, so far they have not participated in the Buddhist cultural exchange programs, as indicated by my Buddhist monastic informants (see Schedneck 2018).

22 I conducted interviews with sixteen novices, three monks, and the abbot of the center at Plik Wiwek from July 15 to July 17, 2016. The discussions with these monks revolved around the annual gap year program participants from America and Australia that Plik Wiwek hosts for a few weeks every year as well as irregular English-teaching volunteers, some who have stayed for over three months.

References

Chidester, David, and Edward T. Linenthal, 1995. "Introduction." In *American Sacred Space,* edited by David Chidester and Edward T. Linenthal, 1–42. Bloomington and Indianapolis: Indiana University Press.

Choe, Jaeyeon, and Michael O'Regan. 2015. "Case Study 2: Religious Tourism Experiences in East Asia." In *Religious Tourism and Pilgrimage Management: An International Perspective,* 2nd ed., edited by R. Raj and K. Griffin, 191–204. Oxfordshire, UK: CAB International.

CM108.com. 2014. "Foreigners practice yoga, stretching arms and legs, in the middle of an old famous temple in Chiang Mai" [Farang Len Yoga YokKhen ThāngKhā Klāng Wat Kao Kæ Chūa Dang Khaung Chiang Mai]. Accessed March 23, 2016. https://www.cm108.com/bbb/topic/4263.

Coconuts Bangkok. 2016. "Tourist visits Phuket temple in see-through dress, gets cultural education from police." Accessed January 9, 2017. https://bangkok.coconuts.co/bangkok/news/tourist-visits-phuket-temple-see-through-dress-gets-cultural-education-police.

Phra Saneh Dhammavaro. 2009. "Forward." *Thai Buddhism Monk Chat.* Mahachulalongkornrajavidyalaya Buddhist University, Chiang Mai, Thailand.

Eade, John, and Michael J. Sallnow. 1991. "Introduction." In *Contesting the Sacred: The Anthropology of Christian Pilgrimage,* edited by John Eade and Michael J. Sallnow, 1–29. New York: Routledge.

Harrison, Rachel V. 2010. "Introduction: The Allure of Ambiguity: The 'West' and the Making of Thai Identities." In *The Ambiguous Allure of the West: Traces of the Colonial in Thailand,* edited by Rachel V. Harrison and Peter A. Jackson. Hong Kong: Hong Kong University Press.

Kaplan, Uri. 2010. "Images of Monasticism: The Temple Stay Program and the Rebranding of Korean Buddhist Temples." *Korean Studies* 34:127–146.

Kapook! Hilight News. 2015. "Foreigners practice yoga poses in Chiang Mai temple—is it appropriate?" [Farang Len Yoga ChīkKhæng HǣkKhā ChīKhau Nai Wat Chiang Mai Thām Mæsom Lǣw Rư̄]. Accessed January 9, 2017. http://hilight.kapook.com/view/113642.

Kinnard, Jacob. 2014. *Places in Motion: The Fluid Identities of Temples, Images, and Pilgrims.* Oxford: Oxford University Press.

Lenaerts, Sigrid. 2015. "Visitor Experience and Interpretation at Luang Prabang World Heritage Site." In *UNESCO in Southeast Asia: World Heritage Sites in Comparative Perspective,* edited by Victor T. King, 54–74. Honolulu: University of Hawaiʻi Press.

Lewis, Craig. 2016. "Buddhist Temples in Japan Hope to Tap Foreign Tourist Boom." Buddhist Door Global. Accessed January 9, 2017. https://www.buddhistdoor.net/news/buddhist-temples-in-japan-hope-to-tap-foreign-tourist-boom.

———. 2017. "Tourism Boom Threatens to Turn 'Little Lhasa' into a Concrete Jungle." Buddhist Door Global. Accessed January 9, 2017. https://www.buddhistdoor.net/news/tourism-boom-threatens-to-turn-little-lhasa-into-a-concrete-jungle.

McDaniel, Justin. 2011. *The Lovelorn Ghost and the Magical Monk: Practicing Buddhism in Modern Thailand.* New York: Columbia University Press.

Olsen, Daniel, H. 2006. "Management Issues for Religious Heritage Attractions." In *Tourism, Religion, and Spiritual Journeys,* edited by Dallen J. Timothy and Daniel H. Olsen, 104–118. New York: Routledge.

Olsen, Daniel, H., and Dallen J. Timothy. 2006. "Tourism and Religious Journeys." In *Tourism, Religion, and Spiritual Journeys,* edited by Dallen J. Timothy and Daniel H. Olsen, 1–21. New York: Routledge.

Sanook.com. 2016. "Big Drama: Foreign Woman Wears Very Thin See-through Outfit in a Famous Phukhet Temple" [Drāmā Sanan Farang Sāw Sai Chut Sī Thrū Bāng Chīab Wai Phra Wat Dang Phukhet]. Accessed January 9, 2017. http://news.sanook.com/2046794/.

Schedneck, Brooke. 2018. "Religious Others, Tourism, and Missionization: Buddhist 'Monks Chats' in Northern Thailand." *Modern Asian Studies* 52 (6): 1888–1916.

———. 2015. *Thailand's International Meditation Centers: Tourism and the Global Commodification of Religious Practices.* New York: Routledge.

UNESCO. 2015. "Monuments, Sites, and Cultural Landscapes of Chiang Mai, Capital of Lanna." Accessed January 31, 2017. http://whc.unesco.org/en/tentativelists/6003/.

UNESCO Bangkok. 2011. "Chiang Mai Being Developed as a Creative City." Accessed January 31, 2017. http://www.unescobkk.org/news/article/chiang-mai-being-developed-as-a-creative-city/.

Van Esterik, Penny. 2000. *Materializing Thailand.* New York: Berg.

4

Marketing Maitreya

Two Peaks, Three Forms of Capital, and the Quest to Establish a Fifth Buddhist Mountain

Justin R. Ritzinger

SACRED MOUNTAINS HAVE A LONG HISTORY IN China. Since antiquity, various peaks have been seen as thick with numinous power. In Chinese Buddhism, mountains became sacred as the sites of divine manifestations, "sanctuaries" (*daochang*) at which great bodhisattvas were believed to appear. Over time, a standard list of "four great famous mountains" (*si da mingshan*) emerged. Mount Wutai in the northern province of Shanxi became the home of Mañjuśrī; Mount Putuo, an island off the coast of Zhejiang, became home to Guanyin (Skt. Avalokiteśvara); Mount Jiuhua, not far away in Anhui, became home to Dizang (Skt. Kṣitigarbha); and Mount Emei in the western province of Sichuan became home to Samantabhadra. These mountains' reputations spread through legends of wondrous events. Some of these were codified by the elite in the histories and hagiographies of the Buddhist canon and in mountain gazetteers. The imperial state confirmed and magnified these sites' reputations with patronage and recognition recorded in stone stele for all to see.

The situation in the contemporary People's Republic is rather different. Whereas the late imperial state was a religiously constituted entity, concerned to marshal the numinous powers within its borders for the good of the empire, the Chinese Communist Party (CCP) is atheistic. Yet today it too strives to harness the power of mountains and other sacred sites, only now for their wondrous power to draw tourists. As China seeks to rebalance its economy toward domestic consumption and reduce the disparities between regions and localities, developing tourism has emerged as an important task of state and quasi-state agencies at many levels. They see tourism as a particularly useful form of consumption, for its economic effect spreads broadly. The contribution of tourism, the great majority of it domestic, to GDP grew tenfold in twenty years, reaching 139.4 billion USD in 2010. In the same period, employment in tourism nearly doubled to twenty-two million (Chiang 2012). The sacred sites of Buddhism and Daoism are especially attractive because they are often located in precisely the peripheral, mountainous areas that have been left behind by economic development (Ji Zhe 2011, 40–42). They also serve an ideological agenda. These historic sites speak to the glory of the Chinese past at a time when the Party's legitimacy derives in part from its claim to oversee a great "rejuvenation" (*fuxing*) of Chinese civilization. This "traditional culture" is also seen as a way to connect the Chinese people to their roots in an age of dislocation and impart values in a time of cutthroat competition.

In this context, Maitreya represents an attractive cultural property. The future Buddha is an important figure, ubiquitous in Buddhist scriptures and iconography as well beyond Buddhism in the pantheon of popular Chinese religion. Yet unlike other great bodhisattvas he never became firmly associated with a mountain home. Such a site, if established, would have a claim to be a fifth great Chinese Buddhist mountain. Since even the least popular of the already established four drew three million visitors in 2012 (Wang 2014, 193), the creation of a fifth would be an economic boon to the surrounding area. It is therefore not surprising that cases are now being made for two different mountains as residences of Maitreya. The first, Mount Xuedou, is located in the prosperous eastern province of Zhejiang. The second, Mount Fanjing, stands in the interior province of Guizhou. Chinese Buddhism has no Vatican, however, with the power to officially canonize a mountain. The only way to establish a fifth great mountain is to convince the people of its greatness. No court has greater authority than that of public opinion.

Interested parties at both mountains are therefore busily developing their respective sites and staking claims for their status as Maitreya's premier sanctuary. These place-making endeavors draw upon each of the three forms of capital identified by Bourdieu—economic, social, and cultural—in order to pursue strategies shaped by the dynamics of contemporary China. While the strategies pursued are thus convergent, Bourdieu reminds us that our social games are always shaped by the accumulations of the past (1986). As such, Xuedou, located on the economically developed coast and in the traditional Buddhist heartland of Jiangnan, is much better endowed in every respect, whereas Fanjing, lagging in economic, cultural, and perhaps most fatally social capital, is sharply disadvantaged.

A Tale of Two Peaks

Let us begin by considering each of the mountains and their development individually.

Mount Xuedou

Mount Xuedou is a picturesque mountain rising up above the historic town of Xikou. Its tree-covered topography ranges between two hundred and nine hundred meters above sea level and forms part of the Siming range that also includes the famous Mount Tiantai. It is located within the jurisdiction of the county-level city of Fenghua, which is in turn within administrative territory of the municipal-level city of Ningbo, a major port with a population of three and a half million. Though Xuedou and Xikou lie at the periphery of that urban center and have not been developed to the same degree, they are nevertheless easily accessible, just twenty-two kilometers from the city center (Xuedou si zhi bianzuan weiyuanhui [hereafter Xuedou si zhi] 2011, 1).

Midway up the mountain lies Xuedou Monastery, or Zisheng Monastery as it is formally known. Established in the Jin dynasty (265–420), it played an important role in the history of the Chan school. Its real claim to fame, however, is its connection to the eccentric monk Budai (d. 917), who came to be seen as a manifestation of Maitreya. Renowned for his cheery smile and rotund physique, he lived and died in the vicinity of Fenghua, spending time at several local monasteries including Xuedou. When the mysterious monk was at the end of his life, he is said to have recited the following verse:

> Maitreya, the true Maitreya,
> with manifold manifestations
> appears to the people of the time
> yet they never recognize him

Based on this, Budai came to be seen as an emanation of the bodhisattva (CBETA, T51, 2076, 434, a19–b28; see also: CBETA, T50, 2061, 848, b23–c8; Chapin 1933). Over the centuries, he grew in popularity, becoming the primary iconographic form in which the bodhisattva is depicted. Indeed, it is so popular that it has completely eclipsed his original princely form. He has also entered the popular pantheon as a god of wealth.

Given Maitreya's importance and connection to Xuedou it may come as a surprise that Xuedou did not become a destination of pilgrimage in imperial times, though the perceived connection with rebellious movements was certainly a factor. It was not until the 1930s that we find someone first making a case that Mount Xuedou should be seen as a sanctuary of Maitreya and a fifth great mountain alongside the established four. This argument was advanced by the monk Changxing (1896–1939), an associate of the reformer Taixu (1890–1947). Taixu had been a leading advocate of the cult of Maitreya for over a decade and had recently been installed as abbot of Xuedou by Chiang Kai-shek.[1] In Changxing's 1933 preface to the latter's commentary on the Sutra of Maitreya's Ascent, he proposed recognizing Xuedou as a fifth great mountain, holy to Maitreya (Changxing 2006), but the proposal seems to have initially made limited headway.

It was research into the reinvention of the cult of Maitreya that first took me to Mount Xuedou in the spring of 2008. At that time, the monastery was in the midst of a major expansion. The main body of the monastery was well appointed, laid out in the fashion typical of the region with a series of halls and courtyards with dark tile roofs and bright mustard walls. The substantial and prosperous appearance I found in 2008 stemmed from a significant renovation undertaken from 1998 to 2000 by Yizang, the current abbot. This was immediately followed by the construction of the Taixu Reliquary Cloister (Taixu ta yuan)[2] and the Maitreya Seminary (Mile foxueyuan), completed in 2005 (Xuedou si zhi 2011, 26–27, 94–95).

The construction project under way that spring, however, would drastically change the monastery's profile. On the hillside behind the monastery and to the right, a three-story concrete structure was taking shape. Atop it could be seen a nine-meter-high bronze lotus pedestal, where soon a monumental image of Maitreya as Budai would sit. The plan had been hatched in 1999, when the erection of the thirty-three-meter image of South Seas Guanyin was completed on Mount Putuo, becoming the visual symbol of the sacred mountain. Aspiring to likewise instantiate Xuedou's claims in bronze, Yizang partnered with the Fenghua government, which hoped to reap the economic benefits a fifth great mountain would bring, to seek approval for construction. Such an image, however, requires inspections and approvals from municipal, provincial, and national agencies. After some setbacks, the proposal was eventually greenlighted in 2005. Adopting the principle of "the monastery is the agent, the government coordinates, society participates, and Buddhist circles administer" (*siyuan wei zhuti, zhengfu xietiao, shehui canyu, fojiaojie guanli*),[3] a coordinating task force was formed under the leadership of Fenghua city's vice-mayor and Yizang. Designs were solicited and selected, and construction firms were hired. Work commenced in late December 2007 with a foundation laying ceremony attended by a representative of the national Religious Affairs Bureau and a host of provincial officials as well as two famous Olympic athletes, Li Ning and Li Xiaoshuang. Xi Jinping, then provincial secretary now general secretary of the CCP, sent a letter of congratulations (Xuedou si zhi 2011, 36–41).

On that first visit the monastery grounds included several billboards and posters featuring artist renderings of the planned image and the associated complex that was to be built, alongside the original monastery. These and other notices exhorted visitors to make a donation. "Offering a single spade of earth to the Buddha," declared one, "accumulates ten thousand blessings for your descendants." Another offered donors the opportunity to sponsor components of the statue with donations ranging from one hundred to four million RMB (14 to 576,000 USD) and receive their names engraved in stone or brass and, for the generous, invitations to the consecration. Yizang and a delegation also raised funds in Hong Kong where they spoke with the leader of the Buddhist Federation there as well as the Ningbo–Hong Kong Fellowship and the Ningbo Native Place Association, and held an exposition at the Convention and Exhibition Center. By the time the image was complete in 2008, the monastery had raised 120 million RMB (17.5 million USD) from 30,000 donors (Xuedou si zhi 2011, 42). Despite the impressive sum, much of the construction was funded through loans arranged by the government, which the monastery continues to pay off.

The image was completed in October 2008. Dubbed "Human Realm Maitreya" (Renjian mile) it stands 33 meters tall, 56.74 meters including its 9-meter-tall lotus pedestal and three-story supporting structure. Its name refers to the signature idea of the Taixu's movement, Human Realm Buddhism, and is inscribed in the hand of one of his most famous contemporary followers, Master Xingyun of Taiwan's Foguangshan (Xuedou si zhi 2011, 45). The image stands at the apex of the "Buddhaland of Great Kindness" (Daci foguo). This complex runs parallel to the original monastery, forming a new secularized tourist axis running from the entrance, through a large courtyard centered on the Hall of Great Kindness (Daci baodian), a large, tastefully opulent hall in predominantly Song dynasty style enshrining an image of Maitreya, to a broad plaza at the foot of the hillside leading up to the grand Buddha. Viewed from the image's observation deck, the expansive Buddhaland is clearly distinct from the more tightly packed structures of the monastic axis. The effect is one of segregation. While the boundary is permeable—tourists visit the monastery and monks live and work in the Buddhaland—the original monastery continues to look and feel like a monastery rather than a tourist product.[4]

The Buddha and its Buddhaland were inaugurated in grand style in November of 2008 as part of the first annual Maitreya Culture Festival. Although held primarily at Xuedou, it is organized by the Fenghua government and is not open to the public. Five thousand people attend, mostly government officials and business leaders. Opening ceremonies are held in the plaza in front of the Grand Buddha. These include song and dance performances set against computer-animated backdrops shown on billboard-sized LED screens that, if not for their focus on Budai and Buddhist themes, would not be out of place on CCTV's annual New Year's extravaganza (He and Shi 2014). In 2014, other activities included a prayer assembly and vegetarian feast, an academic conference on Taixu's thought, and tour sites related to the life of Budai, but also a session entitled "Forming affinities with Maitreya, following dreams to Fenghua," whose purpose was to gather prominent entrepreneurs and encourage them to invest in Fenghua. This is consonant with the stated goals of the event: to make Fenghua a center of pilgrimage, academic exchange, and cultural tourism, by establishing Xuedou as the fifth great mountain ("Ci yuan sheng guang" 2014).

When I made my second visit to Xuedou in the summer of 2015, it was clear that the Grand Buddha had been a boon to tourism. Even midweek with rather overcast weather, I observed a steady stream of visitors. Although official figures are not available, the vice-proctor at Xuedou estimated that the monastery received six hundred thousand visitors per year, up significantly from years past. This was corroborated by the manager at the Xikou tourism office who told me that the Buddha was a major draw for the area, although it was impossible to measure its contribution, as other areas, such as the Xikou historic district, were also being developed and tourism was growing nationwide.

The authorities are clearly convinced that the construction of the Grand Buddha has had a positive effect on the economy and prestige of Fenghua. When I first visited, Yizang's goal for construction was "one Buddha, three monasteries, and six cloisters," a task already more than half complete. These plans were superseded. In 2013, the Ningbo government approached the monastery to launch an initiative that will vastly increase the Buddhist footprint on the mountain. According to this new plan, there will be three main centers on the mountain: one at the foot, one midway up the mountain, and one at the top. Xuedou Monastery and the Grand Buddha will constitute the midpoint center. At the base will be constructed a vast glass dome topped with a golden hall representing Maitreya's Tusita palace. The enclosed area will accommodate up to five thousand people, allowing it to serve as the site for future Maitreya Culture Festivals. Near the summit will be constructed another large monastery to be dedicated primarily to cultivation. Around these three centers are to be arrayed not the six cloisters originally envisioned, but thirty-three temples. The government is arranging the funding, but once again will allow the Buddhist establishment to administer the completed project without revenue sharing. Clearly it sees much potential in Mount Xuedou as a fifth great Buddhist mountain and is purposefully attempting to foster tourist networks in the hopes of reaping the benefits such a mountain would draw (Xuedou shan fojiao mingshan jianshe gongzuo huibao 2015).

Mount Fanjing

Mount Fanjing is located roughly 750 miles into the interior from Xuedou. It stands primarily in Tongren County, Guizhou, in a mountainous region inhabited largely by ethnic minorities such as the Tujia and the Miao. Where Xuedou is charming, Fanjing is striking. The lush topography surges up dramatically and falls away again into gorges as deep as 1000 meters. Part of the Wuling range, it is composed of two main peaks. One, Fenghuangshan, rises to 2,493 meters above sea level and roughly 2,000 meters from its base. The other, Golden Peak (Jinding), is actually a tower of stone that juts up several hundred meters into the air just short of the summit of Fenghuang and is cleft in two midway up by a crevasse. The mountain and its surroundings are designated as a national nature preserve and a member of the UN "Man and Biosphere" Network, as well as a scenic site (Wang 2014, 7–8, 11, 21). Today, ecotourism is its primary attraction.

Traditionally there were several approaches to the summit. The western route, guarded by Huguo Monastery, was the first to be restored in the 1990s (Zhang 2005, 292). But the construction in 2009 of a cable car, the second longest in China, has led the southern route to eclipse the western, becoming the main focus of tourism. At the base of the mountain on the southern side is a village full of new buildings constructed in hopes of cashing in on tourism. When I visited in 2015, it was at a rudimentary stage of development, filled with indistinguishable guesthouses with restaurants on the first floor and lodging above, and shops selling generic trinkets. From the village it is a forty-minute bus ride to the county seat, Jiangkou. The nearest city with an airport is Tongren, a roughly five-hour bus ride away.

Mount Fanjing's claim to be a sanctuary of Maitreya and the fifth great Buddhist mountain derives primarily from local legends, the mountain's distinctive topography, and a rather tendentious reading of the mountain's history. Legend tells that Śākyamuni and Maitreya cultivated the causes of their Buddhahood here. According to one tale, these "ancient Buddhas" split the care of the world between them, marking the dividing line by slicing the Golden Peak in two with a golden knife. This is the reason that the Śākyamuni Hall and Maitreya Hall face each other across the crevasse. Moreover, viewed from the correct locations the peaks are said to resemble the bodhisattva in various postures. Legend also claims a connection to Maitreya's famous devotee Xuanzang's journey to the West. In this account, the monk returned to China by way of Guizhou. Upon reaching Mount Fanjing, ten thousand rolls of scripture fell from his white horse, emitted a white light, and were transformed into stone by the Tathagatha (Wang 2014, 10–11). On this basis, Zhang Ming has claimed that the mountain was seen to be a sanctuary of Maitreya by the Qing, though it was also said to be the sanctuary of a pratyekabuddha (Zhang 2005, 286), suggesting a multivocal site that was not exclusively identified with Maitreya.[5]

At its eighteenth-century peak, Fanjing was in fact an important regional Buddhist center that boasted five great imperial cloisters on the mountain itself and forty-eight lesser cloisters (Wang 2014, 9–11). Yet the mountain's partisans make the stronger claim that Fanjing was already seen as the fifth great Buddhist mountain in the Ming dynasty. This view is promoted by a cottage industry of scholarship devoted to developing tourism. The central piece of evidence adduced is a Ming stele erected after an imperially sponsored reconstruction of the mountain's monasteries. The key passage proclaims: "Among the enduring things that Heaven has established, among the very lofty things that have stood out from antiquity to today, none match the four great famous mountains. Yet people do not know that here in Qian [present-day Guizhou], there is an ancient Buddhist sanctuary called Mount Fanjing that is first among the famous marchmounts under heaven" (Wang 2012, 259). As evidence that Fanjing was accepted as a fifth great Buddhist mountain, this is problematic,[6] but this is the official line found in contemporary literature about the mountain and duly recited by tour guides whose itinerary includes the stele as a mandatory stop.

The claim that Fanjing was and is the fifth great mountain appears to originate in the campaign to redevelop Mount Fanjing for tourism. The modern era had not been kind to Buddhism there. Most monasteries were destroyed or abandoned in the warfare and disruptions that marked the end of the Qing dynasty (1644–1912). Those that remained were lost to the Cultural Revolution (1966–1976). Limited restoration work was undertaken in the 1980s and 1990s. Only in the mid-2000s did development take off in conjunction with the central government's "Open Up the West" program that sought to bring the benefits of China's economic boom to poor interior provinces (Zhang 2012, 309). This program is likely why the vice-chair of the Religious Affairs Bureau and the secretary of the Chinese Buddhist Association (CBA) gave speeches at a ceremony marking the restoration of Huguo Monastery in 2004 in which they proclaimed, as far as I can tell for the first time, that Fanjing was the fifth great Buddhist mountain. That same year, Tongren designated tourist development as a top priority and initiated work on the cable car that would transform the mountain (Wang 2012, 73–75).

As the cable car was constructed, a handful of Buddhist institutions were built or rebuilt along the southern route defined by the cable car. These include: Cheng'en Monastery at the peak, Longquan Monastery at the base, and the Mount Fanjing Buddhist Culture Park (Fanjing shan fojiao wenhua yuan) a few kilometers outside the nature preserve. The process of development here has taken a very different form than on Mount Xuedou. Whereas at Xuedou the motto was "the monastery is the agent, the government coordinated, society participates, and Buddhist circles administer," the guiding principle adopted at Fanjing was "the government guides, the agencies coordinate, the market operates, and society participates" (*zhengfu zhudao, bumen liandong, shichang yunzuo, shehui canyu*) (Wang 2012, 74). Information about Fanjing is more fragmentary due to the absence of a single authority and more difficult fieldwork environment, but it is clear that in practice this meant that each of the three institutions was (re)built with tourism in mind by different private investors with government involvement.

Let us begin at the summit. Cheng'en Monastery was originally constructed in 1599 and includes several structures. Atop the Golden Peak stand the two halls consecrated to Śākyamuni and Maitreya. Below stands the main body of the monastery, which was restored only in 2009. The initiative for this appears to have come from the provincial government, but the money was put up by the cable car company. According to a volunteer at the temple with whom I spoke, the company agreed to front the money for the restoration on the condition that the government would pay it back at which time ownership would be turned over to the government. It seems likely their motive was to create another anchor attraction beyond the flora and fauna and to meet tourist expectations formed by the aesthetics of traditional landscape art (Li and Sofield 2009, 162). In the end, however, the government reneged on the deal. As a result, only the lower, front portion of the monastery is open to visitors. Should someone wish to go to the upper section of the monastery, they are told that work on that section is not yet complete.[7] In fact, the cable car company is refusing to release that section until the government pays what it owes.

Despite this unusual state of affairs, Cheng'en is an active monastery with a small coterie of resident monks. Yet they do not include the abbot Lingpu, who resides at Guangji Monastery in Beijing, visiting only a few times a year. This contrasts with the constant stream of lay volunteers residing on the mountain. At any given time, the monastery is reported to have half a dozen laypeople staying in the monastery, participating in religious life, and helping out with its day-to-day operation, while basking in the peak's quiet atmosphere and preternatural beauty.

Standing at the foot of the mountain in a narrow river valley, Longquan Monastery is a very different institution. The date of its initial construction is unclear, but it was rebuilt as Guanyin Hall (Guanyin ge) in 1991, and restored again in 2001 at which time it was renamed Longquan Monastery. In that restoration a 28-meter-tall image of Budai was constructed atop a Maitreya Hall. Its consecration was attended by the vice-chair of the CBA as well as the abbot of Shaolin Temple (Zhengxie tongren diqu gongzuo weiyuanhui 2011, 36). After being damaged in a landslide in 2009, the monastery was again restored, this time by a Chinese businessman living in Australia who built a hotel on the land immediately adjacent to the temple. Given the hotel's name, the Longquan Holy Vista Garden of Contented Minds (Longquan shengjing yixin yuan), it seems likely that the temple was an important part of the business plan.

In its current iteration, the monastery is a stop on the tourist route up the mountain. Midway through the bone-jarring ride from the gate to the cable car, the bus stops at Longquan and the passengers are told to disembark for a tour that is "included in the ticket price." What follows can best be termed extractive. The group of tourists is taken in hand by a tour guide employed by Longquan who gives a rapid introduction to the monastery and mountain, using the image of Maitreya as a focal point to discuss Mount Fanjing's status as a Maitreyan sanctuary and the fifth great mountain. Thereafter, the group is taken into a hall to worship the Buddha. No need to believe, the guide assures the group, it is just for good fortune. Tourists are brought before an image and one of the eight resident monks walks them through a simple devotion and instructs them to make three wishes. Foot thus placed in the door, the monk hustles them around the back to a screened-off area where four more monks sit at tables and take donations. Based on my experience, it appears that individuals may be directed to particular tables based on perceived wealth. Every line in the merit book I was invited to sign included donations of 1,200 RMB (180 USD). When I offered a paltry one hundred, I was invited to add another hundred in a second column. Deviation from this program is not welcome. When one group of retirees refused to play along with the devotional exercise they were ejected. After observing this exchange, I too was summarily wished "safe travels" and gestured to the door. I was subsequently told by the manager of the Culture Park that Longquan has a number of complaints lodged to the tourism bureau each year.

The Mount Fanjing Buddhist Culture Park represents yet another model of interaction between state and private interests in the service of religious tourism. Unlike Cheng'en or Longquan, this is a new institution. The initiative came from the provincial government. In the mid-2000s, it invited the layman Zeng Yibin to Fanjing. Zeng comes from a long line of artisans and had made a name for himself and his company by producing fine gold statues of Buddhist figures. To enshrine one such image of Guanyin, he built a Buddhist Culture Park on Hainan Island. This was apparently a successful venture that provincial officials hoped could be replicated at Mount Fanjing. Work began in 2007 and the first phase of construction was completed in 2010. This includes Great Golden Buddha Monastery (Da jin fo si), which consists of a single courtyard centered on a main hall. Although only five years old when I visited, the monastery was already showing wear. Signage was faded and the veneer meant to disguise the poured concrete foundation as brick was peeling. In better repair was the Golden Hall (Jin dian), which stands behind the monastery wall atop a four-story concrete building. Inside stands the Bejeweled Maitreya (Jinyu Mile). The five-meter-tall seated image depicts Maitreya in his princely "true form" (*zhenshen*) rather than as Budai, his more familial manifestation. Composed of two hundred and fifty kilograms of gold as well as precious stones, it is certified by Guinness as the largest such image in the world, as one is reminded by signage and literature as well as a framed certificate placed before the image itself. The image was consecrated in August of 2008 by a group of eighteen prominent monks, representing the CBA and each of the four great mountains, which is touted as confirmation of Fanjing's status as the fifth (Guizhou fanjing shan fojiao wenhua yuan jianjie 2014).

After construction was complete, the monastery was signed over to the Buddhist Association, while the Golden Hall remained the property of the Culture Park. In the second phase of construction, hotels, vacation villas, restaurants, and shops are to be added. It is a profit-making venture that is deeply capitalist while at the same time apparently sincerely Buddhist. According to the manager, eventually they hope that the park will become a place where urban laity can escape their busy lives and enjoy a religious retreat, participating in self-cultivation and Dharma assemblies. This second phase will require an additional three hundred million RMB of investment (46 million USD) on top of the three hundred million spent on phase one. The process has stalled, however, due to permits being refused on environmental grounds.

The park is revising its plans and preparing a new application, but in the meantime, even its manager admitted that the place is a bit "desolate." The monastery has just three affiliated monks and the park receives only seventy to eighty thousand visitors a year. Most visitors, he said, came to Fanjing for the rock formations, not for Buddhism. This was corroborated by a silent survey I performed outside Cheng'en Monastery in which I counted how many visitors wore Buddhist rosaries on their wrists as a loose proxy for devotion. In a half an hour only five of one hundred wore the beads. When the Culture Park originally opened, it had included a vegetarian restaurant and a teahouse, but both of these ventures failed, because a restaurant that followed the Buddhist prohibition on hot peppers held no appeal for the spice-loving locals and tea tasting is a pastime of an upper class that rarely visited. Moreover, most residents of the surrounding villages are members of ethnic minorities who had little traditional interest in Buddhist deities. Those who do are devoted not to Maitreya but to "Mother Guanyin." For now, the park's income derives from the sale of tickets and small replicas of the Bejeweled Maitreya, supplemented by a subsidy from the Culture Park in Hainan.

Three Forms of Capital, Their Tactics, and Transformations

The contrast between the state of development on the two mountains is apparent. To a point, the reason is also clear: money. Zhejiang, and even Fenghua specifically, are simply far more wealthy than Guizhou and Tongren. Zhejiang's provincial GDP stood at four trillion RMB (650 billion USD) in 2014, more than four times Guizhou's 900 billion (147 billion USD) (All China Data Center 2016). This disparity is reflected in the supporting infrastructure for tourism and the resultant mobilities at each site. Due to its proximity to the major city of Ningbo, Xuedou enjoys access to several major freeways, rail and high-speed rail stations, and an international airport. Fanjing, on the other hand, is a five-hour bus ride from Tongren, the nearest city with a train station or an airport. Tongren's airport, moreover, is little more than an airstrip, offering only weekly service to a handful of Chinese cities. In the end, however, airlinks are somewhat beside the point. Urbanites accounted for 75 percent of tourism revenue in 2010 (Chiang 2012, 214) and 80 percent of their tourism activities take place with a 500-km journey from their home city. Within half that distance, Xuedou has some of the wealthiest urban centers in China: not only Ningbo (50 km), but Hangzhou (180 km), and Shanghai (250 km). The nearest comparable urban center to Fanjing is Chongqing, 480 km away. Its immediate vicinity is one of the poorest areas of China. Small wonder Fanjing is less developed.

Yet it would oversimplify the issue, and understate Mount Xuedou's advantage, to view the contrast in terms of economic capital alone. As Bourdieu (1986) has shown, to fully understand the inequalities baked into the social game, cultural and social capital must also be taken into account. Here I use cultural capital to refer to the accumulated prestige and currency of each mountain's associated cultural products. These cultural products are endowed with social value by the Chinese imaginary, which for present purposes we may conceptualize as an economy of symbols in which such goods circulate and are consumed.[8] Social capital refers to the power of the network of agents involved in the promotion of each mountain. It is a function not only of the economic and cultural capital of those agents, but also the strength of their commitment and of the network itself. The role of cultural capital is perhaps especially salient since the parties involved are relatively self-consciously and transparently attempting to turn cultural capital into economic capital. The role of social capital is less direct, but, as Bourdieu observed, it serves as a multiplier, compounding the effects of economic and cultural capital.

If capital is to be seen as a matter of accumulation, it is no surprise that Xuedou is a place more richly endowed in cultural capital. It lies in the Jiangnan region, which has been the heartland of Chinese Buddhism for centuries. Guizhou, on the other hand, was a Buddhist hinterland. As a result, Budai, a figure originally of local importance in Fenghua, has been enshrined in canonical hagiographies. He is iconic, his smiling visage instantly recognizable, and his place in the imaginary well established. In contrast, the legends associated with Maitreya on Mount Fanjing are purely local. Few outside of that region will have heard that once upon a time Maitreya and Śākyamuni divided the world between them there. This is a significant hindrance for place-making endeavors and the development of Buddhist tourism there, for as Salazar (2011) has observed people generally travel to places already known to the imaginary (577).

The process of developing these sites as tourist places, and these symbols as tourist products, necessarily entails commodification. This drives the production of images at both sites. Images serve as attractions, as spectacles to go to see and admire, and also as emissaries of the site that can circulate beyond it in advertisements and as souvenirs. The grand Buddha at Mount Xuedou not only stakes its claim to be a sanctuary of Maitreya but also represents the mountain in brochures. For tourists, it is a superlative spectacle to take in and photograph. On the observation deck, visitors are allowed to get up close to the image: to viscerally feel themselves dwarfed by its size, to hug its massive feet, and photograph themselves doing so. In the supporting structure below there is a small, unobtrusive gift shop where they can commemorate the experience by purchasing expensive images of Budai or inexpensive yellow plush feet, adorned with a smiling face, they can continue to hug at home.

Images are also important at Mount Fanjing. The Bejeweled Maitreya serves a similar function on billboards and in brochures as the visual symbol of the mountain, or at least Buddhism on the mountain. Geological formation such as the Golden Peak also serve this function for the mountain as a whole. Visitors can marvel at the gold and jewels as well as the craftsmanship and even purchase scale models to bring home with them. Longquan Monastery touts its monumental image of Maitreya as a symbol of Fanjing's status, though it does not attempt to capitalize on this image currently. Cheng'en has no signature image, but hardly needs one given its position vis-à-vis the Golden Peak, a more striking visual than any statue. These images serve as symbols of their sites and tokens, which can circulate beyond them, seeding the imaginary. As an attraction, Xuedou's grand Buddha likely holds an advantage for its spectacle and interactivity. As a symbol it represents Maitreya in his immediately recognizable form, whereas the Bejeweled Maitreya portrays the almost unrecognizable Dharma prince.

The process of commodification, however, requires not simply the creation of images but also their marketing. Discourse—be it exegesis, tour guide scripts, or ad copy—frames the images, contextualizing them within the larger site and locating them within broader imaginaries. This too is an important part of constructing the sites as tourist destinations and great mountains, and centering tourist activities there in order to confirm their identity as places worthy of visiting. In this, Xuedou has advantages deriving again from history but also from the skill with which it has been woven into the site and the currents of contemporary Chinese culture. Maitreya is a symbol that resonates with the optimism of twenty-first-century China. Maitreya has long been associated with utopianism in China, and Taixu's version of Maitreyanism gave it a modernist tilt shorn of its rebellious connotations (Ritzinger 2017). As a Chinese manifestation of the bodhisattva, Budai also speaks to growing national pride. It is no accident that the grand Buddha was completed in the year of the Beijing Olympics, when China "came out" as a renewed power. The Olympics have long been an important arena for proving Chinese greatness (Wang 2012, 146–154), and Olympic glory was invoked subtly and overtly in the creation of the image. Former medalists were involved in the inaugural ceremonies and Yizang himself served as a torchbearer. The connection was made explicit when the head of the Religious Affairs Bureau, invoked at the consecration of the image, Maitreya's optimistic spirit and Sinified character (Xuedou si zhi 2011, 56–57). This connection to a bright future is also alluded to in pamphlets for Xikou that organize the local attractions according to a temporal schema in which sites associated with Chiang Kai-shek represent the past; the mountain's natural beauty, the present; and the grand Buddha, the hope for the future (Ningbo xikou lüyou jituan 2015a, 2015b).

Maitreya-as-Budai's associations with more immediate prosperity as a popular god of wealth also have important resonance. These are not directly invoked but the massive bronze image itself naturally evokes wealth and the entire Buddhaland of Great Kindness displays a refined opulence. Appropriately enough, the god of wealth is most directly alluded to in the gift shop, where high-end wooden images of Maitreya, roughly a foot tall, can be purchased for prices such as 188,888 RMB (30,340 USD). "Eight" (*ba*) is considered a lucky number because it rhymes with *fa* as in *facai,* "to get rich." Customers are thus invited to make the association with Maitreya as god of wealth and to presume a special efficacy to an image purchased at his sanctuary.

At Mount Fanjing, several discourses are employed. The official claim is that the mountain is the sanctuary of Maitreya's "true form." Thus, its signature image, the bejeweled Maitreya portrays his princely "Dharma body." A tour guide from the cable car company and the manager of the Culture Park both used this to argue Fanjing's case over that of Xuedou, which was the site of a mere manifestation. They also pointed out that in Indian Buddhism it is the princely form that is worshipped, implying superior authenticity. But Fanjing's iconography is not so unified. There are actually three different images of Maitreya: as Dharma prince (the Culture Park), as Budai (Longquan), and as future Buddha (Cheng'en). This muddies the waters, but one academic advocate claims that this represents the inclusion of all of Maitreya's pure lands (Wang 2014, 196) and the mountain's history as a center of 'Maitreya Pure Land culture.' This idea lacks evidence, however. Worse still it lacks currency. Maitreya Pure Land is a minority position most closely associated in the modern period with Taixu, the former abbot of Xuedou. Although the idea of Pure Land culture has promising resonance with eco-tourism, on the whole Mount Fanjing's cultural products are less effectively marketed.

The disparity in cultural and economic capital is compounded by an even more striking difference in social capital. Social capital is the product of the resources commanded by members of a social network, the strength of that network and of the commitments to that network and its aims. We see again here, as we have throughout the volume, the critical importance of networks to Buddhist tourism. In each respect, Xuedou is the stronger party. Xuedou enjoys a unified leadership that is deeply committed to the advancement of the mountain and quite adept at coordinating with relevant state agencies. Yizang has been abbot of Xuedou Monastery for twenty years. He is the ultimate religious authority on the mountain and he has devoted his career to it. Although like many Chinese leaders, Yizang has a number of bureaucratic positions, Xuedou is his home and his primary post. According to one of the vice-proctors, it is "his life's work." Yizang brought to this work the advantages of an elite seminary education in which he was able to study 'temple management' as well as the intricacies of Buddhist doctrine. This was no doubt an asset in dealing with the authorities. On my visit in 2015, I spoke to a semi-retired man from the Religious Affairs Bureau who had served as a Party representative on the temple management committee. He expressed great appreciation for the abbot, comparing him favorably with other abbots who "do not know how to manage or how to accept management." This ability to build relationships was critical to navigating the process of building the grand Buddha.

Yizang's partners in the project of building a monumental image and establishing Xuedou as a fifth great mountain brought considerable commitment and resources to the project. The Fenghua government brought to bear the resources of one of China's most developed provinces, procuring funding and coordinating logistics. Yizang was also able to draw on nonstate networks tied to the monastery and the locality. Funds were raised from the Ningbo diaspora in Hong Kong, while calligraphic endorsement was secured from Taixu's famous follower Xingyun. Finally, Jiangnan region is the heart of the contemporary Buddhist revival as well as the country's economic boom, allowing Xuedou to readily cultivate support among a pool of devout and wealthy lay people.

Fanjing has far weaker social capital. The agents involved in the promotion of the mountain as a Buddhist center possess fewer resources, weaker commitment, and little or no inclination to coordinate their efforts. Whereas at Mount Xuedou the initiative to construct the grand Buddha and establish a fifth great mountain originated with a monastery, at Mount Fanjing the state played the leading role in conjunction with private business interests while Buddhist leadership was absent. It was the provincial and Tongren governments that first began the process of developing the southern route. Tongren initiated the cable car. The provincial government restored Cheng'en Monastery with funds from the cable car company, courted Zeng Yibin to build the Culture Park, and at minimum approved the construction of the Garden of Contented Minds, which occasioned the rebuilding of Longquan Monastery. Government support appears to be inconsistent, however. Whether this is due to lack of funds, shifts in personnel, or something else is unclear. The cable car company has not been reimbursed for the restoration of Cheng'en and phase two of the Culture Park has been stymied by environmental restrictions, not typically a major hurdle in China. Moreover, it should be noted that jurisdiction over Fanjing is not Tongren's alone. It is actually split amongst three counties. There has been little cooperation in developing the mountain, however (Zhang 2012, 310–311).

As a result, although there are three routes to the peak, one can easily visit the southern approach and never discover the other two. They are not shown on maps found there and no signage at the peak would help the visitor locate them.

The Buddhist network focused on Mount Fanjing has been similarly fractured and weak. Buddhist leadership has been remarkably absent. Huguo Monastery played a role in the early phases of development, but the decision to build the cable car on the southern route effectively sidelined it. The three institutions on the southern route all operate independently with little interaction or even communication and each has weak or absentee leadership. Support among the local populace is rather weak as well. Locals gather at Longquan for the festival of Guanyin's birth, but few are regular temple goers and even if they were, they are of modest means.

Connections between Fanjing and the wider world of Chinese Buddhism appear to be rather uneven. Whereas I was easily able to secure introductions at Xuedou from colleagues in the PRC, I was unable to make any such connections at Fanjing. When one colleague reached out to a friend at the Guizhou Buddhist Association, his friend replied that he had no contact with Buddhist institutions on the mountain and expressed reservations about their "commercial character." In an interesting contrast, the national Chinese Buddhist Association appears to be an important backer of Fanjing and its claims to be the fifth great mountain. The Association first declared for Mount Fanjing in 2004 and has regularly made similar pronouncements since. It has also likely been responsible for arranging for monks representing the four great mountains to attend various ritual events at the mountain (Kaiguang fahui xianchang 2014). Guizhou academics have also been a key source of support. Under a research project funded by the provincial government (Wang 2014, 240), conferences have been held and books produced, often explicitly devoted to developing the site and making the case for its inclusion as the fifth great mountain (Wang 2012; Wang 2014).

The differences outlined here extend beyond the capital available to agents at the two sites and the manner in which it is deployed to the profits gained and the manner in which those profits are utilized. At Xuedou, the construction of the grand Buddha has yielded profits tangible and intangible. The distinction achieved vis-à-vis other sites has helped to turn it into an increasingly important and powerful institution. Although the number of visitors has grown greatly, thus far the benefits have not primarily been economic, since the monastery continues to pay loans taken out to fund the construction. Rather, the benefits have come in the form of prestige. The image serves as a 'token,' in Bourdieu's sense, of membership in the circle of elite Buddhist institutions. It demonstrates not only the wherewithal to complete such a task, but also, given the approvals required, the support of the state at the highest levels. Moreover, the grand Buddha is an investment that keeps paying off in terms of social capital. The Cultural Festival held there each year provides an opportunity for the monastery as well as the local government to network and build relationships with influential government and political leaders. At the same time, the spatial segregation of the tourist axis from the original monastery acts as a buffer, conserving the cultural capital derived from being a 'real monastery.' Now in the second phase of construction the cultural and social capital produced are essentially being reinvested, which in turn will yield more social and cultural capital. Already it has won for Xuedou the right to host the new Zhejiang Buddhist Seminary over Tiantai shan and Qixia Monastery, historically more prestigious institutions.

At Mount Fanjing, tourism has greatly increased but the gains for Buddhist institutions and the project of establishing a fifth mountain are less pronounced. Between 2005 and 2013, visitors to the mountain grew from one hundred thousand annually to six hundred thousand (Wang 2014, 172). This was likely driven by improvements in transportation and the national push to promote eco-tourism that began in 2009 (Chiang 2012, 213) rather than Buddhism. It is unclear whether any of the three institutions on the mountain reaps any significant economic benefit. Cheng'en charges no entrance fee and it seems unlikely that much is donated by visitors. The monastery does generate significant social capital as a site for volunteering. However, the profits appear to accrue primarily to the absentee abbot rather than to the project of establishing Mount Fanjing as the fifth great Buddhist mountain and the home of Maitreya, something that no one I spoke to at Cheng'en seemed particularly interested in. Longquan does tout Fanjing's claim to be the fifth great mountain. It attempts to realize profits, however, by very directly converting cultural capital back into economic capital by extracting donations. To the extent that this becomes known, and online reviews do mention such experiences (Mafengwo 2017), cashing out in this way damages the cultural capital of the monastery and the mountain as a whole. The Culture Park is obviously invested in Fanjing's aspirations, but its state of suspended development makes it difficult to realize any profits at all. It runs at a loss economically and the sale of images and souvenirs in the Golden Hall itself undercut its cultural capital with a taint of commercialization.

In the absence of a central authority with the power to settle such matters, a fifth great Buddhist mountain can only be recognized as the first four were: through a gradually developing social consensus. In China's current age of state capitalism, restricted religion and mass tourism, the path to that consensus has changed. Rather than await a gradual accretion of testimonials to sanctity and numinous power, agents in Zhejiang and Guizhou are attempting to stake their claims through deliberate and rapid development of cultural products for the tourist market. Despite the break from the past, however, the historical accumulations Bourdieu labeled capital still exert their effects. If the disparity were merely economic, it might be more easily overcome. But Mount Xuedou enjoys a host of advantages derived from its location in China's economic center and its Buddhist heartland. Staking its claim to be the fifth great mountain on its connection to the historical monk Budai, it is able to capitalize on a cultural product universally recognized and canonically sanctioned. This symbol, moreover, embodies optimism and prosperity that resonates with the Chinese imaginary in the age of the Chinese dream. In building a monumental image to serve as the visual symbol of the status to which it aspired, the monastery benefited from unified and savvy leadership that was able to cooperate with local authorities to meet the bureaucratic, financial, and engineering challenges involved. That project is now paying dividends in increased prestige and influence, which are being reinvested in further growth and expansion.

Mount Fanjing, on the other hand, suffers from deficiencies in each of the three types of capital. Thus in comparing the case of Mount Xuedou to Mount Fanjing, it becomes clear that constructing a 'place' of Buddhist tourism is not merely reliant upon physical structures and/or landscape. Instead, other factors come into play. Mount Fanjing is located in a province that is not only one of the poorest in the country but also marginal to Chinese Buddhism. As a result, economic capital is limited, but cultural capital is as well. Its landscape may be breathtaking, but its legends are purely local, enjoying no currency beyond the region. Advocates claim it to be the sanctuary of Maitreya's princely true form and the Culture Park has produced a bejeweled Maitreya to serve as a symbol, but that form commands far less recognition than the merry monk of Fenghua. Development has taken place with little Buddhist input and without much coordination among the parties involved. Such leadership as there is on the mountain today is absentee and comparatively uninvested. Though the mountain's fame has grown and the number of visitors risen, the benefits have been limited.

Thus, although developing religious tourism is attractive because it promises to smooth economic inequalities between regions in China, examining the disparities in cultural and social capital between Mount Xuedou and Mount Fanjing in their quest to become the fifth sacred mountain suggests that in many cases inequalities may be even more entrenched than they appear, and the task of creating tourist places more complex and challenging than was hoped.

Notes

1 On the promotion of the cult of Maitreya by Taixu and members of his circle, see Ritzinger (2017).
2 Since renamed the Taixu Lecture Monastery (*jiangsi*).
3 Such sloganeering is common in China. The fact that Mount Fanjing has a similar slogan suggests that the practice is widespread.

4 This is a strategy used for Buddhist tourism in China that Nichols discusses in his chapter in this volume.
5 The legend regarding Xuanzang is also equivocal evidence at best. The Xuanzang of history had no connection to Guizhou and that of legend, no connection to Maitreya. Likely, Xuanzang represents a third tradition on the mountain rather than an example of Maitreya's.
6 First of all, it is not clear that is what the passage is saying at all. The identification of the "four great famous mountains" as those of Buddhism is natural, but somewhat cast in doubt by the fact that just previously the author lists four of the five marchmounts (*wu yue*) and the fact that he refers to Fanjing as a "marchmount," a term never applied to the Buddhist mountains to my knowledge. Even if we grant that he is referring to the Buddhist mountains, it is not clear that he means to add Fanjing to their ranks rather than simply praise it by the comparison. If we were to grant that he meant to add it as a fifth Buddhist mountain, it is still not clear that the "ancient Buddha" he refers to is Maitreya, given that it was also said to be the sanctuary of a pratyekabuddha. Finally, even if we grant that he meant to add it to the list of great Buddhist mountains as a sanctuary of Maitreya, the absence of any corroboration suggests his view was not widely shared.
7 Historically, the upper and lower sections had been two separate institutions: Cheng'en and Zhenguo Monasteries, respectively.
8 My usage of cultural capital here is a bit different than Bourdieu's but in the same spirit. Working on French intellectuals, he was interested primarily in the advantages derived through the consumption of cultural goods, while I am concerned here with the advantages derived from the production and circulation of those goods. My usage shares, however, his core insight into the importance of accumulation to social inequality. Some may wonder if the economy of symbols I refer to might be better analyzed through the lens of symbolic capital, but this form is rather different than the other three for Bourdieu. It refers to power accumulated through the masking of interested action as disinterested, for example the prestige earned by a show of ostensibly altruistic generosity (Bourdieu 1990, 112–121; Schwartz 1997, 89–92). In the case of the two mountains, there is rather little concern to mask the interested nature of their actions.

References

All China Data Center. 2016. China Data Online. Accessed December 7, 2016. http://chinadataonline.org.

Bourdieu, Pierre. 1986. "The Forms of Capital." In *Handbook of Theory and Research for the Sociology of Education,* edited by J. Richardson, 241–258. New York: Greenwood.

——. 1990. *The Logic of Practice.* Stanford: Stanford University Press.

Changxing. 2006. "Guan mile shang sheng jing jiang yao xu" [Preface to "Lecture on the essentials of the Ascent Sutra"]. In *Taixu dashi quanshu* [Collected works of Master Taixu], edited by Yinshun, vol. 30, 928–930. Included in *Yinshun fashi foxue zhuzuo ji* [Master Yinshun Corpus]. CD-ROM, version 4.0. Yinshun wenjiao jijinhui.

Chapin, Helen B. 1933. "The Ch'an Master Pu-tai." *Journal of the American Oriental Society* 53 (1): 47–52.

Chiang, Min-hua. 2012. "The Changing Role of Tourism in China's Economy." *Journal of China Tourism Research* 8:207–223.

"Ci yuan sheng guang" [Kindly springs, sagely radiance]. 2014. Fenghua: Fenghua city government [?].

Guizhou fanjing shan fojiao wenhua yuan jianjie [Introduction to Guizhou Mount Fanjing Buddhist Culture Park]. Accessed August 8, 2014. http://www.fjsfj.com/praise/scenery.

He Jianbo and Shi Yizang. 2014. Ciyuan shengguang: 2014 Zhongguo (fenghua) xuedoushan mile wenhuajie kaimu shengdian [Kindly springs, sagely radiance: Opening ceremony of the 2014 Maitreya Culture Festival of Xuedou shan (Fenghua, China)]. Directed by Xu Qiang, Shi Weixiang, and Fu Na. Shanghai: Xingkuo wenhua chuanbo. DVD.

Ji Zhe. 2011. "Buddhism in the Reform Era: A Secularized Revival?" In *Religion in Contemporary China: Revitalization and Innovation,* edited by Adam Yuet Chau, 32–52. London: Routledge.

Kaiguang fahui xianchang. Accessed August 8, 2014. http://www.fjsfj.com/praise/scenery.

Li, Fung Mei Sarah, and Trevor H. B. Sofield. 2009. "Huangshan (Yellow Mountain), China: The Meaning of Harmonious Relationships." In *Tourism in China: Destination, Cultures, and Communities,* edited by Chris Ryan and Gu Huimin, 157–167. New York: Routledge.

Mafengwo. "Longquan chansi" [Longquan monastery]. Accessed March 15, 2017. https://www.mafengwo.cn/poi/28964.html.

Ningbo xikou lüyou jituan. 2015a. *Xikou shiguang* [Happy time in Xikou (*sic*)]. Fenghua: Ningbo xikou lüyou jituan.

———. 2015b. *Xikou.* Fenghua: Ningbo xikou lüyou jituan.

Ritzinger, Justin R. 2017. *Anarchy in the Pure Land: Reinventing the Cult of Maitreya in Modern Chinese Buddhism.* Oxford: Oxford University Press.

Salazar, Noel. 2011. "The Power of Imagination in Transnational Mobilities." *Identities: Global Studies in Culture and Power* 18 (6): 576–598.

Schwartz, David. 1997. *Culture & Power: The Sociology of Pierre Bourdieu.* Chicago: University of Chicago Press.

Wang Luping. 2012. *Guizhou fojiao wenhua de dianxing tuxiang: Fanjing shan fojiao wenhua yanjiu* [The exemplar of Guizhou Buddhist culture: Research on Fanjing shan Buddhist culture]. Beijing: Guangming ribao chubanshe.

Wang Luping et al. 2014. *Zhuang dian guan shan: fanjing shan fojiao wenhua luyou de kaifa yanjiu* [Adorn hill and pass: Research on the development of Buddhist cultural tourism on Mount Fanjing]. Beijing: Zhongguo wenshi chubanshe.

Wang, Zheng. 2012. *Never Forget National Humiliation: Historical Memory in Chinese Politics and Foreign Relations.* New York: Columbia University Press.

Xuedou shan fojiao mingshan jianshe gongzuo huibao. 2015. [Work report on establishing Xuedou shan as a famous Buddhist mountain]. Fenghua, China.

Xuedou si zhi bianzuan weiyuanhui. 2011. Xuedou si zhi. Ningbo: Ningbo chubanshe.

Zhang Ming. 2012. "Fanjing shan fojiao wenhua baohu yu luyou kaifa." *Renwen shijie* 5:302–312.

———. 2005. "Fanjing shan fojiao yuanliu kao" [Examination of the origins and development of Buddhism on Mount Fanjing]. *Foxue yanjiu* 14:284–293.

Zhengxie tongren diqu gongzuo weiyuanhui. 2011. *Zhongguo fanjing shan fojiao wenhua wenwu yanjiu* [Research on cultural artifacts related to Buddhist culture on Mount Fanjing, China]. Guiyang: Guizhou chubanshe.

PART II

Secularizing the Sacred

5

Cambodian Pilgrimage Groups in India and Sri Lanka

John A. Marston

FOLLOWING ECONOMIC AND POLITICAL DEVELOPMENTS IN THE mid-1990s, there has been increasing openness among Buddhists in Cambodia proper and in Cambodian diaspora communities to the ways that Cambodian Buddhism can connect to a wider world of international Buddhism. This is illustrated through three interrelated phenomena: Cambodian monks going to study in Sri Lanka and India; the building of Cambodian-identified temples in Sri Lanka, India, and Nepal; and Cambodian pilgrims touring sacred Buddhist sites in these countries (Marston 2014). The third Cambodian interface with international Buddhism is the focus of this chapter. All of these projects presume a vision of India and Sri Lanka as sites of transcendent interest for Buddhism. They represent the imaginary of a timeless "elsewhere" to the Cambodians involved in these projects. At the same time they reference and extend the everyday ceremonial and institutional world of Cambodian Buddhism. In their particular Buddhist imaginary, Cambodian Buddhists draw on the underlying logic of merit-making, the ceremonies associated with it, and the ways these practices can and should extend transnationally.

In the case of Cambodian pilgrimage tours, what can be observed is Cambodian pilgrims making donations to Cambodian temples in Sri Lanka, India, and Nepal, as well as efforts to promote these temples upon returning home. Cambodian temples abroad, plus the Cambodian monks who live there, enable pilgrimage tours because Cambodian monks in these South Asian sites facilitate the groups while the newly constructed temples often serve as accommodation. The monks and the temples, being identified as "Cambodian," provide a focus of interest as well as a ready field of merit. Thus, Cambodian pilgrimage groups in India, Nepal, and Sri Lanka, are sacred places very specific to Cambodians. Furthermore, it is also important to acknowledge that at the same time, when traveling internationally, Cambodian pilgrimage groups are choosing to leave cultural comfort behind in order to connect to an international vision of Buddhism.

I approach with caution the concept of *imaginary,* as I approach with caution any scholarly framework that generalizes about collective conceptual systems. My disposition over the years, as a scholar, has been to emphasize what can be concretely observed and let readers draw their own conclusion. However, there is no question but that a whole range of conceptual systems are coming into play for the pilgrimage groups I am concerned with. These include a vision of the importance of places connected to the narrative of the Buddha's life, ultimately derived from Pali scriptures and associated oral traditions. They involve Buddhist practice, much of it at the level of what Bourdieu would call *habitus* (with, in Bourdieu's conception, underlying ideological biases, much like those of more fully conscious imaginaries) (Bourdieu 1977). Such practices are extended and transformed following the logic and logistical requirements of new settings in India and Sri Lanka with Buddhist practitioners from other traditions. Practice is further shaped by state agendas, and those of institutions, which developed in order to manage visiting pilgrims. In the crossing of borders, the imaginary of nation factors also—both that of India and that of Cambodia, which relates as well to the degree to which, among diaspora Cambodians, and among pilgrims from Cambodia proper, Buddhist practice entails the pursuit of national identity. At all these levels, and with varying degrees of consciousness, individuals' conceptual systems come at times to coalesce as shared meaning in what we can call imaginaries.

By using the conceptual framework of imaginaries I suggest something that can be deconstructed. Many times, this implies the negative side of imaginary: we deconstruct it to show underlying secular or political assumptions or the ways it favors a social order. In writing about the imaginary of tourism, there is often the suggestion that the imaginary is shaped by a process of commodification. While recognizing this dimension of the imaginary, I would stress that the synthesis or re-synthesis of imaginary in changing conditions is a necessary cultural process, and at its best can represent, profoundly, a positive creativity.

My short research trips to Sri Lanka and to India focused heavily on interviewing Cambodian monks there, visiting the temples in the countries identified as Cambodian, and at times staying at the temples. I also interviewed monks and ex-monks in Cambodia who had studied in the two countries. All this informs my chapter, although it was only on the December 2016 trip to India that I visited the country during the season of frequent pilgrimage groups.[1] While these research trips are important to the analysis presented here, my principal means of approaching the topic is through videos of Cambodian pilgrimage. These are made and distributed as DVDs by trip organizers, and many videos are available on YouTube. For this chapter I concentrate on a set of eight YouTube videos that documented a trip in late 2007 and early 2008 to India, Nepal, and Sri Lanka, led by the well-known lay Dhamma teacher Buth Savong.[2] I chose these videos because they were among the most widely viewed Cambodian pilgrimage videos on YouTube and because Buth Savong is a highly influential religious leader in Cambodia at the present time.[3] Needless to say, as I will argue, these videos themselves are shaped by and contribute to the imaginary particular to Cambodian pilgrimage groups.

Cambodian Buddhist Pilgrimage in South Asia

There is documentation of Cambodian monks and political elites visiting Indian sacred sites since the time of Cambodian independence, in the 1950s. The history of these sites is closely identified with the career of the Sri Lankan lay specialist Anagarika Dharmapala and the creation of the Maha Bodhi Society in the late nineteenth century—a group that continued to fight for Buddhist control of Bodh Gaya and other sacred sites into the twentieth century. The Maha Bodhi Society's concern with the concrete manifestations of Buddhism extended to the issue of Buddhist relics. One indication of newly independent India's openness to Buddhism was the public welcome given to relics of the Buddha's disciples Sariputta and Mogallana by Jawaharlal Nehru and other government officials when they were returned from England in the 1940s. The relics were greeted with much government fanfare when they toured sites in India and several Buddhist countries in the period immediately after Indian independence with the sponsorship of the Maha Bodhi Society (Rewatha Thero 2013). The last tour of the relics before enshrinement in a stupa in Sanchi was to Cambodia in October 1952.

The Cambodian king at this time, Norodom Sihanouk, visited India in 1955, soon after Cambodian independence and shortly after Sihanouk abdicated to assume a more direct role in Cambodian politics, and there is evidence that the Sanchi relics continued to capture his imagination. Following his meetings with Nehru to set up a framework for diplomatic relations, Nehru arranged for Sihanouk to visit sacred Buddhist sites, including Sanchi, where the relics that had toured Cambodia were enshrined (Sihanouk 1955). In 1955, Indian state policies toward the sites were only beginning to be elaborated. Bodh Gaya had, for example, been under the administration of the Indian government for less than two years. When the Buddha Jayanti was celebrated across Asia in 1956 and 1957, India made an active effort to encourage international Buddhist visitors (Geary 2014; Pryor 2012). A number of prominent Cambodian Buddhists made an effort to visit Sri Lanka or India at that time. An Asia

Foundation document states that sixty Cambodian monks and laypersons were planning to attend the November 1956 Buddha Jayanti celebrations in India.[4] A Khmer-language volume, probably intended for pilgrims, was published in 1958 in Phnom Penh with descriptions of Buddhist sacred sites in India (Luṅ Dū 2500 BCE). In the 1950s and 1960s, several of the highest-ranking Cambodian Buddhist monks visited India and Sri Lanka and toured sacred sites, as did Cambodian monks who began to go for study in these countries following independence and took advantage of being in the countries to also travel.

If this pattern was not interrupted by the cataclysms of the Pol Pot period in Cambodia, the subsequent large diaspora community over time would have begun to achieve economic security. For many of these diaspora Khmer, Buddhism came to be seen as a particularly crucial element of their cultural identity. Overseas Cambodians were already touring Buddhist sacred sites in the 1980s at a time when many were unwilling or unable to go back to Cambodia. Ven. Oung Mean, the abbot of the Cambodian temple in Silver Springs, Maryland, who had studied in India in the 1960s, brought a group to India in the mid-1980s, during a period when he was one of the most visible Cambodian monks in the United States. A former monk still resident in India, Dr. Sam Be, who had gone to India as a monk in the 1970s and stayed on as a doctoral student after the fall of Cambodia to Pol Pot, regularly served as a guide to Cambodian visitors from countries of diaspora. Ven. Poeuy Metta, one of the first Cambodian monks to go to study in India after the war, who is now a major figure in building Cambodian temples and organizing tour groups, had his first experience with pilgrimage groups when he guided overseas Khmer in the early 2000s.

The momentum for groups coming from Cambodia itself took longer to develop but began to intensify in the 2000s. Early trips by well-known Cambodian Buddhist figures gave currency to the idea of the trips and captured the imagination of a larger Buddhist public. The lay Dhamma teacher Buth Savong, who leads the trip in the videos examined in this chapter, became a household name from radio broadcasts of Dhamma talks starting in the late 1990s. He first went to sacred sites in India with a Thai group in 1998. He has since made regular trips to India and began taking Khmer pilgrims with him in 2002. In the meantime there was a *sima* (Buddhist ritual boundary) ceremony consecrating the boundaries of the New Delhi Khmer temple in 2001. This was attended by several prominent figures in Cambodian Buddhism, including the patriarchs of the two orders: radio Dhamma teacher Ven. Sam Buntheourn and well-known Khmer-Canadian monk Ven. Hok Sovann. Both developed interest in sacred sites. Ven. Poeuy Metta began organizing regular trips with Cambodian pilgrims in 2005 and would eventually assume a schedule of two major groups per year, one in November for *kathin* (alms-giving ceremony)—probably representing the largest single institutional framework for bringing Cambodian tour groups.

The tour groups represent different combinations of leaders and organization. Different Cambodian Buddhist figures have organized their own trips as well as going at other times with Poeuy Metta or other temple-building monks. Two well-known lay Dhamma teachers, Thammanon and Kaev Vimuth, younger Dhamma teachers whose careers to a degree follow the model of Buth Savong, have periodically joined Poeuy Metta's pilgrimage groups and made the trips a focus of Dhamma talks in Cambodia. Another conspicuous figure, the wealthy laywoman Nhek Buntha, moderator of the televised Buddhist Forum, has also made regular trips to India and Sri Lanka and supported temple-building projects.[5]

The increasing numbers of Cambodians traveling to international Buddhist sites is a direct consequence of Cambodia opening up politically in the 1990s, growing interaction between diaspora and local Cambodian communities, and greater economic stability, all of which have enabled mobility more generally. This was also a period when Sri Lanka, Nepal, and India were pushing to increase Buddhist tourism—best documented in India, where in 2002 Bodh Gaya was declared a World Heritage Site and international flights began arriving in Gaya (Geary 2012; Singh 2010). In conjunction with the World Heritage designation, the Ministry of Culture and Tourism held an international Conclave on Buddhism and Spiritual Tourism in New Delhi, with representatives of twenty-five countries, including Cambodia. The numbers of pilgrimage groups from Cambodia going to India and other countries since about 2005 is unprecedented, to the extent that it can now be said to be a well-recognized part of institutionalized Cambodian Buddhism among more urban middle-class Cambodians. Importantly, for the Cambodian travelers to India, Buddhist places were not only significant centers for religious activity but were also important destinations for recapturing cultural identities. Thus going on pilgrimage to Buddhist sites in India became integrated into frameworks of being both Cambodian and Buddhist.

Documenting a Transnational Pilgrimage

One pilgrimage group traveling from December 24, 2007 to January 20, 2008 is documented in eight videos, each approximately an hour and a half in length. The tour started in Phnom Penh, beginning with a "flower ceremony" to raise money for donation to Buddhist sites—funds to build Khmer temples in India and Sri Lanka. The tour group then departed from the Phnom Penh airport, flew to Bangkok and on to Sri Lanka, and spent only one night before flying on to New Delhi. In addition to visiting less well-known sites, the group toured the Taj Mahal, Kosambi, Sarnath, Bodh Gaya, Rajgir, Vaisali, and Kuchinaga, as well as Lumbini and other sites in its vicinity. Returning to India, they visited Sravasti and then returned to the Khmer temple in New Delhi. Finally, the tour group traveled to Sri Lanka to visit sites in the area of Anuraddhapura and Mahintale, Dhammabala, Aluvihara, the temple of the tooth relic in Kandy, and Sripada.

As the Introduction to this volume points out, studies have tended to merge the two categories of pilgrimage and tourism. However, for participants themselves, the question of "authenticity" regarding the travel experience—and the suggestion that some spiritual travel is more authentic than others—is an inescapable part of the discourse. The issues raised by the participants are further compounded by the fact that, as the infrastructure for pilgrimage continues to develop, questions of commodification and secularization come increasingly to the fore. While researching the Cambodian temples in India and the Cambodian tour groups who visited them, I heard criticism framed in terms of these projects being "business enterprises." The criticism was sometimes aimed at Cambodian temples and tour groups in India, and other times aimed more specifically at the temples and tour groups affiliated with Ven. Poeuy Metta. At one point in my research I received a number of e-mails from a pseudonymous sender, warning me to be wary of these projects. Furthermore, after giving a presentation in Phnom Penh, a former student of mine took me aside to tell me privately that spiritual travel projects were often criticized as business enterprises. As mentioned above, a laywoman associated with Buddhist television programming, Nhek Buntha, used the same terminology to distance herself from temples and tour groups in India, which she accused of being less than spiritual, even though she had previously been connected to them. I also found that some leaders identified with the tours were defensive when I interviewed them, as though they had previously experienced criticism. They stressed that the tours were genuine pilgrimages and not "tourism." From their perspectives it is clear that pilgrimage aligns with the sacred and a kind of Buddhist authenticity, while tourism comes closer to the realm of the secular.

I raise these issues to acknowledge an element of the discourse that informs the perception of Cambodian Buddhist tour groups:[6] to be workable, multi-destination tours, a tour must consist to some degree of a "package." Especially in the case of tours organized by Ven. Poeuy Metta—tours that include visiting several temples, fundraising for temple building, and undertaking group tours on a large scale—the package tour, with its suggestion of a business model, visits to sites outside of a Buddhist purview, and large amounts of money changing hands, becomes particularly conspicuous. However, if Poeuy Metta succeeds in creating an infrastructure whereby large numbers of pilgrims from Cambodia and elsewhere are able to experience sacred places, the package tour might be viewed as something very positive.[7]

The 2008 trip documented in the YouTube videos I am examining is fairly early and may predate some of this controversy. The trip falls readily into the common categorization of religious pilgrimage; however, there are certainly elements of a "package." Everything was well planned in advance and the pilgrims proceed in orderly fashion in their tour buses on a set schedule with probably very little room for individual variation. Travel agencies were doubtless involved. Much of what they are told at different sites could have come from guidebooks. The fact of the video itself suggests concern with the total package. On the other hand, the tour did not stick to the beaten path. On several occasions, the pilgrims made strenuous climbs over rough terrain, which could not have been easy for some of the elderly members of the group. Although it is never stated explicitly, it seems likely that the difficulties the travel presented for the participants was part of what, in the imaginary of the trip, justified it as "pilgrimage" instead of just "tourism." There was a consistent attempt to have some kind of ceremonial activity at every site—typically circumambulation of the site while chanting. The group was very concerned with ceremonial donation—donations of Buddhist flags and robes, precious objects, and money, as we shall see, at each site. Most of the activities documented in the video seem very routine, but there are moments when, watching the video, we are conscious that the religious experience of the group has intensified. This was all part of the imaginary, if you will, of what is appropriate for a Buddhist pilgrimage.

The roles different figures play in leading the group, undoubtedly of major importance to the experience of the pilgrims themselves, is not always evident in the videos, but comes out over time. The lay Dhamma teacher Buth Savong is the leader of the group to the extent that he is the most charismatic presence, and is the figure who speaks to the group at nearly every site. He is explicitly referred to as the spiritual leader on a few occasions, and the videos on YouTube are titled using his name. For some of the participants, spending time with him may have been almost as important as going to the sites themelves. To some extent, however, he alternates in this role on the trip with Ven. Poeuy Metta, a Cambodian monk who has taken up residence in India. At the time of the 2008 trip, Ven. Poeuy Metta had already founded temples at Bodh Gaya and Lumpini and, as mentioned above, now has several other temple-building projects. Because of this, Ven. Poeuy Metta knows India in a way that Buth Savong cannot. Since Buth Savong is a lay leader, it is also important to have a monk in a prominent role. The 2008 trip probably predates the trips he currently organizes, bringing two groups a year to India. In the video we often see him speaking to the group, like Buth Savong, and giving them information about the sites they are visiting. In the credits for the video we also see the name of Dr. Sam Be, the former monk who has guided Khmer visitors from diaspora countries for many years. In the video he only speaks once and tends to blend in with the other members of the group. However, he represents a continuity of Cambodians visiting these sites over many years and it is likely that he played a significant role in the trip's logistics. Listed in the credits as well are the names of a Cambodian couple from Australia and a woman from

Cambodia who played central roles in the organization of the trip—probably recruiting participants and raising money. They are not spiritual leaders in the same sense of Buth Savong or Poeuy Metta, but are recognized as having helped to set the agenda of the trip. The couple from Australia, in particular, assume a conspicuous role in the videos and are often first in line in ceremonial activities. Above and beyond the visiting of sacred sites, an intensification of the connections between these people and the group of pilgrims is part of what the experience means.

The group includes fifty-four pilgrims, filling two tour buses. Five of these are monks. They are considerably younger than the other members of the group, but their presence and the lead they take in processions and other ceremonial activities legitimates the trip as it serves to make it more clearly religious in character. The majority of the participants were middle-aged to elderly women, but there are a handful of men in the same age category and a handful of younger women.[8] The couple from Australia identified as trip organizers may have been in their late forties, and thus young compared to the majority of the group. The majority of this group may be Cambodian Australians, even though, at the present time, according to Poeuy Metta, most pilgrimage trips participants are from Cambodia proper. Buth Savong, nevertheless, is based in Cambodia, and the narrative of the videos is that of a ceremony held in a Phnom Penh temple, then a trip leaving from the Phnom Penh airport. At the end of the video, they return there. Compared to a 2002 Buth Savong video, where the participants gave the impression of being from an elite social strata, one would not assume, looking at the video, that these participants were particularly well-off—although this is belied by the large donations we see them making in the course of the trip.[9]

Lar Munstock, a leader in the Cambodian community in Minneapolis–St. Paul, recalled in an interview that when the abbot of the Cambodian temple in Washington, DC, Ven. Oung Mean, led a group to India in the 1980s, he wanted all participants to dress in white. The members of the 2008 group also wore white (which Buth Savong, as a lay ascetic, always does). Since the trip was in December and January, the group had a more motley look as they bundled themselves up with different colored scarves and jackets to deal with the cold. Nevertheless, in ceremonial activities at more important sites, they made a point to only wear white. By the time of a 2013 group organized by Poeuy Metta, in addition to dressing in white, many participants wore pink or yellow sashes on which were the wheel of the Dhamma, the flag of Cambodia, and the flag of international Buddhism. Group participants also had white jackets on the back of which was written: Cambodia-India-Nepal. Wearing white is associated with vows to observe precepts, and it is possible that group members had taken vows of this kind. Perhaps the point in general is that the color of dress, with its association with asceticism, becomes standardized as an essential part of the experience, with its own emotional connotations. For participants, and for the audiences of the videos, dress, the undertaking of vows, and the performance of rituals are important elements of place-making at the Buddhist sites in India. These repeated actions performed by the Buddhist pilgrimage groups, function to confirm the tour's religious significance, while adhering to the group's imaginary of international pilgrimage.

The videos set the scene with footage of scenery and of the physical layout of the sacred sites, but they mostly document the activities of the participants. Thus, for instance, if they are circumambulating a stupa at Sarnath or taking the chair lift up to the peace pagoda in Rajgir, we will have long shots in which every single pilgrim will appear as they participate in the activity. Nearly always, at the sites they visit, we see Buth Savong or Ven. Poeuy Metta speaking to the group and explaining the significance of the site for Buddhism. Buth Savong sometimes adds a few words of Dhammic wisdom but mostly the talk is a straightforward description of the site. As at Dhamma talks in Cambodia, the listeners sit with their hands raised in the prayer-like gesture (*sompheah*). One or two take notes. On many occasions, after visiting a site, the group gathered for a group picture and chanted in front of the video camera with their hands in the *sompheah* gesture—again, marking the occasion as purely religious in Cambodian terms. The videos thus represent a most concrete expression of a Cambodian imaginary regarding international pilgrimage. While this is presented through the viewpoint of the videographer, Cambodian expectations are captured.

If Buddhist tourism has intensified in the context of Cambodians' increasing mobility and the growth of an infrastructure that serves pilgrims, the experience is also mediated in new ways by new techniques for recording the experience, exemplified by the videos themselves. The videographer is identified as Ke Palla. On YouTube, video numbers one and eight have many more views than the others—as of early 2016, 17,642 and 16,580, respectively, maybe because prospective viewers just tend initially to view the first or the last videos. The number of views for numbers two to seven is significantly fewer, although in the thousands; they go down with each successive video, from 5,391 to 1,921. The videos have also probably been in circulation as DVDs, so there is viewing of the videos not recorded by the YouTube figures. But these figures give an indication of how the videos are viewed above and beyond the members of the original group.

The videos work on a number of levels. They serve, obviously, as a souvenir for the participants and as a way for them to show family and friends what they experienced on the trip. As YouTube videos, they also function as a travelogue for those curious to see these sacred sites of Buddhism with Khmer-language explanations. Video programming in Cambodian households is often not watched with close attention from beginning to end but serves as background left on while people are involved in other activities around the house, and it is easy to imagine someone—particularly if they are devout Buddhists—letting the videos run while giving them only sporadic attention. Another dimension is added by the fact that Buth Savong is a religious celebrity for Cambodians often associated with the circulation, first of all, of audiotapes of Dhamma talks. Thus some would watch the videos to see Buth Savong and hear his descriptions of the importance of Buddhist sites, and, in addition to showing the pilgrimage and documenting the trip, the video also functions to further enshrine his persona.

Yet another issue is the record of donation. In Cambodian Buddhist practice, financial contributions to ceremonies are systematically written down and very publicly announced. I would argue that, in the same ways, the videos serve as a means of inscribing the act of devotion of the pilgrims, both in the fact of their making the pilgrimage and in the record of the donations that were made in the context of the pilgrimage. Poeuy Metta gave me copies of DVDs from a 2013 pilgrimage, which as far as I know are not available on YouTube. These videos, besides being distributed to participants, are shown at fundraisers in Cambodia and diaspora countries for temple-building projects in India. They are, at the same time, used to capture the imagination of potential future participants.

Experiencing Cambodian Buddhist Pilgrimage

The videos make almost no reference to the more mundane considerations of meals and accommodation, although we see glimpses of the Cambodian temple at Lumpini and a meal prepared at the Cambodian temple in New Delhi, where they had obviously spent the night. There is also a video of a buffet lunch in Sri Lanka to which monks were invited; the obvious enjoyment of the food suggests that this was exceptional on the trip. Other than this we do not know where the pilgrimage group stayed or where they ate. My own experience of staying at Cambodian temples in India during the high season of Buddhist pilgrimage in December 2016 may not totally reflect the situation in 2008, since more temples have been built, and accommodation may be more comfortable in some sites. While staying at Cambodian temples in New Delhi, Sarnath, and Sravathi, I found that the Burmese and Thai pilgrimage groups who came through while I was there would arrive late, sometimes after I had gone to bed myself, and leave early in the morning, sometimes before I had gotten up; they had long days of travel by bus to different sites and did not necessarily linger.

The numbers of rooms in the temples where I stayed was limited. Newer temples being built by Poeuy Metta are much larger and obviously intended to house large numbers of guests/pilgrims. In the temples where I stayed, smaller pilgrimage groups could be accommodated comfortably in rooms with two or three beds. However, it is evident that sometimes temples are used to house much larger numbers of pilgrims, such as the group in the videos, with pilgrims sleeping on mattresses or mats on the floor.[10] These temples did not provide food but they had large kitchen areas designed in such a way that if the pilgrimage groups themselves wanted to bring food and prepare group meals they could do so. Probably Cambodian pilgrimage groups are more likely to spend time at the Cambodian temples in India, Nepal, and Sri Lanka, preparing meals there and getting to know the monks and the other Cambodians resident at the temples—as we see at least briefly in the videos.

Geary (2017) has studied the tensions between temples and hoteliers near sacred sites, who sometimes find themselves in competition. These are complex issues coming into play. The degree to which the temples sustain themselves by providing accommodation for pilgrims certainly has something to do with the criticism, noted above, that they are in some way "business" ventures. However, by lending themselves to ritual activity and being a place where the monks who invariably accompany the groups are comfortable staying, they serve functions that hotels less easily can. Some of the monks associated with these temples, such as Ven. Maha Prasoeurt at New Delhi and Sravathi and, perhaps, Ven. Mok Sophal at Bodh Gaya, had a degree of cult following before their deaths, reminding us that temples can become destinations in and of themselves.

At the Cambodian temple at Sarnath, the abbot told me that he had set fees that he charged for (the more frequent) Thai pilgrimage groups, but that he let Cambodian groups make donations at they saw fit. There is a particular sense of nationalism to this distinction, connected to the temple's self-definition as Cambodian, but it also points to his confidence that Cambodian pilgrims would be more generous in supporting the temple. Cambodian pilgrims played a role in funding the temple from its beginning, and were more likely to make long-term commitments and contributions to ongoing temple support. All this brings out certain nuances to the question of the degree to which temples are functioning like hotels or guesthouses. That is, while there are times when temples do charge fees, like (some would say) a secular enterprise, there are also times when, more in the accepted mode of a temple, they will rely on the freely given donations of pilgrims. It is not always easy to make a clear distinction.

Ceremony and Donation

The videos reviewed for this chapter, understandably give much more emphasis to the pilgrimage *as* pilgrimage—the functional imaginary, the visits to sacred places and the ceremonial activities performed there. Ceremonial activities, which we see in the videos, combine practices common in Cambodia with others that draw on South Asian practices. For example, ceremonies of giving food to monks or circumambulating religious structures while chanting are very much in the repertoire of what one would see in Cambodia. However, we also see pilgrims spraying perfume on structures—an act not common in Cambodia. We see extensive use of the international Buddhist flag—as adopted by the World Federation of Buddhists in the 1950s—such as in chains of small flags connected by strings, which the group as a whole draped on religious sites. Pilgrims also incorporate large versions of the flag, such as the one they lay over the figure of the reclining Buddha at Kushinaga—something I have so far not seen in Cambodia. One may wonder what precisely the use of this flag, a symbol of international Buddhism, represents as an act of devotion at an international Buddhist site. The ceremonial life of the Cambodian pilgrimage, then, is not simply an expression of domestic Cambodian identity nor of an international identity, but rather, is an expression of an identity that mixes them together.

The conspicuous ceremonial donation we see in the videos is one side of the pilgrimage, which is a natural extension of Cambodian Buddhist practices. Some pilgrimages to India are *kathin* ceremonies—that is, the post–rainy season ceremony whereby members of another temple community, who travel as a group to present the robes, give monastic robes to a temple. The earlier 2002 videos of a trip to India led by Buth Savong documented a *kathin* ceremony. At the present time one of the two annual tour groups organized by Poeuy Metta is a *kathin* trip in November. The 2007–2008 trip I focus on here was not a *kathin* trip per se, but had some of the same elements. In particular, saffron robes were donated at some of the sites visited. On at least one occasion, long outstretched strips of saffron cloth were carried by members of the group walking in procession and then folded up and presented as robes at the destination.

At Bodh Gaya, very much in Cambodian fashion, the group organized food and gave it to a long line of monks who parade past one at a time—Cambodian monks apparently first, followed by other Theravada monks, followed by other kinds of Buddhist monks. The pilgrimage group members took turns so that, starting with Buth Savong, each one would have given food to a monk at Bodh Gaya. We learn that a fundraising ceremony was held in Australia to raise money for a Cambodian temple project in Sri Lanka, and the videos begin by showing a similar ceremony held in Phnom Penh at one of the two large temples where Buth Savong regularly gives public talks. At three sites, Varanasi, Nalanda, and New Delhi, the group served food to student monks (some of them Cambodian) at temples or seated in a dining hall, and in Sri Lanka they sponsored a meal in a buffet restaurant. Envelopes with money (identified on one occasion as 20 USD) are given to each of the monks in addition to donations directly to the temples. The videos are often very explicit about how much money is given at each site. They gave 1,770 USD to monks at

Varanasi and 1,300 USD for the Khmer temple there. In Sri Lanka sixty-four monks were given 84 USD each—thus totaling over 5,000 USD. At Mulaghanda Kuti Vihar in Sarnath, a 1931 temple built by the Maha Bodhi Society at the site of the Buddha's first sermon, the video records the resident Sri Lankan monk writing into a book the exact amounts given, including a list of objects of value contributed—jewelry, gold, and silver.[11]

To me the most intense part of the video documenting their time at Bodh Gaya was when the group, seated in a small room in front of an image of the Buddha in the main shrine, after chanting, passed donations forward to Buth Savong, who then placed them into the folds of a cloth on the lap of the Buddha image. There was a bit of the excitement of an auction, as one amount was announced, then pilgrims added money to make it higher and then higher than that. The amounts of 5,500 and 6,000 USD are announced at different times—and finally $6,600. But the most lavish contributions were at the temple of the tooth relic in Kandy, where the camera focuses in on what could almost be a jewelry shop window as Buth Savong opens boxes containing an array of gems, different kinds of jewelry, and decorative gold flowers for donation. The emphasis on gift-giving and recording monetary contributions in precise terms relates, I believe, to practices of long standing in Theravada countries and not necessarily to growing commodification of pilgrimage—although it remains interesting to ask how this fits into the larger political economy of Buddhist tourism and how this may be changing over time.

Viewing Relics

The concrete material exchange associated with the pilgrimage groups includes that of Buddhist relics. For the Cambodian pilgrims, the concrete performative act of donation and contact with relics seemed essential to the imaginary of pilgrimage. In anthropological terms growing out of the classical work of Marcel Mauss, the ceremonial life of the pilgrimage thus includes an element of prestation, with the implication that the iconic enactment of well-recognized forms of merit-making will redound to the spiritual (or even material) benefit of the donor. Visits to these sites, and the importance of the concrete representation of Buddhism they signify, extends to an interest in the power of Buddhist relics—and the spiritual benefits accrued by the possibility of bringing them to Cambodia. Buth Savong was noteworthy, early in his career, for setting up temples and ashrams where monks followed meticulously monastic discipline as stated in the scriptures. In this regard he can be seen as in the reformed tradition of the pre–Pol Pot Mahanikay patriarch Samdech Chuon Nath, who worked to eliminate what he regarded as extraneous, superstitious elements of Cambodian Buddhism. Kate Crosby (2013) has emphasized the degree to which he has tried to eliminate non-reformed (*boran*) traditional elements. But there is also a strong element of devotionalism in the Buddhist practices associated with him that, from the perspective at least of a Western observer, somewhat contradicts the idea of him as a modernizing reformer. His vision of Buddhism is an international one, very much linked to the concrete remains of early Buddhism we see at sacred sites. It also gives great importance to the veneration of relics and Bo trees.

At the Mulaghanda Kuti Vihar in Sarnath a gold cloth is placed on Buth Savong's head. Next, he supports a casket containing relics as he leads the group in a procession around the central shrine. Then the Sri Lankan monk presiding in the temple explains in English that the casket includes three different kinds of relics of the Buddha—a large piece of bone, a smaller piece, and some ash. The casket, he said, dates to the period of Asoka. He then has the pilgrims come up one by one to look at the relics with the glass cover of the casket removed: first the monks, then Buth Savong, then the lay members of the group. This is videotaped but we also see the flash of a camera as each person approaches and peers at the relics. The expression on their faces is one of total awe. The Sri Lankan monk pushes each person aside with the back of his palm so that the viewing by the entire group will proceed quickly—even though in Southeast Asian terms it is unthinkable for a monk to touch even with the back of his hand even an elderly woman. The monk affectionately puts his hand on the head of one older woman as though in a kind of additional blessing. Subsequently, in the same order, the members of the group come up one by one, and the casket with the relics is placed briefly together with a small cushion on each person's head, with a flash photograph once again taken. This was followed by the itemization of donations, as mentioned above, and Buth Savong signing a book naming the donations. Then there is once more a photo opportunity as each member of the group is given a rosary and a piece of cloth—red colored in the case of the monks, white in the case of the lay pilgrims. Because of this, it is fair to say that, for many Cambodian pilgrims, contact with relics is an important part of the imaginary of their experience of pilgrimage.

The Emotional Experience of Pilgrimage

The growing physical exhaustion of the participants is part of the group dynamic and relates, seemingly, to the spiritual dynamic over the course of the trip as we see the group go from site to site in India and Nepal. As noted above, there is very little reference to meals or accommodation in the videos and the fact that we see them at a hotel after they fly to Sri Lanka may mean that they had more comfortable accommodation at this point. The group's energies do seem to revive and they seem refreshed as they begin a new cycle of visits, up to the grueling climb of the mountain at Sripada, which is the final destination of the trip.

One of the most touching moments in the eight videos is the visit to Kushinaga, the site of the Buddha entering *nibbana*. This comes at what must have been the height of their physical exhaustion as they visited the sites in India. We see the group approaching the temple in procession carrying an oversized Buddhist flag. Entering the temple they spread the flag on the large image of the reclining Buddha, as though spreading a blanket over a beloved person in their bed. Later they will add what seems to be a large piece of silk with a simple design. They light incense and candles around the image and chant, with an emotion spreading over the group rather different than what we have seen before. The camera focuses in on one woman as she begins to weep, as though she is enacting the common iconography of the *parinibbana* (complete nibbana). Attention turns to the feet of the Buddha, with the pilgrims, one by one, spraying the feet with perfume and then wiping them with a cloth. Near the end of the time in the temple, while the chanting continues, we see money collected and placed in a donation box.

There are four times when, for me, the videos come alive in ways they don't otherwise. These may have to do with the way the settings lend themselves to being filmed or just that the videographer managed to catch certain things at particular moments by happenstance. But I believe they also have to do with the fact that the emotional experience of the group intensified at certain moments. Three of these I have already mentioned: the veneration of the image of the reclining Buddha at Kushinaga, the viewing of relics at Sarnath, and the donations made in a small room of the central shrine at Bodh Gaya. It is no accident that these occurred at major sites—indeed, three of the four sites, which the Buddha lists, in the Maha Parinibbana Sutra, as worthy sites of pilgrimage.[12]

The video does, however, capture some of the emotional intensity when the group visited the last site, Sripada Mountain, in Sri Lanka, revered for the footprint of the Buddha found there. We see the mountain from a distance as the buses approach it, and, as is typical of the videos we see the group beginning the hike. Buth Savong tells us the height of the mountain and the number of steps. We see the beginning of the climb and pilgrims at various points as they climb. On a previous occasion, in India at Vepira Hill, porters carried two or three elderly pilgrims up the hill on chairs suspended on a pole. Here as well, we see a sort of hammock holding one of the oldest members of the group suspended from a pole carried by two porters. At the top of the hill, it is after dark when Buth Savong speaks to the camera and tells us that the group started the climb at three in the afternoon and different members of the group made the climb in four, four and a half, five, and six hours. The group spends the night at the top of the hill and we see scenes of the spectacular scenery at dawn. The group chants and circles the site carrying offerings, accompanied by local musicians. We sense the exhausted bliss they are feeling. Buth Savong and the lay leader from Australia both speak. This is the last major event on the tour and clearly felt as its culmination.

The pilgrimage described here has, of course, something in common with all pilgrimage: spiritual transformation by means of a journey, where transformation is effected by the timeless qualities of the destination, but also by the experience of the journey itself. The transformation, as performative action, links to the intention and realization of the journey. As the volume's editors state in the Introduction, classical literature on pilgrimage has emphasized the group dynamic of pilgrimage and how pilgrimage groups bond and change in ways that parallel those of groups undergoing rituals of initiation. Part of this may entail entering intensely into a shared system of meaning, or imaginary.

For the purpose of this chapter, I have tried to give flesh to the range of social realities connected to these Cambodian pilgrimage groups in hopes that it will give us some understanding of the meaning of these groups as they flourish in present-day Cambodia. The groups are very much rooted in the everyday practice of Cambodian Buddhism, while they grow out of sociopolitical developments in Cambodia that have brought a degree of prosperity and freedom for international travel. Groups draw on the presence of prominent Cambodian religious figures of the time, like Buth Savong. The groups are also self-consciously Cambodian to the degree that, crossing borders, they choose to present themselves as specifically *Cambodian* Buddhists. In broader terms, the religious practices they participate in at pilgrimage sites, of ceremony and donation, are probably similar to those of other Theravada groups. But at times, they broaden their religious practices to include those they see performed by others groups, as well as those suggested by guides. Buddhism, in the tradition they come from, actively seeks concrete exchange, and the totality of the pilgrimage, including its many acts of ceremonial donation, seems to be related to the devotion to relics and support for Cambodian temples and monks abroad. In the broadest of terms they participate in global processes of place-making, which have led to the intensification of religious tourism, including campaigns to promote Buddhist pilgrimage and the support of infrastructure in India. The groups readily use the most recent techniques of video and the internet to record and extend the impact of their experience, although ways in which this can be seen as a secularized "package tour" have been noted by some Cambodian Buddhists.

Notes

1 During this time, I also observed some non-Cambodian pilgrimage groups coming and going from the temples where I was staying.
2 Links to the *Dhamma Yeatra* 2008 videos (led by Dr. Buth Savong) from which

this chapter derives much of its data: https://www.youtube.com/watch?v=5ZCoU4rtI4M; https://www.youtube.com/watch?v=z9UT8ypem1I; https://www.youtube.com/watch?v=3q9nk-jW59E; https://www.youtube.com/watch?v=VHIPVwHniHA; https://www.youtube.com/watch?v=9a-8IPpTtLc; https://www.youtube.com/watch?v=-mxezazoAJw; https://www.youtube.com/watch?v=nfhY7Y9Tp-o; https://www.youtube.com/watch?v=4Ur7seEaZ5I.

3 I am also drawn to him because of previous research on the ways relics and Bo trees are a salient feature of temples affiliated with him, a development that seems to relate to his trips to India and Sri Lanka and some of the types of devotionalism we see in the videos (Marston 2015).

4 "Travel Grant to President of Pali Association," October 22, 1956, The Asia Foundation Box 175, PALI ASSOC General Cambodia 601.

5 She may have at times been connected to Poeuy Metta, as well, even though in a recent interview she distanced herself from him.

6 I see no evidence that Cambodian monks involved in these projects are pocketing money for personal use. One can accurately say that they want to generate funds that will extend their projects and influence. One can also say that they value projects that, in terms resonant to Cambodian culture as a whole, place them increasingly at the center of social networks and patterns of personal patronage.

7 A factor in all of this is that, in my observation, Poeuy Metta's temple-building projects are overextended and give the impression that they may not in the long run all be sustainable.

8 It has been said that Buth Savong's following is among Cambodians old enough to have lived through the Pol Pot period, and the tour group confirms that, but the makeup of the group may also reflect who would have been most readily available to make the trip.

9 In a table listing "Target Market Profiles" in a report on Buddhist tourism in India (Incredible India! and International Finance Corporation 2014?, 28), Cambodia is placed in a category of "Budget pilgrims" together with Sri Lanka, Thailand, Himalayan Buddhists, Myanmar, Laos, Vietnam, Bhutan, and Refugees from Tibet. The other categories are "Comfort pilgrims" (from more wealthy Asian countries), "Budget explorers," and "High-end explorers."

10 While no pilgrimage groups came through while I was staying at the Cambodian temple in Rajgir, I saw a large stack of mattresses that were obviously used for this purpose.

11 Including a rather bizarre moment when the local monk somewhat officiously insists on clarifying whether a candle holder is silver or silver plate; the Cambodians told him it was a candle holder, not a plate.

12 For some reason, the video record does not show us a similarly intense experience at the fourth site, Lumpini.

References

Bourdieu, Pierre. 1977. *Outline of a Theory of Practice*. Translated by Richard Nice. New York: Cambridge University Press.

Crosby, Kate. 2013. *Traditional Theravada Meditation and Its Modern-Era Suppression*. Hong Kong: Buddha Dharma Centre of Hong Kong.

Geary, David. 2017. "Merit Making and the Politics of Patronage among Indian Hoteliers and Buddhist Monasteries in Bodh Gaya." Paper presented at Association for Asian Studies Annual Meeting, Toronto, March 18.

——. 2014. "Rebuilding the Navel of the Earth: Buddhist Pilgrimage and Transnational Religious Networks." *Modern Asian Studies* 43 (3): 645–692.

——. 2012. "World Heritage in the Shadow of Zamindari." In *Cross-disciplinary*

Perspectives on a Contested Buddhist Site: Bodh Gaya Jataka, edited by David Geary, Matthew R. Sayers, and Abhishek Sing Amar, 141–152. London: Routledge.

Incredible India! and International Finance Corporation. 2014?. *Investing in the Buddhist Circuit: Enhancing the Spiritual, Environmental, Social, and Economic Value of the Places Visited by the Buddha in Bihar and Uttar Pradesh, India, 2014–2018.* India [?]: Incredible India! and International Finance Corporation.

Luṅ Dū. 2500 BCE (1958 CE [*sic*]). *Iṇḍia Yātrāa*. Phnom Penh [?]: Wat Unnalom [?].

Marston, John. 2015. "Buth Savong y la nueva proliferación de reliquias en Camboya." *Estudios de Asia y África* 50 (2): 265–284.

——. 2014. "The Transnationalism of Merit: Diaspora Communities and Cambodian Student Monks, Pilgrims and Building Projects in South Asia." International Association of Buddhist Studies, Vienna, Austria, August 18–23.

Pryor, C. Robert. 2012. "Bodh Gaya in the 1950s: Jawaharlal Nehru, Mahant Giri, and Angarika Munindra." In *Cross-disciplinary Perspectives on a Contested Buddhist Site: Bodh Gaya Jataka,* edited by David Geary, Matthew R. Sayers, and Abhishek Sing Amar, 110–118. London: Routledge.

Rewatha Thero, Ven. Dr. D., ed. 2013. *History of Sacred Relics of Gautama Buddha and Arahants Sariputta, Moggallana*. Gaya, Bihar, India: Maha Bodhi Society of India.

Sihanouk, H. R. H. Norodom. 1955. "Reply by H.R.H. Prince Norodom Sihanouk Varman of Cambodia." *The Maha Bodhi* 63 (4): 143.

Singh, Upinder. 2010. "Exile and Return: The Reinvention of Buddhism and Buddhist Sites in Modern India." *South Asian Studies* 26 (2): 193–217.

6

Buddhists, Bones, and Bats

Thematic Tourism and the Symbolic Economy of Phnom Sampeau, Cambodia

MATTHEW J. TREW

CAMBODIA TODAY IS NEARLY UNRECOGNIZABLE FROM A few short years ago. Streets hiding tiny bistros that were once quiet refuges from the crowded chaos of Angkor Wat are now filled with countless hip young international travelers chronicling their adventures on their blogs. Meanwhile, shiny new Lexus SUVs have overtaken the previously ubiquitous 1980s-era Toyota Camry as the taxi of choice, luxuriously ushering tourists from one destination to the next over newly paved roads once famed for spine-shattering potholes. These changes are symptomatic of the expeditious growth of the tourism industry in Cambodia, which saw tourist arrivals reach five million in 2016—more than double the arrivals from 2009 ("Tourism Statistics" 2016). Predictions for the future are similarly optimistic, with projections estimating an additional 500,000 new tourist arrivals for the next several years, thanks partly to an increasing collection of accolades such as the European Council on Tourism and Trade's 2016 World Best Tourist Destination Award (Qiang 2016). These changes show that mobility is becoming central to the perception and experience of modern Cambodia—in other words, that Cambodia is becoming a place to be encountered, explored, and eventually shared through new technologies. In turn, these new imaginaries of Cambodia as a *destination* and not just a location are creating new opportunities for development in places both large and small.

While most foreign tourists journey to Cambodia primarily to visit the UNESCO World Heritage Site of Angkor Wat, the speedy expansion of the tourist market is also benefiting smaller sites around the country in ways that were almost inconceivable less than a decade ago. The swell in foreign tourist arrivals is creating a significant demand for fresh places to visit, new things to do, and unique memories to be made in order to satisfy the hordes of tourists who often find themselves suffering "temple fatigue" after a few days at Angkor. Meanwhile, the development of Cambodia's roadways is helping locals explore their country's significant sites, with many Cambodian tourists now seeking to experience places that exemplify Khmer heritage and Buddhist tradition. Modern-era Buddhist pagodas, especially those built on scenic hilltops, are prime candidates for satisfying the desires of both domestic and foreign tourists because they provide a change of pace from the ancient ruins found scattered throughout the nation, while giving access to the lived practice of modern Cambodian Buddhism.

From a sensory perspective, these temples gilded in yellow-gold paint and decorated with rainbow-colored banners contrast with the timeworn gray and red stones of Angkor, while the many colorful paintings of the life of the Buddha that are found inside most temples bring vivacity to the religious tales described in guidebooks and advertisements. This style of making Buddhism tangible and animated through tourist experience is leading to new global connections that support growing symbolic economies. Religious scholar Lewis Lancaster argues that Buddhism thrived historically due to its portability, creating networks that linked modes of thought across populations (2012). In a world where networking now includes the ubiquity of social media technologies, Buddhist spaces both stimulate the senses while satisfying the inner narratives that foreign visitors create about the exoticism of Buddhism, all the while allowing them to share their experiences through social media networks in a striking and memorable way. For Cambodians and other Buddhist visitors, these technologies similarly encourage practitioners to explore and share their beliefs in ways that motivate others, especially youth, to experience sacred landscapes and places of meaning, albeit with dramatically different intent.[1]

Both domestic and foreign imaginaries of Buddhism are powerful motivators for inspiring travel to Buddhist sites, from searching for peace in India to viewing fantasy worlds in Southeast Asia (see Geary and Miksic, this volume). In Cambodia, tourist imaginaries often involve perceptions of an oft-exoticized spirituality, the legacies of a violent past, and the beauty of the natural environment in creating a narrative foundation for tourism. From this initial inspiration, these imaginaries also structure new economic forms while creating opportunities for people of differing backgrounds and expectations to interact in Buddhist spaces, thus altering the practice of modern Buddhism itself. In this chapter, I examine one such site—the mountain of Phnom Sampeau in the northwestern Cambodian province of Battambang—as it establishes a new tourist economy reliant upon varied and overlapping imaginaries of Buddhist space, especially the imaginaries of the Cambodians themselves, that result in new debates about what it means to practice Buddhism in a rapidly globalizing world.[2] As new technologies allow the experience of Buddhism to become more accessible, more performative, and more lucrative, practitioners at these sites are forced to reexamine what behaviors are permitted in religious spaces, balancing respect with profitability.

The Symbolic Economy and Thematic Tourism

Commodifying overlapping imaginaries for profit, whether monetary or metaphysical, through the shaping and manipulation of symbolism results in what philosopher Jean-Joseph Goux calls a "symbolic economy." Using the language of Karl Marx and Sigmund Freud, Goux argues that symbols and the process of symbolization have use-value beyond just the metaphorical (1990, 79). Symbols, claims Goux, originate in the individual subconscious where desire creates an imaginary that serves only the "supernatural abstraction" of exchange-value in the form of as-yet disembodied ideas (19). However, when those symbolic desires are satisfied in real life, such as in the touristic visitation of a long-imagined locale, they exhibit use-value. Their use is found in satisfying the imagined narratives that travelers create for themselves, and thus in providing "physical, incarnated, perceptible" benefit to those individuals (Goux 1990, 19, 206). When those internal desires further begin to be shared by more than one individual and then are jointly satisfied through touristic experiences, they create a form of supply and demand that trades on desire. In this way, symbolic economies transform unconscious desires into tangible commodities that can reshape outward social and symbolic structures in turn. As social media becomes more globally pervasive, particularly in smaller countries like Cambodia where Facebook surpasses all other media as the leading source of news, tourists are able to share their experiences with increasingly diverse audiences, establishing joint imaginaries more easily than ever before and resulting in the rise of new symbolic economies (Kaing 2017).

Symbolic economies also provide ideal spaces for the convergence of tourism and pilgrimage because of the necessity of internal desire as the motivating factor for "authentic" experiences. For this reason, religious spaces that have a history of pilgrimage, such as Phnom Sampeau, can often find new life as destinations for both domestic and foreign tourists. Buddhist spaces, being sites long associated with meaningful imaginaries ranging from Orientalist stereotypes to places of merit-making and social transformation, are increasingly reliant on the symbolic economic form for subsistence. In an analysis of Thai Buddhist temples, anthropologist Marc Askew determined that the consumption and commodification of symbols by foreign tourists and domestic pilgrims is what maintains both the financial upkeep and the spiritual potency of increasing numbers of Buddhist sites. As Askew summarizes, "The symbolic economy in contemporary Asia is a reticulating accumulation process that spawns new monuments and revives old sites, generating an ever-proliferating spectacular landscape that perpetuates competition for visitation, income and fame" (2008, 92). As tourism expands across the region and larger numbers of tourists demand engagement with new activities, the dependence on symbolic commodification and the need to satisfy new expectations of thematic authenticity become increasingly critical.

In Cambodia, authentic experiences that involve some form of technological connectivity are likewise becoming progressively relevant as tourists, both domestic and foreign, simultaneously increase in frequency while dropping in average age. James Dion, a sustainable tourism program manager for the National Geographic Society, describes the need for an "experience economy" in which younger tourists can be physically and psychologically stimulated and ultimately earn a sense of spiritual and emotional accomplishment that can be shared via new technologies. As Dion summarized at the 2016 Mekong Tourism Forum in Sihanoukville, "People that are computer programmers, people that are working in technology or the knowledge economy—maybe sitting down and lying on the beach isn't as attractive as it was for other generations" (Connor 2016). These techno-tourists, including a new generation of computer-savvy Cambodians, are on their own pilgrimages to engage with emotionally and spiritually satisfying activities that meet and exceed their expectations, first through lived activity and again afterwards when recounting their journey via travel blogs and social media. Buddhist experiences perfectly satisfy these needs because they are authentic spaces of religious activity and thus provide sensory and emotional stimulation that not only meet foreign travelers' preconceived ideas but also encourage them to disseminate their opinions and inspire others to follow suit through digital proselytization.[3] So too with local visitors and Buddhist tourists, who can share the lived experience and immersive environments of their beliefs with a wider global audience.

To be even more precise, symbolic economies often result from the successful establishment of themes and thematic narratives. Thematic tourism seeks to transcend simply "visiting" a site to instead subject the tourist to full psychological and sensory immersion, often mentally removing the subject to a different time and place from the spaces they physically occupy in a form of postmodern touristic experience. As anthropologist Scott A. Lukas summarizes, "Lived theming indicates the incorporation of the modalities of theming at the innermost psychological and existential realms of the individual. . . . For a themed space to resonate with the consciousness of a customer in a meaningful way, it must weave through the channels of the mind to register a semiotic effect that is palpable and personal" (2007, 13–14). In other words, theming must satisfy the imaginary of the tourist, making their symbolic desires a reality and allowing them to consume those desires in a physical space—thus completing a symbolic economic exchange.

Theming is most often associated with staged environments such as Disneyland or the Las Vegas strip, existing as what a range of scholars from Lukas to sociologist Jean Baudrillard term a "form of simulation" (Baudrillard 1994; Lukas 2007, 8). While I do not wish to equate religious spaces such as Phnom Sampeau with purposefully staged thematic spaces like theme parks, I do argue that these sites operate on similar principles. Whereas Disneyland exists as a lived film experience in which each "land" represents a different narrative genre—fantasy, adventure, science fiction, etc.—into which a traveler can insert themselves as the star, so too does Buddhist tourism rely on the tourist's personal quest for engagement with places they expect to adequately reflect and exceed their spiritual expectations. The goal of thematic tourism at Buddhist sites is to provide experiences where tourists, regardless of national origin or religious belief, temporarily exist in a physical space that embodies the *desired* Buddhist world, and in turn commodify these experiences to sustain the lives of those laborers and practitioners who help make such experiences possible, thus creating a symbolic economy.

As the demographics of tourists broaden to include increasing diversity of backgrounds and nationalities, including locals, multiple imaginaries can overlap. When similar enough, these imaginaries merge to establish dominant but amorphous thematic categories specific enough to evoke distinct genres of narrative yet ambiguous enough to encompass the individual desires of each visitor. Thus, the imaginaries that provoke the establishment of symbolic economies at these sites rely on themes to solidify the transaction of money and desire. In the case of Phnom Sampeau, I argue for three primary thematic elements that drive domestic and foreign visitation: the perceived mysticism of Buddhism and Cambodian folklore, the horror of historical violence, and the serenity and wonder of the natural environment. These three themes summarize not only the most common motivations for tourist visitation, but also the predominant narratives about Phnom Sampeau that are shared on social media, which, in turn, drive the new technology-dependent form of symbolic economy taking root in this ancient religious space.

The Woman Who Let Down Her Hair

Phnom Sampeau is located in the northwestern province of Battambang, a region considered by many Cambodians to be the "Buddhist heart" of Cambodia. From 1795 to 1907, and again briefly from 1941 to 1945, Battambang existed as an informally independent Thai tributary state, which prevented French colonial influence from permeating the region as thoroughly as it did in much of the rest of the nation (Chhoung 1994). This special relationship with

Thailand also allowed Buddhist scholars to seek instruction in Bangkok before returning to establish schools and training centers across Battambang. While the once-popular Thai-derived Thammayut order of Theravada Buddhism is now relatively scarce in Battambang, the region still serves as a primary educational center for monks and scholars, and many Cambodians find the practice of Buddhism to be stricter and more authentic there than in territories solely occupied by the French.[4]

Located approximately seventeen kilometers southwest of the provincial capital of Battambang City, Phnom Sampeau stands directly next to National Highway 57 toward the border province of Pailin. Whereas Battambang is mostly flat rice paddies, neighboring Pailin Province is mountainous, and Phnom Sampeau is one of several small mountains that hint at the gradually changing landscape between the two topographical regions. Over one hundred meters high and nearly one thousand meters in circumference, the "mountain" (*phnom*) is more of a large hill with several steep cliff faces and abundant foliage, as well as numerous caves, walking paths, and temples. With little else reaching higher than the treetops at the base of the mountain, Phnom Sampeau looms imposingly over everything nearby, including an independently operated Vipassana Meditation Center that sits quite literally in the shadow of the mountain.

Upon entering Phnom Sampeau from the main highway, tourists follow a long pathway to the tourist office, passing a giant Buddha head carved into the side of the mountain. Like most sites in Cambodia, Cambodians are not required to purchase an entry ticket. All foreigners who wish to summit Phnom Sampeau, however, are required to purchase a ticket at the cost of one American dollar. American currency is preferred, but only if the bills are crisp, clean, and new, although the Cambodian riel will be accepted somewhat begrudgingly in any condition. Ticket prices occasionally double during national holidays, ostensibly to pay for extra trash collection to prevent pollution of the sacred sites, though much of the extra money is in reality pocketed by tourist officials. In 2016, more than 11,755 foreign tourists from over 40 countries bought tickets to ascend the mountain, a figure that does not include the additional Cambodian tourists who are not required to purchase tickets.[5] Although official records are not kept for these domestic visitors, tourism officials estimate that Cambodians account for approximately 80 percent of all visitors to Phnom Sampeau, meaning that nearly 60,000 Cambodians also ascended the mountain in 2016.[6] These numbers also do not account for the numerous tourists who traveled to the mountain's base solely to visit the bat cave and did not purchase tickets, as discussed below. Regardless of the precise figure, it is apparent that Phnom Sampeau is a popular destination for a significant and still-growing number of domestic and foreign visitors.

Both sides of the road at the base of the mountain are occupied by numerous shops and restaurants, all of which consist of corrugated tin roofs on wooden poles with no walls. Most of the restaurants sell food prepared on small hot plates and cold beer from large orange coolers brimming with ice. Tourists are required to walk past many of these shops on their way to and from the two access roads leading to the top of the mountain, often stopping to purchase beverages or souvenirs. The most difficult route up the mountain is an ancient staircase that consists of over seven hundred uneven stone steps and is not recommended unless traveling downward. An easier paved road curls around the southern portion of the mountain at a steep incline, which can be traversed by hiring a motorcycle taxi (commonly called a moto) for a few dollars for a quick and terrifying trip up or down the barrier-less pathway, or on foot for an approximately half-hour climb. Recently, specially painted pickup trucks began offering their services to larger groups for air-conditioned rides at a higher price, a sign of the increasing tourist demand.

Regardless of the method of ascent, tourists inevitably pass under a gate decorated with a large junk-like ship (*sampeau*), which depicts the folktale that gives the mountain its name. The story of Phnom Sampeau is well known across all of Cambodia, and is recorded in Book Five of the Buddhist Institute of Cambodia's *Prajum Roeung Preng Khmer* (Collection of Khmer Legends) (Hin and Trevor 2012; *Prajum* 2001). According to legend, the region that now contains Phnom Sampeau was once a vast sea that separated rival kingdoms. Once upon a time, a powerful prince named Reachkol seduced a poor woman who was raising a magical crocodile on an island in the middle of the sea. The woman loved Reachkol but he would not marry her because of her low status, instead promising to return to the island after discussing the matter with his father back in his homeland. Upon his return home, however, Reachkol's father betrothed him to Nieng Rumsai Sok, princess of the rival kingdom (sometimes considered to be Chanthaburi, Thailand), in order to establish peace between the two kingdoms. As Nieng Rumsai Sok was known to be the most beautiful woman in the land, Reachkol happily accepted this arrangement and immediately boarded his *sampeau* to sail to Nieng Rumsai Sok's kingdom. Upon seeing the *sampeau* on the horizon, the poor island woman became excited at her lover's return, but as his ship passed by without stopping she realized his betrayal and fell into a deep despair. Seeing her anguish, her crocodile grew many times his normal size and swam out to attack the *sampeau*. Attempting to fend off the giant beast, Reachkol threw all of his belongings overboard, including his chicken and duck cages, but to no avail. Sensing his plight, Nieng Rumsai Sok dipped her long, magical hair into the water and absorbed the entire sea, thus causing the magic crocodile to die from a lack of water. United, Reachkol and Nieng Rumsai Sok were married as the poor woman withered away on her island, while all of the items from Reachkol's ship, including the chicken and duck cages, the body of the giant crocodile, and the *sampeau* itself, transformed into mountains that remain littered throughout the landscape today.

This legend is actually a localized version of the well-known Buddhist story of Preah Thoranee, the Earth Goddess, who witnessed the enlightenment of the Buddha and summoned water from her hair to testify to the Buddha's many meritorious deeds (Guthrie 2004; Harris 2005, 56). Religious scholar Elizabeth Guthrie has shown that Nieng Rumsai Sok, whose name translates as "The Woman Who Let Down Her Hair," is openly acknowledged in Cambodia to be the same as Preah Thoranee, albeit with a seemingly unending number of local variations to the tale (2004, 145–148). Describing the ubiquity with which this story can be found throughout Cambodia, including in the 1885 journal of explorer Auguste Pavie and the 1961 writings of ethnographer Eveline Porée-Maspero, Guthrie summarizes that the popularity of the legend and the method by which it is constantly recounted in new media provide "a fascinating example of how ancient stories and motifs are continually reworked into new formats" (147).

Indeed, the story of Nieng Rumsai Sok has been adapted from oral tradition and the written word to newer audiovisual technologies numerous times over the past several decades, helping younger generations of Cambodians to experience the story in new ways. Famous Cambodian artist, poet, and filmmaker Kong Bunchhoeun cast his daughter Soriyan as Nieng Rumsai Sok in an undated (likely early 1990s) film that ran on Cambodian television for many years and can now be viewed on YouTube (Guthrie 2004, 146). Perhaps more importantly, Cambodian crooner Sinn Sisamouth wrote several songs about Phnom Sampeau in the 1960s that are still frequently played on the radio, and that continue to inspire new adaptations by modern artists, who often film their music videos on location at the mountain.

Rattanak, a twenty-eight-year-old man who sells tickets at the base of the mountain, summarizes the influence of these recordings in attracting Cambodian tourists to Phnom Sampeau: "Many people come here because of the story of Nieng Rumsai Sok. Some come to see where the story happened because they believe it is the true history of Cambodia. Others come because they remember Sinn Sisamouth singing about these beautiful places. They say that he could only sing so beautifully about this place if it truly was a beautiful place, so they come to see what they've been dreaming about since they first fell in love with his voice."[7]

To claim that Phnom Sampeau is popular with supplicants seeking the blessings of Nieng Rumsai Sok would be slightly misleading, however. Although many practitioners do ask for her blessings, other mountains in the region, such as the nearby Phnom Banon where Nieng Rumsai Sok is believed to have lived, are more popular with those seeking her direct aid. Instead, Phnom Sampeau has become a site associated with the veneration of the oral tradition itself. Images of the ship, the crocodile attack, and Preah Thoranee's witnessing of the Buddha's enlightenment (often with the image of a dying crocodile added to the scene) are found in many locations on and near the mountain, and guides carefully recreate the story for those unfamiliar with it, multiple times a day. Buddhist pilgrims often come specifically to visit spaces associated with the legend, and family outings where elders regale youth with tales of Nieng Rumsai Sok's many virtues are popular on holidays. Thus, the value in visiting Phnom Sampeau for many Cambodians is not found in directly enacting Buddhist ritual, although that does occur, but instead in finding new ways to share and experience a well-worn morality tale, reviving and reshaping Cambodian Buddhist folklore for the benefit of new generations.

For foreign tourists unfamiliar with this legend, the mountain fulfills other needs, such as the expectation of experiencing colorful and mystical Buddhist folklore. Many foreign tourists express a fascination with Buddhist imagery and storytelling, but most know little about the intricacies involved therein. Visiting Phnom Sampeau gives them the ability to interact with a folktale that is exciting, somewhat violent, and abundantly magical, thus reaffirming some of the more exotic stereotypes of Buddhism in Asia. In baser terms, the sensationalism of the story alleviates the growing sense of "boredom" that many tourists experience after staring at monochromatic ancient temples for too long—a thought explicitly voiced by many of the foreign tourists I interviewed at Phnom Sampeau. Moreover, it places these tourists within the space of folkloric occurrence. Tour guides often tell this tale at the precise moment when tourists reach the peak of the mountain, where an overlook allows visibility reaching over twenty kilometers on a clear day. Inviting their customers to imagine these lands covered in water, and pointing to the other mountains created from Reachkol's battle with the crocodile, tour guides help tourists enter a new time and place within their imaginations. A space that was not intentionally themed nevertheless allows guests to experience a thematic journey, commodifying the satisfaction of imaginaries in exchange for American dollars.

This folktale and the practice of Buddhism at sites that derive from it are the least powerful of the three themes, however, and are decreasing in popularity. According to Rattanak, younger generations are less inclined to listen to folktales from their elders, preferring the constant satisfaction of social media to the difficulties of religious pilgrimage. In Rattanak's view, the younger generations no longer revere Phnom Sampeau simply because they do not believe that the legends are true. Indeed, during my many interviews with Cambodian visitors, I found that most Cambodians under the age of thirty expressed doubt in the legend, saying they visit the mountain primarily because they seek a socially acceptable place to date or hang out and take pictures with friends. As a religious site, the mountain allows young couples and groups to be alone without risking gossip, even while their behavior at these sites deviates from that of traditional religious pilgrims. Despite his similar age, Rattanak is particularly pessimistic about these changes, stating that he fears that the retelling of Nieng Rumsai Sok on the mountain's peak will soon be almost entirely for the entertainment of foreign tourists instead of any meaningful religious practice.

The Killing Cave

The appeal of Buddhist authority at Phnom Sampeau has not withered spontaneously or without cause—instead, it has merged with a dramatic and impactful narrative of historic violence that provides much more visceral stimulation to the touristic imagination. Like all of Cambodia, Battambang fell subject to the genocidal Khmer Rouge regime in 1975, resulting in years of mass murder, slave labor, and torture. However, unlike greater Cambodia, which was freed from the Khmer Rouge by the Vietnamese in 1979, Battambang remained in conflict for nearly two additional decades. Fleeing Phnom Penh, the Khmer Rouge sought sanctuary in nearby Samlot and Pailin (then a part of Battambang Province), where they continued a guerrilla war against the government's positions in Battambang until a cease-fire was reached in the late 1990s. This continued warfare took place in the villages surrounding Phnom Sampeau and occasionally on the mountain itself, restricting any tourist access until 1998. Since then, the unique role the mountain played in the conflict with Pol Pot's regime has itself become a powerful thematic draw for tourists at home and abroad.

As mentioned, Phnom Sampeau is carpeted with numerous caves whose beauty conceals a dark history of suffering and death that attracts tourists and pilgrims of all nationalities. Upon ascending the mountain, the first stop for most visitors is Wat Kirirom (the Temple of the Mountain), although tourists do not often spend much time admiring this pagoda. Instead, they follow a small concrete pathway to the right of the temple, down a slight slope and toward a concrete staircase with a carving of a protective naga serpent coiled around the handrail that descends into an ominous cavern. This cave, which legend claims was once used for the performance of traditional lkhaun theater, is now known as the infamous Killing Cave of Phnom Sampeau. The Khmer Rouge once threw their victims to their deaths through a small hole at the top of the cave over twenty meters from the ground (Zepp 2006). Those who fell would die either immediately from impact or slowly from their numerous injuries, saving the Khmer Rouge the expense of foreign-made bullets. Tourists can now stand at the bottom of the shaft and gaze upward toward the ethereal beam of light that pours through the opening at the top, or climb down a small staircase below the shaft to see the dark abyss where, under the regime, bones gathered and slowly turned to dust.

Inside the main cavern is a newly paved area that has been designated a holy space requiring the removal of shoes, quiet voices, and displays of respect. A large golden reclining Buddha is entrenched in a wall, and a small glass stupa containing the skulls of many of the Khmer Rouge victims stands on display at the far end of the cavern. This stupa is left unlocked and open during the day, and guests are encouraged to take photos of the skulls and share them on social media so long as they do not disrespect the site. Across from this stupa, near the entrance staircase, is another collection of bones kept locked in a chicken cage to prevent vandalism. While many foreign guests are horrified by the image of the remains of torture victims kept padlocked in death just as they were in life, local monks claim the protection became necessary in the 1990s when Ieng Thirith, wife of the Khmer Rouge's Minister of Foreign Affairs Ieng Sary, offered monetary rewards for any human remains brought to her in an attempt to erase evidence of her crimes.[8] These shocking and sensational images immediately transport guests to Cambodia's traumatic past, surrounding them with horror and tragedy, as well as providing emotionally stimulating images for sharing across social networks.

For Cambodians, pilgrimage to Khmer Rouge sites is often discussed as a necessary evil in order to perform Buddhist rites for those who died but whose bodies could not be located. In my interviews with numerous Cambodian visitors to the cave, most people expressed deep uncertainties about tourism at these sites but reasserted the necessity of access specifically in Buddhist terms. As many of these visitors lost numerous friends and family members during the regime but do not know the location of their remains, these pilgrims travel to the Killing Cave to make merit for their loved ones in a place they know beyond doubt contains the spirits of the dead, whether their relatives or not. They also commonly express the belief that mass graves are more statistically likely to contain the anonymous remains of their loved ones, thus giving them hope that their rituals are being performed in the most appropriate spaces possible. As one woman in her mid-sixties stated, "I cannot prove that my family died here, but I believe they died here because I feel close to them when I come here. I come here to be with my family."

To that end, I found that foreign guests are far more likely to complain about Khmer Rouge sites being open to tourist visitation, as Cambodians often proclaim open access a necessity for Buddhist purposes. Furthermore, these sites are seen as crucial for bearing witness to the events of the past. As one practitioner exclaimed, "If we destroy these places, how will our children know what we suffered?" With discussions between parents and children about the Khmer Rouge considered a mostly taboo topic, if only because children do not want to upset their parents, sites like the Killing Cave of Phnom Sampeau act as thematic history lessons that viscerally illustrate the importance of remembering the past so as not to repeat it. Indeed, many Cambodian visitors

I interviewed enthusiastically defended the practice of sharing images and stories from Khmer Rouge killing sites on social media as a form of "education." Although foreigners sometimes decry such behavior as disrespectful to Buddhism, in my experience most Cambodians view social media usage at dark tourist sites as an important, albeit uncomfortable, method for teaching others about historical tragedies that are often too painful to discuss in person.

In recent years, the Killing Cave has also become popular with those supplicants who believe the spirits of the dead bring luck to worthy individuals or can predict the future with greater precision than non-mortuary sites. The usage of Khmer Rouge sites for luck is not uncommon across Cambodia, as believers are known to visit places like Pol Pot's cremation site in Anlong Veng to pray for everything from assistance in conceiving children to help selecting lottery numbers (Crane 2016; Fitch Little and Muong 2015). In recent years, sixty-eight-year-old Wan Won, a kindly gentleman who was born and raised in the village at the base of Phnom Sampeau, has begun telling fortunes inside the Killing Cave to benefit those who seek spiritual guidance while simultaneously providing financial support to his family.[9] According to Wan, almost every Cambodian who visits the cave seeks their fortune from him, making donations that are split between himself and the temple responsible for the cave shrine's maintenance. Foreigners, on the other hand, rarely seek their fortunes from him either because they do not believe in his abilities, cannot understand Wan's attempts to speak English, or, as Wan suggests, simply do not know the proper procedure for having one's fortune read. Wan believes that most of the foreigners who seek his counsel do so primarily for the purpose of taking pictures for Facebook and Instagram. "I am very popular for selfies!," he says.

Aside from the omnipresent red luck string found at numerous Buddhist sites throughout the country, Wan also performs lottery divination, in which he helps pilgrims apply laundry powder on the skulls of the dead before rubbing it off again to reveal auspicious lottery numbers. As more individuals succeed with their bets, the popularity of the site grows—benefiting both the reputation of the cave as a spiritually and magically significant space and the practical upkeep of the relics and remains. In one oft-recounted instance, a Cambodian-American couple from Long Beach, California, who initially traveled to Phnom Sampeau to make merit for relatives lost during the Khmer Rouge, asked the spirits for luck with the lottery and succeeded. With their winnings, they financed the refurbishment of one of the nearby wat's holy spaces, adding a large painted reclining Buddha and a new resting area for the monks. As gossip turns to legend, promoted by people sharing such stories on social media and elsewhere, so too grows the symbolic economy—desires increase and are satisfied through tangible returns, both spiritual and financial, which in turn leads to renewed investment (again, both spiritual and financial) in the site itself.

The Wonder of the Natural World

The primary thematic draw for Phnom Sampeau has shifted dramatically since my first visit to the mountain in 2009. Today, advertisements are less likely to feature the Killing Cave, in favor of promoting the natural wonders of the mountain's ecosystem, with particular emphasis on a large colony of wrinkle-lipped bats that live inside the mountain and emerge dramatically en masse at sundown each night. Whereas the bats were rarely discussed in 2009, today's tourists gather around the base of the mountain near sundown each evening and await the steady stream of black winged bodies that slowly trail out of a large scar-like opening on the mountain's eastern face. What begins as a thin black line gradually transforms into an imposing mass of hundreds of thousands of bats that flows seemingly without end for nearly an hour. Tourists gasp, take photos and videos to be shared online later, and marvel at the spectacle while their moto and tuk-tuk drivers smoke and gamble nearby, waiting to drive them home.

The thematic shift toward the natural environment as the main attraction for tourists stems from a need to provide new authentic experiences that allow guests to explore modern Cambodia instead of solely promoting heritage sites steeped in past historical narratives. As Dion implied in his statements above, younger tourists seek *active* experiences that provide talking points for their social media–driven lives. While the Killing Cave is a dramatic experience, it is also rooted in the memory of a history long since passed, one with which younger generations often no longer feel a direct connection. The bats, on the other hand, are a part of nature and reward the more socially conscious visitor seeking both emotional and ethical satisfaction, as photogenic ecotourism is a rising priority for many tourists. Furthermore, many foreign guests come to Battambang having already visited the Killing Fields of Chhoeung Ek and/or the former high school–turned–torture center of Tuol Sleng in Phnom Penh. In an emotional reversal from how too much of a good thing causes "temple fatigue" at Angkor, visits to Khmer Rouge spaces often leave these guests feeling emotionally drained and less eager to repeat the experience at other killing sites. As social imaginaries shift toward the desire for more positive and reaffirming experiences, those who rely on tourism at Phnom Sampeau for income need to establish an alternative draw from dark tourism—a new symbol that resonates with changing and technologically motivated tourist desires. The bat cave fills this need, demonstrating how a controlled multiplicity of themes prevents touristic stagnation, thus avoiding a collapse of the symbolic economy.

Interestingly, most Cambodian visitors are less interested in the bats than the lookout on the mountain's peak. As Rattanak summarizes, "Most Cambodians don't care about the bats. Why would they? We have bats everywhere in Cambodia! But nowhere has a view as nice as ours. It's perfect for selfies!" Indeed, the technology-driven desires of young Cambodians have dramatically altered the Buddhist landscape at Phnom Sampeau. Most notably, the mountaintop temple of Wat Prang Lok Ta Yak, the highest and most gilded of the mountain's temples, is no longer the quiet meditative retreat I encountered in 2009. These days, Cambodian teens clamor raucously across the temple grounds, taking photos of the spectacular scenes the temple affords while shooting the local macaque population with slingshots and enjoying ice cream bought from vendors who sell sweets next to the temple's staircase. To many of these younger Cambodians, such behaviors are a manner of experiencing and celebrating their religion while enjoying themselves. As one teenage girl told me on a humid afternoon, "When I selfie at the temple, I am not just taking pictures of myself. I am showing the world I am a good Buddhist and that this is the beautiful place of my religion." Indeed, near a scenic rocky overlook close to the temple's main shrine, one resourceful entrepreneur now offers instant portraits printed on a small Canon laser printer powered by a noisy portable generator. While the monks severely dislike the invasive disruptions of such enterprises, they also recognize the need for tourism to attract financial donations that keep the temples pristine. Thus, the symbolic economy of Buddhist space includes a constant negotiation of financial and spiritual needs, requiring a balance that maximizes returns in both realms.

The Politics and Mechanisms of the Symbolic Economy

The conflict between the traditional practice of Buddhism and tourism at Phnom Sampeau is exemplified in conversations with Lok Yay Hienglay, a fifty-two-year-old *don ji* (precept nun), who spends most of her days in one of the nearby cave shrines (Crosby 2014).[10] Her primary responsibility is to maintain an ancient life-sized statue of a meditating Buddha whose head has been replaced due to looting, located inside a small cavern that opens to reveal magnificent beams of light that illuminate the Buddha figure with dancing specks of gold. The acoustics of the cavern are impressive, leaving little question as to why this cave has long been valued as a place for meditation and reflection. Lok Yay Hienglay has been an attendant in this cavern since 1983 and laments the method by which rapid tourist expansion has altered Buddhist practice. "Before [the tourists came], Phnom Sampeau was quiet and respectful," she claims. "Now it is noisy because of the tourists, especially the children. Parents do not control the children as they should. The children run and scream in our meditative space, and the parents don't even make them remove their shoes before walking through this area." She further elaborates that her disappointment in the behavior of visitors is directed largely at the Cambodian people, as she finds foreigners far more likely to be respectful of the site even if they do not know how to follow all of the precautionary actions expected in a holy space.

"When foreigners disrespect the Buddha, it is because they do not know our customs. Sometimes Christian missionaries come and purposefully disrespect the Buddha, that is true and that is upsetting, but most of the trouble comes from Cambodians not behaving properly. Cambodians should know better than to run around making noise in places of meditation. That they choose to behave improperly is disappointing."[11]

Lok Yay Hienglay does concede to some benefits, almost exclusively financial, from the growing tourist population. While most foreign tourists do not typically give offerings because they do not often partake in Buddhist rituals, Cambodians regularly donate money when they visit the mountain, particularly during important holidays. "We've used donations to repaint and improve some areas," she says, "but people only give small amounts of money and we can't do as much as we like." If given the choice, she would prefer tourism to cease at this site if only because, in her words, "Buddhism should not be used for business."

Wan Won strenuously disagrees with Lok Yay Hienglay and argues that tourism is beneficial to the practice of Buddhism at the mountain. As he states, "I don't know if foreigners come just to see the dead or to learn more about Cambodian culture, but I am glad they come. The money they bring helps us keep our temples beautiful. I want more tourists to come here!" He agrees that Cambodians often disrespect Buddhist spaces, but not to the degree with which Lok Yay Hienglay objects to their behavior. This disagreement likely stems from their respective forms of Buddhist practice. Wan Won is a fortune-teller who communicates with the spirits of the dead to bring good fortune and luck to supplicants, not a monk who practices meditation or textual Buddhist study. Lok Yay Hienglay is a formal adherent of meditative practice and openly rejects the belief in fortune-tellers and spirit mediums as "not real Buddhism," describing Wan as a type of Cambodian snake oil salesman. Nevertheless, while most Cambodians often identify simply as "Buddhists," Wan Won's spirit practices are far more popular than any formal rituals or meditation offered by Lok Yay Hienglay or the temple monks. Thus, Wan Won sees more engagement with and financial benefit from tourism than Lok Yay Hienglay. As tourism increases and the symbolic economy takes root in such activities, it reveals how popular localized interpretations of Buddhist beliefs and practices merge with and often supersede formal Buddhist philosophy in Cambodian daily life.

The debate between Lok Yay Hienglay and Wan Won also reveals the importance of temporal and spatial balance in maintaining the symbolic economy. The multiple themes of Phnom Sampeau help spread the arrival of tourists across the entire year, preventing any long gaps in income from threatening the livelihoods of those reliant on tourist dollars for subsistence. Foreign tourist season is at its peak from November to March, during which time hundreds of international tourists visit the mountain and provide a steady flow of income. The off months are bolstered by Cambodia's two biggest holidays, Khmer New Year and the Pjum Bun spirit festival, which occur in April and early autumn, respectively, and always guarantee large crowds of Cambodian visitors. Pjum Bun is particularly lucrative, as hundreds of families make an annual pilgrimage to the mountain to make merit and "feed" the spirits of the victims of the Khmer Rouge (Harris 2005, 121). Individual families also visit the Killing Cave to venerate their deceased relatives throughout the year, especially on birthdays, anniversaries, and the anniversaries of deaths, albeit with less frequency than during Pjum Bun. Additionally, Cambodians continually desire to improve their fortunes any day of the year, providing constant income for spiritual practitioners like Wan Won. The rainy season is a particularly beautiful time for young Cambodians to come take pictures of the mountain and surrounding landscape, which truly does resemble a small sea during the flooded months.

The dissemination of income is also carefully structured for the benefit of those who maintain the foundation of Phnom Sampeau's symbolic economy. Donations given to spirit mediums are shared between the mediums and the temples where they reside, whereas direct temple donations are immediately put to use in maintaining not only the temple grounds but also the cleanliness and safety of the mountain's many sacred spaces. The numerous vendors at the base of the mountain are assured a constant income from sweaty tourists needing to quench their thirst thanks to the brutal Cambodian heat and can often supplement their income by selling traditional tourist goods like carvings, paintings, and clothing. The single dollar each foreign tourist pays to ascend the mountain is pooled and, after high-ranking officials take their openly acknowledged kickbacks, the remainder pays for the tourist police who ensure safe passage for tourists and pilgrims alike, as well as occasional cleaning services that remove trash and other pollutants from the mountainside. As tourism at Phnom Sampeau gradually becomes more reliant on the bat cave, an attraction which does not require the purchase of a ticket, profits must be found in other forms. Luckily, foreign tourists can always be relied upon to purchase beer while waiting for the bats to emerge, and several seating areas now encourage tourists to relax, take scenic pictures, and splurge on libations for the benefit of the vendors, who make an average of 75 to 200 USD per month depending on the season. The government charges a monthly fee for the usage of these seating areas to guarantee profits from tourists that do not purchase tickets. And all Cambodians who rely on the mountain for income, from tourist police to beer vendor, donate to the temples on major holidays in order to secure spiritual protection and good blessings in their future business endeavors, thus ensuring a cyclical exchange of money up and down the mountainside throughout the year.

As tourism expands across Cambodia and Asia at large, smaller sites like Phnom Sampeau enjoy new opportunities to establish symbolic economies based on the commodification of tourist imaginaries. When sites are able to layer multiple thematic narratives in such a way as to sustain numerous forms of income across time and space, symbolic economies flourish. In this process, new symbolic meanings arise that merge financial, emotional, and spiritual needs as equal parts of a desired goal. In Buddhist spaces such as Phnom Sampeau, symbolic economies provide support for Buddhist practice while simultaneously challenging what it means to be Buddhist in a world of growing global tourism. As more visitors from different ethnic, national, and religious backgrounds, including Cambodians themselves, interact as tourists and pilgrims in these spaces, previously valued symbols adapt to accommodate new expressions of desire and new technologies for their dissemination, requiring reconsiderations of proper behavior in religious spaces that are rapidly being commodified. In summation, the symbolic economies of Buddhist sites such as Phnom Sampeau transform spaces of symbolic meaning into arenas in which profit-making and merit-making symbiotically coexist.

Notes

1 I use the generic term "tourist" to refer to *both* domestic and foreign tourists experiencing Cambodia through thematic experiences, including Buddhist pilgrims at religious sites. In situations needing specification, I employ additional qualifiers to indicate the separate groups. My intention is to compare and contrast how thematic narratives are experienced by Buddhist and non-Buddhist visitors while arguing that each group still operates within similar thematic structures. In this way, I hope to show that the multiplicity of thematic narratives and their tendency to overlap at tourist sites, in this case Buddhist ones, makes tourism a global endeavor while remaining culturally specific in its consumption. In some sense, my approach is an attempt to reflect debates about Eurocentrism in tourism, as notably discussed by Erik Cohen and Scott Cohen in their work on mobilities-based tourism, as well as Victor T. King (Cohen and Cohen 2015; King 2017).

2 The Romanization of the Khmer language is a tricky and unsatisfying process that rarely results in accurate transcription of Khmer sounds to English. For this reason, the spelling of Phnom Sampeau varies widely across tourist literature and signage, most commonly displayed as Sampov, Sompov, Sampeauv, Sompeauv, and so on. I have chosen the spelling "Sampeau" not for its prevalence but because I find it more phonetically accurate and because the suffix "eau" serves as a reference to the history of French colonialism that always lurks behind any discussion of modern Cambodian issues.

3 In my hundreds of interviews with foreign tourists, "I heard about Cambodia from a friend" or "I read about Cambodia on a blog and it sounded amazing" are by far the two most common reasons given for traveling to Cambodia.

4 Although the prevalence of the Thammayut order is in decline in the region, the current Supreme Patriarch of the Thammayut order of Cambodia, Samdech Preah Sanghareach Bour Kry, was notably born in Battambang in 1963.

5 These statistics were gathered in a survey I conducted from January 1 to December 31, 2016, with support from the Battambang Provincial Ministry of Tourism.

6 I can verify from my many years of traveling to and researching Phnom Sampeau that this approximation is likely accurate and a useful estimate for Cambodian visitation.
7 My interviews with Rattanak were conducted in the tourist police ticket office over several months in 2016.
8 Her paranoia was well founded, as she later died in custody awaiting her trial by the Extraordinary Chambers of the Courts of Cambodia tribunal on genocide.
9 Like most Cambodians, Wan Won's name begins with the surname, hence my referring to him as Wan.
10 *Lok Yay* is an honorific denoting status and age.
11 My interviews with Lok Yay Hienglay took place in her cave at Phnom Sampeau in February and March of 2016.

References

Askew, Marc. 2008. "Materializing Merit: The Symbolic Economy of Religious Monuments and Tourist-Pilgrimage in Contemporary Thailand." In *Religious Commodifications in Asia: Marketing Gods,* edited by Pattana Katiarsa, 89–119. New York: Routledge.

Baudrillard, Jean. 1994. *Simulacra and Simulation.* Translated by Sheila Faria Glaser. Ann Arbor: University of Michigan Press.

Chhoung, Tauch. 1994. *Battambang during the Time of the Lord Governor.* Translated by Hin Sithan, Carol Mortland, and Judy Ledgerwood. Phnom Penh: Cedoreck.

Cohen, Erik, and Scott Cohen. 2015. "Beyond Eurocentrism in Tourism: A Mobilities Approach." *Tourism Recreation Research* 40 (2): 157–168.

Connor, Logan. 2016. "Millenials travelling to Southeast Asia for 'authentic' experiences." *Southeast Asia Globe,* August 1.

Crane, Brent. 2016. "Can 'Dark Tourism' Help Cambodia Heal?" *The New Republic,* September 15.

Crosby, Kate. 2014. *Theravada Buddhism: Continuity, Diversity, and Identity.* Malden: Wiley Blackwell.

Fitch Little, Harriet, and Vandy Muong. 2015. "Dark tourism in Anlong Veng." The *Phnom Penh Post,* August 8.

Goux, Jean-Joseph. 1990. *Symbolic Economies: After Marx and Freud.* Translated by Jennifer Curtiss Cage. Ithaca, NY: Cornell University Press.

Guthrie, Elizabeth. 2004. "A Study of the History and Cult of the Buddhist Earth Deity in Mainland Southeast Asia." PhD diss., University of Canterbury, Christchurch.

Harris, Ian. 2005. *Cambodian Buddhism: History and Practice.* Honolulu: University of Hawai'i Press.

Hin, Thon, and Gerald Trevor, trans. 2012. *Cambodian Myth-History: Khmer Texts in Prajum Roeung Breng Khmer (Book 5).* Phnom Penh: Editions Angkor.

Kaing, Menghun. 2017. "Are Cambodians better informed in the internet and Facebook era?" The Asia Foundation, January 11.

King, Victor T. 2017. "Introduction to the Special Issue: Emerging Tourisms and Tourism Studies in Southeast Asia." *Asian Journal of Tourism Research* 2 (2): 1–32.

Lancaster, Lewis. "The Movement of Buddhist Texts from India to China and the Construction of the Chinese Buddhist Canon." In *Buddhism Across Boundaries: The Interplay of Indian, Chinese, and Central Asian Source Materials,* edited by John R. McRae and Jan Nattier. *Sino-Platonic Papers* 222:226–238.

Lukas, Scott A. 2007. "The Themed Space: Locating Culture, Nation, and Self." In *The Themed Space: Locating Culture, Nation, and Self,* edited by Scott A. Lukas, 1–22. New York: Lexington Books.

———, ed. 2007. *The Themed Space: Locating Culture, Nation, and Self.* New York: Lexington Books.

Prajum Rueng Preng Khmer (Book 5). 2001. Phnom Penh: Buddhist Institute of Cambodia.

Qiang, Hou, ed. 2016. "Cambodia named World Best Tourism Destination for 2016 by European Council on Tourism." *Xinhua Asia & Pacific Edition,* June 16.

"Tourism Statistics Report—Year 2016." 2016. Phnom Penh: Ministry of Tourism Cambodia.

Zepp, Raymond. 2006. *Around Battambang*. Battambang: Tean Tor Association.

7

Taking Tourism into Their Own Hands

Monastic Communities and Temple Transformations in China

COURTNEY BRUNTZ

> Rather than making an arduous pilgrimage to a remote temple, those in search of spiritual enlightenment these days can simply log on to their WeChat or Sina Weibo to get guidance from some of the most respected Buddhist masters in the country.
>
> *Ying, "Smartphone Buddha"*

LONGQUAN MONASTERY—A POPULAR TOURIST DESTINATION LOCATED ABOUT an hour from downtown Beijing—sits inside Fenghuangling Nature Park. Also known as Phoenix Mountain or Phoenix Ridge, the area offers hiking trails, attractive rock formations, scenic mountains and views, and most importantly, fresh, un-polluted air. In 2006 when the temple reopened, after rebuilding, it did so with practitioners chanting sections of the sutras in which the Buddha explains how the Dharma will spread through the years, concluding with the Dharma-ending age.[1] Today, with government regulation of Buddhism, economic development, and commercialization, the end of the Dharma (*mofa*) is a common topic across China, and Buddhists are responding in various ways. The following chapter examines some of these.

Concerned with temple autonomy, Buddhists at Famen Temple outside Xian work to alter government policies. At Kongque Temple in Shaanxi Province, given the abbot's interest in creating devotional spaces devoid of commercial operators, the temple's rebuilding occurs solely through lay support. And at Longquan, Buddhist volunteers believe they are not in the age of darkness, and instead claim to be in a period in which true Buddhism (*zhengfa*) spreads.[2] Believing the Buddha Dharma is quite strong, they strive to actively and creatively spread Buddhist teachings. They describe their actions as contributing to a transformation from an age of darkness to an age of truth—a transformation that has been facilitated by Chinese Buddhist monks who disseminate the Dharma through all mediums available, including technology.

When Chinese Buddhist temples began legally reopening after 1979, they did so in the midst of great economic change. The 1980s and 1990s were a pivotal time in China's recent economic history, and with developments in government-supported tourism, Buddhist temples once again received guests. China's State Administration for Religious Affairs, along with Beijing's tourism administration, encouraged Chinese citizens to become mobile consumers of destinations associated with religion, and administrative bodies supported this through constructions of high-speed rail, roadways, ferry services, bus tours, and ski lifts. These alterations initiated quick and convenient means of travel to and around Buddhist locations, similar to the situation of Japan (Reader, this volume). In China, enterprises like the Mount Putuo Scenic Area Management Committee—the official administrative body of the Buddhist mountain[3]—were set up by the state to revive religious sites alongside commercial development (Bruntz 2014). In this burgeoning consumer economy, leisure travel was equated with being a "modern" Chinese citizen (Oakes and Sutton 2010), state-owned tourism enterprises were created to manage travelers (Ryan and Gu 2009), and Beijing's tourism administration controlled religious site development for tourism (Pine, Zhang, and Lam 2005). Constructions of Buddhist Cultural Scenic Areas furthermore integrated political and corporate institutions, and promoted Buddhism as "culture" in order to economically profit from sightseeing.[4] And given that China's Buddhist mountains receive millions of visitors each year, these state-led endeavors succeeded in mobilizing Chinese citizens.[5]

One benefit of commercial tourism is that many individuals—who would perhaps not otherwise know about Buddhism—learn something of the tradition. Many temples are furthermore able to renovate and/or build new temple spaces because of government support. Thus, Buddhists have not been opposed to economic development, with some even being in favor of partnerships with commercial enterprises to expand tourism.[6] With increases in tourist numbers (many from overseas), plus financial resources, monastic communities often view Buddhist tourism as an opportunity to spread religious teachings in innovative ways.[7] But there are many negatives. Tourists create noise and disturb monastic communities engaging in meditation, tourism results in high entry costs for visitors, and overt commercialization causes many to question the sacredness of Buddhist sites. Interviews I conducted with monks and laity in 2016 across three temples around Beijing and Xian revealed a concern not over the tourist economy itself, but rather how to promote Buddhism as a tradition of relevant teachings and practices and not just a product of Chinese culture to consume.

In the following I analyze how three Buddhist communities have responded to this concern by making use of political connections and technological resources to transform tourism and perceptions of the religion. Buddhists are engaging secular forces themselves to promote travel itineraries of meditation, sutra study, and temple stay. In this way, aligning with the state and using technology become ways to infuse into tourism the aspects of Buddhism these communities value and want to share. My study utilizes interviews I conducted with monastic leaders in March of 2016 at three diverse settings. I begin in Xian with the Famen Buddhist School that sits adjacent to a government-supported Buddhist Cultural Scenic Area. For this space, I convey monastic views of tourism shaped by government and corporate activity, and discuss monastic leadership in altering current government policies regarding temple ownership and the building of temples for tourism. Following this, I turn to Longquan Temple outside Beijing to uncover the utilization of technology for the purpose of transmitting Buddhism as a "modern" tradition applicable to the lives of young Chinese. Finally, at Kongque Temple in Shaanxi I meet a monk who also makes use of technology, but does so to disseminate Buddhism as an ancient tradition of mental activity requiring long-term meditation retreats over short-term visits.

All of my interviewees expressed concern regarding the ideology of consumerism that has been layered on top of Buddhist sites. While beneficial for financial survival, economic forces from state and privately owned tourism enterprises have transmitted an image of Buddhism associated with economic growth and thus moneymaking. To combat this, Buddhist communities are creating ways to spread what they deem to be valuable practices within the tradition, and doing so through a variety of projects (Dharma talks, precept training, sutra study, meditation, etc.). In this manner, what we can observe is that while processes of secularization arising from tourism development are often felt as invasive, they also create opportunities for transmitting the religion in innovative ways when Buddhist communities themselves can take control of these resources.

De-tangling Buddhism from Tourism

Famen Temple, outside Xian in rural Shaanxi Province, is well known for multiple reasons. In the Tang dynasty, elaborate imperial ceremonial rituals occurred there as did esoteric Buddhist practices. Further, the temple functioned as a reliquary for one of the Buddha's finger bones.[8] In the 1980s, Famen Temple received fame again, when in 1981 the pagoda collapsed. When the Shaanxi Archaeological Research Treasure Municipal Cultural Bureau and

Fugang County Museum began restoring the pagoda they found underground chambers amongst the remains, chambers that were intricately linked together, which had been untouched since 880 CE. Inside these previously closed temple crypts were Tang artifacts. In discussing these findings, Patricia Karetzky comments that "The majority of the objects comprising the *Famensi* [Famen Temple] horde are a marvel of skillful workmanship in precious matters: many are silver or gilt silver; some are solid gold; others are made of crystal, jade, glass, gold-embroidered silks, marble, and celadon porcelain. Most treasured by the temple are the relic bones of the Buddha" (Karetzky 1994, 78).

When the Chinese government began its "Open Up the West" campaign to integrate Shaanxi Province into national economic markets, tourism was a significant arena for Shaanxi's economic advancement. Key locations for development were cultural sites, museums, and forest parks, including the Famen Temple Park and, in particular, temple artifacts from the crypts (Vermeer 2004). The temple essentially provided resources for tourism advancement. More recently, in 2006, Shaanxi Famen Temple Cultural Scenic Tourism Development Company (a state-owned enterprise) was founded under the Shaanxi provincial government to construct a Famen Temple Cultural Scenic Area ("Tourism Development Project of Famen Temple Scenic Area" 2010). Components of this 150-acre development project include: tea and flower shops; a luxury hotel resort offering bathing in hot springs, yoga, and meditation; vegetarian restaurants; and a monastic villa—promoted in the project description as the ideal place for commercial tourism, health preservation, and recreation ("Tourism Development Project of Famen Temple Scenic Area" 2010). Additionally, a pedestrian street surrounded by golden statues of bodhisattvas has been created to lead to a Grand Hall where the Buddha's finger bone is displayed.[9] Based on the estimated investment, the cost of these components combined is over 200 million RMB (over 29 million USD) with the hot spring hotel resort projecting a large part of this cost. I toured the scenic area in 2016 with a local Xian resident and Buddhist practitioner. According to him, the investment numbers are much higher than the estimated government price.[10]

The Famen Temple Cultural Scenic Area opened in 2009 and exemplifies contemporary entanglements of Buddhists, tourists, corporate bodies, and the Chinese government. The scenic area is intended to boost tourism, and is a realm accessible to anyone able to pay the 120 RMB entrance fee.[11] As told to me by my lay Buddhist tour guide, government bodies collect 70 percent of this tourist revenue, with the remaining going to the Famen Buddhists. With this breakdown, it is not surprising that the entry fee is quite high, for the higher the cost, the more the government financially profits. But with this allocation of revenue, how much ownership do Buddhists have over the relic and Famen as a significant place of pilgrimage?

These questions concern Famen monastics teaching and/or studying at the Buddhist School sitting adjacent to the scenic area. While this school financially benefits from tourism, it also suffers because of it. Entanglements between Buddhism and tourism thrust monks into social situations that interrupt meditative practice and sutra study. When a government official comes with a guest, for example, monks are required to play the role of host and tour guide. The school is thus kept separate from tourists (at both the Tang site and the scenic area), in order to prevent further distractions. And to gain access to the area, one must know a resident master—specifically a monk who can give you proper security clearance necessary to pass through the barrier gates.

Luckily for me, my guide in 2016 was well connected. After the security gates opened and I was able to enter the thriving monastic school, I interviewed a resident monk who made it clear to me that many monks are unhappy with the way tourism inundates temples. In 2015, for example, monks at Haikou Lingshan Temple in Hainan Province were concerned because the temple was undergoing reconstruction. Reconstruction itself did not worry them but the temple fee did, and they demanded its elimination (DHH Law Firm 2015). This was China's first legal case regarding Buddhism in the post-Mao era, representing fervor for reclaiming sacred sites from commercialization. In discussing this case with me, the Famen monk argued that Buddhist temples must have autonomy—they must be given back to practitioners—for at present, devoted laity have little access to their teachers. Famen's Buddhist school is prestigious and competitive, he said, and its graduates are committed to spreading Buddha wisdom through meditation. Meditation sessions with lay practitioners occur only once a week, and too often, he said, the contemplative practices are interrupted by tourist noise.

For the Famen teacher, the concern is over the control of Buddhist spaces, and this is not a unique case. As Ashiwa and Wank (2006) explain, because the state recognizes Buddhism as a legal religion, Buddhists have not had to be concerned with the state authorizing religious practice itself. Buddhism already has legitimization. Buddhists are instead concerned with administrative implementation of state religious policy (338), meaning the management of religious sites and interactions between government and corporate bodies and Buddhists. In their study of Nanputuo Temple in Xiamen, Ashiwa and Wank (2006) found that while government administrative committees like the Nanputuo Temple Administrative Commission set up by the Religious Affairs Bureau in 1982, enable temple revival, such state interference is not always welcomed by monks. In the case of Nanputuo, monastery monks did not agree with how the commission planned to spend temple income. While the abbot Miaozhan wanted to use funds to build a meditation center and library, Religious Affairs Bureau officials criticized this plan and proposed a high-class vegetarian restaurant, hotel, and tour buses to develop the site's tourism market (Ashiwa and Wank 2006, 349).

In a 1982 document from the Chinese Communist Party (CCP) titled "The Basic Viewpoint on the Religious Question during Our Country's Socialist Period," the Religious Affairs Bureau and religious associations were positioned as prominent figures in how religious sites are administered. The document states, "All sites of religious activity are under the administrative leadership of the government's Religious Affairs Bureau, while religious organizations and religious professionals are responsible for their management" (CCP Central Committee 1982/1987, 440). But how sites are managed is open to interpretation, and Buddhist communities are constantly negotiating and framing their interests and actions within state control (Ashiwa and Wank 2006, 341).

These same issues concern the Famen master I spoke to, and he expressed an interest in altering religious policies. He finds it strategic to work with provincial governments. This cooperation, he articulated, will transform Chinese Buddhism, and "it will not be too difficult to alter current policies regarding Buddhist temples." Indeed, on September 7, 2017, a newly revised "Religious Affairs Ordinance" was announced, and its policies began being implemented on February 1, 2018. Policy changes include: 1) addition of protections against ownership of temples from those who give donations for a temple's construction; 2) restriction against organizations and individuals other than religious groups in constructing outdoor statues; 3) prohibition against commercial service outlets setting up vendors outside a religious site without consent of the religious group; and 4) lawful ownership and use of buildings, structures, and facilities by religious groups and schools (State Council of the People's Republic of China 2017). Such policy changes were what the monk spoke of, and they do seem to give more power to religious communities. However, this policy change does not provide monasteries with control of economic resources. Furthermore, as has been the case with previous policies, religious policies, in their implementation, are open to interpretation.

Unlike the next site for study in this chapter, Famen was marked as a government-driven tourism site. Famen is along the historical Silk Road plus a Tang dynasty imperial pilgrimage route. Today, tourist itineraries highlight Famen's pagoda as an emblem of the Tang dynasty, and Buddhist relics are a cultural resource for corporate and government promotions of the "Tang Paradise."[12] One consequence of this is that when Buddha statues in the Buddhist Scenic Area need consecration, monks are required to travel to Famen to perform the rituals. It is not surprising then, that when speaking to a teacher at the Famen Buddhist School, the response to commercialized Buddhism is one concerned with strategies for gaining temple autonomy. With great awareness of how government policies shape commercial development and places of Buddhist tourism, the leadership at Famen has aimed their efforts toward compromising with government entities through building relationships with officials, providing diplomatic tours, and performing rituals at commercially developed

Buddhist tourist sites. Although he has had to act as a subject of the state, the master I spoke to seemed willing to do so for the sake of his interests.

Commercial development of Famen Temple includes tourism companies promoting Buddhism as a cultural commodity, and while companies do not differentiate new constructions like the Grand Hall *from* religion, they make use of Buddhism as a cultural resource to expand tourist opportunities. In this way, the commercialization of Famen is also a process of secularization in which the religious is shaped by state agendas and economic developments. Greater authority over Buddhist site development is one issue arising amidst this context. Another concern is in regard to competition. With Buddhist places of tourism existing in a market of commercial enterprises, many Buddhists wonder how to distinguish their temples as authoritative on the Buddha Dharma. At the next site of study, technology is the enthusiastic answer. Through embracing technological developments, the temple community hopes to offer a variety of ways of experiencing temple life while emphasizing Buddhism as a "modern" tradition.

Animating a "Modern" Buddhism

Located over 1,000 km from Xian, the Longquan Temple community disseminates the Dharma through WeChat (*weixin*),[13] blogs, a cartoon series, bookmarks, calendars, flash animation, and the robot monk Xian'er. On October 1, 2015, Xian'er—a two-foot-tall robot monk—emerged as a means of combining Buddhism and technology to spread Buddhist teachings in the twenty-first century. Xian'er is able to respond to questions, chant sutras, and sing Buddhist songs. After Xian'er's "birth," Longquan welcomed, on average, one thousand visitors each day—visitors hoping to capture a photo with the robot. Inspired to spread the Buddha Dharma to this influx of travelers, Longquan volunteers suggested they connect with Xian'er through his WeChat account, animations, and cartoon series (Ke 2016, 13).

While visiting Longquan, I spoke to half a dozen volunteers, including members of the lay animation team. These individuals create the Xian'er cartoon series that launched in 2011, plus flash animations available on Longquan's website.[14] Prior to his existence as a robot, Xian'er emerged as a cartoon character—a novice monk—created by Master Xianfan. According to one lay volunteer in the translation and textual publication department, Xian'er is a way to reach young Chinese and to make Buddhism popular. Further, the community hopes Chinese citizens will learn about Buddhism from Buddhists themselves, will travel to temples to further Buddhist practice, and will begin implementing Buddhist ideals in their daily lives.[15]

Like so many other visitors, I first learned about Longquan online. I read stories about a robot-monk in residence at the temple, which encouraged me to travel there to gain a better sense of how the Longquan community actively mobilizes young Chinese. Upon arriving, I sat down with the charismatic Venerable Xianqing, director of the temple's education department. Prior to entering the monastery, he received a PhD in engineering thermophysics,[16] but under the tutelage of Longquan's abbot and China's then president of the Buddhist Association—Xuecheng[17]—Xianqing began the difficult monastic lifestyle. What I learned from my host is that Longquan's instructors are interested in "Engaged Buddhism" that includes temple stay programs, meditation retreats, small group sutra study, and volunteerism. The community's vow is to spread the Buddha's teachings into society so that Buddhism is not something one passively tours or consumes but instead is a source of wisdom to implement into one's daily life—a practical means for transforming young Chinese into active, compassionate, engaged citizens, committed to the betterment of society.[18] Tourism does not necessarily prevent this transformation; rather, as many chapters within this volume show, tourism can result in active, engaged visitors—be they Buddhist or not. However, in an overflowing market of tourist destinations connected with Buddhism, monastic communities are confronted with the challenge of differentiating themselves. To reach their intended audience of young adults, Longquan monks must alter strategies for doing so.

Longquan monks are concerned that "because of pressure from family and society, young people are isolated in their journeys and need to have a collective way to change." Xianqing equated this to being like a fish. "How we live our lives is based on habits in our behavior. Like fish, we are polluted by our contexts and cannot resist the circumstances in which we reside." Pollution, he said, is difficult to resist, and one cannot depart from their circumstances. "Great leaders, great masters, are those who have trained their mind to resist such pollutions . . . attachments to fame and wealth. Once students decide to follow a great leader—a leader that embodies a pure mind, circumstances can begin to change. Gradually within oneself, by following such a teacher, one can transform."

Xian'er's WeChat account provides one method for individuals to ask questions of a "monk," and for the Longquan community to share its message. If a user is connected to the Longquan lay volunteer network on WeChat, for example, s/he receives daily digital memes—short aphorisms of Buddhist teachings. Based on a Dharma discourse by the previous abbot Xuecheng, the May 4, 2017 meme stated: "There are many weeds in our minds—greed, hostility, ignorance and doubt, to name a few. These weeds are not going to be cleaned after a few runs of pulling. Even if we pull them out hundreds of thousands of times, they would still grow back because they were not uprooted and their seeds are not eliminated." According to Xianqing, Longquan's community believes young Chinese "need to be reached on an entertainment level they enjoy." Entertainment is not, however, the focus, he argued, but instead is a method to help youth transform from isolated individuals to members of a community.

Turning to technology is thus skillful means for the temple to differentiate itself. Xian'er creates curiosity and individuals travel to the monastery to "meet" his creators and experience his temple.[19] When Xuecheng was the head abbot, he encouraged technological developments for this purpose. As president of the Buddhist Association, and head abbot of many temples, he insisted that monasteries separate themselves from commercial markets. As abbot of Putian Guanghua Monastery in Fujian Province, Xuecheng required that the monastery not charge admission, set up commercial shops, or perform commercialized Buddhist services (Shi 2016, 93). His mission was to rectify "indiscriminate commercialization," and he encouraged monks to emphasize study and promote precepts (96). Using media platforms to spread teachings and advertise temple tours run by the monastery were furthermore encouraged. These gatherings included Dharma learning and precept transmission. Xuecheng defended the use of technology contending:

> China has a population exceeding one billion, therefore, we must employ modern technologies to extensively benefit all living beings... we should spread Dharma speedily with the help of information technology so that people from all walks of life are able to have access.... The agricultural era relies on farming... the industrial age relies on machines and science.... In this post-industrial era, information is valued. If you have a piece of information, you can only succeed when you spread it and make people understand and accept it... being connected as one is collective karma. (Shi 2016, 185)

Xuecheng was thus not against commodification, secular influences, or tourism, but rather, was concerned with a speedy spread of Buddhism.

But if temples are to separate themselves from commercial markets, they must find alternative means to generate public interest. Given that technology is one of the quickest ways to spread information, Xuecheng disseminated his teachings through blogs and posting lectures online. "I believe that if it were possible," he said, "Venerable Master Xuanzang, Venerable Master Kumarajiva and Venerable Master Jianzhen would have set up blogs in their times" (Shi 2012, 177). At 8:08 a.m. on August 8, 2008, the *Voice of Longquan* website launched with links to information about the monastery, Dharma talks, Xuecheng's personal blog, and animation videos for how to cultivate the mind, and by January 2012, Master Xuecheng's blog alone had more than 8.6 million visits (Shi 2016).

Serving as tourist operators, the temples Xuecheng led have held Dharma assemblies for young intellectuals and social elites. Guanghua (Fujian Province), for example, has held a "Tour of Bliss and Wisdom" assembly for experiencing monastic life, learning Buddhist tradition, inspiring young Chinese to improve their lives, purify their minds, reset their life goals, and reflect upon the value of life (Shi 2016, 100). Similarly, at Famen (Shaanxi Province), the "Light of Famen" camp of bliss and wisdom enrolls young Chinese in courses, provides temple tours, and guides students on how to lead a happy life, understand the rules of karma, and perform seated meditation (112). During the 2009 camp, when it was in its fourth year, Xuecheng transmitted the three refuges to camp members, a gathering of over 150 attendees. And at Longquan, in 2005 the temple held its first summer retreat with over 1,000 people attending. At its conclusion, Xuecheng transmitted the precepts to over 200 new Buddhists. Thus at all three of these sites (Guanghua, Famen, and Longquan), Dharma camps and assemblies have become new opportunities for young Chinese to tour Buddhist teachings, places, and practices. And blogs, WeChat, and websites are a means for advertising these events.

While interviewing Xianqing, I inquired whether or not technology defiles how the Buddha Dharma is spread. His response was that the monastery maintains tradition (i.e., follows the vinaya) but does so with innovation regarding how to spread the Dharma. "There are three levels of Buddhism in China," he said, "the first includes letting people know about Buddhism. The second level involves gaining wisdom. The third level consists of the monastic community who seeks only to compassionately benefit society. All levels are necessary." In his view, Buddhist teachings coming from monks who only want to benefit society are not defiled by technological projects because they are spreading wisdom in order that individuals change their behavior. One difficulty monastics face is how to make their ideals popular. This is why, Longquan monks believe, their messages of Buddhism need to be practical and entertaining.

In the Introduction of this volume, we discuss how religious sites are not "fixed" fields. They are instead fluid compositions. Buddhist landscapes in China today are altered by various views of what Buddhism entails, and varying practices orient visitors in particular ways. Although a development of Buddhist sites for tourism has created competition, the Longquan Temple has responded by constructing their own tours of meditation retreats, sutra studies, and Dharma assemblies. Furthermore, amidst commercial tourist operators commodifying Buddhism, the community appears to view secular resources as advantageous for missionization. Making use of technology, monks have developed mediums for enticing individuals to visit the temple, interact with the monastic community online, and view Buddhism as a "modern" tradition.

Spreading an "Ancient" Tradition

To uncover a third response to China's context of commercialized Buddhist tourism, I visit a lesser known temple that a lay Buddhist friend of mine told me about. Kongque Temple—whose head abbot is Venerable Ru—lies in the midst of Shaanxi's lush countryside of orchards. Known for spreading Buddhism beyond the scope of tourism, Ru is a monk who has successfully reconstructed a temple not based on government money, but instead fully funded through practitioner donations. For thirteen years, Venerable Ru has struggled to accrue enough financial capital to build this temple—a temple necessary, he told me, for educating others on "realizing truth." After experiencing the results of government-assisted temple building for tourism, he set out to construct a space free of government development. To do so, he needed enough laypersons to donate to the cause. Ru built this temple in order to give back to Buddhist practitioners.

I met Venerable Ru through my Xian-based Chinese friend who, on the drive to Kongque, explained that in China today there are many reasons for which individuals become monks and therefore there are different kinds of monks. Some individuals are escaping the mundane world, many monks are interested in Buddhist philosophy, and a few, he said, become monks as an occupation. In his view, those motivated to escape the mundane world become recluses in mountains,[20] those interested in the teachings transmit sutras, and the latter make up "fake" monks. "Most [lay] Chinese practicing Buddhism," he said, "are ritual based Buddhists." They travel to temples and offer incense and prayers in order to obtain health, blessings, and/or wealth. This merit economy (discussed in the Introduction to this volume) is an aspect of Buddhism that is commodified by Buddhist tourism operators.[21] Ritual as commodity is the reason for which the third kind of monks—deemed "fake" by my guide—exist. At sites like the Famen Temple Cultural Scenic Area, some young men portray themselves as monks, and receive payment from travelers in exchange for temple tours. This exemplifies the ways in which Buddhism has been indiscriminately commodified.[22] Venerable Ru, he claimed, is a rare visionary, transmits Buddha wisdom with every word he speaks, and inspires monks and laypersons to continue the difficult journey of knowing their true nature.

My guide told me that to move beyond the ritual phase one must: "1) understand and study Buddhist philosophy; 2) practice the precepts and change their behavior according to Buddhist teachings; and 3) become wise themselves by studying Buddhist scriptures." Essentially, in his view, Chinese citizens need to go through an ontological shift—from consuming Buddhism to transforming and embodying Buddhist teachings. When the individual becomes wise, he said, "[they] can then be considered a 'true' Buddhist, one who has their own proof of the Buddha Dharma from sutra study and contemplation." And when I inquired as to how Chinese Buddhists can alter the current situation of commercialization, I'm told that when Chinese citizens themselves progress beyond the ritual level, they will see through the mirage of consumptive based activities. "They will want something more . . . wisdom that comes from the teachings themselves"—wisdom, he explained, that can only be disseminated by a "true" monk.

At Kongque, abbot Ru's goal has been to teach citizens Buddhist teachings and meditation so that they go beyond the ritual stage. He discriminates meditation as the source of true wisdom, and his imaginary of Buddhism has been based on this belief. Lay members, including my guide, financially support Ru to help his vision of a meditation complex come true. One member, for instance, donated sustainable building materials from his furniture company. These supplies have been necessary to revive the ancient Tang dynasty temple structure and construct new temple spaces. When I visited, the community was small with only nine volunteers, but Ru was initiating opportunities for the temple to become a nexus of a variety of Buddhist networks. A non-traditional Chinese school for Buddhist youth, for example, was present in the temple complex. It is a private school that fuses Buddhist teachings with secular studies. Further, once building construction is complete, the temple will be able to house up to one thousand residents for temple stays. Individuals will have choice regarding their length of stay, and during residency, visitors will receive free shared-housing and meals from the temple's organic farm.

During my 2016 visit, the temple had much to complete, including gold finishes on statues, but the abbot was not in a rush to finish these tasks. His construction has not emphasized speed, as temples supported by government allocations have for the purposes of tourism. Instead his concern was "preserving natural resources." The Buddha statues, for example, come from Qinghai Province (as many statues do at other temples). However, the gold paint differs from other locations. Ru hired individuals with knowledge of how to naturally procure raw materials from trees and then sustainably process the material into synthetic gold paint. This deliberate slowness in renovating the Tang dynasty site is to return to the "old" ways—meaning reviving Buddhism (in architecture, meditative practice, and monastic study)—from the Tang dynasty. Ru has wanted to be sure he revives the temple in ways that preserve his ideas of tradition while modernizing at the same time. While explaining this to me, Ru pulled his smartphone out from under his robes and asked: "Do you have weixin? Let me add you to my contacts."

When I asked Ru about Buddhist revivalism following China's political and economic reforms, he replied, "Buddhism was not ready for the great influx of people." From 1978 to 2010, China's economy grew at an average of almost 10 percent each year (Morrison 2015). With this growth, individual citizens could financially afford to travel, and Buddhist monasteries were overwhelmed with curious travelers. Some monks, like Shi Yongxin of the Shaolin Temple (famous for Chinese martial arts), used the attention to build financial wealth. Yongxin received his post as abbot from the government, and he "wished to restore Shaolin to its pristine beauty, valued not only in its own right but also as a means of securing the temple's bid to become a UNESCO-recognized World Heritage Site" (Shahar 2008, 47). Such associations of Buddhists, government bodies, and businesses led to some Chinese questioning monks' intentions. Ru has not made use of financial opportunities as a means of acquiring temple wealth, but instead offers free Dharma talks in Xian to gather lay followers, advertising these lectures on the radio. Once fully complete, Kongque's temple-stay programs will provide laity time to engage in meditation, for "Chinese today," Ru claimed, "need to know their true self."

To explain his point of view to me, Ru grabbed a piece of candy and said:

> It is our grasping that prevents us from seeing truth.... When you eat a piece of candy, you make note of its sweetness and continue to crave that sweetness—over and over again. This is like our constant grasping. Constant grasping prevents one from being flexible or fluid, clinging to desires prevents one from recognizing who they truly are.... This teaching is what Chinese need to hear.... It is only through meditation that one can know themselves. The Mahayana perfections of giving, virtue, patience, effort, and concentration all come from the sixth perfection of wisdom. Wisdom is a result of meditation.... To know Buddhism, you need to know yourself.[23]

Given that he is concerned with spreading meditation, sutra study, and practicing the precepts, Ru's vision of Buddhism is in concert with the previously examined sites in this study, and similar to Longquan's community, has created temple-stay opportunities to encourage long-term engagement with Buddhist teachings. Technology is a means for Ru to communicate with practitioners, but his intention is not to rapidly missionize Buddhism or make it entertaining, as was seen in the case of Longquan. Instead, his focus is on returning to an "old" way of Buddhism.

Ru emphasized Buddhism as an "ancient" tradition when I met with him, and regarded its age as the primary source of its legitimacy. In his twenty years of being a Buddhist monk, he has studied all of China's Buddhist schools, and even studied at the famous Mount Wutai. Ru now roots his beliefs and teachings in the Huayan (Flower Garland) school. This is fitting for an individual who uses great imagery to teach. "By looking at, and knowing, a single flower," he explained, "you can see, and know, the entire universe." His teachings emphasize philosophy, and even his rhetoric incorporates phrases uncommonly heard in modern speech. In addition to this rooting in Huayan,

Ru teaches Chan (Zen) meditation—a meditative form visitors immerse themselves in while staying at the temple. "China," he said, "is very much like dirt. China has historically buried all of the influences that have come its way—both indigenous and foreign. . . . [Chinese] Buddhism has grown out of what has been buried." In current settings, Ru believes that ideals of fame and fortune have been buried into society along with everything else. His goal has been to reclaim Buddhism's roots of contemplation buried deep in the nation's soil.

In comparison with other monks I interviewed for this study, Ru's vision of Buddhism, and response to commercialized tourism, is the most introspective. By this I mean that he interprets Buddhism as a tradition that teaches one to reflect on their "true" self—the self beyond layers of social construction. Along with Famen and Longquan temples, he too emphasizes meditative practices, sutra study, and disseminations of the Buddha's teachings, and he makes use of secular resources (i.e., technological and financial) to connect with practitioners and revive the temple. But his intentions for doing so are quite distinct. At Famen, aligning with secular forces creates avenues for education—in particular, educating officials about Buddhism's autonomy. At Longquan, Buddhist practice is interpreted as a means of social engagement, and technology a skillful means for rapidly spreading Buddhist teachings. At Kongque, neither entertainment nor government policies are emphasized. And Ru is not necessarily "aligning" with secular forces but is instead simply offering an alternative to commercialized tourism. The temple's setting in a remote rural location provides a rarely found quiet landscape for individuals to escape their busy lives, and Ru has adapted the temple space to meet an influx of visitors who will reside in dormitories for long-term stays and not short-term visits. Here, technology offers an effective medium for transmitting Ru's teachings while staying in contact with those who might continue to support the temple and pilgrimage there for Dharma talks, meditation, and/or a temple stay.

When we peel back the layers of corporate tourism taking place at Buddhist sites across China and focus on the travel itineraries offered by monastic communities, we find a variety of experiences available. Buddhist landscapes in China today are expressions of a tradition that reflect diverse visions of what Buddhism entails. For sites entrenched in commercial tourism, Buddhism is often presented as a cultural commodity, and one interacts with the tradition through consumption. To relay different interpretations of monastics responding to such touristic realities, this study has uncovered the viewpoints of diverse communities engaged in transforming how temples are operated and toured. Across these locations, we encounter monks reacting to, and concerned with, contemporary consumerism—not the act of consumption itself but rather Buddhism being passively shaped by consumer markets. None of the masters I spoke with view the monastery as a separate institution from society. Instead, they are imagining methods in which to engage Chinese citizens so that they begin encountering Buddhism from monks themselves. To missionize Buddhism beyond state-run tourism, monks are actively creating settings in which they are able to teach the Buddha Dharma and encourage study and contemplation. And it is this direct encounter that is the concern, for through relationship building, networks of lay practitioners are created and Buddhism is mobilized beyond the scope of commercial tourism. Furthermore, from the monks' perspective, direct encounters with the public, especially young Chinese, enable them to "re-learn" what Buddhism entails. Thus amongst these settings examined, we can identify a few similar patterns of engagement—monks communicate with and build networks of Buddhist individuals and groups through new technological resources; monastic communities offer alternative temple tours (temple stays, sutra study assemblies, meditation retreats, Dharma talks, and digital interfaces); and monks tailor their definitions of Buddhist practice to meet their own experiences and imaginings of the tradition, the presence of Buddhist audiences in the region, and available resources.

In the midst of large-scale government spending on Buddhist tourism, Chinese monks are emerging as activists, Dharma educators, creators of technology, meditation teachers, and tourism operators, and they have formed new avenues for encountering sutras, teachers, and sanghas. In this way, they are building Buddhism's "soft" power in China—power that is established based on attracting a following rather than imposing ideas or creating conflict with state-run tourist operators. Secularization has created challenges for monastic communities, especially in regard to Buddhism's commercialization. However, it has not resulted in an end to religious practice but instead has altered Buddhist practice. Today monks are not opposing tourism but are instead spreading a modern Buddhism that envelops participants in newly constructed online discussions, meditation retreats, and temple stays.

Notes

1 This is especially detailed in the *Dajijing* (Great Collection Sutra).

2 Speaking on behalf of the lay community, a volunteer working in the translation and publication department conveyed this sentiment. Personal interview, March 20, 2016.

3 Mount Putuo is located in China's Zhejiang Province and is one of the four great and famous Buddhist mountains.

4 Sanya Nanhai Guanyin (Guanyin of the South China Sea) in Hainan represents one such promotion of Buddhist tourism for the benefit of the political state. Sanya Nanhai Guanyin is located in the Nanshan Culture Tourism Zone—a zone that includes a Buddhism Culture Park developed to promote tourism focused on Chinese culture. This park includes a 108-meter statue of Guanyin built in 2005.

5 In the case of the above-mentioned Mount Putuo, for example, the number of domestic visitors in 2014 was 6,255,606. Visitor statistics were sourced by the authorized control office of the Mount Putuo Management Committee, accessed June 11, 2015: http://www.putuoshan.gov.cn/Detail/322/112351.html.

6 In 2011, for example, Buddhist monks at Mount Putuo accepted a seven-million-yuan donation from China Rongsheng Heavy Industries Group Holdings Limited—a company involved in large-scale heavy industry including shipbuilding. Coverage of this event was available through the Mount Putuo Buddhist Association Network, accessed June 11, 2015, http://www.putuo.org.cn. Interviews with local Buddhist monks at Mount Putuo, detailed in Cora Wong's 2011 dissertation, furthermore revealed this favorable attitude toward economic development at Mount Putuo. All tourists were described as future Buddhists, and Buddhist monks and nuns had a very positive, welcoming, and supportive attitude toward receiving visitors and tourists. Nichols (this volume) also explores such monastic views.

7 This resonates with the case of temples in Thailand as explored by Schedneck (this volume).

8 According to Indian Buddhist legends regarding King Ashoka (ca. third century BCE), relics of the Buddha were distributed to lands outside of India.

9 While tourist literature promotes the Grand Hall as the place where the Buddha's finger bone is kept, according to my interview (March 22, 2016) with a teacher at the Famen Buddhist school, the actual finger bone is kept at the monastery. The "bone" on display is a replica.

10 Personal interview, March 22, 2016.

11 Entrance fees are based on data collected in 2016.

12 For more promotion of this see: Shaanxi Provincial Tourism Administration, accessed December 12, 2018, http://en.sxtour.com/content/details25_837.html.

13 Weixin or WeChat is an instant messaging application in China.

14 See: Voice of Longquan, accessed June 1, 2017, http://www.longquanzs.org.

15 Personal interview, March 22, 2016.

16 It should be noted that monks at Longquan are known for their doctoral degrees from high-ranking Chinese universities.

17 Xuecheng was president of the Buddhist Association of China from 2015 to 2018. In 2018 he was removed from the position because of allegations of sexual misconduct.

18 It should be noted that Longquan has begun to take its mission abroad, engaging in workshops with Western scholars, monastics, and practitioners regarding how Chinese Buddhism can benefit Western countries. Furthermore, they have created monasteries abroad. In 2015, Longquan Great Compassion Monastery was founded in the Netherlands; in 2016, Longquan Guanyin Monastery in Los Angeles; and Longquan Bohua Monastery was established in Botswana, Africa.

19 With these projects, the temple has gained international fame, and international media, including CNN, Reuters, *Guardian, Boston Globe,* and *New York Times,* has covered the robot-monk who spreads Buddhist wisdom.

20 At present the Zhongnan mountain range has over five thousand recluse monks. Director Peter Berger's film *Amongst White Clouds* provides a portrayal of monastic life in this mountain range.

21 Or in Nichols terms in this volume, "weak" commodification.

22 While president of the Buddhist Association of China, Xuecheng stated the desire to "rectify the current abuses of transmitting precepts, accepting disciples, performing commercialized Buddhist rituals . . . in an indiscriminate way" (Shi 2016, 96). Perhaps "fake" monks are also an example of "strong" commodification from Nichols, this volume.

23 Master Ru is concerned with individuals "seeing truth" and "knowing the self." While he did not go on to explain what it means to "see" truth, it perhaps is important to note that in Chan meditative traditions, especially those from the Tang dynasty Master Huineng, "knowing" is "seeing," and the traditional Chinese term used is *jian,* "seeing." This term is used rather than *kan,* "to look at." One may "look" for truth but not apprehend it. To "see" truth is to successfully apprehend

that which the individual is seeking. Thus in the use of *jian* Master Huineng was transmitting a "seeing" that is perhaps better translated as "experiencing." Thanks to Justin Ritzinger for pointing out this distinction.

References

Ashiwa, Yoshiko, and David L. Wank. 2006. "The Politics of a Reviving Buddhist Temple: State, Association, and Religion in Southeast China." *The Journal of Asian Studies* 65 (2): 337–359.

Bruntz, Courtney. 2014. "Commodifying Mount Putuo: State Nationalism, Religious Tourism, and Buddhist Revival." PhD diss., Graduate Theological Union.

Chinese Community Party Central Committee (Zhonggong Zhongyang). 1982/1987. "The Basic Viewpoint on the Religious Question during Our Country's Socialist Period" (Guanyu woguo shehuizhuyi shiqi zongjiao wentide jiben guandian he jiben zhengce). In *Collection of Important Documents since the Third Plenum of the Eleventh Party Congress* (Shiyijie sanzhong quanhui yilai zhongyao wenxian xuandu), vol. 1. Beijing: People's Publishing House (Renmin chubanshe).

DHH Law Firm. 2015. "Lawyers from Haikou Office Counseled on China's First Religious Case." Accessed May 26, 2017. http://en.deheheng.com/a/NEWS/Achievements/20161205/443.html.

Karetzky, Patricia Eichenbaum. 1994. "Esoteric Buddhism and the Famensi Finds." *Archives of Asian Art* 47:78–85.

Ke, Yun. 2016. "Finding Robot Monk Xian'er: Understanding Buddhism in Longquan Animation." *Journal of Visual and Media Anthropology* 2 (1): 7–24.

Morrison, Wayne M. 2015. *China's Economic Rise: History, Trends, Challenges, and Implication for the United States*. Washington, DC: Congressional Research Service.

Mount Putuo Management Committee. Accessed June 11, 2015. http://www.putuoshan.gov.cn/Detail/322/112351.html.

Oakes, Tim, and Donald Sutton, eds. 2010. *Faiths on Display: Religion, Tourism, and the Chinese State*. Lanham, MD: Rowman and Littlefield.

Pine, Ray, Hanqin Qiu Zhang, and Terry Lam. 2005. *Tourism and Hotel Development in China: From Political to Economic Success*. Binghamton, NY: Haworth Press.

Ryan, Chris, and Gu Huimin, eds. 2009. *Tourism in China: Destination, Cultures and Communities*. New York: Routledge.

Shahar, Meir. 2008. *The Shaolin Monastery: History, Religion, and the Chinese Martial Arts*. Honolulu: University of Hawai'i Press.

Shi Huikong. 2016. *Stories of Ven. Master Xuecheng*. Beijing: China Fortune Press.

"Tourism Development Project of Famen Temple Scenic Area." 2010. China Bidding Network (zhongguo caigou yu zhaobiao wang). Accessed April 1, 2017. http://www.chinabidding.org/projectinfo/810501.

State Council of the People's Republic of China. 2017. "*Zongjiao shiwu tiaoli*" [Religious Affairs Regulation]. Last modified September 7, 2017. http://www.gov.cn/zhengce/content/2017-09/07/content_5223282.htm

Vermeer, Eduard B. 2004. "Shaanxi: Building a Future on State Support." *The China Quarterly* 178 (June): 400–425.

Wong, Cora U. I. 2011. "Buddhism and Tourism at Pu-Tuo-Shan, China," PhD diss., University of Waikato.

Ying, Li. 2015. "Smartphone Buddha." Last modified March 29, 2015. eng.longquanzs.org/monastery/reports/61492.htm.

8

Turning to Tourism in a Time of Crisis?

Buddhist Temples and Pilgrimage Promotion in Secular(ized) Japan

Ian Reader

IN EARLY 2016 EIHEIJI, THE HEAD TEMPLE of the Sōtō Zen Buddhist sect in Japan and long famed as a center of austerity, meditation, and monastic training, announced that it was working with a construction company to build a new upmarket hotel to encourage tourists to visit the temple. In seeking to boost visitor numbers the temple was cooperating also with local and regional authorities, including the government of Fukui Prefecture, where Eiheiji is located. These authoritative bodies are providing logistical support and are including Eiheiji in tourist publicity designed to attract visitors to the region. The Fukui prefectural government was, for example, constructing new paths to improve access to the temple, while its promotions department portrayed Eiheiji as an important part of its strategy to increase tourism and to "strengthen our brand power," as one prefectural official put it (Fujita 2016).

While this venture might contrast with Eiheiji's image of monastic austerity, it fits with a growing pattern in contemporary Japan, of religious institutions interacting with secular, commercial, and government agencies to promote themselves as tourist venues in order to encourage visitors. Such engagements with tourism are nothing new either in the context of Japanese religious institutions or in the field of pilgrimage in general—an area in which tourism has recurrently played a significant role (Badone and Roseman 2004; Reader 2014). In Japan, tourism has long been a feature in the landscape of visits to religious sites, whether Buddhist, Shinto, or associated with the folk tradition. Pilgrimages to places such as Ise (location of some of Shinto's most important shrines), as well as Buddhist pilgrimage routes, provided the genesis of an indigenous tourist industry (Kanzaki 1990; Nishigaki 1983; Reader 2014). Shinto shrines and Buddhist temples alike have long been engaged in putting on entertainment spectacles and exhibitions to attract visitors (Thal 2005), while the presence of hot spring facilities on the way to or near shrines and temples was a factor enhancing the appeal of pilgrimages in premodern times (Vaporis 1994, 240–241). Susanne Formanek (1998, 174–183) shows how entertainment and amusement (along with visits to nearby hot springs) became a dominant theme in pilgrimages to the mountain Buddhist site of Tateyama in the Edo (1603–1868) era. As this happened, Formanek (1998) states that the descriptions that local pilgrimage guides (*oshi*) provided for visitors became more oriented toward amusement, while her study of visitors' accounts indicates that while they continued to spend money on charms and offerings at the religious sites of Tateyama, they focused increasingly on the notion of *monomi yusan* (seeing things and enjoying the mountains)—a term widely used for ludic travel in premodern times (176). Shinjō Tsunezō, Japan's pre-eminent historian of the social and economic dimensions of premodern visits to temples and shrines in Japan, has similarly emphasized the extent to which visits to Tateyama had, by the early nineteenth century, shifted from being primarily concerned with veneration at the temples there to being predominantly focused on enjoying mountain scenery (1982, 730–731). As Okamoto Ryōsuke (2015) has observed, pilgrimage and tourism were so entwined in Edo-era Japan that one could not separate them into distinguishable categories (4–5). While Okamoto notes that in the modern period attempts have been made to set tourism apart from pilgrimage and religious travel, he is clear that in Japan the two remain deeply entwined to the extent that they cannot be categorically separated. This is a perspective that has been broadly accepted in the field, with the general thrust of studies linking pilgrimage and tourism in Japan, and showing clearly how problematic it is to view them through a binary structure in which one element (tourism) is viewed as a disjunctive secular intrusion into, or contradiction of, the "sacred" domain of shrines and temples (Asakawa 2008; Reader 2014; Yamanaka 2012). To that degree tourism, by which I mean travel for the purpose of getting away and/or taking a break from one's normal environment to seek enjoyment and entertainment, as well as looking at interesting places including historical and cultural sites, is an embedded element in Japanese visits to religious sites and institutions.

At the same time, it is also recognized that the rise of modernity has enhanced the emphasis on tourism in increasingly overt forms. Studies of pilgrimage guidebooks for the famed Japanese Buddhist Saikoku Kannon pilgrimage route (which takes in thirty-three historically important temples in the region around Kyoto, Osaka, and Nara dedicated to the Bodhisattva Kannon (Skt. Avalokiteśvara)) show that, especially from the nineteenth century onward, they displayed an increasing emphasis on entertainment, tourist sights, hot spring resorts, places to eat, and other detours, with such diversions becoming absorbed into the framework of the Saikoku pilgrimage experience (Barbaro 2013; Foard 1982). This reached a turning point during the 1920s, when, as Paolo Barbaro (2013) has shown, tourist themes became a predominant element in Japanese pilgrimage guidebooks and promotional literature.

During the rise of a modern travel and tourism industry in the 1920s Japan focused on internal travel. This was supported by government policies encouraging the Japanese to travel in their own country and learn about their traditions, culture, and history, thereby fostering a heightened sense of nationalism and national identity. The expansion of national and private rail networks and the development of increasingly comfortable lodging and eating facilities aided the process, as did the development of a mass publishing industry that produced travel-related literature such as magazines, pamphlets, and other advertising material. A variety of travel magazines from the 1920s onward lauded religious sites such as Buddhist temples as cardinal elements in the Japanese emotional landscape,[1] and the state-instituted Japan Tourist Board (JTB) began to publish pilgrimage guidebooks that encouraged people to do them using buses, cars, and trains. Travel magazines ran features on pilgrimages and temples, too, presenting them as cultural sights and tourist attractions and saying that one did not need to have religious faith to visit them (Mori 2005, 47–55; Reader 2014, 106–108). The travel industry, as well as state institutions, thus utilized religious sites as elements in a strategy to increase custom, build a national tourist industry, and encourage people to travel around their own country. As Japan developed as a modern nation, the idea of tourism for its own sake and of travel as a legitimate leisure pastime became increasingly prevalent.

While modern developments thus made leisure and tourist themes, already embedded within pilgrimage and temple visiting, increasingly overt elements in this process, there has, as I argue in the rest of this chapter, been a shift in the balance between pilgrimage and tourism in the past two decades or so. What was formerly a complementary interaction[2] has altered significantly beyond the patterns evident even in the 1920s and Japan's first engagement with mass modern tourism. In the present day, temples and shrines may continue to serve as places where people can engage in religious practices such as praying for various boons and for the well-being of their ancestors. However, as I will show via a number of examples, they have increasingly been transformed, primarily in publicity and promotional literature—even literature at times emanating from and produced by temples themselves—into tourist locations. As I have discussed above, the notion that pilgrimage and tourism could be separated into different fields of activity, with the former identified with the realms of the religious and the latter with that of the secular, has never been viable in

Japanese contexts. However, the examples that I will turn to shortly indicate that ludic, sightseeing, and entertainment-related activities and concepts that are commonly associated with the idea of tourism, have become increasingly prominent in publicity aimed at attracting people to religious sites such as temples. To that degree it would be fair to suggest that the touristic elements of temple visiting have been paramount in the present day.

The factors behind this are multiple and include Japanese national policies on tourism, a focus on concepts of heritage (and particularly of UNESCO-designated World Heritage sites), and constitutional restraints that frame the ways secular government agencies such as tourist offices can talk about religious sites in their promotional literature. Critically, too, they involve the parlous situation many religious institutions, individual places of worship, and pilgrimage sites such as Buddhist temples are experiencing in contemporary Japan—a context in which religious affiliations have been in decline and in which various religious organizations and places of worship have seen a serious drop in visitor numbers.[3] While people do continue to visit temples and shrines, albeit in fewer numbers than before, questions have been raised about the nature of such visits in the present day. Okamoto (2015, 9), for example, refers to "pilgrims without faith" (*shinkō naki junreisha*) to refer to many of these visitors, while the emphasis on tourist themes in contemporary religious sites suggests that they are being increasingly perceived as places to view through a tourist gaze (Urry 1990) in which religious practices have become marginalized. This process is particularly striking in the context of Buddhist temples and pilgrimages in Japan and it is on such institutions and contexts that I focus in the following sections, where I look particularly at the examples of Eiheiji, the aforementioned head temple of the Sōtō Zen Buddhist sect of Kōyasan; the mountain temple-town headquarters of the Shingon Buddhist sect that since 2004 has been included in the UNESCO list of World Heritage sites; and at Japan's best-known Buddhist pilgrimage route, the eighty-eight-stage Shikoku pilgrimage.

Eiheiji as Tourist Spectacle: Factors and Policies

A key backdrop to the Eiheiji venture is the drive by the Japanese government to stimulate tourism in the present day. Tourism, according to the UNWTO (United Nations World Trade Organization), was by 2008 the world's largest industry. In connection with this, in 2008 the Japanese government expanded its Ministry of Land, Infrastructure and Transport into the Ministry of Land, Infrastructure, Transport and Tourism, with a remit to promote the country—and especially rural Japan—as a tourist destination. This built on earlier government-funded activities through agencies such as the JTB to promote tourism that drew attention to temples, shrines, and pilgrimage centers as manifestations of Japan's cultural and artistic heritage and history.

The award of the 2020 Olympics to Tokyo has intensified this focus on tourism as a matter of national policy, underpinned by Prime Minister Abe Shinzō's plan to attract twenty million visitors to Japan by 2020.[4] As a result money has been poured into regional tourism, which is viewed as a mechanism of rural regeneration for areas suffering severe depopulation and economic malaise. This emphasis on tourism as a national policy has also been enhanced by an awareness that when places acquire accreditation as a UNESCO World Heritage Site they can attract visitors on an international scale. The Japanese government, supported by various prefectural administrations, has actively sought such accreditation for a number of sites, including those with religious affiliations, both as a means of bringing in more overseas visitors and as a means of enhancing Japan's international profile and status.[5]

At the same time, there are constraints on how the state can operate in such contexts. A primary resource in the drive to increase tourism at all levels are the numerous religious sites found throughout the country that are regarded as historically important manifestations of Japanese cultural achievements. And here constitutional prerogatives play a major role. Since Japan's war defeat and the promulgation of a constitution in 1946 that severed links between state and religion, the use of state and public funds to support religion and religious activities has been prohibited. This means that while state tourist agencies and government organizations can emphasize the architectural splendor and historical significance of religious institutions such as Buddhist temples as cultural sites and places of national heritage, they cannot promote them *as* religious institutions or because of what they signify in religious terms. They can draw attention to Buddhist statues, images, and paintings as works of art and issue leaflets with photographs of temples and nostalgic phrases that associate them with notions of belonging, identity, and the idea of a Japanese cultural and spiritual homeland (*furusato*).[6] However, they cannot outline the teachings of the sect that built the temple or talk of them as icons to which miraculous powers are attributed that have drawn worshippers for centuries. The same constraints apply to the national state-funded broadcaster NHK, which is legally obliged by its charter to produce television programs about Japanese culture and history but has to avoid publicizing institutions in religious terms. As the producer of a series of NHK documentaries on the Shikoku pilgrimage commented to me, the pilgrimage was an apt subject for a documentary because of its prominence in the history and contemporary life of one of Japan's main islands. However, the documentary producers had to avoid talking about it in terms that might appear to allude to anything associated with religion and faith.

Institutions such as Buddhist temples have found it pragmatic to go along with such policies and tourist campaigns not simply because touristic elements have always been part of the Japanese engagement with religious sites.

Pertinently, present religious institutions in general—and Buddhist temples and pilgrimage sites in particular—have faced serious problems that threaten their very ability to survive or sustain themselves. At Eiheiji, for example, visitor numbers have dropped from well over one million a year in the late 1980s to less than half a million a year recently (Fujita 2016). The falling numbers are a result not just of fewer group tours run by tour companies but also because the Sōtō sect (along with all other Buddhist organizations) is struggling in the face of declining adherents. As temples across the country have lost supporters, the numbers wishing to visit their sect's head temple have been severely reduced. This has led to a loss of income for the temple (as is the sect's declining support structure, which has led to temple closures and a loss of sect taxes paid by temples), affecting the temple's ability to support the monastic training necessary for future generations of priests. Hence Sōtō sect authorities overseeing Eiheiji have been amenable to links with commercial firms and regional authorities, even to the extent of being incorporated into secular state tourist promotional activities aimed at constructing Fukui Prefecture's "brand power."

The problems facing religious institutions in general include rural depopulation, increased competition in the religious field, and a general turn against organized religion, alongside an increasing tendency to eschew engagement even in customary practices such as the memorialization of the dead—practices rooted in social structure and associated with shrines and temples. While this issue extends across the religious spectrum, it is particularly acute for Buddhist temples, which, as various recent studies have shown, face an erosion of their traditional support structures (Nelson 2012; Reader 2011a, 2012; Ukai 2015).

It also is a problem facing many Buddhist pilgrimage routes in Japan. Although one major pilgrimage route centered on Buddhist temples,[7] the Shikoku pilgrimage, involving a journey around the island of Shikoku to visit eighty-eight Buddhist temples, appears to have done well in recent decades (Hoshino and Asakawa 2011; Mori 2005; Reader 2005). However, it is more of an anomaly than anything else in the current context. Examinations of regional pilgrimages such as the eighty-eight-stage Sasaguri pilgrimage route near the city of Fukuoka in Kyushu, and the eighty-eight-site pilgrimage around the Inland Sea island of Shōdoshima (both of which are modeled on the Shikoku pilgrimage), as well as major nationally known pilgrimages such as the Saikoku Kannon pilgrimage, indicate pilgrim numbers at all these sites have fallen since the 1980s (Reader 2014, 6–8, 34–39; Satō 2004).

In such cases the response from priests and the pilgrimage associations they represent[8] has been to increase cooperation with local businesses, tourist offices, and travel companies to create joint publicity campaigns in which the touristic dimensions of such sites are afforded prominence.[9] The impetus for this increased engagement with tourist agencies and government agendas on tourism has been encouraged also by examples of pilgrimage centers and Buddhist sites that appear to have increased their standing through embracing tourism and its associated images of tradition and heritage. It is two such examples—the Shikoku pilgrimage and the famous Shingon Buddhist center at Mount Kōya (Kōyasan)—that I turn to next. In both cases UNESCO World Heritage recognition plays an important part: Kōyasan has been granted such a status while authorities in Shikoku are in the process of campaigning for this status for the pilgrimage. In both cases it will be clear that this has involved an increased orientation toward tourism and a weakening of traditional religious practices.

Shikoku and Heritage

The Shikoku pilgrimage is often highlighted as a success story in contemporary Japanese pilgrimage terms and as Japan's most popular Buddhist pilgrimage in the present day. However, this was not always the case. Until at least the 1950s it was regarded as a largely ascetic pilgrimage done mainly by devout and poor people. It was only after the development of bus tours in the 1950s and skillful publicity—produced in close collaboration between the temples, regional and national tourist agencies, commercial firms, and transport companies—that the site's image changed. Thereafter it has been portrayed in the guise of a special Japanese spiritual homeland imbued with images of nature and Japanese tradition and identity. Such image construction, along with the development of better facilities for pilgrims—notably from the mid-1980s—helped increase visitor numbers, as well as efforts to displace the Saikoku pilgrimage as Japan's leading Buddhist route (Hoshino and Asakawa 2011; Mori 2005; Reader 2005, 2014, 36–39). Transport companies such as the Shikoku-based Iyo Tetsu Bus Company, which organized the first bus package pilgrimages tours and remains a major carrier of pilgrims, also catered to the wishes of those visiting the temples by including regional tourist attractions and sites into many of their package tours—something that Iyo Tetsu began to do in 1979 (Mori 2005, 165). As officials of various companies have informed me in recent years, it has become increasingly common for people inquiring about pilgrimage tours of Shikoku to ask for some of the island's (non-pilgrimage-related) tourist sites in their itineraries.

Although the Shikoku pilgrimage thus appears to still attract pilgrims—especially in contrast to pilgrimages such as Saikoku, Sasaguri, and Shōdoshima—priests and pilgrimage authorities on the island worry that the broader turn away from religious engagement and from other pilgrimage sites might in turn affect Shikoku (Reader 2014, 174). It is for such reasons that the temple association overseeing the pilgrimage has been a seemingly willing affiliate with campaigns seeking to get the pilgrimage accreditation under

UNESCO's World Heritage charter. This campaign led to a 2008 request to the Japanese government (only national governments can make the formal application to UNESCO) to nominate the pilgrimage. The application was unsuccessful, but recently, with the encouragement of the Japanese government, a revised application was submitted in August 2016.

The campaign has involved a variety of interest groups, all, in different ways, motivated by an agenda centered on strategies to revive the island's depressed economy through tourism. The island, Japan's fourth biggest, is largely an economic backwater these days. Its former industries such as shipbuilding and agriculture are now marginalized, and its population falling. Concerns about the implications for its long-term economic future have led both the national and regional prefectural governments to look for ways to revitalize the area, and tourism, already an element in national economic strategies, has been highlighted as a key element in this potential revitalization. The pilgrimage, which circles the island and passes through all four of its prefectures, has been flagged as Shikoku's most striking cultural and historical resource in this context. Seeking UNESCO World Heritage status for the pilgrimage was viewed by priests and government agencies alike (and by commercial firms with a vested interest in Shikoku) as a key element in such schemes to attract more people—both international tourists and Japanese visitors—to the island (Hoshino and Asakawa 2011, 159–168). Examples of other pilgrimage places that have flourished after gaining UNESCO status (for example Santiago de Compostela in Spain and, as I describe below, Kōyasan in Japan) have also been influential in shaping attitudes to the Shikoku UNESCO campaign.[10]

Yet to ensure they conform to UNESCO guidelines and to Japanese government requirements (which constitutionally mean not supporting any religious activities), the temples have accepted the need to downplay any focus on miracles and even some traditional religious practices, instead emphasizing the pilgrimage as a cultural phenomenon embedded in Japan's history. As I have noted elsewhere (Okamoto 2015, 91; Reader 2014, 180–181) the desire to make the pilgrimage appear suitable for such status (and also to attract better-off visitors keen on seeing sites of cultural heritage) has involved trying to erase some practices (such as begging for alms) that some pilgrims have traditionally done and even the removal of items suggestive of miraculous events in the pilgrimage.[11] The rhetoric associated with the pilgrimage in Shikoku has also been reshaped through this process. The pilgrimage is spoken of as an expression of Shikoku culture (Shikoku *no bunka*) and as an exotic destination redolent of Japanese tradition and culture, rather than anything to do with unseemly superstitions and religious traditions. This rhetorical agenda has been assiduously promoted by interest groups, including nonprofit organizations set up by local Chambers of Commerce, as well as by the island's universities, many of which are state institutions receiving public money. They now offer courses on the pilgrimage and its history that portray it through a nonreligious lens as a cultural phenomenon linked to notions of island identity and community.

Some of the agencies and interest groups involved in the Shikoku heritage campaign have sought to reshape the agenda also by talking of the Shikoku pilgrimage in product terms, as a "brand," while stating that in its modern guise its focus has shifted from faith to health, sports, and exercise (Reader 2011b, 96–97). The pilgrimage is now also promoted as a "hiking trail," with recent studies indicating that many of those who now walk the route view it as a walking tour or hiking holiday rather than as a journey of faith (Mori 2005, 12–42), and has even been described by one campaigning interest group online as a "theme park" (Reader 2011b, 96–97). While such references and terminologies are the product of campaign groups situated in the secular sphere, they are indicative of the recent trend in Shikoku toward increasingly portraying the pilgrimage in ways that distance it from its religious roots while heightening its appeal as a cultural and tourist phenomenon.

Kōyasan and Heritage: More Tourists, Fewer Rituals?

An example that has influenced Shikoku temple and civic authorities in their quest for UNESCO Heritage status is the Shingon Buddhist temple town of Kōyasan in Japan. A recent study by Ian Astley (2015), who has conducted research at Kōyasan over more than three decades, indicates how its UNESCO designation (alongside other places in the Yoshino-Kumano region) has impacted the site's activities. Kōyasan is one of the most striking Buddhist centers in Japan, a temple town amidst the mountains and forests of the Kii peninsula. It headquarters a major Buddhist sect with numerous temples, important Buddhist artworks, and an atmospheric graveyard set amidst avenues of vast cedar trees and centered on the mausoleum of Kūkai (the founder of Shingon in Japan and one of Japanese Buddhism's most important figures). As Astley notes, Kōyasan has been visited by tourists at least since restrictions on access were removed by the government in the late nineteenth century (until 1873 women were forbidden from entering its precincts), and especially since the 1930s when the Nankai railway opened a line linking Kōyasan to the major conurbation of Osaka. One effect of the train line was to reshape visitor itineraries, who began to go directly to Kōyasan by train, thereby missing several temples that pilgrims used to call in at on their way. Via the railway, Kōyasan itself became a single focus rather than an end point on a route. The building of the railway line also helped concentrate visitor donations, offerings, and purchases of talismans on Kōyasan itself. However, temples previously visited by pilgrims but now bypassed due to the railway lost out and even became derelict.

However, it has been the award of the 2004 UNESCO designation that has been most dramatic in altering the landscape. As Astley (2015) comments, the UNESCO Heritage inscription bestowing this status draws on: "the mainstream projection of an exotic Japan promoted by official bodies such as the Agency for Cultural Affairs (which collated and submitted the definitive documents) and the Japan Tourist Board (JTB)" (528). As he notes, the designation led to efforts by the temples and the lodges (*shukubō*) they run, which are the sole means of accommodation in the town, to transform themselves into tourist sites and luxury accommodations for international visitors. One such example is Fukuchiin, the largest *shukubō* (temple lodging at which visitors can stay overnight on payment of a fee) at Kōyasan, which bought the rights to hot mineral water discovered under Kōyasan in 2005, and thereafter marketed itself as Fukuchiin Onsen Kōyasan (Fukuchiin Hot Spring Resort Kōyasan). Astley also shows how recent promotional literature from the town's tourist office and its temples have emphasized the aesthetic and scenic dimensions of Kōyasan, and have talked of it as a place for hiking.

While international visitor numbers have increased since the UNESCO designation, the town's population has decreased, as have Japanese visitor numbers. The former is linked to a fall in the numbers coming to Kōyasan to train for the priesthood and to study at the sect's university there, and the latter to the general pattern I have identified earlier, of a broader Japanese estrangement from religious institutions. Just as Eiheiji has suffered from the weakening structures and support levels of its sect, so too has Kōyasan. The knock-on effect has, as Astley indicates, been a fall in the number of rituals performed and sought at Kōyasan. As this has happened those overseeing the temples of Kōyasan have become more reliant on income from foreign tourists who come to see Kōyasan—the UNESCO World Heritage and tourist site, rather than Kōyasan—a location for Japanese Shingon Buddhist followers to pay reverence at the headquarters of their sect. As the numbers of the latter continue to fall, the reliance on the former will doubtless increase. Likewise, as regional Shingon temples face the problems indicated above, their incomes decline, meaning they send less sect taxes to the headquarters. This thereby intensifies the sectarian headquarters at Kōyasan reliance on foreign tourist income.

Astley's conclusion is that while tourist activities predate modern times,

> the fabric of life on the mountain has changed over the past three decades and that although the aspects of commerce and marketing were readily obvious before, its traditional religious activities have decreased in intensity compared to the touristic elements that the [UNESCO] Inscription has helped to promote. (2015, 540)

A further point to note in this context is that in several interviews with Shingon Buddhist priests running temples in areas away from Kōyasan, I have heard a recurrent complaint that regional temples are becoming increasingly alienated from Kōyasan. As one priest said to me, temples such as his faced serious longer-term difficulties because of falling rural populations along with a general turn away from established religions. In such contexts they needed help from their headquarters—from financial aid, advice, and support to developing sect-wide policies and strategies to counter these problems. Yet they get little or no support because, in his view, Shingon headquarters had become more interested in tourism and foreign visitors than in the needs of sect temples distant from Kōyasan. This is an issue I have heard articulated by other priests concerned that international tourists and a focus on tourism have displaced religious rituals as a driving force at the headquarters of their sect.

A New Campaign: Pilgrimage from the Station

Both Shikoku and Kōyasan appear, at least in the shorter term, to have increased their flows of visitors through the use of tourist- and heritage-related strategies, and their success has encouraged those overseeing temples reliant on pilgrims and worried about falling numbers, to become increasingly active in engaging with themes of tourism. As I have noted above, temple authorities in Sasaguri, Shōdoshima, and Saikoku have been trying to do this for some years, and recent events indicate that their efforts continue unabated. In 2014 for example, the civic authorities that administer the Sasaguri District sponsored an event to promote the local pilgrimage as a tourist resource that could boost the local town's economy.[12] The pilgrimage has held promotional events, with the cooperation of the area's commercial firms and civic authorities, at several locations within easy access of Sasaguri. This serves to publicize the pilgrimage, while regional tourist offices try to attract overseas tourists to the temples, notably from nearby Korea and China, who are increasingly visiting Japan.

Similarly the Saikoku temples are continuing to work with agencies such as Japan Rail West (hereafter JR), the national rail company that serves the area where the Saikoku temples are. On a recent visit to Japan (in June 2016) I went to three Saikoku temples and talked to officials there. Each temple office displayed posters of a joint campaign between the Saikoku temples and JR initiated in 2014 and designed to run for five years. I was aware that they had run previous campaigns (such as the one in 2008, mentioned in Reader 2014, 91) and so asked about the new one. The answer I received at each temple was the same: pilgrim numbers were still falling and so the temples needed new promotions, while JR was keen to increase passenger numbers in an era when more and more people owned cars and used trains less.

The types of image depicted on the posters had not changed much from earlier campaigns: photos portrayed the temples and route through a lens of beauty, history, and culture, and as sights to see and places to engage with Japanese cultural tradition and heritage. For example, one of the posters advertising the 2008 campaign depicted at its center a long wooden corridor and stairs leading up to a temple, framed by hanging paper lanterns, alongside a Buddhist statue and a photograph of a temple gateway set against hills and blue skies.[13] The posters also offered a variety of goods and souvenirs that could be claimed by those who visited a set number of temples. The campaigns had all used the phrase "starting from the station" (*eki kara hajimaru*) as a key slogan, and had indicated that the Saikoku temples and JR were joint participants in the campaign. Yet there were also perceptible differences from the posters and offerings I had noted from previous campaigns, and the 2008 and 2014 poster content that seemed especially indicative to me.

In 2008 a key poster (see Reader 2014, 92, for an illustration) depicted a long wooden walkway and steps with lanterns leading up to a temple, a Buddhist temple gate set against a largely cloudless sky, and a side view of a Buddhist statue. Across the top were the words: *eki kara hajimaru kokoro no michishirube: Saigoku sanjūsankasho junrei no tab*i (starting from the station, a guide to the spirit: A journey to the Saikoku thirty-three-stage pilgrimage). The involvement of JR was noted at the bottom of the poster, as well as items related to pilgrimage and prayer such as *sange* (leaf-shaped cards with Buddhist inscriptions) that would be given as presents (*purezento*) to those who did the pilgrimage.

In 2010 the posters I saw featured JR's involvement much more outwardly and the title of the campaign as depicted on the posters and JR's website was different. It stated *eki kara hajimaru Saikoku sanjüsankasho meguri sutanpu rari*[14] (starting from the station, the Saikoku thirty-three-site pilgrimage stamp rally). The poster and website both offered a variety of items for those who did this, including *sange,* but also small daypacks, watches, and DVDs. The types of goods one received depended on how many temples one visited. In 2016 the posters (associated with the campaign that began in 2014) used the same terminology as 2010 but without the depiction of goods such as daypacks and with more emphasis on resplendent temple scenery. However, JR's website offered a variety of goods from watches to rosaries for those who visited various numbers of temples.

There were two things that stood out for me. The first was the change of terminology since 2008 when one started from the station (as in later years), but in which the pilgrimage was cited as a guide (*michishirube*) to the spirit (*kokoro*), and in which the traditional term for pilgrimage (*junrei*) was used. After 2010 the journey was described as a *meguri*—another term associated with pilgrimage although not the formal term traditionally associated with Saikoku, and one more associated with simply "going around" an area. The idea of the pilgrimage as a guide to the spirit had disappeared, while the pilgrimage was referred to as a "stamp rally"—a term used in Japan to refer to the popular custom of stamping a plain book or sheet of paper with the rubber stamps of different places. At numerous sites in Japan—not just temples and shrines but tourist spots such as castles and museums, and also at stations, hot springs, and the like—one finds a red ink pad plus special stamp for the location, which people can use to stamp into whatever item (a notebook, a special commemorative book, or even a sheet of paper) they carry for the purpose. Traditionally on pilgrimages one carries either a special pilgrim's book or scroll onto which the temple seal (*shuin*) is stamped by temple authorities as a sign one has visited the religious site, and a completed book or scroll from a pilgrimage bearing such temple stamps has come to be viewed in Japan as an item of special religious meaning. Stamp rallies, by contrast, have normally had no specific religious connotation and are more associated with tourist excursions and places.[15] By referring to the pilgrimage as a "stamp rally" it appeared that the railway authorities had in effect transformed it into a secular event on a level with the activities of Japanese tourists who, on visiting hot spring resorts, do a "stamp rally" and collect the seals of the local sights.

Moreover, in order to qualify for the various items being offered, participants had to do two things: to get the *shuin* of the temple in their pilgrim's book and then take this to the nearby JR station and show this to the station staff—who would then affix a station stamp on a special stamp card provided by JR. In other words, JR staff would serve along with temple officials as validators of the journey; the goods given as a reward were for visiting not simply the temples but the stations as well. The campaign to boost visitors to the Saikoku temples had, in other words, by 2016, been transformed from a pilgrimage into a stamp rally that linked stations and temples together as joint validators of a pilgrimage (*meguri*) that would entitle visitors to claim goods as rewards.[16]

Tourism and pilgrimage are interlocking categories. In Japan historically, visits (pilgrimages) to sites such as Buddhist temples have been interwoven with ludic and sightseeing themes. The development of a modern travel and tourist industry as Japan emerged as a modern nation from the mid-nineteenth century onward has meant that the "tourist" dimensions of travel to religious sites have assumed an increasingly prominent position in the promotional literature produced about pilgrimages and temples, and in the minds of those who visit such places. These developments have been intensified by processes that have conditioned attitudes to religion and religious sites in Japan—notably the retreat from religious engagement and the eroding structures of the religious establishment to which Buddhism belongs, as well as factors such as rural depopulation and national policies that emphasize tourism as a mechanism of economic growth and regional regeneration.

While such developments have not impacted Buddhist temples alone, it has been the Buddhist temple tradition that has been the most affected by current patterns of decline, as discussions about the disappearance and closures of Buddhist temples throughout Japan indicate (Ukai 2015). The falling number of visitors to pilgrimage routes such as Saikoku and the worries about the longer-term viability of many pilgrimages have encouraged temple priests and pilgrimage associations to be ever-more accommodating to the various secular, commercial, and state agencies that want to promote their sites through the lenses of heritage and tourism.

This has had a number of implications. At Kōyasan tourism has been stimulated by its UNESCO Heritage status, while religious rituals and visits by Japanese people (many of whom, earlier, would have been visiting because of their membership in the Shingon sect) have declined. On Shikoku the increased emphasis on heritage and tourism has gone hand in hand with a downplaying and marginalization of religious practices such as begging for alms by pilgrims. Prominent monastic institutions such as Eiheiji, long revered for their austerities and as centers of meditation, now allow themselves to be promoted as tourist sites. In a secular state where civic authorities are precluded from supporting religion yet want to utilize famed temples and pilgrimage sites for the purpose of tourist development, the weakening support structures of religious institutions have opened the door for secular agencies to push forward their tourist strategies while making religious institutions more amenable to cooperate with them.

Studies of how temples and shrines used attractions such as hot springs and tourist attractions to stimulate visits to their institutions in the past show that priests have historically been in the vanguard of such activities. As Thal (2005) has demonstrated, throughout the Edo era and beyond, priests at the Konpira shrine—a major Shinto shrine in Shikoku—put on theatrical events, Sumo wrestling tournaments, and markets in order to encourage more visitors, reasoning as they did that a lively economy of entertainment would not simply complement the religious activities of the shrine but would please the gods venerated there (74). As I have discussed in the context of Shikoku (Reader 2005, 167–183), the association of pilgrimage temples and the priests running it, were deeply involved in working with bus companies to develop the pilgrimage in the postwar era. Temple priests continue to play a role in this context, as can be seen in their cooperation in Shikoku heritage campaigns, their encouragement of the growth of international tourists at Kōyasan, and Eiheiji's collaboration with a construction firm and the prefectural tourist agency. Yet it is hard to avoid the view that control of the agenda has shifted toward the secular agencies involved. Rather than shaping the agenda and the context in which tourist activities and attractions fit into the ambit of a temple or pilgrimage site, Buddhist priests are becoming subsidiary agents operating from a position of weakness compared to government agencies and tourist offices whose remit is squarely focused on portraying religious institutions in ways designed to maximize tourist visits and economic success.

In their Introduction Courtney Bruntz and Brooke Schedneck have drawn attention to themes such as commodification, secularization, and the construction of imaginaries as salient elements in the relationship between Buddhism and tourism in the modern world. The Japanese examples I have highlighted here in many ways express such themes. The landscape of temples and pilgrimages has, as the depictions of scenery, tradition, and heritage indicate, been reshaped at places such as Kōyasan and Shikoku, to produce new imaginaries of the exotic and to re-present them as tourist sites imbued with nostalgic notions of heritage and tradition that can appeal to people both in and beyond Japan. The new imaginary is one where heritage, culture, and representations of Japanese tradition take precedence while prayers are hidden. The processes of inducing and encouraging visitors by offering goods and stamps (provided by station staff) for those who visit pilgrimage sites, would appear to be a further example of a continuing process of commodification. From the perspective of government officials charged with implementing national strategies or seeking to revive a failing local economy, a famous temple or pilgrimage is a vital commodity, to be used as such to hopefully attract tourists.

Yet I would suggest a further and more deep-seated development is also at hand here; rather than just a process of (re)imagining and of commodification, there is also one of reshaping what we might consider as the domain of religion and of the secular. Okamoto Ryōsuke (2015) has recently examined the emergence of the concept of sacred sites (*seichi*) as it is being used in present-day Japan. A term long associated with traditional religious sites such as Buddhist temples and Shinto shrines, with traditional pilgrimages such as Shikoku, and with mountains that have been viewed as abodes of the gods, the term has in recent times also been applied to new types of places and new modes of sacralization. It has, for example, been appropriated by fans who visit sites and locations associated with and depicted in popular anime films. They have created the concept of *anime junrei* (anime pilgrimages), appropriating, as they have done so, the traditional Japanese term (*junrei*) for pilgrimage. Other places not formally associated with religious traditions but that have acquired a special significance in modern Japanese popular culture, such as the stadium where Japan's annual high school baseball tournament is held, have been incorporated into this notion of *seichi*.[17] Okamoto (2015) attributes these phenomena to the secularization of society and the weakening of established religions, arguing that in a sense such practices and concepts are filling the spaces created by the waning of traditional religions (207). Rather than simply being a process of secularization, it is, he contends, a sign that the very notion and nature of religion is changing and being reshaped in modern society in ways that absorb and incorporate new phenomena such as anime sites that are grounded in the secular and commercial worlds yet are increasingly assuming the shape of sacred places.

Such ideas to a degree resonate with my discussions of the advancing emphasis on tourist images and agendas in the context of Buddhist pilgrimage places in Japan. Yet, while this may involve a reshaping of notions of religion and, as such, of pilgrimage—issues that require fuller discussion and analysis[18]—it is also a sign of the continuing marginalization of traditional modes of religious practice associated with Buddhist temples, and a changing balance in the nature of interactions between temples and the interest groups and civic agencies keen to promote them. Temples are increasingly becoming commodities to be used in pursuit of national economic policies. The secularizing tendencies of society and the turn away from religious institutions have placed them in a position where accepting their status as entities and commodities to be used for secular agendas looks like a viable survival strategy. As this has happened, space has opened up for other interests (for example, fans of anime films) to make claims about notions such as the sacred, and to claim their position in the framework of pilgrimage. The ramifications of this are a matter for future discussion. What is clear is that the ways in which the agendas of temples worried by fears of decline and the loss of clienteles, are increasingly shaped by secular agencies of government and of transport and travel firms, illustrate far more than just an increased focus on tourism as a key element in the dynamics of Buddhist temples. They suggest that the very landscape in which Buddhism, temples, and the pilgrimages associated with them operate in Japan, is being reshaped in ways that give weight to the forces of secularization and to the erosion of notions that temples are specially religious spaces.

Notes

1 This is a term I used in Reader (2005, 5–6, 39–41) to refer to the ways in which both physical landscape and stories, legends and narratives of identity are interwoven to create a sense of belonging that simultaneously idealizes the landscape and affords it special meaning.

2 I borrow this notion from the work of Knut Aukland (2016).

3 In Reader (2011a, 2012) I discuss these issues at length and provide statistical data to illustrate the severe decline in affiliations, especially relating to Buddhist temples, and to the widespread closure of temples throughout Japan.

4 This target has already been reached and it is now being suggested that a new target of forty million is being considered for 2020.

5 For fuller discussion of earlier tourist policies in Japan, see Leheny (2003), on religion and UNESCO Heritage, see the essays in Yamanaka (2012), and for insights into the notions of regional and national economic regeneration via tourism, see Motani and Yamada (2016).

6 There are numerous discussions of how nostalgia and nostalgic images—notably the idea of *furusato* (a term meaning native village or homeland), and *kokoro no furusato* (spiritual homeland)—have been co-opted in Japan to create a sense of nationalistic nostalgia, belonging, meaning, and identity centered on specific loca-

tions, including religious sites (Ivy 1995; Reader 1987; Robertson 1988).

7 It should be noted that in Japan the most common pattern of pilgrimages in Buddhist contexts is for pilgrimages to consist of linked circuits of a number of pilgrimage sites—usually Buddhist temples or wayside halls of worship—rather than just one pilgrimage destination. On the structure of Japanese Buddhist pilgrimages see Reader and Swanson (1997).

8 Because Buddhist pilgrimages in Japan commonly involve a number of temples linked together within a single pilgrimage framework, they invariably have one pilgrimage association (*reijōkai*) that coordinates and oversees pilgrimage activities and the production of publicity materials.

9 I have discussed these examples (Shōdoshima, Sasaguri, and Saikoku) elsewhere and drawn attention to an increasing engagement, in each case, with tourist agencies as pilgrim numbers have continued to fall (Reader 2014).

10 I base these comments on discussions with a number of interested parties including temple priests in Shikoku between 2008 and 2010, and have written in more detail about the issue and the original 2008 application (Reader 2014, 173–182).

11 As I noted in Reader (2014), a collection of crutches and similar aids that had long been displayed at Iyataniji, one of the Shikoku temples, as markers of claimed miraculous events that had occurred there, was removed in 2005 as part of efforts by the temples to project a more "modern" image of the pilgrimage—one that was not associated with elements of "superstition" and miracle tales (169–170). In addition, temple authorities have banned pilgrims from carrying out the traditional Buddhist practice of *takuhatsu* (soliciting alms) in the precincts of the temples. This practice was a staple mode of economic support for pilgrims in earlier eras, and had largely died out in modern times. However, some pilgrims continued to use the practice, leading temple authorities to enforce a ban, because they felt that begging pilgrims would upset other visitors and would not fit with the campaign to get the pilgrimage World Heritage status (Reader 2014, 170).

12 Information from Yamanaka Hiroshi, October 25, 2014.

13 See Reader (2014, 932) for the photograph of this poster.

14 See: http://www.jr-odekake.net/navi/saigoku/#station, accessed March 1, 2017.

15 For example, on a recent visit to Japan in March 2017, I visited Tawarayama Onsen, a small rural village with hot springs claimed to be good for one's health. The local inns and businesses there were holding a Tawarayama Onsen hina meguri sutampu rari (Tawarayama Hot Springs Doll's Festival pilgrimage stamp rally) of displays of *hina* (traditional Japanese dolls) in a numbered route around the town, as a means of attracting custom.

16 https://www.westjr.co.jp/press/article/items/140526_00_saigoku.pdf.

17 In a sense Okamoto is rearticulating arguments made by Reader and Walter (1993) and by Margry (2008) in extending discussions of pilgrimage and "sacred places" beyond the traditional boundaries of religious institutions.

18 It is my plan to develop these issues (along with the themes explored initially in Reader [2011a, 2012]) in a book that looks at secularizing processes and the meanings and (re)definitions of "religion" in twenty-first-century Japan.

References

Asakawa Yasuhiro. 2008. *Junrei no bunkajinruigakuteki kenkyū: Shikoku henro no settaibunka*. Tokyo: Kokon Shoin.

Astley, Ian. 2015. "Space, Time and Heritage on a Japanese Sacred Site: The Religious Geography of Kōyasan." In *The Changing World Religions Map: Sacred Places, Identities, Practices and Politics,* edited by Stanley D. Brunn, 523–544. Dordrecht, The Netherlands: Springer Science and Media.

Aukland, Knut. 2016. "Tours, Trade and Temples: Hindu Pilgrimage in the Age of Global Tourism." PhD diss., University of Bergen, Norway.

Badone, Ellen, and Sharon R. Roseman, eds. 2004. *Intersecting Journeys: The Anthropology of Pilgrimage and Tourism*. Urbana and Chicago: University of Illinois Press.

Barbaro, Paolo. 2013. "*La mise en discours des pèlerinages au Japon depuis l'époque d'Edo: Pour une théorie de l'interversion réciproque entre expérience et récit.*" PhD diss., École Pratique des Hautes Études, Paris.

Foard, James. 1982. "The Boundaries of Compassion: Buddhism and National Tradition in Japanese Pilgrimage." *Journal of Asian Studies* 16 (2): 231–251.

Formanek, Susanne. 1998. "Pilgrimage in the Edo Period: Forerunner of Modern Domestic Tourism?: The Example of the Pilgrimage to Tateyama." In *The Culture of Japan as Seen through Its Leisure,* edited by Sepp Linhart and Sabine Fruhstuck, 165–193. Albany: SUNY Press.

Fujita, Junko. 2016. "Japan's rural temples see the light in luxury tourism." *The Japan Times,* January 5. http://www.japantimes.co.jp/news/2016/01/05/national/japans-rural-temples-see-the-light-in-luxury-tourism/#.VrN2SkvRc07.

Hoshino Eiki and Asakawa Yasuhiro. 2011. *Shikoku henro: samazamana inori no sekai*. Tokyo: Furukawa Kōbunkan.

Ivy, Marilyn. 1995. *Discourses of the Vanishing*. Chicago: University of Chicago Press.

Kanzaki Noritake. 1990. *Kankō minzokugaku e no tabi*. Tokyo: Kawade Shobō

Leheny, David. 2003. *The Rules of Play: National Identity and the Shaping of Japanese Leisure*. Ithaca, NY, and London: Cornell University Press.

Margry, Peter Jan, ed. 2008. *Shrines and Pilgrimage in the Modern World: New Itineraries into the Sacred*. Amsterdam: Amsterdam University Press.

Mori Masato. 2005. *Shikoku henro no kindaika: modan henro kara iyashi no tabi made*. Osaka: Sōgensha.

Motani Kosuke and Yamada Keiichirō. 2016. *Kankō rikkoku no shōtai*. Tokyo: Shincho Shinsho.

Nelson, John K. 2012. "Japanese Secularities and the Decline of Temple Buddhism." *Journal of Religion in Japan* 1 (1): 37–60.

Nishigaki Seiji. 1983. *O-Ise mairi*. Tokyo: Iwanami Shinsho.

Okamoto Ryōsuke. 2015. *Seichi junrei: sekai isan hara anime no mutai made*. Tokyo: Chūkō Shinsho.

Reader, Ian. 1987. "Back to the Future: Images of Nostalgia and Renewal in a Japanese Religious Context." *Japanese Journal of Religious Studies* 14 (4): 287–303.

———. 2011a. "Buddhism in Crisis? Institutional Decline in Modern Japan." *Buddhist Studies Review* 28 (2): 233–263.

———. 2005. *Making Pilgrimages: Meaning and Practice in Shikoku*. Honolulu: University of Hawai'i Press.

———. 2014. *Pilgrimage in the Marketplace*. New York: Routledge.

———. 2012. "Secularisation R.I.P? Nonsense! The 'Rush Hour Away from the Gods' and the Decline of Religion in Contemporary Japan." *The Journal of Religion in Japan* 1 (1): 7–36.

———. 2011b. "The Shikoku Pilgrimage Online." In *Japanese Religions on the Internet: Innovation, Representation and Authority,* edited by Erica Baffellii, Ian Reader, and Birgit Staemmler, 80–100. Routledge Studies in Religion, Media and Culture. New York: Routledge.

Reader, Ian, and Paul L. Swanson. 1997. "Editors' Introduction: Pilgrimage in the Japanese Religious Tradition." *Japanese Journal of Religious Studies* 24 (3–4): 225–270.

Reader, Ian, and Tony Walter, eds. 1993. *Pilgrimage in Popular Culture*. Basingstoke, UK, and New York: Palgrave.

Robertson, Jennifer. 1988. "Furusato Japan: The Culture and Politics of Nostalgia." *Politics, Culture and Society* 1 (4): 494–518.

Satō Hisamitsu. 2004. *Henro to junrei no shakaigaku*. Kyoto: Jimbo Shoin.
Shinjō Tsunezō. 1982. *Shaji sankei no shakai keizaishiteki kenkyū*. Tokyo: Hanawa Shobō.
Thal, Sarah. 2005. *Rearranging the Landscape of the Gods: The Politics of a Pilgrimage Site in Japan, 1573–1912*. Chicago: University of Chicago Press.
Ukai Hidenori. 2015. *Jiin shōmetsu: ushinawareru 'chihō' to 'shūkyō.'* Tokyo: Nikkei BP Sha.
Urry, John. 1990. *The Tourist Gaze*. London: Sage.
Vaporis, Constantine Nomikos. 1994. *Breaking Barriers: Travel and the State in Early Modern Japan*. Cambridge, MA: Harvard University Press.
Yamanaka Hiroshi, ed. 2012. *Shūkyō to tsūrizumu: seinaru mono no henyō to jizoku*. Tokyo: Sekai Shisōsha.

PART III

Commodification and Its Consequences

9

Interrogating Religious Tourism at Buddhist Monasteries in China

Brian J. Nichols

TOURISM CAN BE DESTRUCTIVE TO AN ENVIRONMENT conducive to contemplative religious practices, yet temples and monasteries actively promote themselves as tourist sites. It is tempting to read such commercially motivated behaviors as examples of commodification at the expense of religiosity, but what we now call tourism has arguably enjoyed a long history in Buddhism. This chapter aims to contextualize religious tourism within Buddhist history in China, seeking to determine what may or may not be new in the growing religious tourism industry in China. In addition, this work, based on two years of fieldwork in China spread out over ten years from 2005 to 2012, will examine how some temples may mitigate the ill effects of tourism, how conflicts related to tourist development sometimes boil over in protests or violence, and how such incidents have been resolved.

Several monks I have interviewed recognize the harmful effects of tourism on Buddhist temples. In the words of one of my interviewees at Quanzhou Kaiyuan Monastery in Fujian: "Monks should practice meditation, the monastery should be peaceful and quiet, but on account of the tourist industry we have too many visitors which destroys the peaceful atmosphere of the monastery."[1] Travelers may have an impression of Buddhist decline in China after visiting any number of popular tourist temples such as Beijing's Yonghe Gong (Lama Temple), Beijing's Baita Temple (White Pagoda Temple), Shanghai's Jade Buddha Temple, Famen Temple outside Xian, or Shaolin Temple near Luoyang. However, as I have written elsewhere, such touristically oriented temples are only part of the story, and increasingly, perhaps, the smaller part. What is arguably more common is the rebuilding of temples by clergy driven to reclaim sites for the sangha and the restoration of monastic Buddhism (Nichols forthcoming).[2]

In this chapter I interrogate what seems to be a facile opposition between economic development and religious cultivation. In particular, I examine the question of commodification and the complaint of negative impacts of tourism on religious sites. These issues have been identified as two of the four dominant themes in research on religion and tourism by Timothy and Olson (2006).[3] These two issues, which are often treated together in discussions of tourism and religion, should be distinguished.[4] I investigate commodification and negative impacts separately based on the following two questions: Is commodification contrary or corrosive to the principles of Buddhism as manifested in the history of Chinese Buddhism? Is tourism destructive to the religious environment of Buddhist temples in China? Answering the first question requires carefully defining commodification, identifying the traditional place of commerce in Chinese Buddhism, determining what commercial transactions are new, and the potential problems they may cause. To answer the question about the impact of tourism on the religious environment I will draw on my own fieldwork at Quanzhou Kaiyuan Temple, a Tang dynasty temple which survives with relics from each imperial dynasty since its founding. It receives thousands of tourists per week and is home to about one hundred monks engaged in various forms of monastic practice. I also draw on the research of other scholars studying Mount Putuo, Mount Wutai, and other sites (Ryan and Gu 2010; Shackley 2006; Wong, McIntosh, and Ryan 2012).

The Question of Commodification

In interrogating the claim that touristic or economic development is destructive to the character or principles of Buddhism, my principal interlocutor will be Venerable Dr. Jing Yin, former director of Buddhist Studies at Hong Kong University and currently abbot of Po Lin Monastery in Hong Kong. In particular I will analyze the ideas he presented in a 2006 book chapter titled "Buddhism and Economic Reform in Mainland China." Jing Yin presents a view that emphasizes the dangers of tourist development at religious sites.[5] He notes the dramatic increase in income of monasteries that have developed tertiary industries, such as vegetarian restaurants, souvenir shops, and guesthouses as a means of generating income. Jing Yin notes that many of these monasteries have not only been able to become self-sufficient, but have also been able to make significant contributions to charities. He notes, for example, that Fujian's Nanputuo Monastery had donated more than 118 million RMB to social welfare projects between 1993 and 2002 (Jing Yin 2006, 89). Despite these advantages, Jing Yin argues that the focus on economic development is destructive to the religious character of the monasteries:

> Economic independence has improved the standard of living of the sangha, helping to renovate monasteries and to contribute to the general welfare of Chinese society. However, becoming rich has also brought with it problems that *challenge the very survival of Buddhism in China*. (2006, 90, emphasis added)

He elaborates his concern for the "very survival of Buddhism in China":

> From a Buddhist perspective, one can say that the one-sided economic development in many monasteries has made them *lose their distinctively Buddhist characteristics*. . . . Monasteries commonly operate vegetarian restaurants, guest houses, souvenir shops, and food and drink booths. Some even go to the extreme of running factories and operating companies. The long-term effect is that the market economy is *seriously hurting the religious nature of the monasteries*. Once monasteries become large-scale enterprises, it is difficult for them to back out. And when monasteries become principally tourist attractions, the danger is that the energy of monks becomes devoted chiefly to receiving tourists, leaving no time for the sangha or to engage in Buddhist practice. (2006, 91–92, emphasis added)

He identifies a "lack of character" appropriate to Buddhism and specifically mentions tourist development of monasteries as taking monastics away from their religious cultivation. He repeats his assessment of the economic development leading to "a certain decay in Buddhism," which leads monks to focus on "the *mundane* business of making money" (92–93, emphasis added). He considers this a "severe challenge [to Chinese Buddhism]" (92–93). After noting the Chinese Buddhist tradition to "balance agriculture and meditation" stemming from Mazu (700–788) and his disciple Baizhang (720–814), author of the *Pure Rules* for monks (*Baizhang qinggui*), Jing Yin expresses concern that monastics are overemphasizing "agriculture" (i.e., income generation) and thereby contribute to the commodification of monasteries:

> Unfortunately, it is clear that some communities today emphasize agriculture and income over practice and meditation. Monasteries are now becoming active participants in the process of commodification that characterizes contemporary Chinese economic life, a phenomenon that is equally familiar to North American society. Needless to say, this commodification runs the risk of impairing the ability of Buddhists to concentrate on their fundamental work, which is, in Buddhist terms, to liberate sentient beings from suffering and to propagate the dharma. (96–97)

The view that commodification accompanying tourism damages the religious character of sites is expressed by Jing Yin as well as other scholars of religious tourism. Shi Fangfang has stated that "tourism development and the subsequent commercialization phenomenon are contradictory to the Buddhist ascetic principle and need for a secluded environment for meditation and other practices" (2009, 200). Xuan Fang of Beijing's Renmin University has been quoted as stating that "[t]he commercialization of Buddhism has already become quite common, and this is causing a great deal of concern for a lot of people because it *goes against the function of Buddhism as a religion*" (Tschang 2007, emphasis added). Before challenging the assumptions of these critiques, I'm interested in investigating the nature of the negative view of tourism at religious sites that one finds in views like the one expressed in Jing Ying's essay.

When considering the binary nature of this view, the opposition portrayed between religion and tourism, seems to share a structural affinity with the opposition between sacred and profane as elaborated from Durkheim to Eliade. Durkheim argues that all religious phenomena fall into two categories, namely, beliefs and rites (1995, 34). Durkheim makes the special nature of rites contingent upon belief. Belief, for Durkheim, thus supersedes ritual action. All religious belief, for Durkheim, is based on "the division of the world into two domains, one containing all that is sacred and the other all that is profane—such is the distinctive trait of religious thought" (34). For Durkheim, the sacred and profane are absolute opposites:

> ... nothing but their heterogeneity is left to define the relation between the sacred and the profane.... It is absolute. In the history of human thought, there is no other example of two categories of things as profoundly differentiated or radically opposed to one another. The traditional opposition between good and evil is nothing beside this one: Good and evil are two opposed species of the same genus, namely morals, just as health and illness are nothing more than two different aspects of the same order of facts, life; by contrast, *the sacred and profane are always and everywhere conceived by the human intellect as separate genera, as two worlds with nothing in common.* (36, emphasis added)

Durkheim goes on to write: "*The mind experiences deep repugnance about mingling,* even simple contact, between the corresponding things, because the notion of the sacred is always and everywhere separate from the notion of the profane in man's mind, and because we imagine a kind of logical void between them" (37, emphasis added). Is "deep repugnance" what Jing Yin felt when asked to pay an entry fee to the ancestral home of Chan, Shaolin

Temple? Reflecting on the event he simply wrote: "I consider it a great pity that a monk has to buy a ticket to return to his own ancestral shrine" (2006, 91). Gareth Fisher has written about a lay Buddhist named Wang Xiaolan who took him to Beijing's White Pagoda Temple (*Baita si*) and refused to pay the fifteen RMB entrance fee, insisting that she was a lay Buddhist and there to worship.[6] Daniel Olsen has pointed out that for some religious devotees "charging entrance fees is anathema" (2006, 108).

Feeling wronged at having to pay to enter a religious site of one's faith is an understandable feeling, but what about the presence of tertiary enterprises that provide services for tourists as well as lay and monastic Buddhists, such as vegetarian restaurants, teahouses, or souvenir shops? These are the activities that Jing Yin singles out as at odds with the proper vocation of monastics, namely, self-cultivation and propagation of the dharma. Jing Yin feels that such commercial operations increasingly direct the attention of monastics away from cultivation and threaten the "survival of Buddhism." Such concerns over commodification or commercialization are frequently cited in studies of religion and tourism. A common view is that commodification is perceived as incompatible with religious ideals (Berkwitz 2002; Shi 2009; Tschang 2007; Vukonic 2002; Yu 2007; Zaidman 2003). The most productive approach to this question is not to examine it based on abstract principles, such as the sacred and the profane. We should first examine the attitude toward commerce in the phenomenal world both historically and among Buddhists in China today. The other reason to do this is to determine what is or is not newly commodified. The reason this is important is because it: 1) alerts us to what may have developed as part of modern tourism, and 2) enables us to determine what has been commodified in a strict sense.

I want to distinguish two uses of the term "commoditization," a strong sense and a weak sense. The strong sense is when something is newly commodified and is thus the making into a commodity (commodification) of something that was previously not for sale. The weak sense is used to simply speak of buying and selling (in a religious context or in the vicinity of a religious site). Jing Yin is using "commoditization" in the weak sense to indicate something that is simply for sale in the vicinity of a religious or sacred site. The way that Jing Yin uses the term "commodification" is in line with the usage of "commodification," "commoditization," or "commercialization," and their derivatives in some of the literature on religion and tourism. Myra Shackley, for example, considers the sale of religious souvenirs outside of religious shrines as "commercialization" and remarks: "This level of commercialization is a common phenomenon at most visitor attractions, and sacred sites are no exception" (2006, 99, 2001).[7] Yet souvenir items have long been sold at the type of Catholic site Shackley is examining. While specific souvenirs made of plastic, for example, may be new, the phenomenon of buying and selling souvenir items is not. This is why I consider this a weak form of "commodification," because the items for sale are not newly made into commodities.

A strong sense of "commoditization" would be to indicate the monetization of something previously not for sale. As described by Erik Cohen:

> "Commoditization" is a process by which things (and activities) come to be evaluated *primarily in terms of their exchange value,* in a context of trade, thereby becoming goods (and services)...the principal question in this context is, what happens to the other meanings (particularly religious, cultural and social) of things (and activities) once they become commoditized, particularly under the impact of tourism. (1988, 380–381)

A good example of the strong sense of commodification as I intend it is given by Shirley Yee in her study of the commodification of Buddhist talismans in Thailand and Singapore. "In this cosmology, suffused with the spirit of modem consumerism, everything is potentially commodified to be sold and re-sold in an endless circulation of goods in the vast marketplace. This ironically encompasses the commodification of Buddhist fetishes which *began as gifts* to merit-makers" (1996, 15–16, emphasis added). This is a clear example of commodification because the talismans in question began as *gifts* to devotees by charismatic monks.[8] These talismans are then *sold* on a market that values such talismans. Yee elaborates: "The highest priced and most valuable talismans are the scarce objects produced and/ or blessed by deceased charismatic monks followed by living charismatic monks. The cheaper talismans which flood the market are those blessed by ordinary monks, either dead or alive" (3). Importantly, this form of "commodification" takes place outside of temples at "Buddhist enterprises" run by lay businessmen or "ex-monks" (Yee 1996). The commodification under investigation in this chapter takes place in Chinese Buddhist temples that serve as places of practice as well as sites that attract tourists.

In order to determine which kind of commodification (weak or strong) is taking place we must distinguish what is newly commodified from what has a history of being bought and sold. As is well known, institutional Buddhism in China and beyond has long engaged in mercantile and commercial activities (Shi 2009). When it comes to the operation of monasteries there seems to have long been a gap between ideals and reality. Although the vinaya has long prohibited monastics from handling money or acquiring personal wealth, for example, the evidence from the first century B.C.E. onward suggests that monks did (Gernet [1956] 1995; Kieschnick 2003; Schopen 1997; Walsh 2010; Yu 2007). Speaking of the Chinese case, Gernet writes: "It was the introduction of *commerce* into the circuit of *giving* that turned a community of mendicant monks into a great economic power" ([1956] 1995, 78, emphasis added). Not only did monasteries accrue great wealth, manufacture and sell goods, they also introduced new loan instruments from Indian Buddhism into Chinese society. Taking note of this, Gernet remarks: "Buddhism was certainly not extraneous to the accelerating development of commerce under the Tang" (93).

Research by scholars examining the realities of monastic life find that a small minority of monks dedicate themselves to meditation while the others have myriad duties and jobs (Buswell 1992). Monasteries require a number of monastics to take part in administrative roles and financial management of the monastery.[9] Michael Walsh has looked at the economic life of Chinese monasteries during the Song, Ming, and Qing dynasties and found records of monks trading shiploads of grain and selling other goods such as medicine or oil, which they *manufactured at their monasteries* (2010, emphasis added). His work builds on the foundational work done on Buddhist economics in earlier dynasties by Gernet ([1956] 1995) and Ch'en (1956, 1973). Other examples of commercial enterprises located at Buddhist temples throughout history could be detailed.[10] The point I want to make here is that Buddhist monastics have long been involved with economic enterprises in China and running a vegetarian restaurant or tea shop is not something so radically new that it threatens the integrity of the sangha if the actual sanghas of the past are our models. Jing Yin's appeal to the *Pure Rules* of Baizhang is an appeal to prescriptive accounts in a text that does not take into account these historical realities of Buddhist institutions.

Concerning the question of commodification, tertiary businesses have long played a role in supporting Buddhist monasticism and are not to be considered forms of commodification in the strong sense. Contemporary manifestations of teahouses, restaurants, guesthouses, and shops selling religious goods and books are not sufficiently novel to be considered commodified in the strong sense. There are, nonetheless, objects and services that may be considered commodified in the strong sense at temples. There is, for example, the increasingly common practice of temples placing "prices" on ritual services or special sticks of incense. This happens at temples that are popular with tourists as well as temples that receive few or no tourists. Thus, I argue that these are "marketed" for devotees and pilgrims (*xiangke*) rather than tourists (*youke*).[11] Fees for such items and services may be understood as "donations" by the faithful, which provide access to merit dispensed by the religious economy of the temple. Such a system of pricing or "recommended donation" may be seen as an effect of a spreading market mentality rather than an impact of tourism.[12] Thus, while "selling such goods and services" may serve as a strong sense of commodification, these activities are not ones developed within the context of tourism.

DeBernardi has examined the issue of commodification in contemporary Penang, Malaysia, and Wudang Mountain in China with respect to the selling of exorbitantly priced sticks of incense during the double ninth festival celebrating the Nine Emperor Gods, who control fate (2008). Devotees mark the climax of the festival in both Penang and Mount Wudang by climbing sacred mountains topped by temples to one of or all of the Nine Emperor Gods. Mount Wudang is now a World Heritage Site, which marks the site of a once vibrant Daoist temple complex.[13] At Mount Wudang individuals pay 1,000 RMB (123 USD) to have their names added to a bushel basket representing heaven and earth; this basket also represents health, wealth, happiness, and longevity and is thought to be responsive to the prayers of the virtuous (DeBernardi 2008, 60–61). On the climax of the festival, the privilege of making the first offering of incense costs 1,000,0000 RMB (12,370 USD), 30,000 RBM for the second incense. Successful businesspeople, the mayor, and local officials paid large sums such as these to offer incense (DeBernardi 2008, 63). In Singapore and Malaysia there are typically auctions held at the end of festivals where patrons bid on items such as statues, brandy, and black gold (blessed charcoal), which fetch thousands of dollars. It is a way to donate to temples, demonstrate one's wealth, and earn moral merit in the community (DeBernardi 2008, 64).

DeBernardi (2008) contends that those who spend large sums of money to light incense or bid on objects, are not buying blessings (which is the superficial context of the transaction). Rather, she argues, that these individuals are translating their personal resources into a social distinction, a social distinction that Simmel has called an "unearned increment" of the ownership of wealth, which is only available to the wealthy who are able to exhibit public benevolence ([1900] 1978, 220). Such munificence sets them apart from the poor for whom such generosity is not an option. In addition to expressing public benevolence, it is also clearly a means of demonstrating or establishing one's elite status.[14]

DeBernardi (2008) offers a helpful perspective on exorbitant expenditures in Chinese religious contexts. Commodification in such circumstances should not be seen as a simple exchange of money for blessings. In the Buddhist context we might call the exchange of exorbitant fees to light incense a form of *upāya* (skillful means). The temple provides an opportunity for people of means to publicly demonstrate their wealth in a moral context, thus gaining moral face (a social value with potential political value), at the same time the individuals earn merit (a religious good) because their funds help support the (meritorious) activities of the temple. Being recognized for financially supporting the temple is a venerable tradition well attested at Dunhuang in the medieval period and all across China today. It is also a venerable tradition in a Euro-American context with the listing and ranking of donors to all sorts of not-for-profit institutions and causes. Compare such exchanges with the exchanges made at a car dealership, the buying and selling of a genuine commodity. They do not post your name on a wall for being the proud owner of a new vehicle, but they do put the names and photos on their walls of employees who sell the most vehicles. Selling/productivity is the value embraced and publicly heralded, not the virtue of generosity. Compare that with the posting of donors' names at temples or charities or arts programs. It may be easier to see when the donor is a corporation. Like the wealthy Chinese businessman purchasing rights to light the first incense, corporations get to have their names associated with public benevolence and goodness. They both receive a form of social distinction or cultural capital.

A genuine commodity, like the talismans discussed by Yee, responds to market pressures in more dynamic ways than incense at temples. The talismans must be marketed as authentic in a sea of counterfeit items.[15] As Yee was informed by her interviewees, the free talismans given by monks are more authentic than the ones in shops, yet the shops continue to do a brisk business thanks in part to advertising campaigns. While paying high fees for incense at temples is a strong form of commodification, it seems to differ from the commodification described by Yee. Lighting the first incense at Mount Wudang or any number of Buddhist sites on January first is a set value determined by the temple, there is no negotiation or unpredictable market pressures in the same way that genuine commodities are vulnerable. This should alert us to possible differences between the commodifications of ritual within a gift economy and mundane commodifications in a market context.

So far the activities we have examined have not been explicitly related to the tourist industry. In other words, these are commodified activities that happen in the absence of any tourist development. Let's now turn to commodification in the strong sense that happens at Buddhist sites that have become tourist attractions, using these perspectives on commodification in religious contexts. The most prevalent example of commodification in the strong sense at Buddhist sites that serve as tourist attractions is one of the specific complaints of Jing Yin, the entrance fee. Such entry fees are charged to individuals who do not have a Buddhist identity card or who are not recognized as "insiders" by the gate monitors. Lay or monastic Buddhists who are asked to pay entrance fees to visit Buddhist temples are rightly offended. No one wants to "pay to pray" (Olson 2006, 108; Shakley 2001). We need to examine this entry fee closely to see who benefits and who runs it.

At Quanzhou Kaiyuan this fee was a modest 10 RMB (just over 1 USD) and was divided between the temple management committee of government-appointed bureaucrats who monitor the gates and collect the fees and the clerics who reside at the monastery. The abbot claimed that he would abolish this entry fee if he could, indicating it was the non-clerical management committee that was preventing this since it was the source of their salaries.[16] After a decade of working on the problem, Quanzhou Kaiyuan was able to abolish the entry fee in 2015 agreeing to pay salaries from other sources. Nanputuo Temple, located in the same province, eliminated its entrance fee in 2011, indicating the possibility of other temples following suit. The reasons these temples can eliminate this entry fee is because the vast majority of their temple income derives from donations from pilgrims and devotees and "fees" for ritual services. While other sites may have very different dynamics, the examples of these sites suggest that this form of commodification is one that successful temples are not committed to promoting or even preserving. The challenge will be at sites where larger and more entrenched non-clerical stakeholders such as tourist bureaus are funded by such entrance fees. Additional research needs to be done to bring a more complete picture of these dynamics at different sites.

At monasteries in Fujian, monks expressed little concern over the issue of commodification except in instances that were considered extreme such as the ambitions of the abbot of Shaolin Temple. Shaolin Temple provides an example of what happens when commodification and tourist development are taken to extremes by a monastic population. This site has been successfully marketed as the "Home of Kung Fu" by the current abbot, Yongxin, who considers himself the "business manager" (*jingying*) of the temple and has been nicknamed the "CEO monk" (Yu 2007, 8). Yongxin speaks of a new path for Buddhism based on developing business and services (*shangyefuwu*). Products are marketed with the Shaolin trademark, tickets are sold to view kung fu performances, fees are paid to bless (*kaiguang*) cell phone numbers, and a wedding ritual has been invented (Yu 2007). His embrace of business tactics to run the monastery has been widely criticized by other monks and "netizens" in China (Beam 2015). This type of commodification appears to be a special case at the moment, but it can serve as a warning to how an unfettered business approach can harm the reputation and religious character of a Buddhist site (Yu 2007). Jing Yin rightly, I think, recognizes the danger of such rampant commercialization at a site like Shaolin Temple, but the problem is his unwarranted linking of such unfettered commercialization to the phenomenon of tourism more broadly.

The expensive entrance fee to the Shaolin complex and the amusement park–like effect of the approach to the temple, featuring shops and kung fu movie theme music, arguably diverts attention in a non-contemplative manner. But what about other Buddhist sites that serve as sites of practice as well as tourist attractions? How does tourism impact the religious environment of these sites? Given that tourism is a fact of life for many Buddhist sites throughout Asia, the more pressing concern is to understand the impact of tourism on the Buddhist tradition more broadly, to understand how tourism affects life at the average Buddhist temple, not the home of kung fu under the CEO monk.

Disturbance of the Environment and Religious Atmosphere

As already noted, the literature on tourism and religion frequently recognizes concerns over the negative impacts of tourism on the religious environment and atmosphere for religious practice (Buswell 1992, 227; Kaplan 2010; Olsen 2006; Shackley 2006; Shi 2009). Is there evidence for such problems in China? I will examine the reports of other scholars working on China as well as my own research to determine perceptions of impact, steps taken to mitigate such impacts, and situations where disturbances become intolerable. Studies examining perceptions of tourism have been conducted at the two most popularly visited of China's four famous Buddhist mountains, Mount Wutai and Mount Putuo. I will examine the findings of these before turning to my own research and the views expressed by Jing Yin. The phenomenon of commodification will also come up in this section as it is a factor thought to impact the religious environment of temples. In this section I am not interested in evaluating strong and weak senses of commodification or identifying what is newly commodified, but rather the perceptions of activities associated with tourist development that impact the life of temples.

Using qualitative interviews to assess visitor experiences at Mount Wutai, mythological home of the Bodhisattva Mañjuśrī, the Buddhist bodhisattva of wisdom, Shi Fangfang found mixed reactions to the site and, in particular, to perceptions regarding commercialization. He notes that just as governments and clergy have different views so do different visitors. One group generally accepted the commercial developments with varying levels of tolerance. Among those accepting the commercialized aspects of the experience were individuals who noted the benefits of such development in introducing people to Buddhism and propagating interest in Buddhist culture. These same individuals often recognized the need to keep such developments separate from the temple grounds. Another group expressed resentment at the commercialization due to perceived incompatibility with Buddhism.[17] This latter finding supports the view of Jing Yin that commercialization threatens to interfere with the religious goals of the monastery. This, however, was not a unanimously agreed upon perspective; his small sample also included individuals who expressed no serious concerns over commercialization.

Attempting to understand the differences in view, Shi correlated levels of acceptance and resentment to travel experience, age, religious background, and levels of Buddhist knowledge (2009, 210). Older visitors with more travel experience, for example, were found to be less shocked and more tolerant of commercialization. Buddhist visitors were more inclined to be more resentful than non-religious visitors. Senior Buddhists tended to be more nuanced in their perceptions, whereas Buddhist novices were more likely to respond with their immediate impressions, positive or negative.

A significant finding of Shi's involves the role of "critical events" in shaping visitors' perceptions about their trips. These significant events, whether good or ill, left impressions that colored the memories of visitors. He provides two examples. One was a woman sorely disappointed after being cheated on a box of incense; she paid 490 RMB and was later offered a similar box for 60 RMB. She was upset at being cheated by the vendor and left Wutai on that same day. Another example was a nun who attended a special Buddhist ceremony and was positively impressed that it was a spectacle like no other (Shi 2009, 207–208). For the first visitor, the atmosphere of Mount Wutai had been tarnished by the dishonest practice of vendors encountered outside the temples. The second visitor passed by the same vendors, but was left with a positive impression of the site having witnessed a striking spectacle. Shi concludes that while there are patterns to propose regarding differences in perceptions, such patterns can be trumped by "critical events" that can color one's experience positively or negatively. Given the different perceptions of visitors, Shi was only able to conclude that there were "contrasting attitudes" over the impact of commercialization at Mount Wutai.[18]

A more nuanced view of tourism was also found to be operative at Mount Putuo in Zhejiang in research carried out by Wong, McIntosh, and Ryan (2012). The study of Mount Putuo, sacred home of Guanyin, the bodhisattva of compassion, focused on the perceptions of clerics residing at the temples. They were asked two primary questions: 1) Who do you think are the people who come to Putuo? and 2) How do you perceive having tourism and receiving visitors in your monastery/nunnery? (219). Twenty-five monks and nuns were interviewed by Wong who was described as a Buddhist herself, which helped give her access to her interviewees (221). The first question was designed to explore perceptions of visitors in an effort to understand views about pilgrims and tourists.[19] The second question is more relevant to this chapter as it concerns perceptions regarding the impact of tourism on the temple's environment. Parallel to Shi's findings, the authors of this article find a link between higher knowledge of Buddhism and greater tolerance of visitor disturbances.[20]

In addition to this supposedly experiential dimension of tolerance the monks also expressed the need to spread the dharma.[21] Recall the concern expressed by Jing Yin that commodification would take clerics away from the important task of propagating the dharma. What this study and others find is the recognition that being open to tourists and accommodating their needs is precisely a means of propagating the dharma. In my own research on Buddhist monks in contemporary China and in the work of Holmes Welch on Buddhism in early twentieth-century China, we both find that one of the paths to becoming a monk is by first visiting temples as a casual visitor or tourist and becoming introduced to and attracted by the life witnessed (Nichols 2017; Welch [1967] 1973).

Both Shi and Wang and colleagues find that higher levels of Buddhist learning or cultivation are thought to help one tolerate disturbances.[22] This view, expressed by monastics in all the studies where they have been interviewed, is an important counter to Jing Yin's view that tourism and commercial activities threaten Buddhism. It is important because it comes from *within* temple compounds at busy pilgrimage and tourist sites. While this may not be a majority view, it remains a significant finding because the potential for monks to practice the dharma within such tourist sites is critical in determining whether or not tourism is inherently detrimental to Buddhist religious goals. Finding that insiders, in this case monastics, perceive the situation differently and more sanguinely than some outside observers was pointed out as a pattern at religious tourism sites by Erik Cohen:

> While to the external observer, commoditization may appear to involve a complete transformation of meaning as a cultural product. . . . In many situations of commoditization, the performers themselves do not necessarily perceive that such a transformation had in fact occurred . . . *rather than assuming the destructive impact of commoditization* on the authenticity and meaning of cultural products, *such impact should be submitted to a detailed empirical examination,* if possible within an emic, processual, and comparative framework. (1988, 382–83, emphasis added)

This chapter is contributing to just such a comparative study of emic views of commodification of religious sites. While further research needs to be conducted, we have evidence from multiple sites that monastics are able to continue their practice in the midst of disturbances brought about by tourists.

While Wong and colleagues make a reasonable final conclusion that researchers need to note the perceptions of host communities, I find other points in the article somewhat overstated. The fact is that the monks and nuns did complain about disturbances and annoyances as they have at other temples such as Famen Temple, discussed by Bruntz in this volume. Wong and colleagues write: "The majority of respondents acknowledged that there were 'intrusions' and 'disturbances' caused by some visitors; yet they also commented from their Buddhist perspective that the external disturbances had no effect on their Buddhist mindset" (Wong, McIntosh, and Ryan 2012, 229). One way to understand what the clerics are saying is that they *shouldn't be* annoyed because they know the Buddhist teachings and (likely) feel obligated to represent the best face of Buddhism to their fellow Buddhist interviewer. In other words, they may be saying how they *should* see tourists, rather than how they *do* experience them. As with the view that monastics accept tourism, the view that they find it disruptive needs additional research following different lines of inquiry in order to sort such questions out.

Turning to my own research at Quanzhou Kaiyuan Monastery, I too have heard complaints from clerics about the noise and disturbances caused by tourists at temples. When I asked one of the more educated monks about the influence of the tourist industry on Buddhism in China he replied:

> There is definitely an influence, but I cannot exactly say exactly what the influence is. Having said that, the most obvious influence, is a benefit, namely it provides monasteries with much income. The baleful influence is the change in our traditional way of life. Traditionally, under the agricultural society, Chan monasteries were self-sufficient (*ziji zizu*). Most monasteries technically belong to the Chan school; monks should practice meditation, should be peaceful and quiet, but on account of the tourist industry have too many visitors [and] the peaceful atmosphere of the monastery is destroyed (*anjing de qifen jiu puohaui*). Many Chan school monasteries simply keep the name while the real thing has fled (*mingcun shiwang*).[23]

What this monk considered the "real thing" was an environment and organization supporting meditation and Chan cultivation. It is this focus on contemplative cultivation that he considered hampered by the daily disturbances of dealing with visitors and busloads of tourists. He also felt that such values were not sufficiently emphasized or enforced by the abbot.[24] When I have pushed monks on this point, counterarguing that temples have always hosted visitors, the reply is that there are now *more* visitors and they have a greater influence on the temples that host them. This seems to be a reasonable rejoinder, given the growth of China's population, combined with advances in both personal and mass transportation, and rising incomes and a corresponding growth in leisure travel. These factors combine to bring in busloads of tourists and pilgrims, sometimes in matching caps led by tour guides toting a flag, but always generating a small crowd that interferes with the flow of devotees seeking to prostrate, burn incense, or chant the Buddha's name (*nianfo*). Such large groups inevitably produce more noise and disruptions than even a steady trickle of visitors and tourists, which would have been the worst-case scenario for most sites before the advent of essentially ubiquitous mass transportation in the form of trains, buses, and airplanes within a rapidly growing economy.

While such problems are real, they are limited to temples receiving large numbers of tourists. While famous temples that receive busloads of tourists are the ones most likely to be visited by scholars, pilgrims, and tourists alike, they are not, nor have they ever been, the most common form of Buddhist temple in China. In my research I have visited dozens of small temples primarily in Fujian that serve a small resident population and the surrounding community and receive no tourist visitors at all. After the evening service at one of these small temples in the mountains, I yielded to a cow passing between buildings, no tour buses. Such small temples vastly outnumber the large famous temples most impacted by tourism. When observers like Jing Yin or Yu Xueming question the future of Chinese Buddhism as being threatened by tourism and the attendant commercialization of temples, it is important to point out that Chinese Buddhism is much larger than those famous temples. Even if a handful of once important Buddhist temples such as Shaolin Temple or some of the temples on Mount Wutai become consumed with catering to tourists and lose a focus on Buddhist cultivation, this simply doesn't spell the end of "Chinese Buddhism." This would be like saying weak coffee at Tim Horton's will bring about the collapse of Starbucks. A corrupt monastery may tarnish the image of Buddhism, but it does not vitally damage those dedicated to cultivating the path in monasteries across China and beyond or even all the monastics or lay Buddhists practicing at those very touristic locations. As researchers have pointed out, some monastics recognize tourist disturbances as an opportunity to practice and, as I will discuss below, there are methods used to mitigate disturbances from tourists and pilgrims.

Even at temples receiving large numbers of tourists, steps can be taken to reduce the harmful effects of tourism. At Xian's famous Famen Monastery, home of the famous/infamous finger relic of the Buddha, a split is emerging between the historic side of the temple complex with a newly developed museum and a living temple space for monastics off-limits to general tourists. I had noticed such a split emerging when I visited Famen Temple in the summer of 2009 and asked the vice abbot if this was the case and he agreed that something like that was happening. In such an arrangement it is possible for the majority of resident monks to pursue a traditional monastic lifestyle while a few in the leadership are left to deal with the management of tourism and engagement with the public (Nichols forthcoming).[25]

Another more common method of mitigation is to restrict commercial activity to vendors and shops located outside the gates of the monastery so that residents and pilgrims can at least visit the shrines and halls of the monastery without being exposed to potential distractions and haggling that occurs outside temples at Mount Wutai, Badachu Temple Park near Beijing, and elsewhere. Still another common means of mitigating the impact of tourism on the life of the monastery is to restrict tourist access in a variety of ways. The first way is to open the gates to tourists and visitors for strictly set hours, for example from 8 a.m. to 5 p.m. While this is a full day, it does provide dedicated clerics and devotees opportunities to meditate, chant, circumambulate, read, practice calligraphy, and so on during early morning and evening hours. The basic communal forms of daily practice, the morning and evening services and meals, are undertaken largely away from the eyes, cameras, and megaphones of tourists. Monasteries are not open to tourists during the morning service, and by 4 p.m., when the evening service typically begins, tourist numbers have sharply declined.

Another way that access is controlled is by keeping the living quarters of monastics off-limits to visitors and tourists. Monks not required to deal with the public through their monastic jobs, can almost entirely stay away from tourists. In addition to restricting access to living quarters, temples often prevent visitors from entering halls where monks are engaged in ritual practice, such as chanting sutras or meditating. I have witnessed such restrictions in effect at Putian's Guanghua Temple in Fujian, Jiangsu's Gaomin Monastery, and Quanzhou Kaiyuan Monastery.

While there are ways to limit the disruptions caused by large numbers of visitors, there are also times when even the most tolerant monks have had enough and actively protest against such disturbances. Three examples of monastic protests of disruptive situations related to touristic development occurred at Hebei's Bailin Temple and Xian's Famen Temple in 2009, and Kunming's Panlong Temple in 2014 (Nichols forthcoming). In each instance monks at these temples closed their sites in protest of tourism-related incidents. Bailin Temple closed to the public for two months after a scuffle broke out between incense sellers, their patrons, and security personnel just outside the temple. Famen Temple was closed for one day after monks tore down a wall that was being erected by a tourist developer to encircle the monastery (Li 2009), and Panlong Temple closed its doors for one morning to protest commercialization and corporatization (*shangyehua he gongsihua*) by local government bureaus (Tang 2014). Such instances reveal the flashpoints between clerics and other stakeholders in the tourist industry. Such points of contention between different stakeholders is a theme of scholarship on tourism and religion.

Michael Stausberg published the second book-length study on the phenomenon of religious tourism in 2011.[26] He drew upon extant studies to present overviews and framings of the issues surrounding religious tourism. After noting that there are various interested parties when it comes to developing or preserving a particular site, such as businesspeople, government, and religious leaders, he writes: "Religious sites transformed into tourism destinations are therefore naturally contested sites" (Stausberg 2011, 100). "Naturally contested sites," suggests two or more parties pitted against one another in competition for control or influence over a given site. While this is generally true, there are also cases of religious sites promoting themselves as tourist sites and working to accommodate tourists. In such cases, the paradigm of "contestation" doesn't seem to fit, at least not in the way it is conceived as a conflict between two distinct interested parties, like indigenous people against outside tourists (Stausberg 2011, 100–102). Expecting an inevitable conflict to arise seems to reflect a dichotomous way of viewing pilgrims and tourists, influenced by the tradition of separating sacred and profane as discussed earlier. Such a view does not reflect the reality of tourism explored in this volume. The situation in China is generally one of *negotiation,* rather than *contestation.* Nevertheless, as noted, there have been cases of contestation and these cases reveal when the impacts of tourism have crossed a line in the eyes of the clerical management.

The nature of the contestations noted here have to do with violence and disruptions initiated by vendors and overreach by tourist developers seeking to alter the built environment of temple sites in ways found unacceptable by the resident clergy. In both cases of developer overreach the conflict was resolved in less than twenty-four hours, with the developers quickly acquiescing to the demands of the monastics. This suggests, in these cases at least, clerics held the upper hand and were able to swiftly stop particular aspects of development plans. In the case of the altercations outside Bailin Temple, the temple has attempted to keep incense sellers outside the gates of the monastery by moving a large incense burner outside the gates. In addition, the local government stepped in to help mend the situation by developing a system of licensing and registration of tour guides.[27] In sum, the ability of clerics to resolve these disruptions may be seen as part of the growing pains of a reviving system of Buddhist monastic life and temple activity where clerics are confronted with the task of negotiating the terms of their autonomy with local residents as well as local bureaus and governing agencies.[28]

Regarding the question of the impact of tourism on the environment of temples, the answer is that yes, tourism brings disturbances and annoyances to the resident clerics as well as religiously oriented visitors. This has been marked by all the research cited. At the same time, researchers note that resident clerics and pilgrims alike express varying degrees of tolerance due to the benefits derived from tourism. The most often cited benefits are economic support for the site and the ability to spread Buddhist teachings, practices, and cultures to new audiences. The other point made is that clerics have the ability to mitigate the disruptions caused by tourists in a variety of ways such that it is common for many resident clerics to have little or no interactions with tourists. When disruptions reach a breaking point, clerics have successfully asserted themselves and their right to manage their sites. The greatest threat to the integrity of monastic life comes from within the clerical community in the form of unscrupulous monks who may sacrifice Buddhist principles in the pursuit of wealth, fame, or power. The most dramatic example of such a questionably managed site is Shaolin Temple.

The tourist industry is a powerful economic force in the world today. Domestic tourists in China are estimated to have made a staggering 1.6 billion trips in 2007 spending 777.1 billion RMB (Ryan and Gu 2009, 5). In addition, religious sites are a significant percentage of tourist sites around the world (Stausberg 2011). Of China's top eighty-four national tourist sites, sixty-three are related to religion—that's 75 percent (Mu et al. 2007, 105, as cited in Stausberg 2011, 97). The fact that many of these are also World Heritage Sites necessitates their public accessibility and general promotion.[29] For many of China's Buddhist monasteries tourism is an inevitable fact of life. On the one hand it brings financial benefits, which enable monasteries to carry out renovations and expansions and contribute to charitable causes. On the other, the noise and disturbances from crowds damages the contemplative atmosphere conducive to meditation and other ritual activities. At the same time, crowds and noise are a welcome and expected part of most religious celebrations, including those held at Buddhist monasteries.[30]

As for the commercialization that accompanies the development of popular tourist attractions such as the sites at the heart of this chapter, I have proposed the notion of strong and weak forms of commodification to help nuance the question of corruption. I have found that the strongest form of commodification directly associated with tourism is the charging of an entry fee to visitors. Technically, Buddhist visitors with Buddhist IDs (*guiyi zheng*) are not supposed to pay these entry fees. Nevertheless, as attested by Fisher and Jing Yin, such rules are not uniformly applied and both lay and monastic Buddhists can be hassled, to their great consternation, to pay a fee to enter Buddhist temples such as Beijing's White Pagoda (*Baita*) Temple or Shaolin Temple. This is a legitimate concern that Buddhists have, which some temples like Xiamen Nanputuo and Quanzhou Kaiyuan have begun to address by eliminating the entry fee altogether.

Other commercial aspects such as the operation of vegetarian restaurants, tea shops, or religious goods shops present nothing categorically new in the history of Chinese Buddhism, which has a long history of such activities. That monasteries would engage in commercial activities as a means to support their institutions is in line with hundreds of years of institutional Buddhist practice throughout Asia. As suggested above, such commercial activities should only be understood as commodification in a weak sense.

In short, tourism can be disruptive to religious cultivation, but it is not at odds with the larger goals of Buddhism, which include the propagation of the dharma, nor does it prevent religious cultivation from happening. In addition, tourism is a phenomenon at a minority of Buddhist temples in China, the majority of which remain small temples tended by one to five monastics. From this broader perspective, the economic benefits of a tourist industry arguably outweigh the costs, which can be mitigated by a creative and committed sangha using a selection of strategies outlined above. As stated above, the greatest threat to the integrity of Buddhist monasteries is not tourism or any other outside influence, but from within in the form of unscrupulous monks seeking to enrich themselves. Monastics are aware of the problems and are actively taking steps to mitigate the potentially harmful influence of tourism, while keeping their sites open to tourists, if only partially, taking a characteristically Buddhist middle way.

Notes

1 Personal interview at Quanzhou Kaiyuan, February 2009.

2 I have found that there are three general paths taken by Buddhist monasteries in contemporary China; these three paths of development lead to tourist temples, places of practice, or a combination of these two identities. At the extreme end of development as a tourist temple is a process I call museumification in which no active clergy is present and the site has been developed as a place of interpretive display. Gareth Fisher (2011) borrowed the term "museumification" in his article "In the Footsteps of Tourists: Buddhist Revival at Museum/Temple Sites in Beijing." An example of complete museumification is Yangzhou's Tianning Temple, which has become known as the Yangzhou Buddhist Culture Museum. In this volume, Nanshan Buddhist Cultural Park discussed by Bruntz would be another example of a "tourist temple." As for places which receive few to no tourists and are dedicated to Buddhist cultivation I note Mount Taimu's Pingxing Monastery in Fujian as the home of a dedicated group of clergy focused on vinaya-based practice. In this volume, Bruntz discusses Longquan Monastery, which serves as a place of practice. Regarding places that combine Buddhist practice while actively catering to tourists I note my field site of Quanzhou Kaiyuan as well as Xiamen's Nanputuo, both in Fujian.

3 The other two themes are the pilgrim-tourist dichotomy and characteristics and travel patterns of religious tourists (Timothy and Olsen 2011).

4 Uri Kaplan (2010), for example, examines issues with the temple-stay program developed at Buddhist sites in Korea and doesn't clearly distinguish issues of commodification from the negative impacts of tourists. Jing Yin (2006) also makes no clear distinction between these two issues nor does Shi Fangfang (2009) in his discussion of tourism and commercialization at Mount Wutai.

5 Now that Venerable Jing Yin has become abbot of a large important temple in Hong Kong it is entirely possible, if not likely, that his views have changed from the time of his 2006 article. In this chapter I am addressing the sentiment and views he expressed then that are still found among Buddhists, both lay and clerical, in China today.

6 Ignoring the pleas of the ticket agent she walked on through, leaving Fisher to pay both entrance fees (Fisher 2011, 512). At some monasteries in China waivers are available for lay and monastic Buddhists who have the proper identification cards. This is comparable to dual fee systems set up at other religious sites (Olsen 2006, 108–109).

7 Shackley is examining the Catholic shrine of Our Lady of Knock in Ireland where a vision of Mary was seen in 1879. Shackley discusses the sale of Irish souvenirs, souvenirs unique to Knock, such as small statues of the shrine, as well as devotional items of various kinds and considers these aspects of commercialization and commoditization (2006, 96–99).

8 This may also be considered a form of exchange within a merit-based economy. The individual has typically made an offering to the temple or in some way supported the temple before being *given* the talisman.

9 Jonathan Silk (2008) has examined the early history of such administrative monks in *Managing Monks: Administrators and Administrative Roles in Indian*

Buddhist Monasticism. See also Nichols (2015) on the place of administrative work in monastic life in contemporary China.

10 Chinese monks also served as technical advisors, planners, and fundraisers in building bridges and other structures; records indicate, for example, that monks in the city of Quanzhou were actively involved in the construction of dozens of bridges from 900 to 1300 (Nichols 2011, 76–80). Monastic engagements with construction work to expand and develop temples in the contemporary period is noted by Bruntz in this volume. See discussion of merit with special reference to the building of bridges in Kieschnick (2003, 191–219).

11 This does not mean that tourists (*youke*) do not sometimes participate in rituals or purchase incense, but that when they do their identity, which this volume recognizes as fluid, may be thought to shift from being a "traveling guest" to an "incense guest."

12 They are also a response to the loss of landed wealth in the modern period. Monasteries have turned to other forms of support, and regularizing ritual fees is part their means to generate supportive income. Such trend was noted by Welch in his study of Buddhist practice in early twentieth century China (1967).

13 Today there is a group of Quanzhen Daoists in residence as well as a martial arts academy (DeBernardi 2008, 57).

14 In addition, although Chinese religious culture embraces a morality of karmic cause and effect, there also operates a belief in fate and luck. These individuals may be seeking to influence their luck with their wealth.

15 "According to informants, there is a difference between a talisman given as a gift from a monk and one that is sold in shops; they perceived the former as authentic whereas counterfeits could be sold in shops. Thus advertisements by Buddhist enterprises must necessarily construct myths about the authenticity and scarcity of the products, since people might otherwise prefer to obtain them from monks in temples. . . . Indeed, the construction of authentic Thai images and talismans as scarce goods amidst a host of powerless counterfeits is central to the commercial discourse of entrepreneurs" (Yee 1996, 12–13).

16 For more on the conflict between this management committee and the clerics, see Nichols (forthcoming) and Wank and Ashiwa (2006).

17 Shi Fangfang writes: "The primary reasons [for disapproving commercialization] were that it was incompatible with the religious atmosphere of the Buddhist site and the secular trade of religious souvenirs was disrespectful to the Buddha . . . the sacred mountain was losing its own features" (2009, 210).

18 The rest of his conclusions have to do with recommendations to management of such destinations on how to anticipate different needs of visitors and accommodate them. This is a concern with much of the literature on religion and tourism given that it is published in journals catering in part to tourist industry professionals.

19 This is important to the authors of this article published in a tourism studies journal, as the distinction between pilgrims and tourists is one of the main themes of religion and tourism literature.

20 "It seems that the more enlightened, in the Buddhist sense, the monks and nuns are, the better they are mentally prepared to welcome visitors" (Wong, McIntosh, and Ryan 2012, 231). What the authors seem to mean by this odd assertion regarding relative levels of "enlightenment," is that some monks exhibited a greater awareness of Buddhist doctrines about non-attachment, impermanence, and such, and linked these to a need for a practitioner to not let such adventitious disruptions disturb one's peaceful state of mind.

21 "Though they acknowledge the existence of disturbances created by visitors, the majority of the respondents perceived tourism positively, and they viewed it as a channel that allows people to learn about Buddhism while fulfilling the key Buddhist role of helping others find nirvana" (Wong, McIntosh, and Ryan 2012, 230). It is unfortunate that the authors use this term "nirvana" as an immediate goal of

visitors when ethnographers have long revealed that Buddhists tend to focus on more mundane and immediate goals, reserving nirvana for a future life.

22 In the words of one of the monks interviewed: "Having more visitors come to the monastery will of course make it more crowded, but people just come in and leave... this has no effect on my personal Buddhist practice... our life will not change according to the number of visitors" (Wong, McIntosh, and Ryan 2012, 229).

23 Personal interview at Quanzhou Kaiyuan, February 2009.

24 The role played by the abbot is a factor unrelated to the question of tourism or commodification. It was a matter of not enforcing discipline or modeling and enabling meditative cultivation as an institutional practice.

25 See further discussion of Famen Temple by Bruntz (this volume).

26 The first book-length study was Boris Vukonić's *Tourism and Religion* (1996). A difference in approach between these two studies is the relative positive approach to tourism as fulfilling spiritual needs taken by Vukonić.

27 The self-trained guides were a concern of the monks due to complaints that they would sometimes pressure people to accept their services. The supportive relationship between the local government and Bailin Temple has been noted and explored by Yang Fenggang and Wei Dedong (2005).

28 Such negotiations betweens clerics and government agencies at Xiamen's Nanputuo have been explored by Wank and Ashiwa (2006).

29 See Robert Shepherd's *Faith in Heritage* (2013) for details of the effects of World Heritage status on local communities at Mount Wutai in China.

30 A *renao* (hot and noisy) atmosphere is part of a successful religious celebration throughout Chinese culture (Chau 2006).

References

Beam, Christopher. 2015. "The Rise and Fall of Shaolin's CEO Monk." Bloomberg, December 28. Accessed March 19, 2017. https://www.bloomberg.com/news/features/2015-12-28/the-rise-and-fall-of-shaolin-s-ceo-monk.

Berkwitz, Stephen C. 2002. "Recent Trends in Sri Lankan Buddhism." *Religion* 33:57–71.

Buswell, Robert E. 1992. *The Zen Monastic Experience: Buddhist Practice in Contemporary Korea*. Princeton: Princeton University Press.

Chau, Adam Yuet. 2006. *Miraculous Response: Doing Popular Religion in Contemporary China*. Stanford: Stanford University Press.

Ch'en, Kenneth K. S. 1973. *The Chinese Transformation of Buddhism*. Princeton: Princeton University Press.

——. 1956. "The Economic Background of the Hui-ch'ang Suppression of Buddhism." *Harvard Journal of Asiatic Studies* 19 (1/2): 67–105.

Cohen, Eric. 1988. "Authenticity and Commoditization in Tourism." *Annals of Tourism Research* 15:371–386.

DeBernardi, Jean. 2008. "Commodifying Blessings: Celebrating the Double-Yang Festival in Penang, Malaysia and Wudang Mountain, China." In *Marketing Gods: Rethinking Religious Commodifications in Asia,* edited by Pattana Kitiarsa, 49–67. London: Routledge.

Durkheim, Émile. 1995. *The Elementary Forms of Religious Life*. Translated by Karen E. Fields. New York: Free Press.

Fisher, Gareth. 2011. "In the Footsteps of Tourists: Buddhist Revival at Museum/Temple Sites in Beijing." *Social Compass* 58 (4): 511–524.

Gernet, Jacques. (1956) 1995. *Buddhism in Chinese Society: An Economic History From the Fifth to the Tenth Centuries*. New York: Columbia University Press.

Jing Yin. 2006. "Buddhism and Economic Reform in Mainland China." In *Chinese Religions in Contemporary Societies,* edited by James Miller, 85–100. Santa Barbara, CA: ABC CLIO.

Li Raymond. 2009. "Rampaging Monks Drive Back Developers." *South China Morning Post,* March 25, A1.

Kieschnick, John. 2003. *The Impact of Buddhism on Chinese Material Culture.* Princeton: Princeton University Press.

Kaplan, Uri. 2010. "Images of Monasticism: The Temple Stay Program and the Rebranding of Korean Buddhist Temples." *Korean Studies* 34:127–146.

Nichols, Brian J. 2011. "History, Material Culture and Auspicious Events at the Purple Cloud: Buddhist Monasticism at Quanzhou Kaiyuan." Ph.D. diss., Rice University.

——. 2017. "Taking Welch and *The Practice of Chinese Buddhism* into the 21st Century." *Studies in Chinese Religions* 3 (3): 258–280.

——. Forthcoming. "Tourist Temples and Places of Practice: Charting Multiple Paths in the Revival of Monasteries." In *Buddhism After Mao,* edited by Ji Zhe, Gareth Fisher, and Andre Laliberte. Honolulu: University of Hawai'i Press.

——. 2015. "Typologizing Religious Practice at Buddhist Monasteries in Contemporary China." In *Chinese Buddhism: Past, Present, and Future,* edited by Xie Da-ning, 411–436. Yilan, Taiwan: Fo Guang University Center for Buddhist Studies.

Olson, Daniel H. 2006. «Management Issues for Religious Heritage Sites.» In *Tourism, Religion and Spiritual Journeys,* edited by Dallen J. Timothy and Daniel H. Olsen, 104–118. New York: Routledge.

Ryan, Chris, and Gu Huimin. 2010. "Construction and Culture in Research: Understandings of the Fourth Buddhist Festival, Wutaishan, China." *Tourism Management* 31:167–178.

——. 2009. *Tourism in China: Destinations, Cultures and Communities.* London: Routledge.

Schopen, Gregory. 1997. *Bones, Stones, and Buddhist Monks: Collected Papers on the Archaeology, Epigraphy, and Texts of Monastic Buddhism in India.* Honolulu: University of Hawai'i Press.

Shackley, Myra. 2006. "Empty Bottles at Sacred Sites: Religious Retailing at Ireland's National Shrine." In *Tourism, Religion and Spiritual Journeys,* edited by Dallen J. Timothy and Daniel H. Olsen, 94–103. New York: Routledge.

——.2001. *Managing Sacred Sites: Service Provision and Visitor Experience.* London: Continuum.

Shepherd, Robert J. 2013. *Faith in Heritage: Displacement, Development, and Religious Tourism in Contemporary China.* Walnut Creek, CA: Left Coast Press.

Shi Fangfang. 2009. "Evaluation of Visitor Experience at Chinese Buddhist Sites: The Case of Wutai Mountain." In *Tourism in China: Destinations, Cultures and Communities,* edited by Chris Ryan and Huimin Gu, 197–212. London: Routledge.

Silk, Jonathan A. 2008. *Managing Monks: Administrators and Administrative Roles in Indian Buddhist Monasticism.* Oxford: Oxford University Press.

Simmel, Georg. (1900) 1978. *The Philosophy of Money.* London: Routledge.

Stausberg, Michael. 2011. *Religion and Tourism: Crossroads, Destinations and Encounters.* London: Routledge.

Tang Yunyun. 2014. "Kunming Panlong Temple closed its doors to guests for the first time to protest 'commercialization.'" *China News Service.* August 8. Accessed September 17, 2014. http://www.chinanews.com/cul/2014/08-18/6503559.shtml.

Tschang, Chi-Chu. 2007. "In China, Dharma Confronts the Dollar." *Businessweek Online* 20.

Timothy, Dallen J., and Daniel H. Olsen, eds. 2011. *Tourism, Religion and Spiritual Journeys.* London: Routledge.

Vukonić, Boris. 1996. *Tourism and Religion.* Oxford: Pergamon.

Walsh, Michael J. 2010. *Sacred Economies: Buddhist Monasticism and Territoriality in Medieval China.* New York: Columbia University Press.

Wank, David, and Yoshiko Ashiwa. 2006. "The Politics of a Reviving Buddhist Temple in

Contemporary China: State, Association and Religion in Southeast China." *The Journal of Asian Studies* 65 (2): 337–359.
Welch, Holmes. (1967) 1973. *The Practice of Chinese Buddhism, 1900–1950*. Cambridge, MA: Harvard University Press.
Wong, Cara, Alison McIntosh, and Chris Ryan. 2012. "Buddhism and Tourism Perceptions of the Monastic Community at Pu-tuo-shan, China." *Annals of Tourism Research* 40:213–234.
Yang Fenggang and Wei Dedong. 2005. "The Bailin Buddhist Temple: Thriving under Communism." In *State, Market, and Religions in Chinese Societies*, edited by Yang Fenggang, 63–86. Leiden: Brill.
Yee, Shirley. 1996. "Material Interests and Morality in the Trade of Thai Talismans." *Southeast Asian Journal of Social Science* 24 (2): 1–21.
Yu Xueming. 2007. *Fojiao de fazhan he fazhan de fojiao: cong dangdai shaolinsi kan zhongguo de weilai* (Buddhist development and the development of Buddhism: The future of Chinese Buddhism as seen from the contemporary phenomenon of Shaolin Temple). *Henan Social Sciences* 15 (3): 7–12.
Zaidman, Nurit. 2003. "Commercialization of Religious Objects: A Comparison Between Traditional and New Age Religions." *Social Compass* 50 (3): 345–360.

10

How I Meditated with Your Mother

Speed Dating at Temples and Shrines in Contemporary Japan

MATTHEW MITCHELL

ONE JAPANESE DATING WEBSITE BEGINS WITH THE following:

> It's difficult to find other people who like temples and shrines. It is thought of as a hobby for elderly people, one that is outdated or plain, and so it's hard for you to tell anyone about it. However, there are many younger people who like temples. So, we've created a space where men and women with this same hobby can connect and seek marriage partners. We created these events to support you. Enjoying an event at a temple or shrine can be the key to meeting your special someone. (Jisyacon 2016d)

This company, Jisyacon (www.jisyacon.com), is among a growing number of matchmakers who specialize in activity-centered speed dating events. What sets Jisyacon apart is its focus on Buddhist temples and shrines. Though this may seem a difficult sell amongst the increasingly secularized youth of Japan, as I will show below it does draw in those who are seeking a match made in Maitreya's Tushita Heaven.[1]

In this chapter, I analyze information from websites such as dating forums and matchmaking company homepages to discuss how companies and priests in contemporary Japan are commodifying Buddhist spaces so that, in addition to being centers of Buddhist activities, they are also centers for events directed at seeking a spouse. In other words, they are being sold as locations valuable for finding love. Below I discuss how this type of speed dating began, what happens during a session, how these activities are considered efficacious for matchmaking, who participates and why, and what temples receive from their participation. As I largely focus on the events planned by Jisyacon, I introduce its founder and his motivations as well.

A number of things come to light from this examination. First, companies such as Jisyacon are successful at marketing their events to both participants and Buddhist priests, which they do by promoting the experience to both groups as a way to overcome the challenges they face. For participants, the challenge is finding a temple-loving mate; for priests, it is attracting visitors to their temples. Second, priests and tour companies expand their explanations of rituals, temple space, and even their roles in order to convince participants of the efficacy of looking for love in Buddhist places. Third, singles events at temples fill a niche in the domestic Buddhist tourism market that is not filled by other tour companies that largely cater to an older clientele.

From the above, it should be clear that this research is placed at the intersections of Buddhist tourism, commodification, and marketing. To encourage compatibility between the event and the temple, the matchmakers promote these events, which may seem too secular and beyond the purview of Buddhist temples (more on this below), to priests as an efficacious means of drawing an interested crowd of youth to their temples. Priests partner with the matchmakers, and they try to attract young love seekers who have an interest in Buddhist temples. In the process, they often reinterpret Buddhist rituals, space, and deities to promote them as efficacious for matchmaking.

Seeking marriage by traveling to a temple or shrine is not new in Japan. Usually, however, it involves traveling to a temple or shrine famous for "making connections,"[2] praying or having a ritual done, purchasing an amulet, or participating in other tourist and consumer activities (Reader and Tanabe 1998). Likewise, in recent years, temples are not unusual locations to have marriages performed, though they have not reached the popularity of Christian chapel weddings.[3] Some temples, such as Shunkō-in in Kyoto, have even paired with hotel and tour companies to encourage foreign LGBTQIA tourists to have Buddhist wedding or friend ceremonies.

Speed dating at temples, however, is a relatively recent phenomenon. It is a twist on the basic form of singles events, speed dating, or marriage-seeking activities, called *konkatsu*[4] in Japanese, where a group of an even number of men and women meet somewhere, usually a restaurant or bar, and spend some time talking in the hopes of meeting that special someone.[5] In the mid-2000s and 2010s, the number and variety of these types of activities increased and came to include hiking, barbeque parties, snowboarding, and so on.[6] Some of these companies eventually branched out to temple- and shrine-related activities. Temples and Buddhist sects have also organized temple speed dating events. But, in some cases these temple-organized events are a way for future head priests of temples/shrines to meet wives, largely to ensure that there is a successor to the typical family-run temple.[7]

Speed dating at temples and shrines is called *jishakon* in Japanese, which is an amalgamated word. The first portion, *jisha* means temples and shrines. The *kon* has one of two origins: the first is from *konpa,* which means a "get-together" or a "group party." The other origin is *konkatsu,* itself an amalgam (of the characters of *kon* from marriage—*kekkon*—and *katsu* from *katsudō,* or activity) meaning "marriage-seeking activities," or seeking that special someone.[8] Because of these origins, the word *jishakon* can therefore mean "a group party at a temple or shrine" or "searching for marriage at a temple or shrine."

Though many dating companies hold singles events at temples and shrines, Jisyacon specializes in them. Jisyacon is pronounced the same as Jishakon, but it utilizes a slightly different Romanization. It began organizing these events in 2009 after its founder, Horiuchi Katsuhiko, was repeatedly told "I like temples and shrines, but it's difficult to find people who have the same interests." So, he founded the organization as a way to bring men and women who like temples and shrines together. As of 2016, he and Jisyacon had organized over two hundred temple/shrine speed dating events. Horiuchi is not a priest, but a layperson with an interest in temples and shrines. Before he founded Jisyacon, he organized temple-stay events through his organization called "temple-stay research society" (*shukubō kenkyūkai*), an activity he continues. His research society and Jisyacon temple dating ventures have been certified as official tour agencies in Japan, joining many other tour agencies that focus solely or in some part on temples or pilgrimage. However, Jisyacon's concentration on romance hints at an expansion of Buddhist-related touristic activities that draws from and yet moves beyond religious, cultural, and ludic reasons.[9]

Meet, Pray, Love: What Happens at a Temple Singles Event

Jisyacon advertises their events a few months in advance. Participants have ample opportunities to learn about the events through Horiuchi's or the company's social media accounts, newspapers, and word of mouth. They can sign up online a month or so in advance. The participation form asks questions one would expect: selected event, name, e-mail address, cell phone number, area where participant lives, gender, where the person heard about Jisyacon, number of times participated in Jisyacon events, and space for a message. Staff at Jisyacon use this information to try to group people according to the area they live in, age, etc., so that it is more likely that people will be able to find a match that will work out.

On the day of the event, the group will meet at a nearby train station, introduce themselves, and then walk to the temple/shrine. The group's time at the temple, which is facilitated by both Jisyacon employees and priests or employees of the temple, can last anywhere from a few hours for a short activity to two days for a temple-stay event. During this time, the priests will give a Dharma talk, which can include information about the history of the temple/shrine, its icon, the sect's teachings, and so on. If the temple or its deity is said to be an efficacious matchmaker, the priest will emphasize this. For example, Uno, the head priest of Shōrinji in Kyoto, discussed how his temple's *Bishamonten* (Skt. *Vaiśravaṇa*) and *Kichijōten* (Skt. *Laksmi, Mahasri,* or *Sri-mahadevi*) are powerful in making love matches if one prays to both icons. He then added another layer of mystique to his temple by highlighting how until the 1870s, this was a popular spot with the female dancers (aka *geisha*) of the Gion entertainment district (Jisyacon 2016q).

The group will then do an activity that is centered on the special features of the temple/shrine, the season, and so on. These can include viewing the temple's Buddhist images, drawing a Buddhist image, copying sutras, doing seated meditation, performing waterfall austerities (chanting a sutra or mantra underneath a waterfall), receiving "luck in making connections" rituals,[10] touring the temple grounds, and so on. After this, the group moves into the speed dating portion either in a large room at the temple or at a nearby restaurant. If this is at the temple, it may include Buddhist vegetarian food. The Jisyacon staff will periodically direct the participants to switch seats so that they can talk with as many people as possible. This staff member will also pay attention to people's personalities and other aspects of their lives, and Horiuchi has even been known to direct participants to others he thinks they will match well with. At the end of this initial party participants can exchange contact details if interested. Of course, participants can refuse or give false information. Some organize after-parties as a group or as a couple, but participation is optional and Jisyacon staff do not attend. In the days that follow, participants can then arrange dates if they are lucky.

These events are not cheap. A basic event costs around 4,000 yen (roughly 40 USD) for participation and around 4,000 for the party. This does not include transportation and the fee for entering the temple, if there is one. Longer or more involved events cost more; for example, a visit to Hōkekyōdera and a ritual by one of its ascetics cost 6,000 yen, and another special *konkatsu* night event at Mt. Mitaka near Tokyo was free to participate in but cost between 8,000 and 10,000 yen per person per night for lodging and two meals.

How much of this goes to Jisyacon? At Jisyacon events, there are as few as twenty, and as many as fifty, participants. If the participation fee is 4,000 yen per person, the total the company receives for a typical event is at least 80,000 yen and at most 200,000 yen. Presumably, Jisyacon gives some of that to the priest or other speakers for their role in the event.[11] The 4,000 yen for the party afterward (for regular events) is roughly the going rate (perhaps on the cheap end for Tokyo or Kyoto/Osaka) for a dinner and drink set menu party at a restaurant, so Jisyacon probably does not receive anything from that. Events are typically held in the Tokyo area or the area surrounding Kyoto, Osaka, and Kobe. This is because these are the largest population centers in Japan, and they are easily accessible for many potential participants. This geographic proximity also means that people can participate in multiple events if they so desire (as seen in the case of Mr. "S,"[12] who participated in nine! (Jisyacon 2016n)), or if they miss one in their area, they can catch another without too long of a wait.

Second, these areas are home to some of the most famous temples in Japan. It is logical that Jisyacon and other organizing companies would hold events at these temples because their name power alone would draw in participants. However, a quick review of the list of Jisyacon hosts shows a fairly even mix of famous and not-so-famous temples.[13] The Jisyacon website says that it is possible to arrange events outside of these areas. However, to do so requires a local organizing sponsor, payment of Jisyacon staff hotel and meals, and an additional fee based on distance that ranges from 15,000 yen for areas near Tokyo to 85,000 yen for the western island of Kyūshū.

Must Love Temples: Demographics and Reasons for Participating

According to the Jisyacon site, most participants are office workers in their twenties, thirties, or forties.[14] Many of them have an interest in Buddhism, temples, art, or history, though people can attend if they know nothing about any of these topics but are interested in learning. Jisyacon and similar companies thus cater to a much younger crowd than many other temple and shrine tours, such as bus tours of the famous Shikoku pilgrimage circuit, whose participants are typically over sixty (Reader 2005, 78). To participate in a speed dating event, Jisyacon says that participants must "1) be single, without a girlfriend or boyfriend. 2) Be seeking a serious meeting/relationship. 3) Like temples/shrines" (Jisyacon 2016e). Many say they joined because they were looking for a serious relationship, and they did not want to participate in a regular singles event. For some, other types of events were just not interesting. One participant said that other singles events were mostly sitting around, but temple singles events were more active. Most come to these events by themselves, though some bring a friend or two. Some are first-time participants, while others have joined Jisyacon events multiple times.

Jisyacon and other companies make sure that there are even numbers of men and women involved in the events. However, this means they have to turn away some who want to participate. One participant from one of these other companies with the username QJV97FCr said that she or he heard that there are five times as many women who apply to participate as there are men. This participant suggests that this is because "women are more interested in spiritual events" than men are (QJV97FCr 2012). Putting aside whether women or men are more interested in spiritual matters, it seems that Jisyacon does not suffer from this degree of gender imbalance. On their website one can find as many singles events that are "only taking applications from women at this time," meaning that they have received more applications from men than women, as one can find events asking for more men to apply.[15]

Looking beyond love, there are other reasons for men and women to participate in singles events at temples. One way to find these reasons is to look at how participants rationalize their participation even though they know that they may fail in their attempt to find love. Participants' explanations for this were gendered in interesting ways. Men focused on the connections possible. For instance, a few men said "if I go, perhaps I can just meet someone" even as a friend. Many men did talk about the friendships that they made with other men at these events and how they would organize drinking parties with people they had met. Women took a more experiential approach, saying "even if I don't find love, I will have had this interesting experience that I wouldn't otherwise have had."

Nostalgia was another reason for some people's participation. Several people, like Ms. S and Mr. K, said that their Jisyacon event was "just like a junior high school trip [to see temples and shrines], so it was fun!" (Jisyacon 2016k, 2016m). For others, it was a nostalgic turn to Japan's history or tradition (either real or in the imaginary) that drew them to participate. Not all participants enjoyed the experience, however. On one net forum devoted to topics related to love hosted by the Yomiuri newspaper, a person with the user name Kiriko asked for advice about whether she should attend a nearby temple speed dating event.[16] Kiriko got a number of positive responses including "if I were single, I'd go," "I went and it was fun," and "better to go than regret not going." Kiriko also received some off-target advice. Several suggested, "if you like temples that much, why don't you just marry a priest?"[17] Others related their not-so-positive experiences. A user named Saa said that "many who went were passive... one woman talked the entire time. Even though you all have the same interests, it's not that conversation naturally develops." Another, going by the user name of U, said "the women were respectable, smart, and beautiful, but many of the men were a little odd.... Not everyone was interested in temples, and some people talked about things that were completely unrelated. One even asked about how much I pay in rent!... It was the opposite of what I expected, and didn't match my interests, so I have no plans of going again" (Hatsugen komachi 2013).

I would like to make a small note here regarding the language that

Jisyacon and other companies use to describe their customers, who are goal-oriented (they seek a marriage partner) and local (many come from cities or regions where the temples are located) tourists to the temples. Jisyacon and other companies use the word "participants" (*sankasha*) for the people who have signed up for and participate in singles events at temples and shrines. One reason they may do so is because it encompasses participation in both the temple-oriented and romance-seeking activities. Additionally, although many of these participants are interested in Buddhism, company websites refrain from calling them "Buddhists." Questions of belonging to a religious tradition in Japan are often complicated,[18] and from the late 1990s until now, many young Japanese have become "spiritual but not religious." Furthermore, the number of people claiming Buddhist affiliation has been declining for years.[19] So, even though these events take place at temples and shrines, and the activities that take place there are Buddhist (for the most part), it is a wise strategy for companies to avoid labeling participants "Buddhist," but rather focus on their interests in temples, shrines, history, or meditation. In other words, calling participants Buddhists would risk alienating a large portion of their potential clientele who may have an interest in temples, but not identify as Buddhist.

This labeling of individuals as participants also widens the clientele in regard to religious tourism, especially targeting domestic tourists. It is clear that some participants are motivated to venture to the temples and shrines because of their connections to or interest in Buddhism, but many others are seeking benefits (i.e., nostalgia and/or love) other than religious ones. These travelers venture to a sacred site not (or not only) for a spiritual or religious purpose, but because the site is being marketed and commodified as both a cultural site and a place that is efficacious for matchmaking. As noted in the Introduction to this volume, a tourist is simply someone who "travels temporarily . . . away from home to another region" (Timothy and Olsen 2006, 6). Thus, in the case of Japan, we see that in order to widen a temple's consumer base, domestic tourists are encouraged to journey to temples for a variety of motivations. In the next section, I examine the myriad reasons why young Japanese participate in such singles events at temples. In addition to an interest in Buddhism, participants join Jisyacon's dating tours of temples because of societal pressures, the romance industry, and testimonials.

Love Actually? Marriage and Uncertainties Facing Young People in Contemporary Japan

Like many the world over, young Japanese people face familial and social pressure to marry.[20] Unwed men and women are often stigmatized as freeloaders or "parasite singles" who live with their parents and have no ambition.[21] Women, in particular, face the lion's share of these criticisms; they are seen as lazy if they are unwed and unemployed, and as irresponsible for "their failure to serve the public good as wives and mothers of the nation" if they focus on their careers instead of love (Ambros 2015, 156; Mirza 2016, 27–28).[22] How people look for love has also changed. Arranged marriages had been fairly common in Japan even up to the early 1990s when 25 percent to 30 percent of marriages were arranged (Applbaum 1995; Hendry 2010). However, the number of love marriages has increased significantly, which has given rise to a host of personal concerns over how to find a spouse.

These pressures and concerns have spurred the growth of the Japanese romance industry into what was in 2006[23] a sixty billion yen (roughly 600 million USD) a year industry comprised of at least 4,000 individuals and companies (METI 2006, 14–16). The industry is made up of traditional matchmaking services, Internet dating sites, guidebooks that promise to mold purchasers into marriageable material, advisors who offer strategies to be successful in dating, organizers of singles parties, and others. Organizations that use temples and shrines for singles events are, of course, a part of this industry, and both Buddhist and romance-seeking activities become intertwined commodities. By bringing together people with interests in temples and shrines, Jisyacon attempts to assuage participants' fears "that there is no one else their age with an interest in temples and shrines," and thereby earn money by tackling this area of concern for participants (Jisyacon 2016d).

Organizers of these events are eager to highlight their successes. Horiuchi claims that as of 2015, over two hundred couples met at Jisyacon events and began dating afterward. He also says that in 2015 alone there were five marriages and one or two children as a result of connections made at Jisyacon events (Nikkan SPA! 2015). Not content to simply provide numbers to indicate success, Jisyacon proudly posts stories of successful couples on their website. These testimonials follow a set pattern of how each person found out about Jisyacon, why he or she decided to join, initial feelings at the event, impressions of others at the event, how he or she became calmer in the course of the event either through activities at the temple or the friendly face of another participant, if he or she participated in multiple events, how the person met his or her partner there, what dates the couple went on, how they decided to become exclusive, and if there is discussion of marriage. At the end of the description is an encouragement of others to try the event, and thanks to Horiuchi for organizing it. In this acknowledgements section, one person named Ms. S even called Horiuchi a deity of matchmaking in human form (Jisyacon 2016l). These stories encourage participation by advertising that Jisyacon events are successful, and they lower the anxiety of potential participants by telling them what to expect in terms of the types of people they might meet (people with various interests in temples), and the activities they might do (tours of the temple, sutra copying, meditation, etc., and talking at the after-party).

Many participants state that being at the temple made it easier to connect or talk with other participants. This was in part due to a combination of elements, including shared interests, involvement in the same activities, and freedom to move around during activities (to a certain degree—standing up and talking during a group meditation session is generally frowned upon!), so they could talk with people who interested them. However, these are all reasons that can be replicated in other speed dating events—for instance, a hiking singles event would bring together people with shared interests, they would be involved in the same activities, and they would definitely be moving around.

In addition to participants' testimonials, organizers are clear to indicate the Buddhist-specific reasons for the couple-forming efficacy of their events. In these explanations, we can see Buddhist priests (and others) expanding the purpose of Buddhist rituals to encompass the needs of love-seeking visitors. For example, one of Jisyacon's competitors called Konkatsu Style claims that copying sutras is a form of "prayer for successfully finding a love match," so participation kills two birds with one stone by combining a prayer for a love match with activities to find a marriage partner. Priests also discussed the efficacy of the activities they had planned at their temple, but they used the language of preparing the heart or achieving an open mind as reasons for the activities' efficacy. One priest at a Nichiren temple, Kusano Myōkei, led the participants in what he calls "Tibetan exercises," which helped participants care for their bodies and open their hearts to love, he said (Jisyacon 2016j). Morita Eiryū, a priest at Seiryūji Fudō Hall, said that undergoing waterfall austerities helped people to understand pain and develop compassion (Jisyacon 2016p). Matsumura Kanshō said that drawing the Buddhist image at his temple puts people in a calm mind-set (Jisyacon 2016r). Oka, the vice head priest at En'yūji Temple, said that "copying sutras allows you to put down the baggage that you have in your heart. When your heart becomes lighter, you become more open to forming connections with those around you. Doing that, you are certain to have a wonderful meeting with someone" (Jisyacon 2016a). These then enable participants to be more successful at finding a love match. The debate over whether these adaptations are orthodox or even simply a form of Buddhist expedient means (*upāya*) is beyond the scope of this chapter. Rather, what is important is that they demonstrate how priests and organizers are willing to adapt Buddhist rituals and promote them as efficacious in meeting contemporary visitors' needs in order to draw people to the temple.

Of course, being a Buddhist temple, Cupid's arrows could just as easily have been loosed by buddhas, bodhisattvas, and other Buddhist deities. This is thought to be especially likely if the deities at temples are famous for matchmaking. Companies include this information in their advertisements and the priests highlight it in their Dharma talks. Indeed, these powers may have been a reason why some participants chose to come to an event at a particular temple.[24] One woman called K says that though she was nervous and afraid, she had the courage to talk to her current partner when he sat next to her at the temple "because the temple's Avalokiteśvara led him there" (Jisyacon 2016o).

Sleepless in the Temple: The Uncertainties Facing Priests in Contemporary Japan

While it may sound unusual to scholars of Buddhism in other areas, contemporary Buddhist priests in Japan are facing several types of uncertainty. I have already mentioned one—that many must ensure that they are married and have (male) children who will become priests, so that the temple stays in the family. Having a smooth transition from father to child reduces uncertainty for the temple's parishioners as well, since many will be familiar with the children of the priest, and many would (presumably) prefer a local priest who is familiar with the area and their families, to see to their needs and perform funeral rituals for their family members and memorials for their ancestors.

This hints at another area of uncertainty for priests. Since at least the sixteenth century, many Japanese temples could rely on the income from providing funeral and memorial services for a set group of parishioners in their area (Hur 2007). The parishioner-temple relationship was largely set and difficult to change in the Tokugawa period (1603–1868), and even though it lost quasi-legal support in the late nineteenth century, remnants of this so-called parishioner system can be seen even today. Combined with this is the more recent uprooting of families from the locales of their ancestors. Many people have moved to larger cities, and no longer have connections with their family's old parish temple. Some may not even know what school of Buddhism their family belongs to until a family member passes away. This is exacerbated by the rural depopulation and lowering birthrate, which has also reduced the number of parishioners that support local, rural temples.[25] Furthermore, priests have seen people turn to other types of funerals or memorials that may be nonreligious, or might not come with the obligatory financial connection with a temple that the family has little to no relationship with (Rowe 2011).

This sense of uncertainty has gripped individual Buddhist priests, Buddhist schools, and even scholars of Buddhism. Many have sought to revitalize Buddhism through novel ways of bringing people (especially youth) to the temple, or new ways of providing Buddhist support to society at large (Nelson 2014). Some have opened cafes, a few have started Buddhist rock bands, and others have offered material and psychological support in disaster areas (McLaughlin 2013a, 2013b). Some see these (usually individual) efforts as hopeful, others as futile. However, these activities are viewed, many have declared that Buddhism is dying, or at the least, in need of serious help. Not all scholars see the case of Buddhism in this way. Jolyon Thomas, for instance, has stated that Buddhists have much to gain from saying that their tradition is in danger, and scholars of contemporary Buddhism have taken up this chant as well. According to Thomas, "this narrative of inexorable attenuation does not mesh with the continued reality of Buddhist survival.... In contemporary Japan Buddhist priests and ecclesial organizations use a variety of methods to ensure that their tradition survives and flourishes" (2016, 487). Whatever the case may be,[26] it is clear that many Japanese Buddhist priests themselves do feel some uncertainty about the future of their temple and tradition, and they hope to bring in new visitors to their temples (who they hope will come to learn more about Buddhism) and who will provide them, their temples, and even Japanese Buddhism itself with a new sense of purpose.

Horiuchi from Jisyacon also believes that temples are facing difficulties. He gives seven reasons for this:

1. *The threshold is high.* By this, Horiuchi means that people can be afraid to enter temples for a variety of reasons. Additionally, many priests do not realize that ordinary people feel this way, and "until they realize it, the distance between priests and ordinary people will not close."
2. *There's no reason to go.* Horiuchi says, "temples house wonderful teachings of Buddhism, but many people do not go to them. This is because priests don't show us Buddhism as a thing of splendor. Buddhism is useful in life. It is necessary for priests to concretely embody this."
3. *Technology at temples lags behind.* "One weakness of priests is that they have little contact with technology and information that affects both temples and society. Because of this, they are behind in new technology." Horiuchi thinks that it is essential for temples to enlist new technology and use it effectively. This is one area where Horiuchi has been extremely active, promoting his personal and business activities on Twitter, Facebook, and over e-mail.
4. *Information cannot be found.* "We cannot find information about temples. Putting out information is perhaps one area where temples are the worst. This includes understanding the characteristics of the internet and thinking about things before posting them on the internet."
5. *Priests are feared/afraid.* "This includes the dual meaning of 'priests are to be feared (from an ordinary person's point of view)' and 'Priests are afraid (of ordinary people).'"
6. *People do not gather at temples.* "Temples should be the pillars of communities. However, to do this, it is not effective to call in people at random." He says that priests must think about "what kind of place

would people who come to temples feel comfortable at? And then, in what shape could temples be to easily generate community?"

7. *Sermons don't reach the heart.* "Buddhism has countless wonderful teachings. However, what we seek cannot be found in listening to those teachings until they are exhausted. The way priests live their lives is more important than any talk. We will feel the wonder of Buddhism and find resonance in that way of living." (Horiuchi 2014)

Horiuchi hints at some larger societal issues, saying that "contemporary Japan has lost its balance... and what has been lost is human relations" as a result of contemporary conveniences, which have "cost people balance in their families, neighborhoods, schools, and workplaces" (2014). Temples can play a part in society by making people happy and rebuilding community if they follow his suggestions and solve these seven problems.[27] Additionally, while many trace problems facing priests to issues such as temples' reliance on traditional funerals and memorial services, Horiuchi argues instead that priests have difficulty with communication and creating a welcoming environment for all people. While this may be difficult to fix, he says that it is not impossible for resourceful and thoughtful priests who closely follow his list of specific items, or if they have the guidance of someone like him. In other words, Horiuchi is marketing his expertise to priests: he says that he has the know-how to fix the problems facing priests, and that he can help if they read his e-book or request to act as a host to a singles event or temple stay organized by his company.

Though not made explicit on Jisyacon's website, singles events at temples and shrines are designed to help with all seven of the problems Horiuchi describes. By being the organizer of events aimed at young people, Horiuchi can lower the threshold (#1) for going to a temple by doing things like guiding participants through correct procedures at the temple. Arranging dating events at temples gives participants a reason to go (#2) and to gather at temples, giving priests a reason to think about taking up their roles as pillars in the community again (#6). Additionally, bringing people to the temple will lead priests to be more comfortable around them, and participants to be more comfortable around priests (#5). His use of Twitter, Facebook, e-mail, and the web to advertise Jisyacon events provides an example for priests to follow (#3) when they decide to make information about their temples or events available (#4). Finally, with his guidance, priests can learn how to reach participants' hearts in ways that Dharma talks cannot (#7). Of course, singles events are just one of the ways that priests can combat the difficulties Horiuchi describes.

For Horiuchi, making people happy and reviving Buddhism are the two intertwined goals that drive his various temple tour activities. He says, "even as just one person, I want to create a path where many people can become happy. One way is through the temple stay research society. Another is through temple speed dating" (2014). The final one is through his writings and seminars, where he teaches priests how to revive their temples. Horiuchi says that he intends "not just to revive temples, but through raising them up, to create even a little happiness for me and people who have no connections to me or to temples" (2014).

Of course, Horiuchi charges both participants in Jisyacon events and Buddhist priests for his services. For people involved in the pilgrimage business, professing altruistic motives—in Horiuchi's case promoting happiness and the spread of Buddhism—while at the same time hoping to make money is not uncommon. Ian Reader (2014, 89–90) calls these "moral motives" or "altruistic motives."[28] These are the religious or altruistic motives that companies, merchants, and others who cater to attendees at religious events or pilgrims state as the main reason for their actions, with any profits gained declared to be an unintended consequence. For Horiuchi and Jisyacon the altruistic motives are designed to benefit both the temples and participants. For temples, Horiuchi hopes to use his expertise to help temples overcome the problems facing them. Singles events at temples are one way that he can assist with this. However, it is obvious that there are limits to this type of method. The most obvious one is that Jisyacon operates largely in the population centers near Tokyo and Kyoto/Osaka, and that they will most likely have participants come to temples that are larger or more well known. This means that he is unable to assist the smaller temples in rural areas, and unfortunately, they are the ones in most need of help to overcome difficulties due to depopulation.

On the other hand, Jisyacon's outwardly altruistic motive for working with participants is to assist people who are interested in temples to find others like themselves. In this, they may be more successful. However, they do face limitations such as the numbers of participants they can feasibly allow to participate in an event, and that they largely restrict their activities to urban areas in central Japan.

Looking for a Few Good Priests

Jisyacon is not only looking for people to come and participate in these events, they must have temples and shrines to act as hosts, otherwise they will not have a service to sell. The Jisyacon website thus introduces temple and shrine singles events to both participants and priests. In the section aimed at priests, Horiuchi introduces the origins of temple singles events, saying "they were born out of the voices of those who said 'I can't find people with similar interests who like temples and shrines'" (Jisyacon 2016c). He says,

> We are seeking temples, shrines, Buddhist priests, and Shintō priests who can assist with temple and shrine speed dating. Seated

> meditation or sutra copying, vegetarian temple food, or special viewings of Buddhist icons, Dharma talks about or rituals for making love matches, or cultural experiences where the temple or shrine is the location. We will accept anything for a theme as long as it can be connected with temples or shrines. Our plan is to coordinate well so that [this event] is tied to an increase in activity at the temples and shrines. (Jisyacon 2016c)

At the bottom of this page is a form where temples and shrines interested in participating can ask questions or offer their help.

In a similar manner to successful couples providing their testimonials for potential participants to see, Jisyacon also prominently displays the stories of priests whose temples have hosted events. Priests' testimonials describe to potential temple hosts what they can expect from events and delineate reasons to participate. In other words, these testimonials serve as a way of marketing Jisyacon to temples just as the stories of lucky couples help advertise Jisyacon to participants. One purpose they serve is to allay priests' concerns about hosting such an event. Particularly important is how much of a burden it would place on them, especially if they have busy ritual schedules. All of the priest testimonials emphasize that Horiuchi and Jisyacon staff made hosting these events easy. For example, Kusano Myōkei, the head priest at the Nichiren temple Myōkenji, said that he felt that he could rely on Horiuchi to handle most of the event, leaving him free to take care of his portion, which was to give a Dharma talk and other activities (Jisyacon 2016j).

Priests also were concerned about the types of people who might participate in such events. Who would listen to Dharma talks or sit on their meditation cushions, for instance? The priests in the testimonials state that they were pleased with the participants' involvement in the activities. They commented on how participants wholeheartedly joined in activities from meditation to sutra copying. "They even listened intently to my Dharma talk," said several priests. Kōbōji Temple's Watanabe said that he enjoyed having the Jisyacon participants at his temple so much that he "wanted to say to them that they could come to the temple any time just to talk" (Jisyacon 2016g). Others talked about the joy of having guests with a variety of interests. "They asked questions we don't normally get asked, such as why did you become a priest," said Itō Yūsuke, an administrator at Kōjōji (Jisyacon 2016h). Andō Yuichirō, a historian who led a tour of a temple, said that he enjoyed getting informed historical questions from people this young (Jisyacon 2016p). The participants' level of engagement—listening intently to a Dharma talk, wanting to copy a sutra, etc.—seems to have been a shock to some of the priests, especially coming from young participants. However, these are exactly the types of people many priests hope to get in their temples, so displaying this in the testimonial would encourage other priests to offer to host events. Many priests talked about how it was rare to have visitors there for something besides a funeral or memorial ritual.

We can see this in priests' reasons for hosting events. Sōgen Eikai, a priest at Kōtakuji, said that he set up his event so young people could get a feel for Buddhism and an experience they wouldn't normally have (Jisyacon 2016i). Matsumura Kanshō from the Nakanobō sub-temple of Taimadera, said he is grateful that his temple was able to help people develop relationships, but was also happy to see young people at the temple. "Temples were at the cutting edge of culture historically, so it is my wish to see temples washed over with young people's energy now," he says (Jisyacon 2016r). Bidō, head priest at Honkōji Temple, said that pairing the search for a spouse with sutra copying isn't the first thing that a Buddhist priest would think of, and that he was nervous at first about what kind of sermon to give and whether participants would enjoy their time at the temple. However, he sees this as a good opportunity to talk with people about Buddhism. "Rituals and memorials are important, but this activity is so much more so. Temples need to be active in their communities," he says (Jisyacon 2016b).

Some priests have been seeking ways to engage a broader segment of the population—to make Buddhism relevant. The testimonials state how singles events helped them engage people in their communities while re-envisioning their roles and that of their temples. Oka, vice head priest at En'yūji Temple said,

> My initial response was What?!? Searching for a spouse at temples? With sutra copying? This has got to be a mismatch. . . . However, when I thought about it more, what is important in Buddhism is connections, or "*en*." The duty of a temple is to connect people to each other. It's not a mismatch, rather, there is no more appropriate place to do activities to find a partner than at temples! (Jisyacon 2016a)

Morita Eiryu agrees, saying,

> Originally, the purpose of temples and shrines across Japan was to lead people to happiness, but now Horiuchi has been doing that important task, acting as a representative of the Shintō and Buddhist deities as well as the representative of the temples and shrines. All the temples and shrines in the country would agree and cooperate [with Horiuchi on this project]. (Jisyacon 2016p)

The sole Shintō priest represented on Jisyacon's website agreed, saying that "setting up connections is an important part of being a shrine priest. I am grateful to have had Jisyacon at my shrine" (Jisyacon 2016f). By showcasing the voices of participating priests, Horiuchi demonstrates how they can bring in some non-funeral-related income, interact with younger people, enable connections between people, and introduce Buddhism to the participants either through meditation, sutra copying, or Tibetan exercises. At the same time, these testimonials help Jisyacon market the events to priests. This is vitally important for Horiuchi because without temples to host his events, he would not have a service to market to lovers of temples.

Jisyacon and other companies organizing temple singles events fill a niche in the matchmaking industry and at the same time serve a group long overlooked by the Buddhist tourism industry. As I mentioned above, participants in many temple and shrine tours in Japan such as the famous Shikoku pilgrimage circuit are over sixty (Reader 2005, 78). For the most part, if young people were interested in going to temples and shrines before the advent of Jisyacon and similar companies, they would have to either go by themselves (and miss out on many of the benefits of going with a group, such as guided tours of the temple grounds), or travel with people their parents' or grandparents' age. By creating matchmaking events, Jisyacon and other companies have made a way for young people interested in temples and shrines to gain the benefits of organized tours with the comradery of people their own age. They do, however, add a stipulation that participants must be looking for a love match, so it does prevent some potential young participants from joining. But the point remains that they have created a new category of tourists—individuals visiting temples not only to perform a religious act but also to potentially make a love match.

Priests have been responsive to this change, and to those who are interested in finding love at temples. They have sought to re-envision Buddhism, their roles, and those of their temples to meet these interests. We can see this, particularly, when priests declare that connections are important to Buddhism and temples were originally supposed to create happiness. At the same time, priests and matchmaking companies have marketed Buddhist rituals as efficacious in making love connections. In some cases, little effort is required on their part to emphasize this, such as when there are existing rites, amulets, or deities that already create "good [love] connections." In other cases, priests rethink even seemingly unrelated practices such as sutra copying or sketching a Buddhist image so they can be seen as efficacious in helping find a partner. Of course, priests modifying rituals, amulets, and their roles, or that of their temples to meet a demand from petitioners is not new (Reader and Tanabe 1998, chap. 6; Thomas 2016). It is also an element of John Nelson's experimental Buddhism, which are the changes priests have been making to remain relevant in contemporary society. For Nelson (2014), the impetus for change comes from the Buddhist priests he interviews. While this chapter has discussed changes to rituals and spaces, what is interesting is that change has been adopted after being suggested from a company external to Buddhism. An outside company has alerted priests to the demands of Japanese singles, and therefore helped shape dialogue about rituals and spaces, and how they are marketed. To put it another way, priests have worked with non-Buddhist groups (Jisyacon and other organizers) to redefine Buddhist rituals and temple places to include secular ideas (romantic love, for example), thereby promoting engagement with Buddhism by young Japanese tourists to local temples.[29]

I have also discussed how Jisyacon addresses feelings of uncertainty from two types of consumers. On the side of the participants, it is the uncertainty that they might not find someone to marry, an anxiety that has been compounded by politicians and pundits. Those with an interest in temples may be especially concerned about finding someone with whom they will share an interest in visiting temples and shrines. This most obvious group of consumers is seeking access to marriage partners with similar interests, and at the same time, is hoping to gain an experience at a temple that matches their imaginary of what Buddhist temples should be (austere, ritually awe-inspiring, historical, architecturally pleasing, ascetically challenging, etc.). On the side of the priests, it is that they feel they need to be more engaged in the outside world and that they need to attract people to their temples. Buddhist priests in Japan have for decades been criticized for not being more involved in society and for only performing funeral and memorial rituals. As consumers, priests hope to gain Horiuchi's expertise and/or access to willing and interested groups of young (potential repeat) visitors. Jisyacon markets itself to both types of consumers at the same time, attempting to assuage the uncertainty of unmarried people who like temples and Buddhist priests who would like more people to visit their temples. However, as stated above, Jisyacon largely limits its reach to fairly well-known temples near the population centers of Tokyo and Kyoto/Osaka, which means that smaller rural temples and young people outside these areas cannot receive assistance.

Horiuchi has made himself into a matchmaker, creating successful matches between participants. At the same time, he also matches priests with a willing and interested group of young people who they hope will breathe new life into their temples. Whether couples will return to temples after finding a love match, however, remains to be seen.

Notes

1 I would like to thank the participants in the workshop "Buddhist Tourism in Asia: Sacred Sites within Global Networks" and Courtney Bruntz, Hannah Gould, Jessica Starling, and Brooke Schedneck, for comments that have greatly improved this chapter.

2 *Enmusubi* in Japanese.

3 For more about chapel weddings in Japan, see Fisch (2001) and LeFebvre (2015).

4 Dalton and Dales state that "*konkatsu* is understood to include activities that are actively directed towards finding a marital partner, including but not limited to engagement of marriage introduction agencies, participation in singles events (dinners, parties, excursions, sporting events) and self-development geared towards increasing marriageability." *Konkatsu* activities are generally less formal than traditional matchmaking (*omiai*). Additionally, literature on *konkatsu* suggests "that *konkatsu* is a tactical response to a decline in structures that had previously fostered romantic relationships leading to marriage, including workplace practices and employment trends" (Dalton and Dales 2016, 3).

5 LGBTQ+ parties may exist, but I have not heard about them.

6 Dalton and Dales state that online dating sites are not popular amongst Japanese because "there is a widespread fear and distrust of meeting people online. The anonymity of the world wide web is, for many, an unreliable and untrustworthy substitute for traditional mediators, such as friends and family, who tend to at least partially know both parties" (Dalton and Dales 2016, 7).

7 Japanese Buddhist priests are typically not celibate, and the leadership at many temples passes from father to son (typically). For more on this, see Jaffe (2011).

8 As Emma Dalton and Laura Dales note in their examination of *konkatsu* literature, ~*katsu* is an activity or action with a sense of devotion or obligation to perform it (Dalton and Dales 2016, 2–3).

9 Jolyon Thomas discusses *anime*- and *manga*-inspired pilgrimage/tourism to Shintō shrines and Buddhist temples. For more, see Thomas (2012, 31, 117–19; 2016).

10 *Enmusubi* or *ryōen jōju*.

11 In this way, Jisyacon and other companies that organize singles events at temples can be compared to funeral homes (or even, more recently, Amazon, which has begun marketing priestly services on its site!). These homes hire priests to come in to perform funerals, and they only pay the priests a portion of the money from the service.

12 I follow the Jisyacon website's use of pseudonyms. They supply pseudonyms for all participants, but not for company employees, nor for Buddhist priests at temples where Jisyacon events have been held.

13 Part of this may be because temple priests may not want to host events. For more on this, see below.

14 Jisyacon does organize events for people older than 40. These are clearly marked as such, as are "under 40" events.

15 However, it is interesting to note that in the mid-2000s, data suggested that 60 percent of the roughly 600,000 people involved in *konkatsu* activities were men (METI 2006, 15).

16 In this paragraph, I use the usernames provided on the discussion board. I am also associating feminine pronouns with Kiriko, since it is a feminine name, but of course, it could just as easily have been a man writing.

17 There have been hints at growing interest in women seeking to marry priests; this has been spurred on by handsome priest (*ikemen bōzu*) contests and romantic TV shows involving priests such as "*5-ji kara 9-ji made*."

18 For example, some people will state that they are not religious one moment, and then perform overtly religious acts the next (for example, Reader (1991)).

19 This is despite the fact that many people have familial ties with a Buddhist parish temple, which they will turn to for funeral and memorial rites. For more on the decline in Buddhist affiliations, please see Covell 2006; Nelson 2014; Reader 2011; Rowe 2011.

20 In Japan specifically, social and political pressure to marry stems from fear of

lowering birthrates and aging population These trends have even been picked up in the Western media in venues such as *The Economist* ("Marriage in Japan: I Don't," 2016), and *The Guardian* ("Why Have Young People in Japan Stopped Having Sex?" Haworth 2013) and "For Japan's 'Stranded Singles,' Virtual Love Beats the Real Thing" (McVeigh 2016).

21 For example, Yamada Masahiro, a sociologist at Tokyo Gakugei University, has written extensively on "parasite singles" (2001).

22 The general trend, however, is for men and women to marry later in life, after they feel economically stable. Women also put off marriage because they have personally fulfilling careers, and do not want to give them up once they marry or have children (Dalton and Dales 2016, 5).

23 This is the most recent year I could find data for.

24 Guidebooks for sale in bookstores throughout Japan list temples famous for various this-worldly benefits, from creating good connections, breaking bad connections, making money, quitting smoking, and others. For more on this, see Reader and Tanabe (1998).

25 A recent survey suggests that at least 20 percent of Buddhist temples are currently operating without a resident priest. Martin (2017) suggests that this is due to depopulation, lowering birthrate, and a turn to alternative funeral practices in contemporary Japan.

26 Rather than an either/or situation, it may be that both are true. In other words, it could be that Buddhism is declining and Buddhists are benefiting from this narrative of decline. Thanks to Hannah Gould for this insight.

27 On his website, Horiuchi never states outright what actions priests can take to solve the problems. For that, presumably, one must pay to attend a class or purchase his self-published e-book.

28 For more, see Reader (2014, chap. 4).

29 This matches with the editors' introduction to this volume, and David McMahan's discussion of Buddhist secularities, especially "secularity . . . serves as a driver of change and reconfiguration of religious belief, practice, and interpretation" (2017, 114).

References

Ambros, Barbara. 2015. *Women in Japanese Religions*. Women in Religions. New York: New York University Press.

Applbaum, Kalman D. 1995. "Marriage with the Proper Stranger: Arranged Marriage in Metropolitan Japan." *Ethnology* 34 (1): 37–51.

Covell, Stephen. 2006. *Japanese Temple Buddhism: Worldliness in a Religion of Renunciation*. Honolulu: University of Hawai'i Press.

Dalton, Emma, and Laura Dales. 2016. "Online Konkatsu and the Gendered Ideals of Marriage in Contemporary Japan." *Japanese Studies* 36 (1): 1–19.

The Economist. 2016. "Marriage in Japan: I Don't." September 1. http://www.economist.com/news/asia/21706321-most-japanese-want-be-married-are-finding-it-hard-i-dont.

Fisch, Michael. 2001. "The Rise of the Chapel Wedding in Japan: Simulation and Performance." *Japanese Journal of Religious Studies* 28 (1/2): 57–76.

Hatsugen komachi. 2013. "Jishakon Tte Dō Nan Deshō" (How are Jishakon?). *YOMIURI ONLINE*. September 3. http://www.yomiuri.co.jp/komachi/hatsugen/.

Haworth, Abigail. 2013. "Why Have Young People in Japan Stopped Having Sex?" *The Guardian*. October 20, sec. World news. https://www.theguardian.com/world/2013/oct/20/young-people-japan-stopped-having-sex.

Hendry, Joy. 2010. *Marriage in Changing Japan: Community & Society*. New York: Routledge.

Horiuchi. 2014. "Otera Wo Moriageru Nanatsu No Akushon" (7 actions to make temples more lively). June 1. http://syukubo-blog.com/book01.

Hur, Nam-lin. 2007. *Death and Social Order in Tokugawa Japan: Buddhism, Anti-Christianity, and the Danka System*. Harvard East Asian Monographs 282. Cambridge, MA: Harvard University Asia Center, distributed by Harvard University Press.

Jaffe, Richard. 2011. *Neither Monk nor Layman: Clerical Marriage in Modern Japanese Buddhism*. Honolulu: University of Hawai'i Press.

Jisyacon. 2016a. "En'yūji Oka Fuku Jūshoku No Taikenki" (En'yūji's vice head priest Oka's experience). Accessed March 18. jisyacon.com/voice/tjvoice001.html.

———. 2016b. "Honkōji Bidō Jūshoku No Taikenki" (Honkōji's head priest Bidō's experience). *Jisyacon*. Accessed March 18. http://jisyacon.com/voice/tjvoice002.html.

———. 2016c. "Jishakon Kyōryoku Jisa Bōshū" (Seeking temples and shrines to assist with temple and shrine speed dating). Accessed March 18. http://jisyacon.com/contents/jisya.html.

———. 2016d. "Jisyacon." Accessed March 16. http://jisyacon.com.

———. 2016e. "'Jisyacon' Ni Tsuite" (About "Jisyacon"). Accessed March 18. http://jisyacon.com/contents/first.html.

———. 2016f. "Kawagoe Hachimangū Kannushi Sakakibara-San No Taiken" (Kawagoe Hachimangū Shrine priest Sakakibara's experience). Accessed March 18. http://jisyacon.com/voice/tjvoice003.html.

———. 2016g. "Kōbōji Watanabe Fukujūshoku No Taikenki" (Kōbōji's vice head priest Watanabe's experience). Accessed March 18. http://jisyacon.com/voice/tjvoice004.html.

———. 2016h. "Kōjōji Itō Yūsuke-San No Taikenki" (Kōjōji's Itō Yūsuke's experience). Accessed March 18. http://jisyacon.com/voice/tjvoice011.html.

———. 2016i. "Kōtakuji Sōgen Eikai Jūshoku No Taiken" (Kōtakuji's head priest Sōgen Eikai's experience). Accessed March 18. http://jisyacon.com/voice/tjvoice009.html.

———. 2016j. "Myōkenji Kusano Myōkei-San No Taikenki" (Myōkenji's Kusano Myōkei's experience). Accessed March 18. http://jisyacon.com/voice/tjvoice012.html.

———. 2016k. "Seiritsu Kappuru No Koe 1" (The voices of successfully matched couples 1). Accessed March 18. http://jisyacon.com/voice/voice001.html.

———. 2016l. "Seiritsu Kappuru No Koe 2" (The voices of successfully matched couples 2). Accessed March 18. http://jisyacon.com/voice/voice002.html.

———. 2016m. "Seiritsu Kappuru No Koe 4" (The voices of successfully matched couples 4). Accessed March 18. http://jisyacon.com/voice/voice04.com.

———. 2016n. "Seiritsu Kappuru No Koe 8" (The voices of successfully matched couples 8). Accessed March 18. http://jisyacon.com/voice/voice008.html.

———. 2016o. "Seiritsu Kappuru No Koe 10" (The voices of successfully matched couples 10). Accessed March 18. http://jisyacon.com/voice/voice010.html.

———. 2016p. "Seiryūji Fudōin Sōryo Morita Eiryūsan No Taikenki" (Seiryūji Fudōin's Morita Eiryū's experience). Accessed March 18. http://jisyacon.com/voice/tjvoice007.html.

———. 2016q. "Shōrinji Uno Jūshoku No Taikenki" (Shōrinji's head priest Uno's experience). Accessed March 18. http://jisyacon.com/voice/tjvoice008.html.

———. 2016r. "Taimadera Nakanobō Matsumura Kanshō Innushi No Taiken" (Taimadera Nakanobō's head priest Matsumura Kanshō's experience). Accessed March 18. http://jisyacon.com/voice/tjvoice006.html.

LeFebvre, Jesse R. 2015. "Christian Wedding Ceremonies: 'Nonreligiousness' in Contemporary Japan." *Japanese Journal of Religious Studies* 42 (2): 185–203.

Martin, Alexander. 2017. "Thousands of Japanese Buddhist Temples Left 'Priestless.'" *Nikkei Asian Review*. Accessed April 30. http://asia.nikkei.com/Life-Arts/Life/Thousands-of-Japanese-Buddhist-temples-left-priestless.

McLaughlin, Levi. 2013a. "What Have Religious Groups Done after 3.11? Part 1: A Brief Survey of Religious Mobilization after the Great East Japan Earthquake Disasters." *Religion Compass* 7 (8): 294–308.

——. 2013b. "What Have Religious Groups Done after 3.11? Part 2: From Religious Mobilization to 'Spiritual Care.'" *Religion Compass* 7 (8): 309–325.

McMahan, David L. 2017. "Buddhism and Global Secularisms." *Journal of Global Buddhism* 18:112–128.

McVeigh, Tracy. 2016. "For Japan's 'Stranded Singles,' Virtual Love Beats the Real Thing." *The Guardian*. November 19, sec. World news. https://www.theguardian.com/world/2016/nov/20/japan-stranded-singles-virtual-love.

METI. 2006. "Shōshika Jidai No Kekkon Kanren Sangyō No Arikata Ni Kan Suru Chōsa Kenkyū Hōkokusho" (Report: Research on the commercial matchmaking/dating agencies in the age of declining fertility). Ministry of Economy, Trade and Industry: Business Information Policy Bureau, Service Industry Division. www.meti.go.jp/press/20060502001/houkokusho-set.pdf.

Mirza, Vincent. 2016. "Young Women and Social Change in Japan: Family and Marriage in a Time of Upheaval." *Japanese Studies* 36 (1): 21–37.

Nelson, John K. 2014. *Experimental Buddhism: Innovation and Activism in Contemporary Japan*. Honolulu: University of Hawai'i Press.

Nikkan SPA! 2015. "'Honki No Deai' o Motomeru Nara 'Jishakon' e Ikou" (If you are seeking a "real meeting," go to "Jishakon"). *Nikkan SPA!* July 21. https://nikkan-spa.jp/861613.

QJV97FCr. 2012. "Jishakon Ni Sanka Shimashita" (I participated in Jishakon). *Yametai Toki Wa Yameru to Ii*. January 8. http://irumashinjuku.net/?p=84.

Reader, Ian. 2011. "Buddhism in Crisis? Institutional Decline in Modern Japan." *Buddhist Studies Review* 28 (2): 233–263.

——. 2005. *Making Pilgrimages: Meaning and Practice in Shikoku*. Honolulu: University of Hawai'i Press.

——. 2014. *Pilgrimage in the Marketplace*. New York: Routledge.

——. 1991. *Religion in Contemporary Japan*. Honolulu: University of Hawai'i Press.

Reader, Ian, and George J. Tanabe. 1998. *Practically Religious: Worldly Benefits and the Common Religion of Japan*. Honolulu: University of Hawai'i Press.

Rowe, Mark Michael. 2011. *Bonds of the Dead: Temples, Burial, and the Transformation of Contemporary Japanese Buddhism*. Chicago: University of Chicago Press.

Thomas, Jolyon Baraka. 2016. "The Buddhist Virtues of Raging Lust and Crass Materialism in Contemporary Japan." *Material Religion* 11 (4): 485–506.

——. 2012. *Drawing on Tradition: Manga, Anime, and Religion in Contemporary Japan*. Honolulu: University of Hawai'i Press.

Timothy, Dallen J., and Daniel H. Olsen, eds. 2006. *Tourism, Religion and Spiritual Journeys*. New York: Routledge.

Yamada Masahiro. 2001. "Parasite Singles Feed on Family System." *Japan Quarterly, Tokyo* 48 (1): 10–16.

11

Buddhism

A Unique Selling Proposition (USP) in Ladakh

ELIZABETH WILLIAMS-OERBERG

IN JANUARY 2010, NEWSPAPERS IN INDIA CARRIED the news: "Ladakh, the world famous trans-Himalayan land of myriad culture which houses age-old monasteries is all set to become a Spiritual Tourism destination."[1] Nawang Rigzin Jora, a Ladakhi Buddhist and the Minister of Tourism and Culture for the Jammu and Kashmir state in India at the time, was reported as declaring: "Apart from being a foreigners' paradise and an ideal place for trekkers, Ladakh in Jammu and Kashmir will now come up as a Spiritual Tourism destination." He continued by saying: "Here Buddhism is our USP. Under the project, Buddhist culture, heritage, way of life and landscapes will be promoted and infrastructure will be developed for starting Spiritual Tourism in the region." Throughout this chapter we take a closer look at how Buddhism has been positioned by government officials as well as tourism operators as a Unique Selling Proposition (USP)[2] for Ladakh as both a means to stimulate increased tourism to the region and also to establish Buddhism as the main marketing strategy in the face of competing strategies, such as adventure tourism and Bollywood tourism. The "imaginative value" of Buddhism as peaceful, spiritual, and ancient, I suggest, is what helps to create an element of distinction—a necessary element of a USP—as well as an attempt to invoke what marketing analysts term an "emotional selling point" or ESP in order to move the consumer to part with valuable time and money to visit the region.

When newspapers in India carry the headline, "Ladakh set to become Spiritual Tourism destination," at first glance this does not seem like a new development. Visitors have been drawn to this arid, high-altitude mountainous region in Northwest India to catch a glimpse of Buddhism for decades. Travelers and travel agencies alike often refer to Ladakh as the "Last Shangri-La" and the last remaining bastion of Tibetan Buddhism. Ladakh, while previously an independent kingdom, is also frequently described as "Little Tibet" due to its close geographical, cultural, political, and religious association with the Tibetan empire since the thirteenth century (Michaud 1991). For many travelers who faced difficulty in gaining access to Tibet, Ladakh has been positioned as the next best thing. Ladakh was a favored destination among colonial adventurers who, since the early nineteenth century, wrote about their exotic travels. By the twentieth century, travel for government, business, and leisure had become a major industry (van Beek 1998, 6).

While the region is divided into two autonomous districts of Leh, with a total population of 133,487 and a Buddhist majority,[3] and Kargil with a total population of 140,802 and a Muslim majority,[4] most of the tourism activity takes place in the Leh district due to the prominence of Buddhism in the region. When Ladakh was re-opened to tourism in 1974, the region was positioned along the so-called Himalayan Hippie Trail with foreigners seeking entry into "Little Tibet." a portrayal that continues today.[5] During this time, the initial visitors were 500 foreign and 27 domestic tourists. While the number of tourists visiting the region has increased dramatically since the 1970s, foreign tourists outnumbered domestic tourists until around the year 2003 when the numbers started to even out with 15,315 foreign and 12,958 domestic tourists. It was not until 2010 when domestic tourism exploded with 77,800 Indian and 22,115 foreign visitors to the Leh region of Ladakh, and since then the numbers have been increasing dramatically, up to a 121,996 domestic and 59,305 foreign tourist arrivals in 2014.[6]

Accompanying this tourism boom is the rush to build the necessary infrastructure to support these visitors, such as turning homes into guesthouses, turning established guesthouses into hotels, establishing new restaurants and souvenir shops, as well as an increasing number of travel agents and taxi drivers to facilitate and transport tourists once they arrive in Leh. Buddhist institutions as well have expanded their tourism-related services through renovating and expanding monastery infrastructure, building adjacent guesthouses and restaurants, and charging entrance fees to cover the maintenance and building of new structures and statues. Monastery festivals are advertised as central tourist attractions for the region, and tourists are informed about the dates of these festivals on most travel agent websites and encouraged to book their trips to coincide with these festivals. In some cases, the monastery festival calendar has shifted toward the summer when tourists are more likely to visit the region (Jina 1994, 186).

Hence, when Nawang Rigzin Jora, the Jammu and Kashmir tourism minister declared Buddhism to be the USP of Ladakh, this did not appear novel. What is perhaps newsworthy about this proclamation, however, is the explicit positioning of Buddhism as the USP, in other words, the main "brand" of Ladakh, and hence the main marketing strategy for developing the tourism sector in the region. Whereas previously Ladakh has attracted mostly foreign tourists interested in "Little Tibet" and catching a glimpse of this last remaining bastion of Tibetan Buddhism, declaring Buddhism as the USP makes the "Buddhism brand" explicit. Furthermore, within the context of a current shift in the tourism industry with an overwhelming majority of domestic tourists who seem to be more interested in the landscape and scenery than Buddhism, why, then, was Buddhism chosen to be the USP when other tourism marketing strategies such as landscape, adventure, and Bollywood tourism might draw more tourists? What might be the value of defining and maintaining Buddhism as a USP? Furthermore, when over half of the population in Ladakh is Muslim, how can the region be defined and marketed as "Buddhist"?

As will be explicated below, Buddhism as the Unique Selling Proposition is not only a strategy to draw future tourists to the region, but also a strategy to position Buddhism as something "unique" to Ladakh and as the primary brand image of the region, drawing upon the "imaginative value" of Buddhism and the cultural resources that Buddhism as a globally attractive and popular religion may bring. This chapter is based on ethnographic research in the region since 2011, and includes over eighteen months of fieldwork among Ladakhis in India. My methodology draws upon qualitative data gathered through fieldwork stays, formal and informal interviews, participant observation documented through field notes, long-term and ongoing social media research, and analysis of marketing materials such as websites, brochures, and guidebooks. This chapter contributes to our understanding of Buddhist commodification through investigating the positioning of Buddhism as a Ladakhi "brand" and the imaginative value that Buddhism brings to tourism marketing.

Maintaining the Value of Buddhism in Ladakh

The importance of Buddhism—as the last remaining bastion of Tibetan Buddhism, but also as a main marketing strategy to promote tourism—has led to the widespread assumption that Ladakh is primarily a Buddhist place, while neglecting to take note of the long history of Islam and the prominence of Muslims in the region. Ladakh was an important part of the Central Asian cultural and economic sphere due to its geographic position and ancient caravan routes (Sheikh 2007). If Buddhism is the USP of Ladakh—wouldn't this contribute to the marginalization of Muslims and Christians in the region? During a visit to Ladakh in October 2015, I met with Ladakhis who were connected with the tourism industry. During this visit I spoke with hotel owners, taxi drivers, travel agents, tour guides, government tourism officials (of Ladakh and Jammi and Kashmir), Buddhists, Christians, and Muslims. What I encountered was very little ambiguity as to the recognition and importance of maintaining Buddhism as the USP for Ladakh. This was surprising, especially among the Muslim and Christian hotel owners and tour operators. Considering the context of previous and sporadic social conflict between Buddhists and Muslims, and also between Buddhists and Christians in the region, which seem to be an ongoing underlying source of tension (Pirie 2007; van Beek 2000)—wouldn't this add fuel to a potential conflict and struggle over social and economic resources in the region? And for Buddhists in Ladakh, wouldn't the marketization and commodification of religion somehow lessen the value of Buddhism as is typically assumed?

Based on interviews with tourism operators, government officials, and monastery leaders, there was an overall consensus that with Buddhism as the USP, there exists a symbiotic reciprocity between Buddhism and tourism: Buddhism helps tourism, and tourism helps Buddhism. Buddhism has helped attract potential consumers, thus stimulating economic growth in a region that is often considered to be in need of economic development. Through Buddhist-focused tourism promotion, Ladakh is positioned as a Buddhist site and the importance of sustaining Buddhism in the region becomes of economic importance. Among Buddhists there was very little expressed ambiguity about the explicit commodification of Buddhism in Ladakh. Buddhism as the USP has helped to strengthen the identity of the region as Buddhist. Moreover, Buddhist-based tourism has led to large sums of money being invested in building Buddhist infrastructure. When Nawang Rigzin Jora declared Buddhism to be the USP, he was able to procure funds from the central government, 25 crore rupees or close to 372,000 USD for developing spiritual tourism and Buddhist-related infrastructure. Similar to other Buddhist places such as Burma and China, local and state officials promote and invest in the restoration and building of Buddhist monuments with the hopes of attracting increasing numbers of tourists, thus leading to economic development (Fisher 2011; Philip and Mercer 1999). In this way, Buddhism is a cultural resource that can be restored, built, and commodified for tourist consumption as a strategy for increasing economic growth (Olsen 2006, 104).

The economic growth that tourism has brought to the region should not be underestimated. As Jigmet,[7] the president of the All Ladakh Tour Operator Association (ALTOA), proclaimed during an interview at his well-established travel agency, 60 to 70 percent of the people in Leh are directly or indirectly benefiting from tourism.[8] Buddhism, as he recognizes, was the first USP for Ladakh, attracting foreigners interested in catching a glimpse of the last remaining bastion of Tibetan Buddhism. Furthermore, Buddhism as the USP helps to create an image of the region as peaceful and spiritual, which then is understood to draw potential consumers and promote tourism in Ladakh. This is particularly important due to the history of border conflict and the wars waged against both Pakistan and China. Ladakh as part of the Jammu and Kashmir state is often juxtaposed as the peaceful region of a Muslim-majority state that is ravaged by internal conflict and strife. For these reasons—the economic advantages as well as the image of the region as peaceful—there seems to be a widespread acceptance of Buddhism as the USP of Ladakh.[9] Jigmet explained:

> It is a peaceful place, and it has been a peaceful destination. People have benefitted out of the Buddhist tradition that Ladakh enjoys. There are our Muslim brothers, they have also benefitted, they know this fact. It is the Buddhist community in Ladakh, the Buddhist tradition, the Buddhist monasteries, entire ambience in Ladakh is a Buddhist tradition. The whole culture of Ladakh, the whole ambience of Ladakh, the whole peace... has come out of the majority of the people being Buddhist.

However, most travel agents I spoke with, while not disagreeing that Buddhism should be the USP for Ladakh, also acknowledged that the majority of tourists do not come to Ladakh for religious or spiritual purposes, but for adventure tourism, including trekking, river rafting on the Indus river, mountain climbing, wildlife spotting, or for sightseeing and taking in the beautiful and awe-inspiring landscapes. An additional magnet for drawing tourists to Ladakh is that of Bollywood tourism. In 2009, the blockbuster Bollywood movie *3 Idiots* (Hirani 2009), starring the immensely popular Bollywood actor Amir Khan, became the highest grossing Bollywood film in history (2010). The film showcased the beautiful landscape of Ladakh, particularly the remote Pangong Lake that has since become a major tourist destination for domestic tourists. Since 2009 the number of domestic tourists has increased drastically, now far outnumbering foreign tourists. In my interviews and conversations with Indian tourists, it was mostly the movie *3 Idiots* that sparked their interest in visiting Ladakh, even years after the release of the film. I asked a young Indian woman sitting next to me on the plane to Leh from Delhi, what brought her to Ladakh. She explained that ever since she was a young aspiring engineering student her dream had always been to visit Ladakh and the places shown in the movie *3 Idiots*.[10] In this sense, rather than Buddhism, it seems that Bollywood has become the largest draw for tourists to the region. As Tundup, a Ladakhi travel agent, explained during one of our conversations, "There are many USPs in Ladakh... adventure, Buddhism, trekking, mountaineering, rafting... Ladakh is a popular destination."[11] Later in the conversation he explained: "you have to mix all of these USPs," yet for "Ladakhi operators also, the cultural traditions of

Ladakh, that's a very important USP," alluding to the importance of maintaining Buddhism as the primary USP for Ladakh, especially for Ladakhi Buddhists in order to maintain the identity of the region as "Buddhist."

Some Muslim and Christian tourism operators have chosen to highlight other aspects of tourism besides Buddhism, interpreting cultural tourism as Ladakhi rather than Buddhist (highlighting Ladakhi food, dance, and clothing), as well as avoiding Buddhist symbols in their decorative choices for hotels and restaurants, etc. While I sat with Thomas, a Ladakhi Christian hotel owner, in a hotel garden surrounded by Buddhist symbols such as the wheel, banner, and lotus flower, as decorations on the menu card, the coffee cups, on the walls and logo of the hotel, he mentioned how he does not use any Buddhist imagery in his hotel. Instead, he has hung photos of wildlife he has taken while guiding tours into the mountains in search of the infamous snow leopard. At the same time, he acknowledged the widespread interest in Buddhism among his guests.[12] And during a conversation with a Muslim hotel owner, he claimed that the inspiration he uses for decorating his four-star hotel is Ladakhi rather than Buddhist, yet it is hard to mistake the inspiration gained from the aesthetics of a Tibetan Buddhist monastery in the decorative designs in bright primary colors painted on walls and pillars, which contrast to the dull earth-tone colors normally found in Ladakhi homes.[13] For these non-Buddhists who attempt to avoid Buddhist symbolism, the attractive draw of Buddhism, along with the ambience and imagery of Buddhism, is all-pervasive, attesting to the powerful imaginative value that Buddhism continues to bring to tourism marketing tapped into by Buddhists, Christians, and Muslims alike.

No matter what it is that draws tourists to Ladakh, almost all tourist itineraries include monastery tours on their first day during their period of acclimatizing to the high altitude. While sitting and chatting with Angchuk in his travel agency office while he was waiting for a possible walk-in from the street, he explained how the foreign tourists might see twenty monasteries and never tire of seeing them, but for domestic tourists, one, two monasteries were enough, relating the common sentiment he hears from domestic tourists: "If you see one monastery, you've seen them all."[14] This sentiment was somewhat conveyed by a young Indian couple I met in the restaurant of Thiksey Monastery, who while resting out of the hot sun and eating a bowl of instant noodles, explained how they came to the monastery just to have a look around. For them Buddhism was like a "shade," or a colorful backdrop—an added bonus for a trip to the mountains and the scenic Pangong Lake, yet not the main attraction.[15]

Very few of the tourists who visit Ladakh come for organized religious purposes, that is, for going on what is self-identified as religious pilgrimage, or to participate in organized religious practices such as Buddhist rituals or meditation retreats. Exceptions include large monastery festivals such as Naropa 2016 at Hemis Monastery, the annual summer visits of the Fourteenth Dalai

Lama to Ladakh to give public teachings, including the Kala Chakra festival that took place in Ladakh in 2014, as well as various other monastery festivals. The Mahabodhi International Meditation Center (MIMC) is one of the only established Ladakhi-run initiatives to organize meditation retreats, in addition to the Dhamma Laddha Vipassana Meditation Centre, and Dhamma house run by Mr. Tsewang Norbu Vivek, although these centers run a Theravada-inspired or vipassana meditation instruction rather than Tibetan Buddhist–inspired techniques. A few travel agencies run "meditation trekking" or "spiritual treks" such as Mindruk Trek and Meditation,[16] and Spiritual Trek-Ladakh.[17] Phuntsok, the owner of Mindruk Trek and Meditation, explained how he started offering his meditation treks after demand from his foreign guests who frequently asked about whether he could offer meditation instruction or organize a meditation retreat. Besides meditation, the Leh market features a plethora of spiritual goods and services, such as yoga, tai chi, reiki, and ayurvedic cooking. Mostly these services are provided for Westerners by long-term foreign tourists who set up shop in Leh during the busy summer tourist season. Travel agencies, hotels, and restaurants bear the names of "Shangri-La," "Little Tibet," and "Zen peace garden" even while it seems as if the majority of the tourists, the domestic tourists, come more for sightseeing and adventure than for Buddhism. How, then, is the symbolic value of Buddhism maintained? What are the processes behind the marketing strategies chosen and the establishment of Buddhism as the main "brand" of Ladakh? I turn now to discuss the processes of commodification, marketization, and branding of Buddhism and the underlying strategies and resources behind positioning Buddhism as the USP for Ladakh.

Commodification, Marketing, and Branding of Buddhism

When Buddhism is marketed and branded as Ladakh's USP, the commodification of Buddhism becomes explicit. Commodification occurs when a previously non-market object enters the market. With commodification, Buddhism becomes a "commodity": "an item with use value that also has exchange value" (Kopytoff 1986, 64; see also Bruntz and Schedneck, this volume). In considering religion as a commodity, it is not only through the material goods that are produced as symbolic resources of that religion, that is, statues, paintings, and rosaries, but also the "religious services" that are bought or exchanged in the marketplace (Usunier 2014, 30). Religious services on the market in Ladakh include attending monastery festivals, visiting Buddhist monasteries and museums, and taking part in a meditation retreat for a nominal fee, as mentioned above.

The commodification of Buddhism, however, and of religion more generally, is not a new or even recent phenomenon (Kaelber 2006). Religions such as Buddhism have long been in the marketplace through offering products and services to "consumers" (Usunier and Stolz 2014, 4), who give donations in exchange for ritual services, statues, paintings, rosaries, among many other items (Schopen 2004). What is perhaps new in this case is the explicit marketing of Buddhism as a brand, as the USP of Ladakh, in order to promote tourism to the region. Marketing and branding, according to Usunier, are not separable from commoditization "because they are the practical, everyday servants of commoditized markets" (Usunier 2014, 43).[18] Marketing entails the creation of brands in order to consolidate the good or service being offered to consumers.[19] Brands can be understood as "creating economic value" (otherwise referred to as brand equity) that involves "meaning-based activities," which draw upon pre-existing meanings or imaginings and can create new meanings (Usunier 2014, 30). The branding process, moreover, occurs when an "idea or image is marketed so that it is recognizable by more and more people, and identified with a certain service or product" (Usunier and Stolz 2014, 13). Religions are particularly strong brands in that their ideas and images are recognizable by a large population. Buddhism is a well-known and recognizable "brand" that Ladakhis can draw upon in their tourism marketing, especially considering the widespread global popularity of Buddhism today.

Since the 1950s, religions and spirituality have become increasingly "branded" while religious marketing and branding has become increasingly viewed as acceptable (Usunier 2014; Usunier and Stolz 2014). Furthermore, with globalization, religious and spiritual "place-brands" seem to be growing in importance as sites that are attractive for both spiritual and secular tourists (Usunier and Stolz 2014, 20). Religion and religious sites are commonly used in tourism promotional literature as "cultural resources to be consumed by tourists" (Olsen 2006, 112). Some religions, such as Buddhism, carry more positive connotations than others (Tweed 2008), especially due to the global popularity and appropriation of Buddhism. Where religion is another marketable commodity and individuals are able to choose "packaged meaning systems" (Digance 2006, 38), Buddhism fares well in today's consumer society (Borup 2016; Brox and Williams-Oerberg 2016; Obadia 2011).

When Nawang Rigzin Jora, the Ladakhi Minister of Tourism and Culture for the Jammu and Kashmir state, declares Buddhism to be the USP for marketing tourism in Ladakh, what does this entail? The term has come to stand for a company's, or in this case, a region's "brand." American marketing guru Rosser Reeves in his best-selling book *Reality in Advertising* ([1961] 1970) narrows USP down to the three characteristics of the most successful advertising campaigns: 1) It must make a proposition and say to the consumer, "buy this product, and you will get this *benefit*"; 2) It must be *unique* (as the name suggests); and 3) It must have *the power to move the consumer in order to make a sacrifice and spend money on the commoditized good* (28, emphasis added). Jora, in declaring Buddhism to be the USP has recognized that Buddhism is unique for Ladakh, can offer a benefit to the potential consumer, and has what is necessary to convince a consumer to part with valuable time and money to travel to Ladakh.

In tourism marketing, the USP is commonly that which differentiates one place or region from another. In India, compared to other states that have a Buddhist presence and mountainous landscape, USPs include: "A hidden paradise" for Sikkim; the "sunshine state" for Arunachal Pradesh; adventure tourism for Himachal Pradesh; and Buddhist pilgrimage or the Buddhist tourism circuit claimed by Bihar where Bodh Gaya is located, the place where the Buddha is said to have attained enlightenment (Geary, this volume).[20] The way in which Ladakh becomes "unique" is as a place where Buddhist religion and culture have thrived since the tenth century. It is quite possibly a place in India where Buddhism never disappeared (Singh 2010). Other Buddhist tourism sites in India, such as Bihar, draw spiritual pilgrims from all over the world, and are locales where Buddhist tourism is vast (Geary 2008). However, Buddhism in these locations is not a predominant *living* religion. Buddhism exists as attractions to visit—locations preserving relics, caves, and archeological sites tracing back to the historical Buddha. In Ladakh, on the other hand, Buddhism is not primarily promoted vis-à-vis objects to consume, but instead is advertised as a dominant, living, albeit ancient, tradition. Ladakh is thus not only full of Buddhist places, such as ancient monasteries and monuments, but has a continued history and thriving living religious culture that tourists can immerse themselves in when stepping out of the airplane, jeep, or private car. As one guidebook for Ladakh states: "Through time immemorial, this region has preserved and nurtured the typical Buddhist culture which is the USP for the tourist interested in Oriental culture, religion and mythology" (Jamwal and Thsangspa 2013, 2). In this way, Buddhism as USP is Buddhism as an entire, embodied experience. This uniqueness helps differentiate Ladakh from other Indian regions where sun, mountains, and Buddhist tourism are also prominent. In this sense, the importance of positioning Buddhism as the USP becomes clearer in the Indian context in the face of competing strategies and place identities.

Furthermore, while differentiation is said to be a key marketing and branding tool, how does this form of marketing actually work? How might a USP have the power to move the consumer to part with precious time and cash to buy the commoditized good, in this case a trip to Ladakh? What "benefits" does Buddhism offer potential consumers and tourists? The imaginative power of Buddhism and its associated cultural values of peace and spirituality, Ladakhi tourism promoters hope, have this power to "move the consumer" to part with valuable time and money to visit the region.

More recently, the USP theories in advertising have been debated recognizing that the "hard sell" approach that utilizes a direct, rational appeal may not necessarily move the consumer as much as assumed (Haygood 2016). As

Hirschle has recognized, "contemporary sociologists and marketing experts seem to agree that marketing is not capable of designing new wants, but they try to attach a positive cultural value, or imaginative value, to a 'use-value' product to improve its desirability" (2014, 127). Philip Kotler has observed how the difficulty firms have in creating uniqueness has made some focus on emotional associations as a "unique emotional selling proposition (an ESP)" instead of a USP.[21] The focus on emotions was also apparent at a B2B (Business to Business) session on tourism that I participated in as part of the Northeast Festival in Delhi on October 18, 2015. The B2B session was organized to discuss how states in the northeast region of India could expand upon and develop the tourism sector. At the roundtable session, in speeches and questions to experts in the field of tourism, representatives from various travel agencies, state tourism ministries, and stakeholders referred to their work in the tourism industry as creating "dreams." One representative from the International Chamber for Service Industry stated matter-of-factly that "tourism is a fantasy, a dream" and travel agents were "dream machines." Another representative urged every state to not only establish an identity, a USP, but to build upon this brand through producing aesthetically pleasing films to showcase their region on TV and media to move the potential consumer to purchase a tour. The "dream" of experiencing Buddhist Ladakh is also that which has been aesthetically packaged in tourism marketing materials.

Tourism operators are in the business of producing intangible goods, in the form of dreams and desires drawing upon emotional associations and cultural resources in order to motivate consumers to part from valuable time and money to experience this dream.[22] As one tourism agency in Ladakh proclaims:

> If you are also planning for a Ladakh tour to attain peace of mind by seeking blessings from the Gods, you can visit the numerous monasteries in Ladakh and make your dream come true! Here are some of the most pious and devotional monasteries in Ladakh that will help you relax and cleanse your mind and soul while on a Ladakh tour.[23]

In this sense, it is not only tangible goods being bought and sold, but a "meaning system" in the form of experiences and symbols (Philip and Mercer 1999, 47). The "meaning system" of Buddhism as a source of peace, relaxation, and blessings from "Gods"[24] is promoted as a more universal form of Buddhism, which can be tapped into by everyone, not only Buddhists.

Tourism operators in Ladakh engage the imaginative value, the cultural resources, and emotional associations of Buddhism to promote their goods and services to tourists, attaching the imaginative value of Buddhism to the use-value of other USPs, such as adventure tourism, sightseeing, and Bollywood tourism. For example, one guidebook states:

> The natural landscape is the ultimate USP of Ladakh.... A peaceful, tranquil and serene environment encompasses an ecosystem with rare elements of nature. Buddhist culture and traditions conserved and nurtured in its purest form, are all there on a platter for a visitor to experience and savor from... it is definitely a niche for hikers, trekkers, bikers, cyclists, water games enthusiasts, climbers, adventurers, nature lovers and, of course, for those looking to simply unwind while elevating their spiritual states. (Thsangspa and Raina 2011, 5)

Even while asserting that the natural landscape is the ultimate USP, Buddhist culture and traditions, along with spirituality, are attached to other use-values such as adventure sport. For tourism operators, Buddhism has provided a central symbolic resource to draw upon for promoting and marketing tours in Ladakh. As Tundup, a Buddhist tour operator, exclaimed while we sat in his office looking at his marketing material, "if you take away the monks and monasteries there is nothing left!" pointing at his travel brochures and the interspersing of red-robed smiling monks and brilliantly colorful monasteries perched on arid, brown mountaintops.[25] The question then becomes: how did Buddhism come to be associated with this imaginative value that is perceived as beneficial and has the power to move the consumer to purchase Buddhist-related goods and services? I turn now to discuss the production of the imaginative value of Buddhism in Ladakh, the historical roots, and the continual feedback loop between producers and consumers of these imaginings, including the (re)production of this imaginative value among travel writers and travel agents.

The Imaginative Value of Buddhism in Ladakh

Colonial officers and adventurers such as Francis Younghusband and Marco Pallis who wrote about Ladakh in travelogues set the stage for future travelers and tourists, as well as how the region would be represented for years to come. Western imaginings as evident in these travelogues experienced a shift from places of little redeeming value in the early twentieth century, such as in the case of Younghusband's writing that refers to Himalayan persons as "childlike" and "ignorant" (Anand 2008, 44, 45), to places of great imaginative value as "sources of wisdom, necessary for personal growth and societal growth and development," as in the case of Pallis' writings in the mid-twentieth century (Bishop 1989; McKay 2001; van Beek 1998, 15). Since these early travel accounts, Westerners have had a deep fascination with the Himalayas as the "roof of the worl" and an inherently spiritual place (Bishop 1989, 1993; Moran 2004). Ladakh has often been referred to as the "Last Shangri-La" and the last remaining bastion of Tibetan Buddhism in the Himalayas (Bertelsen 1996; Bestaggini 1998; Bishop 1989; Gillespie 2006; Michaud 1991). This understanding is often confirmed not only by Ladakhis, but also by the Fourteenth Dalai Lama who has repeatedly stressed the importance of preserving the Tibetan Buddhist culture and religion in Ladakh, especially due to the Chinese incursion in Tibet and the closing of the borders in 1959.

The term "Shangri-La" appears for the first time not in a Buddhist text, but in a fictional account of the Himalayas. The "myth" of Shangri-La (Bishop 1989) entered Western imaginations through the popular novel *Lost Horizon* written by James Hilton (1933) that was later turned into a movie of the same name (Capra 1937). Shangri-La, which is said to be based on Tibetan Buddhist conceptions of the mythical kingdom of Shambala, in Hilton's novel is a place in the Himalayas, most likely Tibet.[26] Today Shangri-La connotes the antithesis of modernity and the West (Gillespie 2006, 56), as a sacred place where culture, tradition, and spirituality can still be found, in contrast to a materialistic, discontented, unhappy West (Bishop 1989; Lopez 1999). The dichotomy of a spiritual East and a material West has been a widely accepted and implemented discourse about Buddhism, a form of affirmative orientalism (King 2009), and has been disseminated by advocates of Buddhism reaching back to the World Parliament of Religions in 1893 (Lopez 2002; McMahan 2008). The Himalayas, over the centuries, became "a landscape to which the soulful imaginings of many Westerners were drawn" (Bishop 1989, 10), and as Bishop argues "can be seen as one of the modern sacred sites of western pilgrimage" (Bishop 1989, 11). This ideal of travel to a premodern romantic Shangri-La is furthered if we understand pilgrimage as travel "undertaken by a person in quest of a place or state that he or she believes to embody a valued ideal" (Morinis, in Timothy and Olsen 2006, 5). The timelessness of Ladakh and the "valued ideals" of peace, spirituality, and self-realization are what is promoted in marketing brochures and travel writing about Ladakh today.

Places ensconced in mythical, utopic imaginings such as Ladakh have become tourism resources that are commodified and sold to tourists interested in the ideal of a spiritual, timeless landscape and people (Timothy and Olsen 2006). In one guidebook, the authors write about Ladakh, "Here you will see an ancient, nature-based society with centuries of accumulated knowledge" (Thsangspa and Raina 2011, n.p.) In this way, travel to the Himalayan region of Ladakh as the "Last Shangri-La" taps into Western imaginings of the East, of spirituality and timelessness in search of a bygone era, and as an escape from a rapidly developing and materialistic modern world. One guidebook even asserts that "[t]hanks to its remoteness, Ladakh was one of the last cultures on earth to come in contact with Westerners" (Banerjee 2014, 2). As Schedneck (2014) has similarly found in relation to meditation retreats in Thailand, life in rural and peripheral places like Ladakh are often represented as "time-frozen" and "premodern" to tourists. The "myth of the unchanged" is a recurring myth in tourism to developing or non-Western places.[27] Currently, tourists from around the world are spending considerable money and time to catch a glimpse of this last remaining "Shangri-La" (Gillespie 2006, 56).

The "Myth of Shangri-La" (Bishop 1989) is heavily marketed and disseminated in tourism literature and often posits a spiritual alternative to a discontented, stressful lifestyle. As one travel agency promotes it on their website:

> Spiritual tour in Ladakh is something to die for.... We all feel stressed out and freaked out because of fast paced lives. We have thousands of tensions to deal with every day. The tiresome city life never gives us any time to connect with our inner self.... By going on such a spiritual tour to a paradise like Ladakh, it is an amazing opportunity to break free from such unwanted ties which have been pulling us into the world which is full of stress. It is a way to explore your inner self, to know who you are and to explore what you want in life.[28]

Accompanying this myth of Shangri-La is the positioning of Ladakh as a peaceful, spiritual paradise where one can realize one's own potential and come closer to self-realization. As one guidebook asserts: "A journey to Ladakh is an inherently spiritual one" (Norzin 2016, 9). One travel agency markets their services in a place where, "A horde of spiritual tourists from all over the blue planet comes to Ladakh every year in the quest for spirituality."[29] In addition to the spiritual landscape, Buddhist monasteries and monuments, one can also visit "mystics, oracles, and shamans"[30] in Ladakh, alluding to the conflation of Buddhism and New Age spirituality among Western tourists (Timothy and Conover 2006).

In this way, as Salazar highlights, historically laden imaginaries, such as that of Shangri-La as a spiritual utopia in contrast to modern dystopias, have become "representational assemblages" that have been "used as meaning-making and world-shaping devices" (2011, 56–57). This myth draws heavily on widely disseminated imaginaries of orientalism, colonialism, and imperialism, which tap into romantic and nostalgic dreams of tourists (Bishop 1989). Tourism marketers, including Ladakhis, borrow from the essentialization and representation of Ladakhi Buddhists as peaceful, inherently spiritual and exotic, with a static and unchanging culture, in their efforts to promote the region in tourism literature.[31] In this sense, the narratives invoked in promoting tourism in the region utilize the discourses surrounding Buddhism—both by non-Buddhists and Buddhists alike.

Not only for foreign tourists, but for domestic tourists who visit Ladakh is the imaginative value of Buddhism invoked. Most of the domestic tourists who visit Ladakh come from urban areas such as Delhi and Mumbai. In marketing material aimed at domestic tourism, the "mystical" place on the borderlands is highlighted, as in the case of a travel article in the *Economic Times*, an Indian site that claims: "Ladakh, a mystical land of famed passes, is one of the highest visited tourist destinations in India."[32] A travel site for domestic tourists lists the possible tours to choose from in Ladakh as: "Amazing Ladakh tour: Magical Ladakh tour; Tour to Ladakh: a Timeless journey; Enchanting Ladakh tour…"[33] On Make My Trip, a popular Indian travel site, Ladakh is described as "an unexplored Himalayan wonderland. Leh, the capital of Ladakh is set amidst snowcapped hills and is the center of Tibetan-Buddhist culture. Ladakh is dotted with colourful monasteries and is also a popular destination for adventure buffs." Not only is Buddhism highlighted, but also the premodern, timelessness of the place: "Still untouched by modernity, Ladakh is where you'll see life come to a standstill and (really) witness a true communion with nature. The stillness of this place can make anyone go nostalgic."[34] In this way, the imaginative values of Buddhism as peaceful, spiritual, and ancient help to broaden the conceptualization of Buddhism from a specific religion with a set of beliefs, to the general ambience of Ladakh that not only Buddhists, but Muslims and Christians also wish to promote in order to increase tourism.

Contemporary travel writers also (re)produce these discourses in their descriptive writings about Buddhist Ladakh. One writer declares: "You can't walk far in Ladakh without seeing something spiritual," in her article that declares Ladakh to be a "Spiritual 'Mega-Destination'" (Sugden 2012). As one headline of a travel section asserts, "It's peaceful here on top of the world: Ladakh 'Little Tibet.'" The article continues with the byline: "Ladakh, known as 'Little Tibet,' is a bastion of Buddhist calm in a wild, remote region," as the author "gets a taste of traditional life in the Himalayas" (Barrell 2008). And another travel article affirms, "If you want to find real inner calm, the peaceful Buddhist region of Ladakh in northern India will rebalance you better than any spa retreat" (Marshall 2016). The writing about Ladakh, in both travel writing and tourism brochures, as a Buddhist place and inherently peaceful, spiritual, and ancient has produced a continual feedback loop among tourism marketers and tourism consumers in which the producers of these imaginings perpetuate the imaginative value of Buddhism in Ladakh as the "Last Shangri-La," which then informs tourist expectations and perceptions, who then also become producers of these imaginings in their travel writing and stories.

The oversimplified picture of Ladakh as peaceful and traditional, needless to say, does not really match the daily struggles that Ladakhis have faced and continue to face in a harsh climate, with the threat of incursion from both China and Pakistan, social inequalities, and underlying tension between Buddhist and Muslim communities. Moreover, the rapid processes of development and modernization that have occurred in Ladakh are mainly spurred by the income generated through the tourism industry, which threatens to unravel the imagining of Ladakh as "traditional"—a tension that can be found in developing countries across the globe (Salazar 2012, 876). Ladakhis have also been "complicit in the perpetuation of biased global tourism imaginaries of time-frozen social identities and cultural traditions" (Salazar 2011, 584). As we have seen, the image of Ladakh as peaceful, spiritual, and premodern is also an important image that Ladakhis promote about themselves in order to increase the number of tourist arrivals, hence leading to economic gain, as well as to position Buddhism as a prominent and necessary aspect of Ladakhi society and culture to achieve this economic gain, hence securing the future of Buddhism.

Buddhism as a USP draws upon the imaginative value and emotional associations of Buddhism as peaceful, spiritual, mystical, and ancient. In this sense, the valued ideal, or the imaginative values that Buddhism conveys, helps to package and promote tourism to a peripheral, high-altitude region of India. Likewise, the imaginative power of Buddhism, or the Emotional Selling Proposition (ESP) of Buddhism—as a salve for modern dystopias, a resource for the spiritual self while in pursuit of material wealth and the intangible values of peace and spirituality—are attached to more secular or profane use-values of trekking and sightseeing in order to improve their desirability. Furthermore, this more universalized "meaning system" of Buddhism as a source of peace and spirituality helps to position Buddhism as less of a religion and more of an experience for tourists to consume, helping also to maintain the importance of Buddhism as the USP for Ladakh among not only Buddhists, but for Muslims and Christian tour operators as well.

The importance of maintaining Buddhism as the USP for Ladakh remains, even while other attractions such as adventure, its dramatic landscape, and Bollywood seem to draw more tourists. With Buddhism as the USP, Ladakhi Buddhist sites and Buddhist people have been maintained as one of the central tourist attractions, as well as the engine behind the entire economy of the area. Tourism is important for the region not only for stimulating economic growth and bringing in resources, but also for maintaining the prominent position of Buddhism and securing its survival in the future. In this way, possible negative impacts such as the disruptive effects of tourists on Buddhist rites and rituals (Shackley 1999), and environmental degradation are outbalanced by the economic and religious benefits of promoting Buddhist tourism in Ladakh. Not only do tourists come and visit the area, stay in hotels, and take jeep tours to visit monasteries, but they also buy Buddhist-oriented souvenirs, such as singing bowls, prayer flags, thangkas, and statues, which not only bring increased income, but also aid in the dissemination of Buddhist symbols when tourists take these Buddhist objects home with them and display them on shelves or bestow them as gifts. While tourists may not come for Buddhist pilgrimage or even spiritual tourism, the "shade" of Buddhism and the maintenance of Buddhism as the USP of Ladakh helps to differentiate Ladakh from other scenic mountainous areas of India, as well as help to maintain the prominence of Buddhism over other religions and cultural resources in the region, thus helping to maintain the intangible and tangible value of Buddhism in Ladakh.

Notes

The research integrated in this chapter was supported by a generous stipend by the Carlsberg Foundation, Denmark. I wish to express thanks to the participants in the workshop, "Buddhist Tourism in Asia" at Oregon State University, April 6–8, 2016, and especially to Brooke Schedneck and Courtney Bruntz for their insightful editing suggestions.

1 See: "Ladakh Set to Become Spiritual Tourism Destination," accessed March 29, 2016, http://www.travelbizmonitor.com/Ministry/ladakh-set-to-become-spiritual-tourism-destination-.

2 A USP or Unique Selling Proposition is "[t]he particular benefits that a product, brand, or service offers to consumers which differentiate it from its rivals in the marketplace" (Chandler and Munday 2011). The term Unique Selling Proposition was originally coined at the American advertising firm Ted Bates & Company in the 1940s. It is premised on the understanding that differentiation is one of the most important strategies that companies or producers can use to sell their product.

3 Leh District: Census 2011–2018 Data, accessed February 6, 2011, http://www.census2011.co.in/census/district/621-leh.html.

4 Kargil District: Census 2011–2018 Data, accessed February 6, 2017, http://www.census2011.co.in/census/district/622-kargil.html.

5 "Ladakh, 'Little Tibet' Comes of Age." *New York Times*, http://www.nytimes.com/2006/08/27/travel/27surf.html.

6 District Leh-Ladakh, accessed February 6, 2017, http://leh.nic.in/pages/handbook.pdf.

7 All names throughout this chapter have been changed to provide anonymity.

8 Personal interview, Leh, Ladakh, October 22, 2015.

9 One possible reason as to why I did not hear overt criticism regarding Buddhism as the USP among Muslim and Christian tourism operators is a desire to avoid expressing communal sentiments and the impending risk of communal conflict in the region. Social conflicts between Buddhists and Muslims and Christians have occurred in the past, leading to social boycotts including one in Leh between Buddhists and Muslims lasting for three years from 1989 to 1992. Since 2012, there has been an ongoing Buddhist-led social and economic boycott of ties between Buddhists and Muslims in Zanskar, a Buddhist majority area in the district of Kargil in Ladakh. Based on recurring statements I have heard throughout the years, there is an underlying apprehension that a conflict between Buddhists and Muslims may arise again in the near future. The relations between Buddhists and Muslims in Leh, however, seem to have improved throughout the past few years. Aziz, a Ladakhi Muslim friend, suggested that this because "everyone is too busy doing business and making profits in order to worry about the other community" (pers. comm., Delhi, October 16, 2015).

10 Pers. comm., October 16, 2015. *3 Idiots* mostly chronicles competitive engineering education in India.

11 Personal interview, October 20, 2015.

12 Personal interview, Leh, October 17, 2015.

13 Personal conversation, Leh, October 23, 2015.

14 Pers. comm., Leh, October 25, 2015.

15 Pers. comm., July 25, 2016.

16 See: http://www.mindruktrek.com/meditational_tour.html.

17 See: http://www.spiritualtrekladakh.com.

18 Marketing can be defined as "the performance of business activities that direct the flow of goods and services from the producer to the consumer, to satisfy the needs and desires of the consumer and the goals and objectives of the producer" (Barna, in Usunier and Stolz 2014, 13).

19 A "brand" is "[t]hat which is signified by a brand name: the characteristics (both physical and connotational) associated with a particular company, product, or service that distinguish it from others" (Chandler and Munday 2011).

20 See: "Bihar Is Witnessing a Growing Trend in Both Domestic and Inbound Segments," accessed March 31, 2016, http://www.travelbizmonitor.com/In-Conversation/bihar-is-witnessing-a-growing-trend-in-both-domestic-and-inbound-segments—dr-deepak-prasad-ias-principal-secretary-department-of-tourism-bihar-25949.

21 "Unique Selling Proposition," *The Economist*, http://www.economist.com/node/14301696.

22 See also Schedneck (2014).

23 See: "Spiritual Ladakh—A Journey to the Sacred Monasteries in Ladakh," accessed March 9, 2017, https://www.ekashmirtourism.com/leh-ladakh-packages/blog/spiritual-ladakh-journey-sacred-monasteries-ladakh/.

24 A poor yet common translation of the complex cosmology of Tibetan Buddhism, which encompasses buddhas, bodhisattvas, and *lha*.

25 Pers. comm., Leh, October 25, 2015.

26 See also Lopez (1999); Gillespie (2006); Bishop (1989).

27 See also Salazar (2011, 581).

28 See: http://www.simplyladakh.com/blog/spiritual-tour-enjoy-with-simply-ladakh#sthash.dDEKxaod.dpuf.

29 See: "Ladakh Spiritual Tour Package," accessed March 9, 2017, https://www.tourmyindia.com/states/jammu-kashmir/ladakh-spiritual-tour.html.

30 See: "Journeys of the Spirit," accessed March 9, 2017, http://www.journeysofthespirit.com/spiritual-ladakh-tour/.

31 See also Salazar (2011, 582).

32 "Misty Mountain Ranges of the Himalayas and Karakoram Are Hot Tourist Destinations this Summer!" *Economic Times*, last modified April 9, 2015, http://economictimes.indiatimes.com/articleshow/46849024.cms?utm_source=contentofinterest&utm_medium=text&utm_campaign=cppst.

33 See: "Ladakh Tour Packages," accessed April 18, 2017, https://www.ekashmirtourism.com/leh-ladakh-packages/all-packages/.

34 See: "Ladakh Tour Packages," accessed April 18, 2017, https://www.makemytrip.com/holidays-india/ladakh-travel-packages.html.

References

"Aamir Khan's '3 Idiots' becomes Bollywood's biggest grosser." 2010. Accessed June 8, 2013. http://www.independent.co.uk/arts-entertainment/films/news/aamir-khans-3-idiots-becomes-bollywoods-biggest-grosser-1859492.html.

Anand, Dibyesh. 2008. *Geopolitical Exotica: Tibet in Western Imagination*. Minneapolis: University of Minnesota Press.

Banerjee, Partha S. 2014. *LADAKH, Kasmir, Manali: The Essential Guide*. Calcutta: Milestone Books.

Barrell, Sarah. 2008. "It's peaceful here on top of the world: Ladakh 'Little Tibet.'" *Independent*. Last modified November 2, 2008. Accessed March 3. http://www.independent.co.uk/travel/asia/its-peaceful-here-on-top-of-the-world-ladakh-little-tibet-983580.html.

Bertelsen, Kristoffer Brix. 1996. *Our Communalized Future: Sustainable Development, Social Identification, and the Politics of Represenation in Ladakh*. PhD diss., department of Ethnography and Social Anthropology, Aarhus University.

Bestaggini, Antonella. 1998. "The Last Shangri-La." *Geographical Magazine* 70 (8): 24–30.

Bishop, Peter. 1993. *Dreams of Power, Tibetan Buddhism and the Western Imagination*. London: Athlone Press.

———. 1989. *The Myth of Shangri-La: Tibet, Travel Writing, and the Western Creation of Sacred Landscape*. Berkeley: University of California Press.

Borup, Jørn. 2016. "Branding Buddha—Mediatized and Commodified Buddhism as Cultural Narrative." *Journal of Global Buddhism* 17:41–55.

Brox, Trine, and Elizabeth Williams-Oerberg. 2016. "Buddhism, Business, and Economics." In *The Oxford Handbook of Contemporary Buddhism*, edited by Michael Jerryson, 504–517. Oxford: Oxford University Press.

Capra, Frank. 1937. *Lost Horizon*. USA: Columbia Pictures.

Chandler, Daniel, and Rod Munday. 2011. *A Dictionary of Media and Communication*. Oxford University Press.

Digance, Justine. 2006. "Religious and Secular Pilgrimage." In *Tourism, Religion, and Spiritual Journeys*, edited by Dallen J. Timothy and Daniel H. Olsen, 36–48. New York: Routledge.

Fisher, Gareth. 2011. "In the Footsteps of the Tourists: Buddhist Revival at Museum/Temple Sites in Beijing." *Social Compass* 58 (4): 511–524.

Geary, David. 2008. "Destination Enlightenment: Branding Buddhism and Spiritual Tourism in Bodhgaya, Bihar." *Anthropology Today* 24 (3): 11–14.

Gillespie, Alex. 2006. *Becoming Other: From Social Interaction to Self-Reflection*. Greenwich, CT: Information Age Publishing.

Haygood, Daniel M. 2016. "Hard Sell or Soft Sell? The Advertising Philosophies and Professional Relationship of Rosser Reeves and David Ogilvy." *American Journalism* 33 (2).

Hilton, James. 1933. *Lost Horizon*. London: Macmillan Publishers.

Hirani, Rajkumar. 2009. *3 Idiots*. India.

Hirschle, Jochen. 2014. "Adding Imaginative Value: Religion, Marketing, and the Commodification of Social Action." In *Religions as Brands, New Perspectives on the Marketization of Religion and Spirituality*, edited by Jean-Claude Usunier and Jörg Stolz. Farnham: Ashgate Publishing Ltd.

Jamwal, SDS, and TL Thsangspa. 2013. *Destination Ladakh: A Complete Guide on Travel, History and Culture*. Jammu, India: Ingraphix Publications.

Jina, Prem Singh. 1994. *Tourism in Ladakh Himalaya*. New Delhi: Indus Publishing Company.

Kaelber, Lutz. 2006. "Paradigms of Travel: From Medieval Pilgrimage to the Postmodern Virtual Tour." In *Tourism, Religion, and Spiritual Journeys*, edited by Dallen J. Timothy and Daniel H. Olsen, 49–63. New York: Routledge.

King, Richard. 2009. "Orientalism and the Study of Religions." In *Routledge Companion to the Study of Religion*, edited by John R. Hinnells, 275–290. New York: Routledge.

Kopytoff, Igor. 1986. "The Cultural Biography of Things: Commoditization as Process." In *The Social Life of Things: Commodities in Cultural Perspective*, edited by Arjun Appadurai, 64–94. New York: Cambridge University Press.

Lopez, Donald S. 1999. *Prisoners of Shangri-La, Tibetan Buddhism and the West*. Chicago: University of Chicago Press.

——, ed. 2002. *A Modern Buddhist Bible: Essential Readings from East and West.* Boston: Beacon Press.

Marshall, Lee. 2016. "High Spirits in the Himalayas." *Condé Nast Traveller.* Accessed April 6, 2018. http://www.cntraveller.com/recommended/amazingjourneys/highspiritsinthehimalayas.

McKay, Alex. 2001. "'Truth,' Perception, and Politics: The British Construction of an Image of Tibet." In *Imagining Tibet: Perceptions, Projections, and Fantasies,* edited by Thierry Dodin and Heinz Räther, 67–89. Boston: Wisdom Publications.

McMahan, David L. 2008. *The Making of Buddhist Modernism.* New York: Oxford University Press.

Michaud, Jean. 1991. "A Social Anthropology of Tourism in Ladakh, India." *Annals of Tourism Research* 18 (4): 605–621.

Moran, Peter. 2004. *Buddhism Observed: Travelers, Exiles and Tibetan Dharma in Kathmandu.* New York and London: Routledge.

Norzin, Jigmet. 2016. *Forever Ladakh: The Crown Jewel of India. A Guide to Ladakh in the Himalayas.* New Delhi: Roli Books.

Obadia, Lionel. 2011. "Is Buddhism like a Hamburger? Buddhism and the Market Economy in a Globalized World." *Research in Economic Anthropology* 31:99–120.

Olsen, Daniel H. 2006. "Management Issues for Religious Heritage Attractions." In *Tourism, Religion, and Spiritual Journeys,* edited by Dallen J. Timothy and Daniel H. Olsen, 104–118. New York: Routledge.

Philip, Janette, and David Mercer. 1999. "Commodification of Buddhism in Contemporary Burma." *Annals of Tourism Research* 26:21–54.

Pirie, Fernanda. 2007. *Peace and Conflict in Ladakh: The Construction of a Fragile Web of Order.* Edited by Henk Blezer, Alex McKay, and Charles Ramble. Vol. 13, *Brill's Tibetan Studies Library.* Leiden and Boston: Brill.

Reeves, Rosser. (1961) 1970. *Reality in Advertising.* New York: Alfred A. Knopf.

Salazar, Noel B. 2011. "The Power of Imagination in Transnational Mobilities." *Identities* 18 (6): 576–598.

——. 2012. "Tourism Imaginaries: A Conceptual Approach." *Annals of Tourism Research* 39 (2): 863–882.

Schedneck, Brooke. 2014. "Meditation for Tourists in Thailand: Commodifying a Universal and National Symbol." *Journal of Contemporary Religion* 29 (3): 439–456.

Schopen, Gregory. 2004. *Buddhist Monks and Business Matters: Still More Papers on Monastic Buddhism in India.* Studies in the Buddhist Traditions. Honolulu: University of Hawai'i Press.

Shackley, Myra. 1999. "The Himalayas: Masked Dances and Mixed Blessings.(People and Tourism)." *UNESCO Courier* 28.

Sheikh, Abdul Ghani. 2007. "Ladakh and its Neighbours: Past and Present." In *Recent Research on Ladakh 2007,* edited by John Bray and Nawang Tsering Shakspo, 11–24. Leh, Ladakh: J&K Academy for Art, Culture & Languages, International Association for Ladakh Studies.

Singh, Upinder. 2010. "Exile and Return: The Reinvention of Buddhism and Buddhist Sites in Modern India." *South Asian Studies* 26 (2): 193–217.

Sugden, Joanna. 2012. "Religion Journal: Trekking in a Spiritual 'Mega-Destination.'" *The Wall Street Journal,* June 19. Accessed March 9, 2017. http://blogs.wsj.com/indiarealtime/2012/06/19/religion-journaltrekking-in-a-spiritual-mega-destination/.

Thsangspa, Tashi L., and Ajay K Raina. 2011. *Ladakh Simplified: An Unofficial Handbook of Buddhist Ladakh.* Leh (Ladakh): LAY Publications.

Timothy, Dallen J., and Paul J. Conover. 2006. "Nature Religion, Elf-spirituality and New Age Tourism." In *Tourism, Religion, and Spiritual Journeys,* edited by Dallen J. Timothy and Daniel H. Olsen, 139–155. New York: Routledge.

Timothy, Dallen J., and Daniel H. Olsen, eds. 2006. *Tourism, Religion, and Spiritual Journeys*. New York: Routledge.

Tweed, Thomas A. 2008. "Why Are Buddhists so Nice? Media Representations of Buddhism and Islam in the United States since 1945." *Material Religion: The Journal of Objects* 4 (1): 91–93.

Usunier, Jean-Claude. 2014. "'9591': The Global Commoditization of Religions through GATS, WTO, and Marketing Practices." In *Religions as Brands, New Perspectives on the Marketization of Religion and Spirituality*, edited by Jean-Claude Usunier and Jorg Stölz. Farnham: Ashgate Publishing Ltd.

Usunier, Jean-Claude, and Jörg Stolz. 2014. *Religions as Brands, New Perspectives on the Marketization of Religion and Spirituality*. Farnham: Ashgate Publishing Ltd.

van Beek, Martijn. 2000. "Beyond Identity Fetishism: 'Communal' Conflict in Ladakh and the Limits of Autonomy." *Cultural Anthropololgy* 15 (4): 525–569.

——. 1998. "Worlds Apart: Autobiographies of Two Ladakhi Caravaneers Compared." *FOCAAL* 32:55–69.

List of Contributors

Courtney Bruntz is assistant professor of Asian religions and director of Asian studies at Doane University. Her research takes an interdisciplinary approach to analyzing contemporary Chinese Buddhism, drawing together religious studies, economics, and anthropology. In her current research, based on ethnography conducted in China, she focuses on monastic and lay revitalizations of Buddhist rituals and traditions that occur within a context of great economic growth. In this, she is interested in the spread of Buddhism through new technologies, contemporary alterations of Buddhist landscapes and practices, and monastic and lay efforts to disseminate Buddhism through temple-stay programs, meditation retreats, entertainment, and digitization.

David Geary is assistant professor of anthropology in the Department of Community, Culture and Global Studies at the University of British Columbia (Okanagan). He has held research and teaching positions at IIAS (Leiden), the Antioch University Buddhist Studies Program in Bodh Gaya, India, and at the University of Oxford. His research interests include pilgrimage, tourism and diaspora, the spatial politics of UNESCO World Heritage, and the contemporary Buddhist revival movement in India. He is the author of the book *The Rebirth of Bodh Gaya: Buddhism and the Making of a World Heritage Site*, and co-editor of *Cross-Disciplinary Perspectives on a Contested Buddhist Site: Bodh Gaya Jataka*.

John A. Marston is a professor at the Center for Asian and African Studies of El Colegio de México in Mexico City. He is co-editor (with Elizabeth Guthrie) of the book *History, Buddhism, and New Religious Movements in Cambodia* and editor of *Anthropology and Community in Cambodia: Reflections of the Work of May Ebihara*. His third edited volume is *Ethnicity, Borders, and the Grassroots Interface with the State: Studies on Southeast Asia in Honor of Charles F. Keyes*. His articles have appeared in journals such as *Estudios de Asia y África, Crossroads: An Interdisciplinary Journal of Southeast Asian Studies, Journal of Southeast Asian Studies, International Journal of Comic Art, Southeast Asian Journal of Social Science,* and *Critical Asian Studies*.

John N. Miksic is professor in the Southeast Asian Studies Department, National University of Singapore (NUS). His current research projects include the archaeology of ancient ports on the shores of the Straits of Melaka; early cities in Indonesia, Cambodia, and Myanmar; and ceramic analysis. He also manages the Archaeology Laboratory for the Department of Southeast Asian Studies, Faculty of Arts and Social Sciences, NUS. He has authored and co-authored over thirty books and has published over fifty-eight articles and chapters in these fields.

Matthew Mitchell is a graduate of the Asian Religions track of Duke University's Graduate Program in Religion. His dissertation, which was awarded the Stanley Weinstein Dissertation Prize for best dissertation on East Asian Buddhism 2014–2016, focused on a group of Buddhist nuns of the Daihongan sub-temple of Zenkōji in Japan's early modern period. His research in Japan and writing have been funded by the Japan Foundation's Dissertation Fellowship, the Anne T. and Robert M. Bass Fellowship for Undergraduate Instruction, and the Robert H. N. Ho Family Foundation Dissertation Fellowship. He received his MA from the Religion Department of the University of Hawai'i at Manoa.

Brian J. Nichols studied philosophy, literature, and history at Duke University (1994) and earned his PhD in religious studies with a concentration in Buddhism from Rice University in Houston (2011). Before joining the Department of Humanities at Mount Royal University in 2012, he taught at the University of Houston and Central Michigan University. His most recent research examines the revival of Buddhism in modern and contemporary China, where he has conducted research from 2005 to 2012, supported in part by a Fulbright fellowship and a grant from the Asian Cultural Council. He is interested in broadening the conception of Buddhist monasticism by examining it in practice, through ethnographic means. He regularly teaches courses on Buddhism, Chinese religions, meditation, and contemporary East Asia.

Ian Reader is professor emeritus at the University of Manchester where he also served as professor of Japanese studies. He has also held academic positions in Japan, Scotland, Denmark, and Hawaii. His research focuses on contemporary religious issues in Japan, pilgrimage, and studies of religion and violence. Among his books are *Religious Violence in Contemporary Japan: The Case of Aum Shinrikyo* (2000), *Making Pilgrimages: Meaning and Practice in Shikoku* (2005), *Pilgrimage in the Marketplace* (2014), and (with Peter de Smet), *Health-Related Votive Tablets from Japan: Ema for Health and Well-Being* (2017). He has also published numerous articles and chapters on issues relating to pilgrimage in the modern world. His current project is a book with Erica Baffelli (University of Manchester) on the trajectory of new religious movements in late twentieth- to early twenty-first-century Japan.

Justin Ritzinger is associate professor of Chinese religions at the University of Miami. His work examines the transformations of Chinese Buddhism in the modern period in relation to the new ideas and values of the era. He is the author of *Anarchy in the Pure Land: Reinventing the Cult of Maitreya in Modern Chinese Buddhism.*

Brooke Schedneck is assistant professor in the Department of Religious Studies at Rhodes College. Her work focuses on contemporary Buddhism in Thailand, where she has lived and conducted research for over eight years. Her first book is titled *Thailand's International Meditation Centers: Tourism and the Global Commodification of Religious Practices.* She has published articles in *Contemporary Buddhism, The Buddhist Studies Review, Modern Asian Studies, Religion,* and *The Journal of Contemporary Religion.*

Matthew J. Trew is a PhD candidate in anthropology at the University of Wisconsin–Madison. His research focuses on thematic tourism as a strategy for establishing competitive symbolic economies in smaller urban areas of the developing world. He has worked in Battambang, Cambodia, for many years, learning from and assisting locals with tourism management and an ongoing application for UNESCO World Heritage Status. Other interests include cultural heritage management, postcolonial space, thanatourism/dark tourism, narratology of space and place, and visual anthropology. He currently runs the website BambooTrain.com to help promote and preserve Battambang's endangered bamboo train attraction, the city's largest tourist draw.

Elizabeth Williams-Oerberg is co-director of the Center for Contemporary Buddhist Studies and assistant professor in the Department of Cross-Cultural and Regional Studies, University of Copenhagen. She is currently working on the collaborative research project "Buddhism, Business and Believers," with a particular research focus on spiritual tourism and the Unique Selling Proposition (USP) of Buddhism in Ladakh, India. She has a PhD in Anthropology from Aarhus University, Denmark, where she wrote her PhD thesis, "Young Buddhism: Examining Ladakhi Buddhist Youth Engagements with Migration, Modernity and Morality in India," which highlights the particularly prominent role that modern education and youth play in forwarding contemporary transformations of Buddhism.

Index